This is the first comprehensive study of the House of Lords in the reign of Charles II. It examines the House's institutional and political activities, and reveals the vital role played by the peerage in Caroline parliaments.

Andrew Swatland draws on an extensive range of sources to analyse the membership and procedural development of the House of Lords, relating these to legislative, judicial and political issues in Restoration England. He sheds light on the Lords' relations with the king and the Commons, and assesses the contribution made by peers and bishops to the Restoration church settlement. He also describes the emergence of political parties, reinterpreting 'Toryism' and 'Whiggism' during the succession crisis of 1679–81. This detailed and balanced study is both a major institutional history and an important contribution to the history of Restoration politics and political culture.

Cambridge Studies in Early Modern British History

THE HOUSE OF LORDS IN THE REIGN OF CHARLES II

Cambridge Studies in Early Modern British History

Series editors

ANTHONY FLETCHER
Professor of History, University of Essex

JOHN GUY
Professor of Modern History, University of St Andrews

and JOHN MORRILL
Reader in Early Modern History, University of Cambridge, and Fellow and Tutor of Selwyn College

This is a series of monographs and studies covering many aspects of the history of the British Isles between the late fifteenth century and the early eighteenth century. It includes the work of established scholars and pioneering work by a new generation of scholars. It includes both reviews and revisions of major topics and books, which open up new historical terrain or which reveal startling new perspectives on familiar subjects. All the volumes set detailed research into broader perspectives and the books are intended for the use of students as well as of their teachers.

For a list of titles in the series, see end of book.

THE HOUSE OF
LORDS IN THE REIGN
OF CHARLES II

ANDREW SWATLAND

Published by the Press Syndicate of the University of Cambridge
The Pitt Building, Trumpington Street, Cambridge CB2 1RP
40 West 20th Street, New York, NY 10011-4211, USA
10 Stamford Road, Oakleigh, Melbourne 3166, Australia

Printed in Great Britain at the University Press, Cambridge

A catalogue record for this book is available from the British Library

Library of Congress cataloguing in publication data

Swatland, Andrew
The House of Lords in the reign of Charles II / Andrew Swatland.
p.   cm. – (Cambridge studies in early modern British history)
Includes bibliographical references and index.
ISBN 0 521 55458 6 (hc)
1. Great Britain. Parliament. House of Lords – History. 2. Great
Britain – Politics and government – 1660–1688. 3. Great Britain –
History – Charles II, 1660–1685. 4. Great Britain – History –
Restoration, 1660–1688. I. Title. II. Series.
JN623 1660
328.41'071'09032 – dc20 95–40685 CIP

ISBN 0 521 55458 6 hardback

For Rosemary, Edmund and Alastair

CONTENTS

TABLES

ACKNOWLEDGEMENTS

The research for this book was made possible by a three-year grant from the Department of Education and Science, culminating in 1985. Further research has since been undertaken. During the course of this research I have accumulated numerous debts to many people and institutions. My chief professional debt is to my former research supervisor at the University of Birmingham, David Allen, whose constructive criticism and encouragement over the years have been of inestimable value. I am obliged to David Johnson, Deputy Clerk of the Records, at the House of Lords Record Office, Clyve Jones of the Institute of Historical Research, John Morrill of Selwyn College, Cambridge, Paul Seaward, formerly Research Fellow at Christ's College, Cambridge and Mark Knights of the University of Leicester for their many useful suggestions and stimulating discussions. I am deeply indebted to Bruce Yardley, formerly of Worcester College, Oxford, who has read drafts of this book and made many helpful criticisms.

I am grateful to the staff of the House of Lords Record Office, the British Library, the Bodleian Library, the Public Record Office, Dr Williams' Library, and to those at all the local record offices that I have visited during the past fourteen years. For permitting me to consult manuscripts in their possession, I am obliged to the Trustees of the Chatsworth Settlement, the duke of Bedford, the Trustees of the duke of Northumberland, the marquis of Bath and Major R. B. Verney of Claydon House.

Finally, and most important of all, my profoundest thanks go to my wife, Rosemary, who has helped me in so many different ways during the research for and writing of this book.

ABBREVIATIONS

Add. MSS   Additional Manuscripts, British Library
BIHR   *Bulletin of the Institute of Historical Research*
BL   British Library
Bodl.   Bodleian Library, Oxford
Burnet   *Burnet's history of my own time. Part I: the reign of Charles II*, edited by O. Airy, 2 vols. (Oxford, 1897–1900)
Cal. Cl. SP   *Calendar of the Clarendon state papers preserved in the Bodleian Library*, edited by O. Ogle, W. H. Bliss, W. D. Macray and F. J. Routledge, 5 vols. (Oxford, 1869–1970)
Cal. SP Dom.   *Calendar of state papers, domestic series, of the reign of Charles II*, edited by M. A. E. Green, F. H. Blackburne Daniel and F. Bickley, 28 vols. (London, 1860–1939)
Cal. SP Ven.   *Calendar of state papers and manuscripts relating to English affairs, existing in the archives and collections of Venice*, edited by R. Brown (1864–1947)
Carte MSS   Carte Manuscripts, Bodleian Library, Oxford.
CJ   *Journals of the House of Commons* (1742–   )
Clarendon, *Life*   Edward Hyde, earl of Clarendon, *The continuation of the life of Edward, earl of Clarendon, 1660–67*, 3 vols. (Oxford, 1827)
Clarendon MSS   Clarendon Manuscripts, Bodleian Library, Oxford
Committee   Committee Minute Books, House of Lords Record Office,
   Minutes   House of Lords, London
DNB   *The dictionary of national biography*, edited by L. Stephen and S. Lee, 63 vols. (1885–1900)
EHR   *English Historical Review*
Foster   E. R. Foster, *The House of Lords 1603–1649: structure, procedure and the nature of its business* (Chapel Hill, 1983)
GEC   *The complete peerage*, new edition, edited by G. E. C[okayne] and V. Gibbs, 13 vols. (1910–40)

Hist. MSS Comm.	*Historical Manuscripts Commission*
HLQ	*Huntington Library Quarterly*
HLRO	House of Lords Record Office, House of Lords
Hutton	Ronald Hutton, *The Restoration: a political and religious history of England and Wales, 1658–1667* (Oxford, 1985)
LJ	*Journals of the House of Lords* (1767–)
Manuscript Minutes	Manuscript Minute Books, House of Lords Record Office
Parl. Hist.	*The parliamentary history of England, from the earliest period to 1803*, edited by W. Cobbett and J. Wright, 36 vols. (1806–20)
Pepys	*The diary of Samuel Pepys*, edited by R. Latham and W. Matthews, 11 vols. (1970–83)
PRO	Public Record Office, London
RO	Record Office
Seaward	Paul Seaward, *The Cavalier Parliament and the reconstruction of the old regime, 1661–67* (Cambridge, 1989)
Statutes	*Statutes of the realm*, 11 vols. (1810–28)

NOTE ON THE TEXT

The spelling and punctuation of quotations from original manuscripts have been modernised and contractions have been expanded. All dates are in old style, but as in modern usage the new year is considered to have begun on 1 January, rather than on 25 March.

All works cited in the footnotes were published in London unless otherwise stated.

$\cdot\!\!\cdot\!\!\langle\!\!\langle\!\!\cdot$ 1 $\cdot\!\!\rangle\!\!\rangle\!\!\cdot$

Introduction

For many years historians of Tudor and Stuart parliaments have neglected the House of Lords, concentrating on the House of Commons. Only recently have scholars begun both to recognise and to study parliament as a trinity consisting of king, Lords and Commons. For the early Tudor period Lehmberg's two books on Henry VIII's parliaments emphasise the interaction between the Lords and the Commons.[1] Michael Graves and Jennifer Loach have demonstrated the significance of the House of Lords in the government of mid-Tudor England, whilst G. R. Elton has emphasised its business functions during the reign of Elizabeth I.[2] For the early Stuart period most of the work on the Lords remains unpublished.[3] One notable exception is Elizabeth Read Foster's institutional study covering the years 1603 to 1649.[4]

The later Stuart period is even more neglected. Most of what has been written on the parliaments of Charles II's reign has focused on the relations between king and Commons.[5] A recent attempt to minimise the assertiveness of the Commons has done so without reference to the Lords.[6] The standard work on the upper House is still A. S. Turberville's two-part narrative essay published in 1929/30, which made little use of manuscript sources, and no use of the documents in the House of Lords Record Office.[7] Both C. H. Firth

[1] S. E. Lehmberg, *The Reformation Parliament* (Cambridge, 1970); *The later parliaments of Henry VIII, 1536–1547* (Cambridge, 1977).

[2] M. A. R. Graves, *The House of Lords in the parliaments of Edward VI and Mary I* (Cambridge, 1981) and *The Tudor parliaments: Crown, Lords and Commons, 1485–1603* (1985); J. Loach, *Parliament under the Tudors* (Oxford, 1991); G. R. Elton, *Parliaments of England, 1559–1581* (Cambridge, 1989).

[3] For example, J. B. Crummett, 'The lay peers in parliament, 1640–1644' (University of Manchester PhD thesis, 1955); J. Stoddart, 'Constitutional crisis and the House of Lords, 1621–1629' (University of California PhD thesis, 1966); and J. S. A. Adamson, 'The peerage in politics, 1645–9' (Cambridge University PhD thesis, 1986).

[4] E. R. Foster, *The House of Lords, 1603–1649: structure, procedure and the nature of its business* (Chapel Hill, 1983).

[5] See, for example, D. T. Witcombe, *Charles II and the Cavalier House of Commons, 1663–1674* (Manchester, 1966) and J. R. Jones, *The first Whigs: the politics of the Exclusion Crisis, 1678–1683* (1961).

[6] J. Miller, 'Charles II and his parliaments', *Transactions of the Royal Historical Society*, 5th series, 32 (1982), 1–23.

[7] A. S. Turberville, 'The House of Lords under Charles II', *EHR*, 44 (1929), 400–17 and 45 (1930), 58–77.

and M. Schoenfeld have written on the actual restoration of the House in
1660, while E. S. De Beer has produced an interesting though brief sketch of
the Lords in 1680.[8] Richard Davis has widened our knowledge of committee
procedures and the activities of the government's critics in the chamber, and
James Hart has illuminated aspects of the Lords' judicial functions.[9] A
detailed study which combines both politics and the governmental functions
of the House is therefore long overdue.

The House of Lords was an extremely important organ of government.
Nearly all Charles II's ministers and privy councillors sat not in the
Commons but in the Lords where they influenced proceedings in both
Houses. The House had a decisive impact on the character of legislation;
drafting bills, amending countless others and, in some instances, re-writing
those sent up from the Commons. Occasionally it rejected bills which a
majority of lords disapproved of, the most famous being the Exclusion Bill in
November 1680. In contrast with the Commons, the Lords was a court of
law; indeed, it was the highest court of appeal in the land. It received a
steady stream of petitions and provided an invaluable service to litigants who
could not find redress elsewhere by giving a settlement that was final. With
regard to impeachments initiated by the Commons, the peers acted as judges
and jurors, conducting the trial of the accused and pronouncing judgment.

Much of the religious and political history of the reign is inexplicable
without reference to the Lords. The House played a major role in the enactment of legislation which constituted the church settlement in the early
1660s. Many of the subsequent attempts to secure a broader Anglican church,
incorporating peaceable Protestant dissenters, originated in the Lords. By
studying the Lords the history of political parties may be seen in perspective.
From the mid-1670s, when the Commons was split between the Court and
Country parties, political opinions in the Lords were also polarised along
similar party lines. In fact the embryonic parties which first appeared in the
Lords in 1675 had, by 1681, transformed themselves into the 'Tory' and
'Whig' parties.[10]

If we are to deepen significantly our understanding of the political history
of the reign an examination of the House of Lords is essential. The purpose
of this book is to examine the political and institutional aspects of the Lords,

[8] C. H. Firth, *The House of Lords during the Civil War* (1910); M. P. Schoenfeld, *The
restored House of Lords* (The Hague, 1967); E. S. De Beer, 'The House of Lords in the parliament of 1680', *BIHR*, 20 (1943–5), 22–7.

[9] R. W. Davis, 'Committee and other procedures in the House of Lords, 1660–1685',
HLQ, 45 (1982), 20–37 and 'The "Presbyterian" opposition and the emergence of party in the
House of Lords in the reign of Charles II', in C. Jones (ed.), *Party and management in par-
liament, 1660–1784* (Leicester, 1984), pp. 1–35; J. Hart, *Justice upon petition: the House of
Lords and the reformation of justice, 1621–1675* (1991).

[10] The labels 'Whig' and 'Tory' were not in common usage until 1681. See Mark Knights,
Politics and opinion in crisis, 1678–81 (Cambridge, 1994), pp. 110–11.

and in doing so we will consider several important questions. Why and how was the chamber restored in 1660 following its eleven-year abolition? How effectively did the House execute its business functions, and how did these compare with the functions of the House of Commons? Was the Lords a rubber-stamp for royal policies and in what ways did the king exert influence over the peers? Why did the chamber so frequently become embroiled in conflicts with the Commons over issues of parliamentary privilege? What religious views did peers hold and what contribution did they make to the character of religious legislation during the reign? Why did political parties develop in the Lords during the 1670s? What were their aims and how were they organised?

A major difficulty facing scholars of this period is the inadequacy of unofficial sources on the proceedings of the House of Lords. Unlike the Commons, for which one has Milward's diary and Grey's comprehensive *Debates*, there are comparatively few surviving accounts of debates in the Lords.[11] Bishop Henchman's parliamentary journal provides a useful insight into debates between 1664 and 1667, though, unlike Lord Wharton's fuller account of two debates in 1663 and 1665, it does not recount the speeches of individual peers. By far the best-documented sessions are those of 1675, 1679 and 1680, for which reports of key debates and voting lists survive.[12]

Among the most informative sources are the official records preserved in the House of Lords Record Office, an archive that has been under-used by historians of the period. These include the Manuscript Minute Books containing the draft notes of proceedings made by assistant clerks in the House. Together with other material – protests, reports of conferences and lists of committee appointments – they provided the basis of the Manuscript Journals, which were published in the eighteenth century as *The Journals of the House of Lords*. The Manuscript Minutes contain a wealth of information not found in the printed *Journals* and sometimes record the figures for votes in the House. By far the richest source for the Lords' handling of legislation is the series of three Committee Minute Books covering the years 1661 to 1681. These books, which contain notes taken by an assistant clerk during the meetings of committees appointed to scrutinise legislation, provide a step-by-step account of proceedings and list proposed amendments. Two further sets of minute books, those for the Committees for Privileges and

---

[11] *The diary of John Milward Esq.*, ed. C. Robbins (Cambridge, 1938); A. Grey, *Debates of the House of Commons from the year 1667 to the year 1694*, 11 vols. (1763).

[12] Bodl., Rawlinson MSS A. 130. For the evidence confirming Henchman as the author of the diary, see R. W. Davis, 'Committee and other procedures', *HLQ*, 45 (1982–3), 29. Wharton's report of the 1663 debate on the earl of Bristol's attempted impeachment of Lord Clarendon is in Carte MSS 81, fols. 226–7 and that of 1665 on the Five Mile Bill has been printed: C. Robbins, 'The Oxford session of the Long Parliament of Charles II, 9–31 October 1665', *BIHR*, 41 (1946–8), 214–24.

Petitions, shed light on the peers' attitudes to their privileges and illuminate judicial procedures. Besides these, there is a virtually complete series of Proxy Books for the period, which record both the names of peers making a proxy and those instructed to cast votes on their behalf in divisions of the House. Lists of proxies are extremely useful for any analysis of political alignments as peers normally entrusted their proxies to their friends, relatives or, more often than not, to their political allies. The Record Office also has an extensive collection of Main Papers, incorporating draft bills, amendments, petitions and a variety of miscellaneous documents. Together these official sources explain how the House processed legislation, dealt with legal cases and interacted with the House of Commons: occasionally they illuminate government policies and show how ministers and privy councillors endeavoured to manage the House.

These official records have been supplemented by private correspondence, newsletters, ambassadors' reports and contemporary memoirs. Particularly useful for this study was the voluminous correspondence of the duke of Ormond and of the earl of Essex, deposited respectively in the Bodleian (Carte MSS) and British Libraries (Stowe MSS). These lords, in their capacity as Lord Lieutenants of Ireland, spent long periods away from England and were kept informed of parliamentary affairs by the letters of their friends and associates. Many of the parliamentary papers of the earls of Anglesey, Arlington and Huntingdon and Lord Wharton are also in the Bodleian Library. Lord Treasurer Danby's vast collection of papers in the British Library provides a clear insight into the management of the Lords during the 1670s.[13] The regular despatches from the French ambassador and the Venetian Resident in England frequently spotlight events in the House, but need to be treated with caution especially as foreign diplomats did not possess a thorough grasp of English parliamentary politics. Few peers from this period have left memoirs; by far the most important to have survived are those written by the first earl of Clarendon, the king's Lord Chancellor until 1667. The *Continuation* of his *Life*, which he completed in exile in France in 1672, contains lengthy passages on the upper House, though these are not . necessarily entirely accurate as he wrote largely from memory.[14]

What follows is divided into five sections: the first considers the actual restoration of the House in April 1660. The second examines both its membership and business functions from 1660 to 1681 when Charles II dissolved

---

[13] See BL, Add. MSS 28,042–103 and Egerton MSS 3,328–32, 3,345–6 (Papers on the duke of Leeds).

[14] E. Hyde, *The continuation of the life of Edward, earl of Clarendon, 1660–67*, 3 vols. (Oxford, 1827).

his last parliament. Relationships with the king and the House of Commons are analysed in the third section. Religion provides the focus of the fourth, and in particular, the Lords' involvement in the Restoration church settlement and in later endeavours to moderate the severity of the penal laws against Protestant nonconformists and Catholics. The final section discusses factions, interest groups and the development of organised political parties in the chamber during the 1670s.

Part 1

FROM ABOLITION TO RESTORATION

2

In the wilderness, 1649–1660

On 6 February 1649 the House of Lords assembled for the last time for eleven years: the peers did not occupy their chamber again until 25 April 1660. Early on that inauspicious February day the recently purged House of Commons resolved 'that the House of Peers in parliament is useless and dangerous and ought to be abolished'.[1] A bill for that purpose was accordingly drafted and debated, passing the Commons on 19 March. The abolition of their House divested peers of their parliamentary powers and privileges, swept away their personal privileges (enjoyed by virtue of their nobility), which had reinforced their exalted position in the social order and, above all, abruptly ended the key role played by those lords who had remained at Westminster during the Civil War in helping to shape the course of parliamentary politics. Yet when peers eventually re-assembled at Westminster in 1660 they successfully reasserted their own authority and that of their chamber. The restored House of Lords proved to be a robust institution, enjoying considerable influence in the government of the realm.

I

The character and composition of the House of Lords changed enormously during the 1640s. In February 1642 the bishops were formally excluded and were closely followed by the Catholic peers. Gradually Royalists ceased to attend, many rallying to the royal standard at Nottingham and later drifting to the king's Oxford headquarters. Only a fluctuating group of about thirty lords remained at Westminster for the duration of the Civil War and its aftermath, and even this group dwindled to below ten on numerous occasions towards the end of the decade. Such a denuded rump could scarcely claim to represent the interests of the English nobility in parliament let alone those of the nation as a whole. In fact 136 peers were alive in 1649. Of these ninety-four were Royalists, having suffered sequestration of their property and only forty-two were either Parliamentarians or neutral.[2]

[1] *CJ*, VI, 132.
[2] I. Ward, 'The English peerage 1649–1660: government, authority and estates' (Cambridge University PhD thesis, 1989), p. iii.

Yet the House of Lords was not seen by contemporaries as an ailing component in the legislative process. On the contrary, the peers played an increasingly significant function in shaping the outcome of parliamentary business in both houses of parliament.[3] Resolutions and pieces of legislation which formally started life in the Commons were often the work of peers operating through their friends, clients and political allies in the lower chamber. Rather than there being a division between the Houses, with the Commons attempting to erode the powers of the Lords, divisions were vertical, slicing across the boundaries of each chamber. Groups of like-minded members in each House formed 'coalitions' to advance their common ends: this was also a feature of parliamentary politics after 1660.[4] The Lords was not abolished for being useless, but because its continued existence posed a threat to the aims of the radicals. One of the reasons why the army purged the Commons in 1648 was that the independence of that chamber had been suppressed by the dominance of the House of Lords.[5] Following the purge of the Commons the Lords remained the major obstacle to the radicals' 'reforms'. It refused to countenance the Rump's ordinance for the king's trial. When this document was read in the chamber on 2 January 1649 not one of the twelve peers present had anything to say in its favour. This refusal to participate in the proceedings against Charles I aroused the Rump's animosity to such an extent that two days later it declared that as the representative of the people it had 'the supreme power in this nation' and that legislation no longer required the assent of the Lords or the king to become law.[6] This resolution paved the way for the abolition of the monarchy and the House of Lords, institutions which at that time many MPs and army leaders considered were incompatible with any lasting settlement of the kingdom.

Although the abolition of the House of Lords denied the nobility any formal participation in the government of the country, individuals continued to exercise political power in various capacities. Lords Pembroke, Salisbury and Howard of Escrick were elected members of parliament and sat in the Commons. Five of the forty-one nominated members of the Council of State established in 1649 were peers, and of these five all but the earl of Mulgrave took their seats.[7] During the Protectorate Lords Eure and Fauconberg briefly sat in Cromwell's second chamber, and Salisbury, Stamford and Dacre sat in

---

[3] J. S. A. Adamson, 'Parliamentary management, men of business and the House of Lords, 1645–9', in *A pillar of the constitution: the House of Lords in British politics, 1640–1784*, ed. Clyve Jones (1989), pp. 29–50.

[4] Ibid. For examples of bicameral groups of peers in the post-Restoration period, see below, chapter 7.

[5] Adamson, 'Parliamentary management', pp. 49–50.

[6] *CJ*, VI, 111.

[7] B. Worden, *The Rump Parliament* (Cambridge, 1974), pp. 73, 95, 97, 178.

the Commons. The impoverished 'Godly conservative', Lord Eure, who had considerable influence in North Yorkshire local government, served on thirty-three committees in the Protectorate Commons. A few peers, most notably Denbigh, Pembroke, Salisbury, Hereford and Warwick, served as assessment commissioners. Twenty-five served as JPs during the Interregnum, the majority of whom were Parliamentarians. None, apart from Viscount Hereford, served on county committees.[8]

By the vast majority of peers who withdrew from politics altogether after 1649 the actions of such men were viewed with contempt; the three peers who sat in the Rump were associated with those who had openly sought the abolition of the Lords. This betrayal of their order was not forgotten; there were rumours in April 1660 that the restored House of Lords was considering punishing Salisbury and Pembroke.[9]

This decline in the political fortunes of the nobility was mirrored by the erosion of its status in the social order. Along with their House vanished all their privileges. Immunity from arrest and the right of trial by one's peers could no longer be claimed. A nobleman was now just like any other Englishman; he could not even avoid arrest for non-payment of debts, which he had been able to do during a parliamentary session.

Severe financial burdens almost became synonymous with being a nobleman in the 1650s. Since a majority of peers had fought for the king, few were able to avoid the effects of financial impoverishment. Most had experienced financial difficulties before the Civil War, and the burdens of the war bore heavily upon them, accentuating their indebtedness. I. Ward argues that all Royalist peers and many Parliamentarians were in debt by the late 1640s.[10] Many Parliamentarians had lost huge sums in the first Civil War. Approximately seventy zealous Royalists, mostly peers, had their estates confiscated.[11] Composition fines, which delinquents were forced to pay if they wished to recover their estates, ranged from a tenth to two-thirds of their value, depending on the degree of delinquency. In the case of Viscount Campden and Lord Belasyse these amounted to fines in excess of £10,000. The assessment and decimation tax (paid by lords involved in conspiracies against the government from 1655) bit even deeper into the purses of Royalist peers. Twenty-four peers were charged with this tax, though a third were discharged after petitioning.[12] The impact of these financial burdens was not

---

[8] Ward, 'The English peerage', pp. 33, 37, 128, 130, 136.
[9] Schoenfeld, *Restored House of Lords*, p. 72; *Hist. MSS Comm.*, 5th report, appendix, pt 1 (1876), MSS of the duke of Sutherland, 194 Gower to Langley, 7 July 1660; West Sussex RO, Winterton MSS, File 52, Lord Salisbury to Edward Turner, 26 April 1660.
[10] Ward, 'The English peerage', pp. 311–16, 459–61.
[11] Ibid., p. 351; J. Thirsk, 'The sale of Royalist land during the Interregnum', *Economic History Review*, 2nd series, 5, 2 (1952), 188; Schoenfeld, *Restored House of Lords*, pp. 35, 39–40.
[12] Ward, 'The English peerage', pp. 113, 118.

uniform. Peers were able to reduce their impact through a variety of expedients, such as mortgages, raising rents and land sales, which for many preserved part of their landed bases in the localities.[13]

It is well known that a few peers plotted to recover England for Charles Stuart. Late in 1653 Royalist conspirators, including Belasyse and Loughborough, organised themselves into the 'Sealed Knot' for this purpose. They failed to rally significant support from among the peerage largely because of the serious risk a rising posed to their lives and possessions were it to fail. The fate of Lords Derby and Capel at the hands of the Parliamentarians in the second Civil War was still being lamented by noblemen after the Restoration.[14] Nevertheless, six peers, the earl of Lindsey and barons Willoughby, Newport, Maynard, Lucas and Petre, were imprudent enough to plot against Cromwell in 1654 and suffered imprisonment. Penruddock's ill-fated rising of the following year — whilst not actively involving members of the nobility (Newport, Windsor and Sandys were implicated because they were seen hunting nearby), together with the June assassination plot which did — led to the introduction of the decimation tax and the major generals, effectively dousing the flames within even the most zealous Royalist until Booth's rising in 1659.[15]

II

During the mid-1650s discussions about the traditional structure of parliament revived. James Harrington, writing in 1656, proposed a bicameral system with one of the Houses consisting largely of the nobility.[16] Cromwell too entertained ideas about a second chamber that could act as a restraint on the actions of the Commons and at the same time strengthen his own position in parliament and assist with the settlement of the kingdom. Accordingly, in the spring of 1657 Cromwell persuaded MPs to agree to the establishment of an 'other House', comprising between forty and seventy members nominated by himself. Its precise role and powers were left ill-defined by the 'Humble Petition and Advice'. Members would not be able to exercise proxies, judicial authority was to be severely limited and their legislative functions were unclear. In part this was because the Cromwellians, who had framed the 'Humble Petition', hoped Cromwell would accept the Crown and then the 'other House' would be transformed into a traditional

---

13 Schoenfeld, *Restored House of Lords*, pp. 40–2.
14 HLRO, Committee for Privileges Minute Book, 1660–4, pp. 37–8, 49.
15 D. Underdown, *Royalist conspiracy in England 1649–1660* (New Haven, 1960), pp. 85–6; A. H. Woolrych, *Penruddock's rising, 1655*, The Historical Association (1955), pp. 10, 15, 17, 23.
16 R. H. Tawney, 'Harrington's interpretation of his age', *Proceedings of the British Academy* (1942), 205, 212.

House of Lords. Many in the Commons, however, envisaged the 'other House' as the junior member of the parliamentary 'partnership'. The Lord Protector issued 63 writs of summons on 10 December 1657 for the meeting of parliament on 20 January 1658. Seven were addressed to English peers (the earls of Manchester, Mulgrave and Warwick, viscounts Saye and Sele and Fauconberg and Lords Eure and Wharton); five were sent to the sons of English peers; one each to an Irish and a Scottish peer and the remainder went to Cromwell's kinsmen, government officials and to military men like Desborough, Skippon and Whalley. Yet when parliament met, only two English peers – Fauconberg, Cromwell's son-in-law, and Eure – actually attended. Warwick and Mulgrave were indisposed; Saye and Sele would only sit in a house of lords with its customary powers and privileges; and Wharton and Manchester's non-attendance probably reflected their increasing dissatisfaction with aspects of the protectorate.[17] The absence of these hereditary peers further undermined the 'other House's' authority and standing at Westminster.

Criticism of this second chamber was not of course confined to members of the hereditary nobility: a sizeable proportion of the House of Commons was openly hostile. The Presbyterian element resented its establishment as this seemed to rule out the restoration of the traditional House of Lords. Lacking the same substantial landed interest as the pre-Civil War Lords, it did not have the authority to act as an impartial arbiter of the differences between Cromwell and the Commons. Republicans on the other hand feared that a second chamber was the prelude to the restoration of the monarchy.[18] Although procedures during the chamber's thirteen sittings closely mirrored those of the pre-1649 House of Lords, nothing tangible was achieved. It examined the laws relating to drunkenness, profaneness and fasting, but the Commons refused to do business with their 'lordships', leaving their messages unanswered. This left Cromwell with no option but to dissolve parliament: his experiment with a second chamber had proved unworkable in the prevailing political climate.

Barely a year later his heir and successor repeated the experiment, though this time with more success. Like his father, Richard regarded the establishment of a compliant second chamber as a way of strengthening his grip on parliament and effecting a workable constitutional settlement. The very same myopic constitutional formula which had failed in 1658 was dusted down in 1659, for Richard Cromwell issued writs of summons to the same categories of members as prescribed by the Humble Petition and Advice. He did not

---

[17] Carte MSS 80, fol. 749, Saye to Wharton, 21 Dec. 1657; G. F. T. Jones, *Saw-pit Wharton: the political career from 1640 to 1691 of Philip, Fourth Lord Wharton* (Sidney, 1967), p. 147.

[18] Thomas Burton, *Diary*, ed. J. Towill, 4 vols. (1828), II, pp. 298–300; Schoenfeld, *Restored House of Lords*, pp. 50–1.

follow George Monck's advice and widen the composition of the chamber by summoning further Parliamentarian members of the old nobility and representatives of the leading gentry.[19] From the opening of parliament on 27 January until its dissolution on 22 April the 'other House' met for sixty-four sessions and debated issues of major importance during thirty-three of these. Topics included the recognition of Richard Cromwell as Protector, confirmation of the sales of Church, Crown and Royalist lands and a bill against Charles Stuart: not a single bill reached the statute book.

Legislation on these key issues could only come to fruition if the Commons was prepared to transact business with the Lords. Even before Parliament assembled, the Venetian Resident had voiced a general fear that 'differences and disputes will arise between them in the first sessions because the House of Commons seems indisposed to accept the House of Lords'.[20] Such fears were quickly realised because about half the members of the Commons refused to assemble in the Lords' chamber for the opening ceremony.[21] There was no further communication with the Commons until mid-April. During this time the government made a concerted effort to persuade the Commons to recognise the upper House and transact business with it. Upon the Commons' decision rested the fate of the constitutional settlement, embodied in the Humble Petition and Advice, and ultimately that of the Protectorate itself. Three main questions featured prominently in the Commons' debates on the 'other House': the principle of a second chamber, its powers and its membership. The first was settled on 8 March when the Commons recognised the existence of the second chamber by a narrow majority of 195 to 188.[22] The issues of the composition and powers of the 'other House' were not resolved before the dissolution on 21 April 1659. Few MPs advocated the conferral of extensive legislative and judicial powers on a body that lacked the landed status of the old House of Lords and was dominated by more than twenty military officers. As in 1658 the chamber was viewed as a rubber-stamp for the protector's policies. With the dissolution of this last Protectorate parliament the Cromwellian 'lords' were stripped of their powers and denied the right to voice their opinions in parliament. No one writing in April 1659 could have predicted that in the space of a year hereditary peers would be journeying once more to Westminster to sit as the House of Lords.

---

[19] Schoenfeld, ibid., p. 56.
[20] *Cal. SP Ven.*, 1657–9, 277–84.
[21] Burton, *Diary*, III, p. 2.
[22] I. Roots, 'The debate on the "Other House" in Richard Cromwell's parliament', in *For Veronica Wedgwood these studies in seventeenth-century history*, eds. R. Ollard and P. Tudor-Craig (1986), p. 200.

III

The restoration of the House of Lords is generally regarded by historians as a landmark in English constitutional history. It has been seen as part of a conscious effort to return to the old order that existed before the Civil War. Apart from Maxwell Schoenfeld in *The restored House of Lords*, the re-establishment of the upper House has been treated superficially by historians. More attention is normally paid to the restoration of the monarchy than to the House of Lords.[23] Even in Schoenfeld's monograph key questions about the restoration of the House are not addressed and the answers to others are drowned in a sea of detail. Several questions are central to an understanding of the re-establishment of the upper House in April 1660: why and how was the traditional House of Lords restored and to what extent did it resemble the pre-1649 body? The answers to the first two questions are the province of this chapter; the third will be considered in later chapters.

The failure of both Cromwells' experiments with a second chamber made the revival of a traditional House of Lords more likely. Their 'other House' had proved unpopular essentially because its membership reflected the power and the influence of the army. The debates in the Commons in 1658 and 1659 demonstrated a deep hostility on the part of many MPs to the presence of swordsmen in the 'other House'. Seen as the Protector's pawns, these men did not represent the interests of substantial landowners. In the debates on Richard Cromwell's 'other House' there were demands for the summoning of more hereditary peers to this body. After Oliver's death the main advocates of a second chamber with nominated members were the army grandees in the General Council of Officers who were anxious to retain their authority and influence at Westminster.[24]

From the autumn of 1659 pamphlets and printed petitions began to agitate for a Stuart restoration and, in some instances, for the return of the House of Lords.[25] An energetic William Prynne wrote pamphlets arguing the case for the nobility to sit in Westminster.[26] Prynne emphasised the advantages to litigation from the Lords' judicature and the chamber's proven ability to protect subjects' legal rights and interests.[27] Prynne's efforts may have helped to rally public opinion to the cause of restoring the old constitution.[28] This was certainly the view of Charles II, who stated: 'I have not only received

---

[23] Ronald Hutton, in *The Restoration*, devotes one paragraph to the restoration of the House of Lords (pp. 117–18).

[24] Ibid., p. 79.

[25] G. Aylmer, *Rebellion or revolution?: England 1640–1660* (Oxford, 1986), p. 197.

[26] W. Prynne, 'Loyalty Banished: or England in Mourning' (1659), pp. 6–7; 'Conscientious, serious, theological and legal quaeres ...' (1660), pp. 4, 17, 21, 47–8.

[27] Hart, *Justice upon petition*, p. 221, note 11.

[28] G. Davies, *Restoration of Charles II* (San Marino, 1955), p. 96.

particular information of your great services and indefatigable endeavours to awaken my people of England from the deplorable condition they have run themselves into, but have had the perusal of some of your labours myself; and I must believe that the efficacy of your pen has been so prevalent in the discovery of such designs that it has and will facilitate my restoration.'[29]

But it was members of the nobility who were to be prime movers in the re-establishment of the House of Lords. A strong conservative breeze was blowing across the estates of ex-Parliamentarian (or Presbyterian, as they were sometimes referred to by contemporaries) peers in the opening months of 1660. John Mordaunt, ennobled for his services to Charles II, and Alan Broderick, both representing the interests of the exiled court in England, were in close contact with members of the nobility.[30] Two of the greatest Presbyterian magnates, the earls of Manchester and Northumberland, were persuaded to the Stuart cause by Mordaunt. Others, including Denbigh, Willoughby, Fauconberg, Wharton, Robartes, Saye and Sele, Stamford and Delawarr, gradually accepted the idea of a monarchy as the only solution to their country's problems.[31] Together with leading gentry like Sir George Booth, Arthur Annesley and Denzil Holles they began organising themselves early in 1660 with the intention of achieving both a conditional Stuart restoration and the re-establishment of the House of Lords. Annesley had strongly argued in parliament in 1659 in favour of a house of lords to act as a 'balance between the supreme magistrate and the people, and to supervise and protect the laws'.[32] To Northumberland the 'restoring of the peers unto their rights' was an essential precondition for the 'peace and settlement of the nation'.[33]

The 'peace and settlement of the nation' was also the prime objective of General George Monck as he marched down through England in January. Monck's role in the restoration of the monarchy has been the subject of scholarly attention and does not warrant repetition here.[34] His involvement in the restoration of the House of Lords has in contrast received less scrutiny.[35] Monck favoured a traditional style of Lords: in January 1659 he

---

[29] Quoted by Schoenfeld, *Restored House of Lords*, pp. 72–3.

[30] For Broderick's unpublished letters see Guildford Muniment Room, Brodrick MSS, vol. 1 (1627–1720), fols. 64–75, Broderick to Hyde, February–March 1660. Most of Mordaunt's letters are published in *Cal. Cl. SP*, IV.

[31] Schoenfeld, *Restored House of Lords*, pp. 65, 74–5.

[32] Burton, *Diary*, IV, p. 27.

[33] Duke of Manchester, *Court and Society from Elizabeth to Anne* (2 vols., 1864), vol. I, 395, Northumberland to Manchester, 5 March 1660.

[34] Recent work on Monck includes, F. D. Dow, 'The English army and the government of Scotland, 1651–1660' (University of York PhD thesis, 1976); Hutton, pp. 67–74, 79, 83–9, 103–22, 127–9, 135–40; and D. F. Allen, 'From George Monck to the Duke of Albemarle: his contribution to Charles II's government, 1660–1670', *Biography*, 2, 2 (1979), 95–124.

[35] The most thorough account of Monck's role in the restoration of the House of Lords is contained in Schoenfeld's *Restored House of Lords*, pp. 68–83.

had written to Richard Cromwell urging him to admit former parliamentarian peers to his second chamber. As Ronald Hutton has convincingly argued, his intervention in English affairs was largely prompted by his fear of religious radicalism and by his desire to achieve a conservative Presbyterian Church settlement.[36] Many ex-Parliamentarian peers also preferred a similar religious settlement – a point which Monck was almost certainly aware of immediately prior to the meeting of the Convention Parliament.[37] It is not inconceivable therefore that Monck initially encouraged the re-establishment of the House of Lords controlled by Presbyterians in order to bring about his intended religious settlement.

Following the general's arrival in London events culminating in the restoration of the House of Lords moved rapidly. His re-admission of the secluded members of the Long Parliament at the end of February encouraged Presbyterian peers to believe their own restoration was imminent.[38] They exerted pressure on Monck for the reopening of their chamber. Manchester argued that two Houses were legally necessary and would confirm the Interregnum land sales.[39] Aware that the army would still not countenance the return of the Lords Monck stood firm, keeping the chamber's doors locked and guarded.[40] The other consequence of the re-admittance of the secluded members was that the influence of republican MPs was diluted, enabling Monck to achieve his aim of securing a 'full and free' parliament. The Act of Dissolution (16 March) contained a proviso upholding the right of those peers who had fought against Charles I to sit in their own House. The key phrase was that these lords 'had and have to be part of the parliament of England', which could be interpreted as support for the revival of a separate House of Lords.[41] The Convention was set to meet on 25 April.

In the weeks leading up to this event the influence of the Presbyterian peers was stronger than at any time since 1648. Their faction enjoyed a majority on the recently created Council of State, which had been set up by the Commons to provide a caretaker government until the election of the Convention. No fewer than six of their close associates, Pierrepont, Crew, St John, Holles, Waller and Grimstone, sat on the Council. With the return of the secluded members the Presbyterians also had a majority in the

---

[36] Hutton, p. 71.
[37] D. R. Lacey, *Dissent and parliamentary politics in England, 1661–1689* (New Brunswick, 1969), pp. 6–8; Schoenfeld, *Restored House of Lords*, pp. 70, 75–6.
[38] Hutton, pp. 96–7; Schoenfeld, *Restored House of Lords*, p. 73.
[39] Firth, *House of Lords*, pp. 271–2; *A chronicle of kings of England from the time of the Romans government, unto the death of King James ... by Sir Richard Baker*, ed. E. Phillips (1674), p. 714.
[40] Sir G. Warner (ed.), *The Nicholas Papers* (Camden Society, 3rd ser., vol. 31, 1920), IV, 200.
[41] BL, Egerton MSS 1016, 'A perfect diurnal of every dayes proceedings in parliament, March 13–16, 1660'; G. Davis, *Restoration of Charles II*, p. 305; *Hist. MSS Comm.*, 7th Report, Appendix, pt II: MSS of Sir Henry Verney, p. 463.

Commons.[42] By early April some of Sir Edward Hyde's correspondents in England reported that the Presbyterians believed they had Monck's support for a conditional restoration and his agreement that only ex-Parliamentarian peers should sit in a revived house of lords.[43]

The central figure in the 'Presbyterian Knot' or 'Junto', as contemporaries termed it, was the 58-year-old earl of Manchester. This former Parliamentarian general had been prominent in the House of Lords during the 1640s, managing the House and chairing committees. His efforts at organising his fellow ex-Parliamentarian peers in March and April 1660 ensured that there was a house of lords in the Convention. A few days before the dissolution of the Long Parliament he had written to most of those lords who had sat in 1648, directing them to take their seats when parliament assembled on 25 April. He urged as many as possible to meet in London prior to this date to formulate plans for the settlement of the kingdom.[44] By early April peers and leading gentry met regularly at Manchester's, Wharton's and Northumberland's London houses, and among the topics for discussion was the terms upon which they would accept the restoration of the monarchy.[45]

With strong memories of Charles I's personal rule they intended to restrict the powers of the monarchy along the lines prescribed by the ill-fated Treaty of Newport of 1648.[46] Parliament would have the right to nominate all great officers of state, councillors and judges and would control all military forces. It would be empowered to raise money for public uses, if necessary without the monarch's consent. All acts against the monarchy would be consigned to oblivion and those peerages and titles bestowed after 20 May 1642 would be void. Junto peers advocated the establishment of a Presbyterian form of Church government, though by the end of April some, including Manchester himself, were prepared to accept a modified form of episcopacy.[47] They desired the confirmation of Interregnum land conveyances and for themselves the major ministerial offices under a monarchy. Presbyterian peers were so

---

[42] Hutton, pp. 96–7; Firth, *House of Lords*, p. 269; Schoenfeld, *Restored House of Lords*, p. 69.

[43] M. Coat (ed.), *The letter-book of John Viscount Mordaunt* (Camden Society, 3rd ser., vol. 69, 1945), 95–6; earl of Clarendon, *The history of the rebellion and Civil Wars in England begun in the year 1641*, ed. W. D. Macray (Oxford, 1888), p. 897; BL, Egerton MSS 2618, fols. 75–6; Lansdowne MSS 1054, fol. 772. *Cal. Cl. SP*, IV, 665–6, Mordaunt to Hyde, 19 April 1660.

[44] Baker's *Chronicle*, 658; *Hist. MSS Comm.*, 8th Report, Appendix, Part II, MSS of the Duke of Manchester (1881), 65, series 58, MSS of the Marquis of Bath, II (1907), 144; Schoenfeld, *Restored House of Lords*, pp. 74–5; J. Cartwright, *Sacharissa: some account of Dorothy Sidney, Countess of Sunderland, her family and friends, 1617–1684* (1893), p. 162.

[45] Schoenfeld, ibid.; Jones, *Saw-pit Wharton*, pp. 153–5.

[46] Guildford Muniment Room, Brodrick MSS 1, fol. 73, Broderick to Hyde, 30 March 1660; *Cal. Cl. SP*, IV, 665–6, Mordaunt to Hyde, 19 April 1660.

[47] Ibid., 654, J. Baker to Hyde, 13 April 1660.

obviously the main beneficiaries of these proposals that at least one contemporary feared that the country would be governed by an aristocratic clique.[48]

The re-establishment of the House of Lords was an essential component in their scheme of securing a conditional restoration. Having failed to persuade the Council of State to agree to impose limitations on the powers of Charles II they intended to exert pressure on the Convention Parliament to achieve their ends. If the Convention were to place conditions on the king's return, Junto peers would require a pliant House of Commons, which they could manage through their political allies in that chamber, and also control the upper House.[49] This was why Manchester only wrote to the seventeen Presbyterian lords still alive who had sat in 1648, many of whom were known to favour restricting monarchical powers. The Junto leaders, Manchester and Northumberland, were firmly opposed to Royalists or young peers who had come of age since 1642 being admitted to the House. Apparently Monck, whose soldiers still guarded the Palace of Westminster, initially acquiesced in this strategy because he believed his control over the army would be in jeopardy if Royalist peers were permitted to sit.[50] Lord Mordaunt was quick to perceive the danger of an exclusive House of Lords. Writing to Hyde he suggested that such a noble rump 'will have a negative voice on the Commons and render ineffectual all those good intentions' they have.[51]

Contemporaries speculated as to whether the peers would sit when the Convention met. Five days before parliament opened Major Wood wrote to Hyde that 'the lords had not decided whether to sit as a house of parliament in their own chamber or elsewhere'.[52] Pepys recorded in his diary that the lords' sitting was uncertain.[53] Lord Salisbury on the other hand had heard rumours that they intended sitting in the Commons.[54] Christopher Hatton, however, had information on 17 April that there would be a rump of the House of Lords in the new parliament.[55] Not surprisingly, most of the Junto peers remained reticent on the subject, perhaps anxious to avoid opposition to their House if they announced their intention of sitting. The earls of Bedford and Clare were less discreet having let it be known in the second week of April that they had resolved to take their seats.[56]

[48] Ibid., 666, Mordaunt to Hyde, 19 April 1660.
[49] The Junto lords miscalculated both the mood of the Commons, which was largely Royalist in sentiment, and its willingness to be managed by noblemen.
[50] Hutton, pp. 117–18; F. P. G. Guizot, *History of Richard Cromwell and the restoration of Charles II* (1956), II, p. 412.
[51] *Cal. Cl. SP*, IV, 666.
[52] Ibid., 671, Major Wood to Hyde, 20 April 1660.
[53] Pepys, I, p. 113, 21 April.
[54] West Sussex RO, Winterton MSS, File 52, Salisbury to Turner, 26 April 1660.
[55] *Cal. Cl. SP*, IV, 665, C. Hatton to Hyde, 19 April 1660.
[56] Carte MSS 214, fol. 65, Legg to Ormond, 13 April 1660.

Further speculation was ended on the morning of 25 April when ten former-Parliamentarian peers entered the Lords' Chamber for the first time in eleven years. The ten: Manchester, Northumberland, Lincoln, Suffolk, Denbigh, Hunsdon, Maynard, Grey, Saye and Sele and Wharton, comprised less than 7 per cent of the peerage; 145 peers were theoretically eligible to sit in parliament that day.[57] This rump of an upper House bore very little relation to the pre-Civil War institution: it was quite unrepresentative of the diversity of political opinion that existed among the English nobility in 1660. The majority of peers were Royalist in outlook: many had been in active service for Charles I and his son. There was no episcopal bench until 1661, the twenty-six bishops having been excluded by act of parliament in 1642. The first act of this tiny body was to declare Manchester temporary speaker. Next the peers sought to consolidate their authority by constituting Northumberland, Saye and Sele, Wharton and Hunsdon a committee 'to consider of such lords as shall have letters written to them to desire their attendance on this House'.[58] It was probably in connection with this business that Wharton compiled his 'List of the Lords of England'. Containing the names of 122 peers categorised largely on the basis of political allegiances during the previous eighteen years, the manuscript would have assisted the committee in deciding which peers to write to.[59] Nine peers who were thought to be in sympathy with the aims of the Junto, Rutland, Nottingham, Delawarr, Bruce, Leicester, Robartes, Bedford, North and Montagu, received letters urging their attendance and several entered the chamber during the next few days.[60]

But the Junto's plans were jeopardised by the unexpected entrance of four lords of a very different political outlook during the afternoon. Dorset, Middlesex, Rivers and Petre were too young to have fought in the first Civil War though, apart from Petre, their fathers had been Royalists. The first three had succeeded to their titles in the early 1650s and were eager to exercise their right to sit in the House of Lords.[61] Their admission established a precedent, for now the old lords had no legitimate excuse in turning away other young lords. Petre was a Catholic, making it extremely difficult for the Junto to exclude lords on the basis of their religious beliefs.

Precisely how these four lords were able to take their seats when General

---

[57] This figure is based on the lists of peers in the *Journal of the House of Lords* (vol. XI) and on a 'Catalogue of the peers of England', in *A collection of scarce and valuable tracts ... of the late Lord Somers* (1812), vol. VII, p. 413.

[58] *LJ*, XI, 3–4.

[59] Carte MSS 81, fol. 63 (List of the Lords of England, 1660).

[60] Add. MSS 32,455 (Draft Journal of the House of Lords, 1660), fols. 6–15; duke of Manchester, *Court and society*, 402–3, Leicester to Manchester, 29 April 1660.

[61] Clarendon MSS 72, fol. 19, Mordaunt to Charles II, 24/26 April 1660; fol. 47, Northampton to Charles II, 27 April.

Monck's soldiers were guarding the Palace of Westminster is a matter for speculation. Perhaps with the large numbers of new MPs entering the building that day they were able to slip in with ease. It is unlikely that Monck had advised them to sit, especially as he deterred other young lords from entering the House at this time.[62] However, once they were in the chamber Monck did not desire their removal. William Powell wrote that shortly after taking their seats the four peers 'left the House and repaired to the General to know his mind, which was so inclinable to unite all interests, that he would not prejudice the right of any person against whom no just exception could be made'.[63] The unification of diverse interests was certainly a prime objective of both Charles and Hyde, as the Declaration of Breda testifies, and it is quite plausible that Monck, who was in communication with the exiled court, was acting on advice from Royalist agents in England.[64] Neither the king nor his advisors relished the prospect of a conditional restoration imposed by parliament. One way to reduce the likelihood of this happening was to undermine the power of the Junto in the Lords. Whatever the general's actual motives were, he did not discourage the earl of Strafford and several other young lords from entering the House on 27 April. Whoever was behind the young lords' asserting their rights on 25 April had almost certainly planned their entrance as a direct challenge to the Junto's policy of exclusion.[65] Mordaunt is the obvious candidate. Earlier he had written to Chancellor Hyde: 'I have made it my business with the earls of Oxford and Strafford to put them to asserting their privileges, who have equal right, without exceptions, with the other [peers] ... I hope at least so far to defeat the old lords as they shall not sit, unless they admit the others.'[66]

The Junto's attitude to the presence of these peers is hard to determine: there is no evidence from the *Journal* of any debate following their entrance. It is likely that the Junto lords felt betrayed by Monck, who had promised only to admit ex-Parliamentarian peers. The earl of Denbigh would have preferred that those peers who had joined Charles I at Oxford should sit, not the young lords, whom he believed would be less moderate and conciliatory.[67] He was soon to be proved right, for in a few days Mordaunt reported that the old lords were finding the young lords unrestrained in their behaviour and views.[68] Their impact on the composition of the House proved decisive: they robbed the Junto of its majority. On 27 April, 35 peers sat in

[62] BL, Egerton MSS 2618, fol. 70, Strafford to Monck, 26 April.
[63] Add. MSS 11,689, fols. 55–6, William Powell to Lord Scudamore, 26 April.
[64] Schoenfeld, *Restored House of Lords*, p. 78; Clarendon MSS 71, fol. 54, Charles II to Monck, 6 April 1660.
[65] Clarendon MSS 71, fols. 305–6, Mordaunt to Hyde, 19 April.
[66] Ibid.
[67] Ibid., 72, fol. 59, J. Butts to Hyde, 27 April.
[68] Schoenfeld, *Restored House of Lords*, p. 83.

the chamber; only seventeen were Presbyterians: the other eighteen were Royalist in sympathy and outlook and four of these were Catholics.[69]

Despite their slight numerical inferiority, Junto peers still sought to put their aims into practice. On 27 April the House appointed a committee composed almost exclusively of former-Parliamentarians to frame an ordinance for establishing a new council of state.[70] It was envisaged that this executive body, consisting of a committee from each House, would manage the affairs of the country as the Committee of Both Kingdoms had done in the 1640s. It would be empowered to levy taxes, control the armed forces, execute all parliament's ordinances, enforce the laws against papists and negotiate a conditional restoration.[71] Later the same day the Lords appointed the earl of Manchester Commissioner of the Great Seal of England, which some contemporaries suspected was a ploy to prevent Hyde from continuing as Lord Chancellor when he returned to England.[72] The entrance of the young lords appears to have shaken the resolve of the Junto to send strict proposals for the king's return. According to two of Hyde's correspondents in London they now decided to take the milder course of petitioning the king to accept the Isle of Wight articles.[73]

No such proposals were ever sent, for on 1 May the king's Declaration of Breda was read in both houses of parliament. Its contents effectively pulled the rug from under the feet of the Junto lords: it anticipated and skilfully dealt with several of their proposals, in particular those concerning religion and land sales. Charles promised a 'liberty to tender consciences' and referred the settlement of the Church to parliament. Likewise he declared all differences over the ownership of land to be determined by parliament 'which can best provide for the just satisfaction of all men who are concerned'.[74] These promises together with the free pardon of the king's enemies (except the regicides) removed fears of indiscriminate royal vengeance and went some way to meeting the demands of the Junto peers.[75] Along with the Declaration, the

---

[69] Add. MSS 32,455 (House of Lords Draft Journal, 1660), fol. 9. The seventeen were: Manchester, Northumberland, Rutland, Nottingham, Pembroke, Suffolk, Denbigh, Lincoln, Saye and Sele, Hereford, Warwick, Delawarr, Maynard, Howard of Escrick, Wharton, Deincourt (Stamford) and Grey. Those lords with a Royalist outlook were: Oxford, Middlesex, Derby, Winchilsea, Bridgewater, Strafford, Conway, Berkeley, Cromwell, Craven, Capel, Rivers, Dorset and Bolingbroke. The Catholics were: Petre, Berkshire, Teynham and Gerard of Bromley.

[70] Add. MSS 32,455, fol. 9.

[71] HLRO, Main Papers, 9 May, Draft ordinance for constituting a committee of both Houses for managing the affairs of the kingdom.

[72] LJ, XI, 5; *State papers collected by Edward, first earl of Clarendon*, ed. T. Monkhouse (1786), III, pp. 738–9, Mordaunt to Hyde, 4 May; Schoenfeld, *Restored House of Lords*, p. 87.

[73] Clarendon MSS 72, fols. 76–7, A. Gillam to Hyde, 27 April; fol. 64a, Warwick to Hyde, 27 April; Cal. Cl. SP IV, 685, Lady Willoughby to Hyde, 27 April.

[74] S. R. Gardiner (ed.), *Constitutional documents of the Puritan revolution, 1625–60* (3rd edn, Oxford, 1951), pp. 465–7.

[75] Carte MSS 214, fol. 109, Mr Buck to Ormond, 4 May 1660.

king's letter was read to the House. In this he recognised the peers' authority, acknowledged their sufferings and asked for their allegiance. Impressed
by the king's sincerity the Lords unanimously voted that the government be
by 'King, Lords and Commons'.[76]

If the influx of young lords deprived the old lords of their control over the
House, the Declaration and royal letter irrevocably split the Junto, which
had never been entirely united. Many accepted that a conditional restoration
was no longer even a remote possibility and were prepared to acknowledge
the king on the basis of his promises at Breda. On 8 May both Houses pro-
claimed Charles king of England. However, Manchester, Saye and Sele and
Northumberland were reported to be still dissatisfied, especially about their
future political standing under a monarchy. They feared Hyde would engross
power and dominate affairs of state.[77] As an incentive to these lords, Charles,
through an intermediary, the earl of Southampton, offered them rewards and
offices in return for their loyalty.[78] Southampton's efforts were not in vain
for shortly after the king's return Manchester became Lord Chamberlain of
the Household; Saye and Sele, Lord Privy Seal; and Northumberland was
made a privy councillor and a lord lieutenant. Other former Junto peers
received rewards and offices, for the government's intention was to bind their
interests with those of the monarchy.[79]

Had the Junto peers managed to exclude the young lords from sitting, the
character of the restoration might have been very different. The earls of
Manchester and Northumberland and their adherents could then have used
their position in the Lords to dictate the terms upon which they would accept
the return of Charles II. These terms would almost certainly have involved a
reduction in the powers of the monarchy. Their failure to exclude other
categories of peers owed much to the unexpected entrance of Lords Dorset,
Middlesex, Petre and Rivers on 25 April. That General Monck, who could
have employed his soldiers to expel these peers, did not desire their exclusion was obviously of the utmost importance in undermining the influence of
the old lords in the chamber. The tactics of Charles and his agents in London
were also significant: the Declaration of Breda divided the Junto and the
promise of rewards and offices in return for their loyalty finally broke the
resolve of hardliners and brought many over to the court.

[76] *LJ*, XI, 8.
[77] Clarendon MSS 72, fols. 187–8, Mordaunt to Hyde, 4 May.
[78] Clarendon MSS 72, fol. 64a, Warwick to Hyde, 27 April.
[79] Jones, *Saw-pit Wharton*, pp. 163–4; Hutton, p. 127.

VI

During the late spring and summer the House of Lords established a satisfactory working relationship with the Commons. On 26 April the lower
House recognised the existence of an upper chamber by transacting business
with it: MPs concurred with the peers for a conference concerning setting
aside a day for a fast and thanksgiving.[80] Only two MPs openly challenged
the peers' right to sit, but the Commons would not countenance any debate
on the issue.[81] The Convention Commons was a very different political
animal from that elected under the Protectorate. It was largely Royalist in
sentiment and most anxious to heal the nation's ills.[82] Its rapid acceptance of
the House of Lords, with all its customary legislative and judicial powers,
served to give the Convention the trappings of a traditional parliament, and
therefore more authority to secure the king's restoration and settle the
kingdom.

The thoughts of most peers, too, were on a peaceful settlement of the
country's problems. From early May few peers seriously considered limiting
the king's powers. The Junto had ceased to be a credible political force in
the chamber. Indeed a spirit of harmony and cooperation existed as the peers
prepared for the king's return, investigated recent infringements of their privileges by commoners and voted money to provide for the armed forces.[83] The
process of filling up the House continued apace. During May former-Royalist
peers who had been living in retirement in England entered the chamber, and
among their number were the influential earls of Southampton, Lindsey and
Portland. On 3 May the House had started the wholesale issuing of
summonses, though it did not despatch letters of attendance to 'those lords
that are recusants until the further pleasure of this House be known'.[84] With
regard to Catholics this statement was really only a cosmetic exercise, as four
peers of that religion had already taken their seats and others were admitted
during the next few weeks. The king, through his intermediaries, was certainly counselling a cautious approach to filling up the chamber, and it is
likely that Monck did not want to alienate former-Parliamentarians who
were particularly sensitive about popery.[85] By mid-May the ranks of the
king's supporters had been swelled so substantially by old Royalist peers that
leading Catholics, including the earl of Shrewsbury, the marquis of
Winchester and lord Arundel of Wardour took their seats in the House,

[80] *LJ*, XI, 3–4.
[81] Clarendon MSS 72, fol. 44, W. Ellesdon to Hyde, 27 April.
[82] Hutton, p. 113.
[83] Add. MSS 32,455, fols. 7–43; HLRO, Committee for Privileges Minutes, 1660–4, pp. 2–51
(3 May–30 July 1660).
[84] *LJ*, XI, 13.
[85] Schoenfeld, *Restored House of Lords*, pp. 78, 81.

helping to rule out any further discussion of exclusion on grounds of religion.[86]

The only category of peers specifically prohibited from sitting were those created since 20 May 1642. On 4 May the restored House had ordered that 'no lords created since 1642 shall sit'.[87] Former-Parliamentarians refused to acknowledge the existence of these peers since they were the political creations of Charles I and his eldest son. To maintain harmony and cooperation in the Lords, Royalist peers temporarily acquiesced in this order until after Charles II had entered London on 29 May. Two days later the king made his wishes plain on the subject, sending a message to the House via the earl of Berkshire 'that those lords who have been created by patent of his late majesty at Oxford do sit in this House of Peers'.[88] Accordingly the House ordered the restriction of 4 May to be lifted and from 1 June peers created since 1642 took their seats in significant numbers. During the same month Royalist exiles, like the dukes of York and Gloucester, the earl of St Albans and Baron Hyde, the Lord Chancellor, likewise sat in the chamber. By July an average of seventy to eighty peers attended each sitting, which proved to be the normal attendance per session for the reign as a whole.[89] The reconstruction of the House of Lords, which had taken almost four months, was virtually complete save for the bishops.

The twenty-six bishops did not begin to exercise their parliamentary functions until November 1661. Unlike the peers, they had been excluded by act of parliament in February 1642 and this act had to be repealed before they could sit in the House. There are several reasons why it took the government eighteen months to restore them to their bench. Only nine bishops were still alive in 1660. It took the court several months to fill all vacancies with suitable clerics. Charles was in no hurry to restore the bishops: he was concerned about the degree of anti-episcopal sentiment that still existed in the Convention.[90] The restored regime was on a precarious footing, with rumours of uprisings and revolts by political and religious radicals and the king did not wish to increase discontent further. The election of the Cavalier Parliament in May 1661 vividly demonstrated to the government the widespread support for Anglicanism in the country as a whole, making the return of the bishops to the Lords almost a foregone conclusion. The government's bill for repealing the statute of 1642 was introduced in the Commons in June and was carried up to the Lords by Clarendon's son, Lord Cornbury, where it was

---

[86] *LJ*, XI, 13, 27–8; Guizot, *History of Richard Cromwell*, II, p. 424.
[87] *LJ*, XI, 13–14.
[88] Ibid., 50; Schoenfeld, *Restored House of Lords*, pp. 83–4.
[89] The *Journal* lists lords attending each sitting.
[90] I. M. Green, *The re-establishment of the Church of England, 1660–1663* (Oxford, 1978), pp. 7, 8, 30.

agreed to with little concerted opposition.[91] The bishops finally took their seats in the chamber on 20 November, ending their nineteen years of political exile and completing the process of restoring the membership of the House of Lords.

[91] Seaward, pp. 165–6.

Part 2

MEMBERS AND THE BUSINESS OF THE HOUSE

Membership, attendance and privileges

I

In contrast with the House of Commons the restored House of Lords was small and intimate. Total membership in November 1661 was 132, which was less than a third of the size of the Commons.[1] This figure showed little variation until the Second Test Act (1678) excluded all but two of the nineteen Catholics, leaving 147 peers.[2] For the 1,549 sittings of the reign average attendance was 74, about half of those eligible to attend.[3] This figure was substantially surpassed when controversial business came before the House, and sometimes as many as a hundred lords packed into the chamber. When Danby's Test Bill was before the House in the spring session of 1675 average attendance was ninety, and for fourteen of the forty-nine sittings over a hundred lords were recorded as present.[4]

Membership was constantly changing, though less dramatically than either in the House of Commons or as it had done earlier in the century. As a consequence of the first two Stuart monarchs' peerage creations the nobility had more than doubled in size, from 59 peers in 1603 to 142 in 1649.[5] Between 1660 and 1685 membership increased slightly from 145 to 153. This was because the rate of peerage extinctions (there were forty-five during these twenty-five years) was running at its highest level for any similar period in the seventeenth century. Charles II actually created more peers than his grandfather and father, a total of sixty-four between 1649 and 1685.[6]

---

[1] *LJ*, XI, 336, call of the House 25 November 1661. The twenty-six bishops have not been included in this figure.

[2] Catholic Lords Morley and Rivers subscribed to the Test Act.

[3] This calculation is based on the attendance lists for each sitting which are printed in *LJ*. Sometimes these lists are slightly inaccurate, perhaps omitting a peer who was nominated to a committee and therefore was present in the chamber that day. A comparison of the printed attendance lists with the draft lists in the Manuscript Minutes reveals that such inaccuracies do not alter the general picture provided by the lists in the printed *Journals*. For further discussion of the reliability of presence lists see C. Jones, 'Seating problems in the House of Lords in the early eighteenth century: the evidence of the Manuscript Minutes', *BIHR*, 51 (1978), 138–41.

[4] *LJ*, XII, 652–728.

[5] Foster, p. 15.

[6] C. Jones, '"Venice preserv'd; or a plot discovered": the political and social context of the Peerage Bill of 1719', in *A pillar of the constitution*, ed. C. Jones, p. 90.

The turnover in personnel was further facilitated by accessions to titles: fifty-five peers who had inherited titles were introduced in the House during the reign.[7] On average two to three peers entered the chamber by descent each session. In addition the king summoned the eldest sons of three peers to parliament in their fathers' peerages.[8] On three occasions he revived titles which had been in abeyance, restoring the baronies of Windsor (1660), Fitzwalter (1670) and Ferrers (1677).

Like his two Stuart predecessors, Charles II decisively influenced the composition of the House through his prerogative of creating and promoting peers. Between 1649 and 1685 he was responsible for 89 creations and elevations within the peerage. In virtually every year of his reign he created or elevated at least one individual. In contrast with his grandfather and father, who had sold titles for money, Charles II's creations were normally determined by political considerations. Of the eighteen titles conferred between 1660 and 1661 half were rewards to former Parliamentarians for helping to secure his restoration.[9] The remainder were bestowed on Royalists in recognition of past services to the monarchy.[10] Some of the king's former enemies also received titles as inducements to remain loyal to the restored regime, since a title, with its associated prestige, might leave the recipient beholden to the king, thereby helping to secure his allegiance in a future crisis.[11] Later in the reign there was a close correlation between royal creations and elevations and the prevailing political climate at court. In the early 1670s, when the king and his ministers were considering schemes to tolerate Catholics, the size of the Catholic contingent in the chamber was enlarged with the creations of Lord Clifford and the earl of Norwich. Following the ascendancy of the earl of Danby, titles were generally bestowed on the Lord Treasurer's Anglican-Royalist colleagues. John Maitland (duke of Lauderdale in the Scottish aristocracy) was given the English earldom of Guildford in 1674 whilst Robert Paston and James Bertie became respectively Viscount Yarmouth and Baron Norreys.[12] Charles II also ennobled men of proven administrative ability, like Sir Thomas Osborne (earl of Danby) and Heneage Finch (Lord Finch). Most of his leading ministers – Clarendon, Shaftesbury, Clifford, Danby, Arlington, Finch and Anglesey – had served apprenticeships in the Commons before being rewarded with a peerage.

---

[7] A. R. Leamy, 'The relations between Lords and Commons in the reign of Charles II' (Leeds University MA thesis, 1966), p. 8.

[8] These were: Lords Mowbray (January 1678), Deincourt (October 1680) and Conyers (November 1680).

[9] The peers were: Albemarle, Sandwich, Anglesey, Carlisle, Ashley, Crew, Delamer, Holles and Townshend.

[10] They were: the dukes of Richmond and Ormond, the earls of Clarendon, Bath, Essex, St Albans and Cardigan and Baron Cornwallis.

[11] See P. Crawford, *Denzil Holles 1598–1680: a study of his political career* (1979), p. 198.

[12] Lauderdale's elevation coincided with attempts by the Commons to impeach him, and his seat in the English House of Lords made him eligible to be tried by his peers.

Unlike his father, Charles II did not create blocks of peers as a method of procuring a government majority in the Lords on a specific issue. One historian has argued that Charles I probably created new barons in 1641 in an attempt to save the earl of Strafford following his impeachment by the Commons.[13] On most occasions during the reign of Charles II a majority of peers supported the government in the chamber. Even during the popish plot and the succession crisis (1678–81) the king added only four peers to the Lords.[14]

The gradual creation and promotion of peers served to strengthen the ties between Charles II and his House of Lords. Two-thirds of all adults upon whom the king conferred a title between 1649 and 1681 were either Anglicans, former Royalists or descended from Royalist families. These men shared the king's distrust of political and religious radicalism, and at the beginning of the reign were enthusiastic about re-establishing monarchical authority.[15] Many were among the government's most stalwart adherents in the House during Danby's ministry when the government pursued conventional Anglican religious policies. In a period of crisis they normally rallied to the Crown. In the decisive division on the Exclusion Bill on 15 November 1680 twenty-seven of the fifty-three lay peers who are recorded as voting to reject the measure owed their titles directly to Charles II. In contrast only eight of the thirty exclusionists had been created by the king.[16] However, royal creations were not sycophantic supporters of court policies: many were openly critical of the king's attempts between 1662 and 1674 to broaden the Church of England to include certain categories of dissenters.[17]

Like his predecessors he also influenced the clerical composition of the House. All of the twenty-four bishops and two archbishops were appointed by the king and were usually amenable to guidance from the court. The prelates were obliged to protect the interests of the church and the government in the chamber. Charles II 'strictly required the personal attendance of every one of them' when parliament assembled to promote his business there.[18] Shortly before the bishops returned to the House of Lords in

---

[13] Foster, p. 16.
[14] Charles summoned Lords Conyers and Deincourt in their fathers' baronies in 1680, created the earl of Rutland's eldest son Baron Manners in March 1679 and ennobled Viscount Campden's son Lord Noel in 1681.
[15] See below chapter 12, pp. 235, 238–9.
[16] In fact forty-nine temporal lords voted to reject the Exclusion Bill. There is no accurate division list for the vote. The figure of fifty-three is derived from three division lists: Add. MSS 36,988, fol. 159; Northamptonshire RO, Finch MSS 2,893, A and C and Carte MSS 81, fol. 669. See A. C. Swatland, 'The House of Lords in the reign of Charles II, 1660–1681' (University of Birmingham PhD thesis, 1985), pp. 394, 398–400.
[17] See below chapter 12, pp. 235–6, 241, 243.
[18] Bodl., Tanner MSS 49, fol. 117.

November 1661 Sheldon of London told Bishop Cosin of Durham that the king 'expects it from all our order' to attend and support 'his great business for his revenue and that of the Church'.[19] For the remainder of the reign the king continued to stress that the prelates' parliamentary duties must take priority over all others.[20] It was deemed to be essential by the king and his ministers that the bishops attended parliament regularly because they could hold the key to the court's control over the House of Lords. When the House was evenly divided on the Irish Cattle Bill in 1666 – a measure which the king opposed – the bishops were instructed by Clarendon to vote against it, which all those present did after its third reading.[21] Though the opponents of the bill were narrowly outvoted, the bishops' votes helped to secure an amendment for protecting the king's dispensing power.[22] When an organised 'opposition' group developed in the 1670s, the bishops' votes and proxies were even more important in determining the outcome of a vote in the chamber. The votes of the fourteen to eighteen prelates who regularly attended during the debates on Danby's Test Bill were decisive twice (on 23 and 26 April 1675) in repulsing the assaults of its Catholic and Presbyterian opponents. Later that year, on 20 November, the votes and proxies of sixteen bishops prevented the court's opponents from carrying a motion to address the king to dissolve parliament.[23]

But the bishops were not uniformly submissive to the wishes of the Crown. On numerous occasions sections of the bishops' bench voted quite independently of the desires of either Charles II or his ministers. For reasons of friendship and justice to their former patron, all but four prelates refused to vote for the commitment of the earl of Clarendon to the Tower on a general charge of treason in November 1667, despite considerable pressure to do so from the king. Frequently when Charles endeavoured to alter the Restoration church settlement in the favour of dissenters a majority of bishops led the opposition in the upper House. When he attempted to suspend the Act of Uniformity with his Indulgence Bill – introduced in the Lords in February 1663 – his most vehement critics there were the bishops.[24] Even during the popish plot not every prelate constantly supported the government. Anxious to dispel criticism from Country peers that they were 'Popishly affected', and concerned by the court's continued sympathy towards Catholics, a few,

[19] G. Ornsby (ed.), *The correspondence of John Cosin, bishop of Durham* (Surtees Society, vols. LII, LV 1868, 1870), LV, p. 26, Sheldon to Cosin, 3 Sept. 1661.
[20] R. S. Bosher, *The making of the Restoration Settlement, 1649–1662* (1951), p. 237.
[21] Carte MSS 35, fol. 148, Conway to Ormond, 27 November 1666.
[22] C. A. Edie, 'The Irish Cattle Bills: a study in Restoration politics', *Transactions of the American Philosophical Society*, new series, 60, 2 (1970), 28–9; Bodl., Rawlinson MSS A. 130, fols. 59, 61.
[23] Add. MSS 35,865, fol. 224; HLRO, Proxy Book 5, proxies held on 20 November 1675.
[24] Clarendon, *Life*, II, pp. 345–6.

including the influential bishops of London (Compton), Durham (Crew), Lincoln (Barlow) and Rochester (Dolben) voted with the Country party on several occasions in the autumn of 1678. Most dramatically, in early November, five, including Compton of London, backed Shaftesbury's motion that the duke of York should be removed from the court and council.[25] The king, Danby and most other Court lords, however, opposed this course of action.

II

Especially when important business was pending in parliament both king and peers were anxious that lords attended regularly. 'By the King's writ your Lordships are summoned upon the most difficult and urgent matters relating to the Kingdom and Church of England upon which you are required to give your counsels and advice', observed one peer in 1680.[26] At all times the regular attendance of peers was necessary if the House was to function properly. On several occasions committee chairmen complained about poor levels of attendance and their inability to obtain a quorum.[27] With the development of political parties in the 1670s the issue of attendance assumed a new importance. No longer did the government seek the attendance of all peers, but only those thought likely to support the Court party. From 1675 the leaders of both parties wrote letters to potential adherents urging them to attend.[28]

There were several methods by which the king could regulate attendance. He might decline a writ of summons to a peer or spiritual lord. Without a writ of summons a peer was not entitled to sit in parliament. When the king decided to call a parliament, or when peers succeeded to a title they received individual writs of summons. Charles I had regarded parliament as an extension of his court and on several occasions had withheld a writ of summons to exclude those who had displeased him.[29] Charles II did not emulate his father. He was aware of the high esteem in which the restored peerage held their privileges – their right to determine their own attendance was highly prized – and rather than antagonise the House for the sake of excluding a few of his opponents he never deliberately detained a writ from any peer eligible to sit in the chamber. Twice, however, he did issue a writ of summons to minors. In October 1667 Charles issued writs to the earls of Rochester and Mulgrave with full knowledge that they were under twenty-one, in the hope that they would vote for the impeachment of ex-Lord Chancellor

[25] K. H. D. Haley, *The first earl of Shaftesbury* (Oxford, 1968), p. 471.
[26] Carte MSS 228, fol. 233, earl of Huntingdon's speech, 13 Nov. 1680.
[27] A quorum was five for a 'select' committee and three for a subcommittee.
[28] See below, pp. 288–9, 251–2.
[29] Foster, pp. 16–18.

Clarendon.[30] Fearful that this would establish a precedent for the king to pack the chamber with minors, and resentful of this attempted encroachment upon their privileges, the Lords refused to permit either peer to take his seat until his majority. The House endorsed the report from its Committee for Privileges that a minor could not sit in parliament, despite a message from the king desiring their lordships to admit the earl of Mulgrave.[31]

Charles II resorted to proclamations, letters to potential absentees and word of mouth as a means of encouraging regular attendance. On one notable occasion in November 1680 he spoke to peers who were present at court, imploring them to attend and vote against the Exclusion Bill when it eventually reached the Lords.[32] Neither the king nor his ministers systematically wrote to government supporters before each session asking them to attend parliament. Temporal lords were only written to when important government legislation was contemplated, or when the court was anxious about the designs of its opponents, as in February 1677 when Danby expected the Country party to try to persuade the House to declare parliament dissolved by the alleged 'illegal' fifteen-month prorogation. On this occasion several Court lords received letters from the Secretaries of State requiring them to attend or return proxy forms.[33]

Only the bishops were systematically reminded of their duties at Westminster. A few weeks before the start of every session the archbishop of Canterbury, and sometimes the bishop of London, wrote to every bishop requiring him to attend, or if infirm, to make a proxy.[34] The initiative for this practice did not always come from the king. On at least two occasions Sheldon urged his brethren to attend and protect the church from royal policies. In December 1662, as bishop of London, he instructed bishops to be present when parliament assembled on 18 February because in his eyes the Church was endangered by the king's recent Declaration of Indulgence.[35] Ten years later as archbishop of Canterbury he implored his prelates to repair to Westminster and, if necessary, oppose the second Declaration of Indul-

[30] HLRO, Manuscript Minutes 15 (21 Oct. 1667); Committee for Privileges Minute Book 2, 27, 35; Bodl., Rawlinson MSS A. 130, fols. 67–8.
[31] Manuscript Mins. 15, 29 Oct. 1667; Bodl., Rawlinson MSS A. 130, fol. 67.
[32] *Hist. MSS Comm.*, 36, 14th Rept, Appendix pt VII, Ormonde MSS, V (1908), p. 486, Conway to Ormond, 9 Nov. 1680; Haley, *Shaftesbury*, p. 601.
[33] *LJ*, XIII, 36; Proxy Book 6: proxies registered by 15 February 1677. Twenty-three Court lords as compared with four Country peers had registered proxies by this date.
[34] Bodl., Tanner MSS 43, fol. 200, archbishop of Canterbury to bishops, Jan. 1677; 42, fol. 46, archbishop of York to Sheldon, 25 Oct. 1673; BL, Harleian MSS 7,377, fol. 6, letter to the bishops, 1669, fol. 39, Sheldon to bishop of Bangor, 28 Dec. 1672, fol. 58, letter from Sheldon's secretary to the archbishop of York, 29 March 1675. See also, N. Sykes, *From Sheldon to Secker, aspects of English church history 1660–1768* (Cambridge, 1959), pp. 22–4.
[35] Bodl., Tanner MSS 48, fol. 69, Frewen to Sheldon, 6 Dec. 1662, *Cosin Correspondence* (ed. G. Ornsby), LV, p. 101, Sheldon to Cosin, 26 Dec. 1662.

Table 1 *Average attendance per session, 1660–1681*

Parliament/session	Number of sittings	Peers	Bishops	Total
Convention				
25 April–13 Sept. 1660	133	62	–	62
6 Nov.–29 Dec. 1660	51	63	–	63
Cavalier				
8 May–30 July 1661	65	82	–	82
20 Nov. 1661–19 May 1662	133	62	18	80
18 Feb.–27 July 1663	89	59	14	73
16 March–17 May 1664	37	73	17	90
24 Nov. 1664–2 March 1665	51	52	14	66
9–31 Oct. 1665 (Oxford)	18	24	9	33
18 Sept. 1666–8 Feb. 1667	91	59	11	70
10 Oct. 1667–9 May 1668	124	62	14	76
19 Oct.–11 Dec. 1669	36	64	13	77
14 Feb. 1670–22 April 1671	184	58	12	70
4 Feb.–29 March 1673	46	69	12	81
27 Oct.–4 Nov. 1673	4	51	14	65
7 Jan.–24 Feb. 1674	40	73	14	87
13 April–9 June 1675	49	75	14	89
13 Oct.–22 Nov. 1675	21	67	15	82
15 Feb. 1677–13 May 1678	117	70	15	85
23 May–15 July 1678	47	58	11	69
21 Oct.–30 Dec. 1678	70	63	11	74
1679 Parliament				
6–13 March 1679	6	57	11	68
15 March–27 May 1679	72	71	12	83
1680/1 Parliament				
21 Oct. 1680–10 Jan. 1681	59	70	11	81
Oxford Parliament				
21–28 March 1681	8	53	13	66

Average attendance for the reign as a whole was seventy-four per sitting.
Sources: Lords' *Journals* and Manuscript Minutes.

gence.[36] Largely as a result of Sheldon's letters at least half of the twenty-four bishops attended every session and when business affecting the church was anticipated the attendance of two-thirds was not uncommon. The average clerical attendance in the session of 1661–2 when the Uniformity Bill was before the House was seventeen.[37]

[36] BL, Harleian MSS 7,377, fol. 39, Sheldon to the bishop of Bangor, 28 Dec. 1672; fol. 42, same to Bishop Henchman, 6 Feb. 1673.
[37] See table 1 for the average clerical attendance at other sessions.

The peers themselves regulated attendance. Particularly when the House was split on an issue of major importance or when the Lords anticipated extremely controversial business, all peers were strictly required to attend. When the House anticipated Viscount Stafford's treason trial in late November 1680 it instructed the Lord Chancellor to despatch letters to all absentee peers to be present within a fixed time.[38] Those who were either too elderly or too ill to attend were only excused on the testimony of two witnesses. The usual practice had been for one peer to offer the excuse and apology of an absentee. During the acrimonious dispute with the Commons over Skinner's judicial case the Lords had ordered that no lord was to leave town whilst the House was sitting, threatening to fine absentees who did not have a reasonable excuse £40.[39] Accordingly on 9 November 1669 Lords Langdale, Stafford, Rivers, Northampton and Derby were fined £40.[40] The threat of such a heavy fine was quite exceptional and was a reflection of the importance the House attached to its judicial privileges when these were questioned by the Commons.

Generally peers did not wilfully absent themselves from their chamber. Some lords were simply not interested in politics and preferred not to attend. Most notable by their absence in the 1670s were the seventh earl of Pembroke, the earl of Sussex and Baron Montagu of Boughton. Pembroke and Sussex were usually preoccupied gambling and womanising whilst Montagu, who never attended after 1673, preferred the rural solitude of his Northamptonshire estate.[41] The primary cause of non-attendance was ill health. This was to be expected in an assembly where a majority of members were middle-aged or elderly. In 1661 44 per cent were over fifty and for the reign as a whole the average age was fifty, higher than in the House of Commons.[42] When the House was called on 25 November 1661 the most common reason given for non-attendance was sickness. Of the seventy-eight absentees, twenty-four were sick, seventeen had left proxies (some of these were due to illness), three were excused and two were abroad.[43] From the correspondence in the Tanner MSS it is evident that sickness, and gout in

---

[38] *LJ*, XIII, 669.

[39] Manuscript Minutes 15, 4 May 1668; 16, 9 November 1669.

[40] Ibid., 16, 19 November 1669.

[41] For the four sessions of parliament between 1675 and 1678 Pembroke attended on twelve occasions and Sussex on fourteen. Even a letter from the Lord Chancellor at the height of the popish plot threatening Montagu with imprisonment if he did not attend immediately was ineffective (*Hist. MSS Comm.*, 45, 15th Rept, Appendix VIII, Buccleuch MSS, I (1899), p. 330, Finch to Montagu, 12 April 1679).

[42] Schoenfeld, *Restored House of Lords*, p. 91; B. D. Henning (ed.), *The history of parliament: the House of Commons, 1660–1690*, 3 vols. (1983), I, p. 1. Seventy-nine peers were under fifty and sixty-one were over fifty in 1661.

[43] *LJ*, XI, 336.

particular, was the main cause of clerical non-attendance.[44] Many aged prelates were too infirm to undertake lengthy and uncomfortable journeys to London. William Lucy, the 81-year-old bishop of St Davids, wrote to Sheldon in 1675 expressing the views of many of his brethren: 'If I should set out now it were odds I should not get to London in my life; truly I would ambitiously desire to be at parliament, but cannot unless it were kept at Brecknock.'[45]

Impassable winter roads and a peer's local business interests also delayed or prevented journeys to Westminster. Richard Sterne, archbishop of York, put off his journey to parliament three times in October 1673 because of the 'ill ways and weather and the high waters'.[46] Lord Rivers had asked the earl of Dorset in September 1665 to inform the House he would 'attend their lordships very speedily, extraordinary business' hindering him 'from attending sooner'.[47] The earls of Marlborough and Nottingham were too impoverished to travel long distances to London and then pay for food and lodgings in the 1670s. Thomas, eleventh Baron Willoughby, was so poor that he could only afford to reside in London for a week after taking his seat in October 1680.[48]

Such impediments affected only a minority of peers. Despite the image of noblemen in Restoration drama as prone to drunkenness and debauchery, political apathy was never a characteristic of the peerage during the reign.[49] The majority of peers took their parliamentary duties seriously. Between 1660 and 1681 the average attendance at each sitting of the House was seventy-four, approximately half those eligible to attend.[50] All the major bills of the reign, and especially those of a religious nature, resulted in an above-average attendance of sometimes ninety or a hundred. In the first session of 1675 when Danby's Test Bill and a serious privilege dispute with the Commons preoccupied the House, 134 out of the 168 peers eligible to sit in the chamber attended.[51] Some sessions witnessed far lower levels of attendance. Fear of the plague deterred lords from the Oxford session in 1665 and the average attendance was therefore only thirty-three. If there was little

---

[44] See for example, Bodl., Tanner MSS 45, fol. 105, bishop of Coventry and Lichfield to Sheldon, 22 Sept. 1666; 43, fol. 68, bishop of Bangor to Sheldon, 13 Jan. 1673; 39, fol. 117, bishop of Norwich to Sancroft, 14 Oct. 1678.

[45] Ibid., 42, fol. 142, bishop of St Davids to Sheldon, 12 April 1675.

[46] Ibid., fol. 46, archbishop of York to Sheldon, 25 Oct. 1673.

[47] Kent Archives Office, Sackville MSS U269, C88/2, fol. 61, Rivers to Dorset, 25 Sept. 1665.

[48] BL, Egerton MSS 3330, fol. 101, Marlborough to Danby, 23 April 1677; *Cal. SP Dom.*, 1676–7, 317; *LJ*, XIII, 610–21; P. J. W. Higson, 'A neglected Revolution family: the Lancashire Lords Willoughby of Parham and their association with Protestant dissent, 1640–1765' (University of Liverpool PhD thesis, 1971), p. 343.

[49] See for example, A. S. Turberville, *The House of Lords in the reign of William III* (Oxford, 1913), pp. 27–44.

[50] This compares favourably with the 1620s, when with only a slightly smaller membership than after 1660 it was rare for more than sixty peers to attend a session.

[51] *LJ*, XII, 652–728. See table 1.

business before the House, or if the business was dull, then only a few dozen peers might attend each day. This was frequently the case towards the end of a session when the House was considering private bills or judicial cases.

Reasons for attending the upper House varied from lord to lord. Some attended because, like the king, they found the debates entertaining.[52] Others sat specifically to promote their own private legislation. The earl of Bedford was often present in the 1660s to sponsor bills for draining the Great Level of the Fens, a scheme in which he had a considerable financial interest.[53] One reason why the earl of Derby attended frequently between 1660 and 1662 was to promote his estate bills. The earl of Berkshire reputedly took his seat in the Convention to avoid paying his debts.[54] Several peers actually stated that it was their duty to serve the public in parliament. By the 'public' they meant the propertied classes, the nobles, gentry and forty-shilling freeholders who comprised the bulk of the political nation. They argued that it was their responsibility to redress national and local grievances.[55]

Ministers and Privy Councillors sat in the House to despatch the king's business. Several times in the 1660s Lord Ashley, the Chancellor of the Exchequer, promoted legislation designed to benefit the Crown's finances. He chaired the committee on a bill to prevent frauds in the customs in April 1662, and in June 1663 sponsored a measure for vesting the profits from alum manufacture in the king.[56] Charles II expected his ministers to obstruct measures which he disapproved of. In July 1661 he told Clarendon to use his influence in the House to ensure that the bill to execute several regicides did not pass.[57] Five years later Charles employed his Lord Chancellor to oppose the controversial Irish Cattle Bill.[58] Since ministers and privy councillors were supposed to represent the king's interests in the House they were expected to

[52] Charles II began attending debates from March 1670. The earl of Bridgewater took great delight in attending parliament, which 'doth agree so much with my nature and disposition that I cannot find in my heart to forebear it' (Hertfordshire RO, Ashridge Collection, AH 1064, Bridgewater to John Halsey, 4 Oct. 1661).

[53] D. Summers, *The Great Level: a history of drainage and land reclamation in the Fens* (1976), pp. 79–83; HLRO, Committee Minutes 2, p. 224; Egerton MSS 2,043, fol. 23 (Diary of Col. Bullen Reymes, 1661–2); Bedford Estate Office, Russell Letters III (1668–79), no. 124, Bedford to Bolingbroke, 27 Sept. 1679.

[54] *Hist. MSS Comm.*, 5th Rept, Appendix MSS of the duke of Sutherland (1876), p. 148, Francis Newport to Sir Richard Leveson, 5 May 1660.

[55] These peers included Dorset, Huntingdon, Shaftesbury and Townshend (Kent Archives Office, Sackville MSS U269/036, fol. 81, earl of Dorset: 'Certain Queries concerning the ancient and Legal government and parliament of England'; Carte MSS 243, fol. 234, Richard Talbot to Ormond, 16 March 1675; 228, fol. 235; Add. MSS 41,654, fol. 30, Townshend to Shaftesbury, 2 Feb. 1677).

[56] Committee Minutes 1, pp. 225, 242, 244, 253, 282, 289.

[57] W. D. Macray (ed.), *Notes which passed at meetings of the Privy Council between Charles II and the earl of Clarendon, 1660–1667* (1896), p. 29.

[58] Carte MSS 35, fol. 124, Burlington to Ormond, 10 Nov. 1666; fols. 197–8, Conway to Ormond, 29 Dec. 1666; BL, Althorp Papers, Burlington Correspondence, B3, Robert Boyle to Burlington, 24 Oct. 1665.

attend regularly. They were among the most conscientious members. Of the twenty-nine privy councillors to sit in the chamber during the spring session of 1675 eighteen attended forty or more of the forty-nine sittings. Twenty-six attended in the autumn session, of whom nineteen were present on sixteen or more of the twenty-one sittings.[59] Such regular attendance meant that privy councillors were better able to influence proceedings to the king's benefit. Frequently they chaired committees, managed conferences with the Commons and transmitted royal messages to the House.[60]

III

Peers regarded their attendance as necessary to preserve their rights and privileges. An important characteristic of the peerage in the seventeenth century was its high regard for privilege. E. R. Foster has recently demonstrated that from 1603 to 1649 lords were ever watchful of their privileges.[61] From 1621 the House appointed a standing committee for privileges at the beginning of each session to prevent its members' privileges being lost through neglect. After 1660 this watchfulness became an obsession. Peers spent more time than ever before on the definition and protection of both their own privileges and those of their House. Over 200 issues of privilege concerning peers, their families and servants were brought to the attention of the House between 1660 and 1680.[62] Barely a session passed without the Lords becoming embroiled in a privilege dispute with the Commons. As one contemporary noticed in 1665, the peers were 'ridiculously tender of their privileges', strenuously resisting any endeavour either by the king or the House of Commons to encroach upon their rights.[63] The earl of Northampton echoed the thoughts of his fellow peers when he observed: 'If you part with one privilege and another you may at last lose all.'[64]

The members of the restored House of Lords had good reason to be attentive to their privileges. For eleven years the nobility had been deprived of all its privileges – an experience no peer wished to repeat. From 1649 to 1660 the distinction between the aristocracy and the gentry had all but disappeared. For the first time noblemen lost their immunity from arrest in civil litigation and suffered imprisonment for debt. Several were humiliated: Lords Chandos and Arundel of Wardour were burned in the hand for duelling.[65]

[59] A. C. Swatland, 'The role of privy councillors in the House of Lords, 1660–1681', in C. Jones (ed.), *A pillar of the constitution*, p. 52.
[60] Ibid., pp. 52–61.
[61] Foster, p. 143.
[62] All privilege cases are recorded in the *Journals of the House of Lords*.
[63] Carte MSS 34, fol. 468, Broderick to Ormond, 2 Nov. 1665.
[64] Add. MSS 28,046, fol. 56, Speech of the earl of Northampton, 2 April 1679.
[65] Firth, *House of Lords during the Civil War*, p. 233.

Most were forced to pay delinquency fines, and Lords Capel, Holland and Derby were executed for their adherence to the Royalist cause. At the restoration of both their House and their privileges peers looked upon the 1640s and 1650s as a period of unparalleled degradation. Early in the Convention the re-established Committee for Privileges was instructed to consider 'the great violation that hath been lately made upon the peerage of this kingdom'.[66] Almost at once the committee investigated the earl of Derby's death, deciding to exclude his 'murderers' from the Bill of Indemnity.[67] Individuals who persisted in violating the peers' privileges were hauled before the bar and were reprimanded, fined or imprisoned.[68] Indeed the experience of the two decades before 1660 was never forgotten by peers and was frequently alluded to in their speeches. After 1660 they vigorously resisted all encroachments upon their privileges. One consequence of this was to bring their House into conflict with the House of Commons.[69]

In the context of parliament the word 'privilege' had several meanings in the seventeenth century. The antiquary John Seldon divided the peers' privileges into two categories in the 1620s: 'things which concern them either as they are one estate together in the upper House or as every of them is privately a single baron'.[70] Some of the rights which Seldon considered concerned the peers as 'one estate in the upper House' were the right to make proxies, enter protests in the Journal, claim exemption for themselves, their families and servants from civil law suits during parliamentary sessions and exercise the right not to be questioned before the Commons without a hearing in the Lords.[71] Privilege also extended to certain functions of the House such as the right to initiate and amend bills and to receive judicial cases.[72] Peers additionally enjoyed individual rights as nobles which were distinct from their privileges as members of parliament. Several involved their rights in relation to the law courts. They testified on their honour instead of on oath; a peer could not be arrested for debt, but was only subject to distraint. In cases of treason, felony or misprision a lord (though not a bishop) was entitled to a trial by his peers. Peers were protected by a special statute, 'Scandalum Magnatum', against any who spread false stories against them. They were allowed a specific number of chaplains under the Statute of Pluralities. By right a peer could appoint a deputy to perform the duties of office entrusted to him. Also, as a consequence of the nobles' traditional role

---

[66] *LJ*, XI, 10.
[67] HLRO, Committee for Privileges Minute Book 1, pp. 15, 37–8, 49.
[68] *LJ*, XI, 26, 35, 75, 79, 87, 198–9.
[69] See chapter 7, section II (pp. 127–41).
[70] HLRO, Main Papers, 15 Dec. 1621, fol. 1.
[71] J. Seldon, *The privileges of the baronage of England when they sit in Parliament* (1689), pp. 7–141.
[72] Foster, pp. 138–9.

as royal counsellors, peers had the right of access to the king. These privileges reinforced the nobility's exalted status in the country and were especially insisted upon in the reign of Charles II as the aristocracy fought to recover the prestige it had lost during the 1640s and 1650s.[73]

One notable feature of the restored House of Lords was its desire for these individual privileges to be recognised in parliamentary legislation. The peers' endeavours to obtain special treatment in acts of parliament resulted mainly from their experiences in the 1640s and 1650s when their privileges, which had not been recognised by statute, were disregarded. Even after 1660 privileges which were not widely known or which were controversial were sometimes ignored. In June 1660 the High Bailiff of Westminster illegally confiscated the earl of Chesterfield's books and papers because of his outstanding debts.[74] A year later the earl of Lincoln's house was illegally broken into by the Under-Sheriff of Middlesex.[75] To safeguard against such intrusions into their privacy peers inserted several of their privileges in legislation during the early 1660s. They amended the 1662 Militia Bill so that lords' houses could only be searched with a warrant signed by the king, and then in the presence of the lord lieutenant or deputy lieutenant of the county, but later the Commons diluted these amendments.[76] In the 1662 Bill against Quakers the House secured a special provision for peers who refused to take an oath in a court of law.[77] Moreover, in the Bill for the Safety and Preservation of the King (1661) the Lords persuaded the Commons to accept a clause confirming that a peer could only be tried by his fellow peers and not by commoners, as had occurred between 1649 and 1660.[78]

Often such amendments were vigorously resisted by the lower House, resulting in disputes between the Houses as was the case with the 1665 Plague Bill. This measure, which was received from the Commons towards the end of the Oxford session, was resisted by the Lords because it empowered a JP to authorise the shutting up of a nobleman's house. The Commons believed this was necessary to prevent the spread of the plague in London, but the peers considered that the bill might establish a precedent which could ultimately lead to the loss of the special status for their residences.[79] Neither chamber made concessions and the bill was lost in the prorogation of parliament. Disputes also arose when the peers insisted on being assessed by lords, not commoners, for their offices in poll bills. Throughout the century

---

[73] Seldon, *Privileges of the baronage*, pp. 142–76; L. O. Pike, *A constitutional history of the House of Lords* (1894), pp. 254–67.
[74] Committee for Privileges Minute Book 1, pp. 15, 17, 18.
[75] *LJ*, XI, 319.
[76] *LJ*, XI, 454–66; HLRO, Main Papers, 13 May 1662, papers 7 and 8; *CJ*, VIII, 418, 421, 426.
[77] *LJ*, XI, 389; *CJ*, VIII, 265–6; *Statutes* (1810–22), vol. V, 350–1.
[78] Committee Minutes 1, pp. 8–10, 25 May 1661.
[79] Carte MSS 34, fol. 468, Broderick to Ormond, 2 Nov. 1665.

the Commons was especially protective of its financial privileges, claiming the exclusive right to levy taxes.[80] With vivid memories of commoners taxing them excessively (as they believed) during the 1650s the Lords sought the right of self-assessment in poll bills. For instance, they added a proviso to a poll bill in August 1660 allowing them to appoint their own commissioners and, after a struggle with the Commons, got their own way.[81] In several subsequent bicameral disputes over the question of who should assess peers, the king and his ministers persuaded the Lords to yield, on the grounds that royal finances would suffer if the money bill failed to pass.[82]

Like members of the Commons, peers enjoyed privileges which were necessary for the effective functioning of their House. Long before 1660 it had been recognised by the Crown that in order for them to expedite parliamentary business members should be exempted from certain obligations to which ordinary subjects were liable.[83] No law suits could be initiated against peers or MPs when parliament was in session. This was an extremely important privilege since creditors frequently used the law to recover debts from noblemen. In July 1661 the marquis of Worcester, Lords Crofts and Howard of Escrick petitioned the House when creditors filed law suits against them during a session of parliament.[84] As in all cases during the reign when peers were implicated in civil suits, the House ordered a stay of proceedings until twenty days after a session, the time when parliamentary privilege lapsed. However, this privilege was abused and used as a means of avoiding debts and other obligations. Thirty-four declarations were filed against Lord Rivers in 1661, and though the House halted all actions against him, it strongly suspected he was evading justice. Shortly after this the earl of Bridgewater expressed his concern about such abuse of privilege, writing that he would never insist on exercising his parliamentary privileges.[85]

The most commonly exercised and most controversial privilege was immunity from arrest for a peer's servants during the period of parliamentary privilege. Of more than 100 privilege cases to come before the House between 1661 and 1669, 42 per cent involved peers' menial servants, and in almost every case the servant had been arrested or prosecuted for debt.[86] Invariably the House ordered the servant's release or halted the legal proceedings against him, and sometimes even ordered those responsible for his arrest to appear at the bar as delinquents.[87] This privilege was extensively abused by

[80] J. P. Kenyon, *The Stuart constitution* (Cambridge, 1966), p. 413.
[81] Schoenfeld, *Restored House of Lords*, pp. 144–5.
[82] *LJ*, XI, 444–5, 459–60, 466–7; *CJ*, VIII, 424, 433.
[83] Foster, p. 140.
[84] *LJ*, XI, 286, 301, 308.
[85] Hertfordshire RO, Ashridge Collection, AH. 1069, Bridgewater to John Halsey, 17 Oct. 1662.
[86] 51 per cent of privilege cases directly concerned peers and 6 per cent involved peeresses (*LJ*, XI–XII).
[87] See Foster, p. 143.

impecunious peers during the reign. Since peers were immune from civil suits during a session of parliament their creditors would often proceed against their servants instead. Even when a lord was absent from parliament he could still claim privilege for his servant, and this was precisely what Lord Windsor did when his servant, Rawlins, was arrested in April 1671 because his master owed money to a local shopkeeper. Windsor wrote to Viscount Halifax asking him to move the House of Lords to order the arrest and punishment of the shop-keeper, his attorney and the bailiffs who had undertaken Rawlins' arrest.[88]

Not surprisingly the House of Lords' vigorous endorsement of members' privileges aroused the hostility of people outside parliament.[89] Lawyers, in particular, felt the Lords' activities in halting law suits was an unwarranted intrusion into the legal processes of the law courts. Creditors in the City of London bemoaned the fact that privilege prevented them from recovering money owed by peers. Similar complaints had been voiced earlier in the century, but because the House and its privileges had been swept away in 1649 people were ignorant of and unaccustomed to the Lords' privileges after 1660.[90] In part this would account for why there were proportionally more reported infringements of peers' privileges early in the 1660s than later in the reign.[91] Contemporaries were highly indignant that peers like the earl of Berkshire should take their seats simply to frustrate their creditors' law suits.[92]

Most criticism was directed against protections. These were certificates issues by lords for the purpose of identifying their servants and dependants and protecting them from arrest upon civil process – usually for debt – during sessions of parliament. The earl of Thanet issued his friend and 'menial servant' John Aubrey with a protection in May 1675 so that he could attend to the earl's affairs in London without fear of imprisonment.[93] Protections were widely circulated and one lawyer calculated that they ben-efited 10,000 men in 1668.[94] Irresponsible lords issued protections to those who were not their menial servants. In 1678 Lord Cromwell was upbraided by the House for issuing illegal protections. Peers' servants sometimes sold protections to bankrupt Londoners, and on one occasion in 1663 Lord Hunsdon's protections were counterfeited and sold for 40 shillings.[95]

[88] HLRO, Main Papers, 47a, Windsor to Halifax, 12 April 1671.
[89] Clarendon, *Life*, II, p. 167.
[90] A. Horstman, 'Justice and peers: The judicial activities of the seventeenth century House of Lords' (University of California PhD thesis, 1977), pp. 68–71, 78, 80–5.
[91] Between 1661 and 1670, 58 cases involving peers' servants came before the House as com-pared with only 29 between 1670 and 1681.
[92] *Hist. MSS Comm.*, 5th Rept, Sutherland MSS, p. 148; F. Newport to R. Leveson, 5 May 1660.
[93] Bodl., Aubrey MSS 13, fols. 217, 218, Thanet to Aubrey, 3 and 4 May 1675.
[94] *Hist. MSS Comm.*, 71, Finch MSS, I (1913), 512, Sir Roger Twysden to Sir Heneage Finch, 3 Aug. 1668.
[95] *LJ*, XI, 491, 512; XIII, 137, 140.

The House itself was not oblivious to this abuse of privilege. 'Sensible of the great complaint of the people of the kingdom', the Lords declared on 3 December 1661 that all protections granted to individuals who were not peers' menial servants or 'persons necessarily employed about their estates' were void.[96] Their lordships also promised to punish severely people who forged protections. This order was reaffirmed two years later. The House investigated abuses involving protections. In March 1663 a man who had purchased counterfeit protections was questioned at the bar, though the forger was not apprehended. Lord Cromwell was reprimanded for the illegal issue of protections in 1678. Nine years earlier the Lords had drafted a bill, which among other things would have removed parliamentary privilege for the servants and estates of members of both chambers. Ironically this measure was rejected by the Commons during a dispute with the Lords over judicial privileges.[97]

Several privileges were restricted exclusively to the peers' activities in their own chamber, most notably the right to vote by proxy and enter dissents and protests in the Journal. Medieval in origin, the proctorial system allowed an absent member to entrust his vote to another who was in attendance. As in the first half of the seventeenth century, peers usually bestowed their proxies on friends, relatives and those sharing a similar religious outlook.[98] The second duke of Albemarle held the second duke of Newcastle's proxy because of his strong ties of kinship with the Cavendish family.[99] With the development of coherent Court and Country parties in the 1670s political considerations frequently influenced the disposal of proxies. Thus, the Presbyterian earl of Bedford held the proxy of his Country party colleague, Lord Crew, in both 1675 and 1678, whilst his rival, Lord Lindsey, one of Danby's lieutenants, held the proxies of Court supporters such as Lords Norreys, Yarmouth and Campden.[100] Proxies had to be renewed each session after a prorogation and were nullified by the presence of the absentee in the chamber.

The House decided when proxies could be used and in Charles II's reign they were only employed in formal votes of the House, and usually then when divisions were close.[101] A good example of the deployment of proxies

---

[96] Committee for Privileges Mins. 1, p. 70; *LJ*, XI, 341.
[97] *LJ*, XI, 481, 512; XII, 265; XIII, 140; F. R. Harris, *The life of Edward Mountagu, K.G., first earl of Sandwich, 1625–1672*, 2 vols. (1912), II, pp. 307–9, 313–15.
[98] Foster, pp. 19–22.
[99] HLRO, Proxy Book 6 (proxies entered 21 Oct. 1678); *Hist. MSS Comm.*, 29, 13th Rept, MSS of the Duke of Portland (1892), II, p. 153, Albemarle to Newcastle, 19 Nov. 1675; Nottingham University, Portland Collection, Cavendish MSS PW1/183, Newcastle to Albemarle, 5 July 1678.
[100] Proxy Book 6. Bedford registered Crew's proxies on 23 October 1675 and on 25 May 1678.
[101] Proxies could not be deployed in committees or in peerage trials.

is at the end of the second reading debate on the highly contentious Roos Divorce Bill in March 1670. Lord Roos, eldest son of the earl of Rutland, promoted a private bill to allow him to divorce his adulterous wife. Many observers noted that if the bill passed it would set a precedent for the king to repudiate his barren queen and remarry. Although Charles discountenanced such speculation, the duke of York was sufficiently alarmed about his own succession to the throne that he mobilised a powerful phalanx of peers and bishops against the measure during the second-reading debate. At the end of a record nine-hour debate on 17 March the question was put for the second reading and after the telling of the House by the duke of Ormond and the earl of Anglesey, the Not Contents actually had one more vote than the Contents, forty-two as against forty-one, until proxies were called. The Contents' fifteen proxies, compared with the Not Contents' six, enabled them to secure both an eight-vote majority and the second reading of the bill two days later. However, proxies were not called for at the end of the third-reading debate because the vote was not sufficiently close, the Contents enjoying an eight-vote majority.[102]

The proxy system was valuable because it enabled less active members to exert influence on the proceedings of the House. In the spring session of 1675 fourteen peers had made proxies before the session opened on 13 April, and only two of these eventually managed to attend. Twelve of the eighteen peers who registered proxies by the first day of the ensuing autumn session never attended at all.[103] Those who had assigned proxies that autumn left their imprint on the course of events in parliament: proxy votes allowed the Court party to thwart the attempt of 'opposition' groups on 20 November 1675 to pass a motion calling on the king to dissolve parliament.[104] Earlier, in 1667, ten proxies had enabled the supporters of an Anglo-Scottish trade bill to ensure that it received its third reading.[105]

It would be wrong to assume that peers who left proxies were necessarily uninterested in politics. Many were elderly, ill or were absent on the king's business.[106] Despite the fact that it cost a peer £2 to register a proxy in the Proxy Book, in several sessions as many as forty registered proxies in the clerk's book. Indeed many made proxies because this helped to demonstrate their loyalty either to the king and the court, or, if they were Country peers, to their own party. Thus a sick Lord Townshend assigned his proxy to the

[102] Harris, *Sandwich*, II, pp. 323–33.
[103] See Proxy Books 5 and 6 (proxies entered 1675); *LJ*, XII, 665–728; XIII, 3–34.
[104] Add. MSS 35,865, fol. 224 (division list, 20 Nov. 1675). The government had sixteen proxies available to the opposition's seven.
[105] Bodl., Rawlinson MSS A. 130, fol. 115v, 19 Dec. 1667.
[106] For instance the earl of Winchilsea was ambassador in Constantinople and the duke of Ormond was frequently absent in the 1660s in Ireland, where he was lord lieutenant.

earl of Shaftesbury, in February 1677.[107] There was always a small proportion of absentees who failed to make a proxy. Several could not afford the fees, like Lord Willoughby in 1680.[108] Others were too indolent or forgetful, and one, Lord Fitzwalter, refused to make a proxy in 1679 claiming he would not be present to hear all the arguments concerning the business in which his vote might be cast.[109]

Proxies were managed for political purposes. Occasionally under the early Stuarts ministers had attempted to persuade peers to nominate proctors who favoured royal policies.[110] This practice became more widespread under Charles II, especially during Danby's ministry when an organised 'opposition' challenged court policies in the Lords. Danby made strenuous efforts to solicit proxies from absent lords, which he assigned to reliable Court peers. On several occasions proxies enabled the government to retain its grip on the chamber.[111] After the Second Test Bill received the royal assent on 30 November 1678 it was much more difficult to manage proxies, since they were not limited to those peers who had attended and subscribed to all the oaths and the declaration against Catholicism in the Act. Only eleven lords registered proxies in the subsequent Parliament (March–May 1679), compared with forty in the last session of the Cavalier Parliament (October to December 1678).[112]

If the number of proxies declined after 1678 the reverse occurred with dissents and protests. Almost twice as many protests were made during the eleven-week parliament of 1679 than had been made for any session of the Cavalier Parliament (1661–78).[113] The situation in 1679 was the direct consequence of differences of opinion resulting from the Popish Plot and the impeachment of the earl of Danby. Although the right of any peer to make a dissent, which involved him signing his name in the Journal below the vote he disapproved of, was as ancient as Henry VIII's reign, the practice of protesting with written reasons was an innovation of the Long Parliament in 1640.[114] By a standing order of March 1642 this privilege had been limited to the sitting following that in which the controversial vote had occurred. Protests were restricted to those who had actually voted. During the

---

[107] Add. MSS 41,654, fol. 30, Townshend to Shaftesbury, 2 Feb. 1677; Proxy Book 6, 13 Feb. 1677.
[108] Higson, 'A neglected Revolution family', p. 343.
[109] Add. MSS 28,053, fol. 150, Fitzwalter to Danby, 22 April 1679.
[110] Foster, p. 20.
[111] See below chapter 12, p. 252.
[112] In Proxy Book 6 there is a note under the earl of Rutland's proxy that the king's assent to the Test Act on 30 November voided all existing proxies.
[113] Protests and dissents are recorded in the *Journals*. Dissents differed from protests in that they did not give the reasons why peers objected to a majority decision in the chamber.
[114] J. E. T. Rogers, *A complete collection of the protests of the Lords*, 3 vols. (1875), I, pp. xvi–xx.

proceedings on the impeachment of the earl of Clarendon in November 1667 Lord Robartes recorded in his diary that the bishop of St Asaph had written his name in the Journal but had later blotted it out because he had not been present when the vote had been taken.[115]

Protests reflected political divisions in the upper House. This was especially so from 1675 when the Lords was split between the Court and Country parties. Whilst less than a third of the sittings of parliament for the reign occurred between 1675 and 1681, 63 per cent of all recorded protests were made during this six-year period.[116] Most were made by members of the Country party since they were normally the minority group in divisions. Country peers were responsible for six of the nine dissents and protests made in the last session of the Cavalier Parliament. In the 1679 parliament they entered nine of the sixteen protests.[117] Six however were the work of Danby's friends and associates who opposed the bills to banish and attaint the former Lord Treasurer.[118]

The privilege of protesting with reasons was particularly valued by members of the Country party. Because protests, which were usually a condensed version of the arguments used in debates, could be published they were an extremely important means of stimulating extra-parliamentary support for their activities. Shaftesbury incorporated several of the protests against the government's Test Bill of 1675 in his widely disseminated *Letter from a Person of Quality*.[119] The names of the noblemen who protested against the rejection of the Exclusion Bill were speedily distributed in manuscript form outside the House, enabling the 'opposition' in the Commons and the City of London to vent their scorn against the bishops and government lords, who had neither protested nor voted for the bill.[120] Opposition groups' frequent recourse to protests for propaganda purposes did not go unchallenged in the chamber. During the spring session of 1675 Court lords questioned the wording of a protest concerning the Test Bill's alleged subversion of the privilege of freedom of speech in parliament. 'Diverse expressions in the protestation' had aroused considerable resentment among Court lords and some suggested that the protesters should be imprisoned in the Tower for their insolent behaviour.[121] Though the Court party succeeded in carrying a motion that the reasons given in the protest reflected

---

[115] BL, Harleian MSS 2243, fol. 60 (Lord Robartes' Parliamentary Notebook).

[116] Thirty-seven separate protests were made between 1660 and 1671 and sixty-three for the period 1675–81.

[117] *LJ*, XIII, 308, 363, 366, 392, 405, 426, 434, 436, 441.

[118] Ibid., 471, 476, 481, 497, 502, 505, 514, 549, 559, 565, 570, 572, 587, 594.

[119] See *Parl. Hist.*, IV, pp. xxxvii–lxvii.

[120] Add. MSS 28,930, fols. 203–4, W. Ellis to J. Ellis, 16 Nov. 1680.

[121] Rogers, *Protests of the Lords*, I, pp. xiv, xx; *LJ*, XIII, 23.

on the honour of the House, the privilege-conscious majority subsequently decided against expunging the protest from the Journal.[122]

One characteristic of the restoration House of Lords was the exploitation of privilege by 'opposition' politicians. This was because they knew that the abolition of the House had made the peerage extremely privilege-conscious, determined to defend every privilege. Any issue which concerned privilege was normally considered sympathetically by the House. Thus the earl of Huntingdon deliberately emphasised the privilege of freedom of speech when he seconded a successful motion on 13 November 1680 for the erasure of the proceedings in the Journal against four Country lords who had been imprisoned in the Tower for contempt in February 1677.[123] In March 1664 the earl of Bristol had stressed Clarendon's alleged violations of privilege in an attempt to revive his impeachment of the Lord Chancellor.[124]

Privileges were exploited to provoke disputes with the House of Commons. Since the restored peerage almost invariably rallied to the defence of its privileges, minority groups used issues of privilege to block controversial legislation. Several Presbyterian peers were anxious to delay the Conventicle Bill in 1663. Lord Wharton devised a list of arguments which played upon every conceivable source of jealousy between the Houses, and most were connected with privilege.[125] Five years later the duke of Buckingham and his adherents fomented the judicial case of *Skinner* v. *The East India Company* into a protracted dispute with the Commons in part to delay a further conventicle bill.[126] Frequently such conflicts led to parliamentary deadlock, in which neither chamber would compromise, as was the case in 1675 when the Country party latched on to the Lords' right to determine appeals from Chancery as a method of blocking Danby's Test Bill. The Commons questioned this privilege largely on the grounds that the disputed cases involved MPs, who themselves were immune from legal actions during the duration of parliamentary privilege.

Privilege was therefore an important feature of parliamentary politics under Charles II. Many privileges ensured that the peers were not distracted by mundane problems when they performed their duties as judges and legislators. Certain privileges were criticised by contemporaries because they were abused or exercised by people who did not attend parliament at all, like peeresses, dowagers and servants. Most privileges reinforced a peer's dignity and

---

[122] *LJ*, XII, 668–9, 671; *The Bulstrode Papers: The collection of autograph letters and historical documents formed by Alfred Morrison* (1897), I, p. 289.

[123] Carte MSS 228, fols. 233–6, earl of Huntingdon's speech, 13 Nov. 1680.

[124] Bodl., Clarendon MSS 80, fol. 153, earl of Bristol's petition to the House of Lords, 19 March 1664.

[125] Carte MSS 81, fols. 170, 178, 240–1; Carte MSS 77, fol. 555, Wharton's material against the Bill; *LJ*, XI, 549, 558, 561, 563, 567.

[126] See below chapter 7, pp. 130–4

social standing, and several underlined the House of Lords' distinctiveness from the Commons. One function of the House considered a fundamental privilege by their lordships was the right to participate in the legislative process, and this is the subject of the next chapter.

4

Legislation

The chief function of parliament in the seventeenth century was the enactment of legislation. This aspect of parliament has been neglected by most historians of the period. Scholars of the Restoration period have focused instead on the political and constitutional aspects of parliament, and especially those of the House of Commons.[1] Yet in the reign of Charles II both Houses devoted more time to legislation than to any other business. Over 900 bills were read in the upper House between 1660 and 1681 – approximately twice the combined number of judicial and privilege cases proceeded with by the House. Two central questions will be addressed in this chapter. First, how did the House process legislation? Secondly, what was the House of Lords' contribution to the legislative process for the reign as a whole?

I

The House of Lords dealt with both public and private bills. Public bills, comprising a third of all bills read in parliament, were those which concerned the nation as a whole, or at least a sizeable section of it. They included bills for the benefit of the church, trade, the poor and any which concerned the 'person, revenue, or household of the king, queen or prince'.[2] Private bills, in contrast, were those intended to benefit individuals or specific interest groups. Promoters of private bills incurred the payment of fees to the clerk, his assistants and to the gentleman usher. In the Lords a private bill normally started from a petition signed by the interested parties. The distinctions between public and private bills were not always as straightforward as this. A bill which had been subject to fees and was sponsored by several individuals could also be a public bill if it affected a section of the country. Conversely, measures which affected one person, like bills for banishment and attainder, were sometimes regarded as public bills, and were assented to

---

[1] Particular pieces of legislation have been studied for how they illuminate the politics of the period: see, for example, Seaward, Hutton.
[2] W. Hakewill, *The manner how statutes are enacted in parliament by passing of Bills* (1659), pp. 131–2, 134.

by the king in the customary manner for public bills – 'le Roy le veult' – not 'soit fait come il est desire', as was usual for a private bill.

On the whole the Lords regarded public bills as more important than private ones, though highly controversial private bills were of the utmost interest, stimulating a good attendance.[3] The House normally gave public bills priority, often relegating the reading of private legislation to before 9 o'clock in the morning or to afternoon sittings when attendance was thinner. When their lordships were engaged on a particularly urgent public bill, like that of Indemnity and Oblivion in the Convention, they might temporarily prohibit the receipt of private bills for a specific period, usually two weeks or a month. Another indication of the high esteem in which the House regarded public bills was that especially after 1674 the most controversial were referred to the committee of the whole House, rather than to smaller 'select' committees, after their second reading.[4] This allowed every peer present – including the king's ministers, who were often too busy with administration to attend 'select' committee meetings, which took place early in the morning or in the afternoon when the House was not sitting – the opportunity of participating in the scrutiny of legislation.

Bills came from a variety of sources. Most often they were sent up from the House of Commons. Just under half of all bills to receive at least one reading had originated there. This was because 70 per cent of all legislation was initiated in the lower chamber during the reign.[5] Traditionally a far higher proportion of bills were introduced in the Commons because of its representative nature. When electors had a grievance or desired a private act to enable them to convey land, for example, they generally turned first to their own MP to act on their behalf in parliament. The Commons was considerably larger than the Lords and therefore had more members capable of sponsoring bills. Also the majority of government legislation began its parliamentary life in the Commons. From the sixteenth century it had been customary for the government to introduce financial bills in the House of Commons. Any attempt to initiate such a measure in the Lords was bitterly resisted by MPs, who considered it their prerogative as representatives of the electorate to initiate all bills which laid a tax upon the people.[6] Bills which

<hr>

[3] The famous Roos Divorce Bill of 1670 witnessed attendances of more than eighty lords per session.

[4] Very little public legislation was non-controversial by this date. 'Select' committee was not a contemporary term. It is used in this study to distinguish between committees of the whole House and those of fewer lords, meeting in specific committee rooms.

[5] There was nothing new about the lower chamber initiating the bulk of legislation: this had been the case in the reign of Elizabeth I. See G. R. Elton, *The Tudor constitution* (2nd edn, Cambridge, 1982), p. 248.

[6] The Commons rejected a government bill introduced in the Lords in 1661 because it laid a tax on Londoners (PRO, P.C. 2/55, fol. 124, note on a bill to repair the streets of Westminster).

definitely or possibly originated with the government accounted for no more than 10 per cent of bills given their first parliamentary reading in the House of Lords during the reign.[7] Like his Stuart predecessors, Charles II did not have a well-defined legislative programme. The king summoned parliament primarily to obtain monetary supplies, and tax bills were introduced in the Commons. However, because of the large number of privy councillors sitting in the Lords it made good sense to employ them to sponsor other categories of bills.[8] The Admiralty Jurisdiction Bill of 1662 and the measure for appointing commissioners to negotiate the king's proposed union between England and Scotland of 1670 were both introduced by privy councillors in the upper House.[9] The Lords was generally more tolerant on most religious subjects than the staunchly Anglican Cavalier Commons and therefore several pieces of religious legislation were introduced in that chamber too. The Lord Privy Seal, Lord Robartes, presented the king's controversial Indulgence Bill in the upper House in February 1663 because Charles II considered this measure, which was intended to enable him to dispense peaceable dissenters from some of the provisions of the Act of Uniformity, would receive a more sympathetic treatment from the peers. During Danby's ascendancy as chief minister, a higher proportion of public bills originated in the Lords than in previous years (see table 2). This was a reflection of the Lord Treasurer's firm control over the upper House and the growing problem of managing the Commons.

The overwhelming majority of legislation initiated in the Lords originated from private individuals, local communities and business interests. Altogether two-thirds of all bills introduced there were private, a comparatively higher proportion than in the Commons. The largest single category (35 per cent) consisted of estate bills. Many were to enable peers and gentlemen to convey land in order to pay their debts, or to raise marriage portions.[10] A much smaller proportion of private bills (5 per cent) were naturalisation bills. Aliens living in England had to be naturalised by private acts in order to hold or inherit property or to engage in certain trades. Two other significant categories of bills included those for river navigation and land enclosure, though these were not as numerous as they were to become in the eighteenth century.

---

[7] It is impossible to be precise about the proportion of bills initiated by the government. The documentary evidence is very scant, particularly as few bills were discussed in formal meetings of the privy council.

[8] For a study of the parliamentary responsibilities of privy councillors see Swatland, 'The role of privy councillors', pp. 51–78.

[9] PRO, P.C. 2/55, fol. 124; *LJ*, XI, 375, XII, 320.

[10] Estate bills were necessary in this period since land held in entail or in trust could not be sold in part or whole without an act of parliament.

Table 2 *Bills and acts, 1660–1681*

Parliament/ session	1	2	3	4	5	6	7	8	9	10	11	12
Convention	45	87	8	37	51	36	62	22	45	35	16	49
Cavalier												
1661	23	95	5	18	42	53	37	9	23	22	5	27
1661/2	42	90	14	28	48	42	60	23	51	32	26	52
1663	29	97	12	17	44	53	32	14	27	14	9	29
1664	9	48	4	5	25	23	18	5	9	10	4	14
1664/5	24	66	4	20	30	36	26	13	25	6	14	16
1665	3	19	2	1	16	3	11	2	7	3	2	8
1666/7	18	61	5	13	35	26	29	12	25	11	9	22
1667/8	17	81	8	9	41	40	32	10	16	17	7	22
1669	6	31	3	3	16	15	1	–	1	–	–	–
1670/1	50	113	5	45	52	61	75	33	73	29	29	65
1673	19	28	5	14	18	10	12	15	14	13	11	10
1673	1	1	–	1	1	–	–	–	–	–	–	–
1674	16	32	6	10	20	12	2	3	1	1	–	–
1675	17	48	9	8	29	19	10	4	4	4	2	3
1675	11	38	8	3	21	17	5	2	2	4	–	3
1677/8	72	80	26	46	45	35	30	42	51	18	25	20
1678	28	32	10	18	22	10	13	17	25	7	11	10
1678	6	6	4	2	5	1	3	5	6	1	–	1
'Exclusion'												
1679	13	24	6	7	17	7	6	6	10	2	1	4
1680/1	8	32	7	1	25	7	8	2	4	3	–	3
1681	1	2	–	1	2	–	–	–	–	–	–	–
Total	458	1,111	151	307	605	506	472	239	419	232	171	358

Key
1 Bills introduced in the Lords and receiving at least one reading
2 Bills introduced in the Commons and receiving at least one reading
3 Public bills introduced and read in the Lords
4 Private bills introduced and read in the Lords
5 Public bills introduced and read in the Commons
6 Private bills introduced and read in the Commons
7 Bills introduced in the Commons and sent up to the Lords
8 Bills introduced in the Lords and sent down to the Commons
9 Bills amended in the Lords and passing the House
10 Unamended bills passing the Lords
11 Lords' bills receiving the royal assent
12 Commons' bills receiving the royal assent
Sources: Lords' and Commons' *Journals*.

Several pieces of legislation were the direct consequence of petitions to the House. On 20 March 1671 the earl of Northampton reported from a committee that had been appointed to consider a petition from imprisoned debtors that his committee had drafted a bill to remedy the prisoners' grievances.[11] The bill of December 1680 to distinguish between Catholic and Protestant nonconformists was also drawn up by members of the committee established to investigate a Quaker petition that alleged that JPs were employing Elizabethan and Jacobean recusancy laws (intended originally for Catholics) to prosecute other dissenters.[12] As in any period bills were drafted as a result of debates in the House: two measures for securing the Protestant religion had their genesis in the anti-Popery debates of February and March 1674.[13]

The chamber from which a bill had originated was not normally of paramount significance. Although most public bills and two-thirds of all private bills were introduced in the Commons, the peers did not regard the initiation of legislation as a symbol of their chamber's importance. An increase in the volume of legislation would only have impeded the Lords' ability to determine judicial cases. As it was, some lords complained about the 'wearisome life' in parliament with 'little satisfaction in it'.[14] The often poor levels of attendance at committees demonstrate that the routine considerations of bills only interested a minority of peers.[15] Moreover, the sheer quantity of bills introduced in the Commons meant that MPs were often overburdened with business. It is perhaps not surprising, therefore, that whereas 52 per cent of bills which originated in the Lords passed the House between 1660 and 1681, only 40 per cent of those initiated in the Commons reached the upper House during the same period. The ability of the Lords to pass a proportionally higher number of bills also stemmed from the calibre of its membership.

II

The members of Charles II's House of Lords were generally well equipped to perform their legislative duties in an efficient manner. The peerage was still the best-educated section of society. Altogether 52 per cent of peers had

[11] Manuscript Minutes 17, 20 March 1671.
[12] Most of the bill appears to have been drawn by the Lord Privy Seal, the earl of Anglesey (Committee Minutes 3, pp. 374–7).
[13] The two bills were: for further securing the Protestant religion and for the more effectual conviction of popish recusants.
[14] *Hist. MSS Comm.*, 27, 12th rept Appendix, pt IX (1891), MSS of the duke of Beaufort (1891), pp. 67, 71, marquis of Worcester to his wife, 6 July and 12 Nov. 1678.
[15] The voting figures for committees, recorded by the clerk in the Committee Minute Books, strongly suggest that even on the most controversial measures it was exceptional for over two-thirds of those appointed to attend meetings.

attended university or an inn of court, and twenty-three had been educated at both. The elementary legal training of the thirty-three peers known to have attended an inn of court was directly relevant to their legislative duties: estate bills, in particular, often raised legal and technical issues.[16]

To function effectively as legislators an essential requirement was administrative experience and expertise. This was particularly important for chairmen and members of committees who drafted, scrutinised and revised legislation. Here the Lords had an advantage over the Commons, for the majority of privy councillors, with their extensive experience of government administration, sat in the chamber. Of the twenty-nine members of the Privy Council in 1660, only five did not sit in the House of Lords. Privy councillors were among the most industrious members of the House, frequently chairing committees and managing conferences with the House of Commons. Several, most notably Lords Anglesey and Robartes and Bridgewater, were at times responsible for drafting legislation.[17] When the House adjourned into a committee of the whole House for freer debate, over 90 per cent of those lords appointed to occupy the chair and direct proceedings were privy councillors.[18]

Most of the lord lieutenants who exercised control over the administration of counties also sat in the upper chamber. A quarter of all peers who sat there between 1660 and 1681 were in fact lord lieutenants at some time during these years. Their intimate knowledge of local government, and particularly the militia, was obviously beneficial to the House as a whole when measures such as those to settle the militia and regulate corporations were scrutinised early in the reign. It was probably no coincidence that the earl of Sandwich, lord lieutenant of Huntingdonshire, chaired the committee appointed to consider a bill to repair the county's highways along with those of Cambridgeshire and Hertfordshire in May 1663.[19]

A significant contribution to the legislative functions of the House was also made by the bishops. Several, in particular Sheldon of Canterbury, Morley

---

[16] Calculations on the peers' education are derived from the following sources: *GEC*; *DNB*; Henning, *House of Commons*, vols. I–III; J. Foster (ed.), *Alumni Oxonienses 1500–1714* (5 vols., Oxford, 1888); J. and J. A. Venn (eds.), *Alumni Cantabrigienses*, pt I (5 vols., Cambridge, 1922–7).

[17] Although the bulk of legislation was drafted by lawyers, such as Bulstrode Whitelock, these peers were especially active in committee, penning revisions and clauses to existing bills. Lords Robartes and Anglesey were closely involved in drafting legislation to relieve Protestant nonconformists. Committee Minutes vols. 1–3 provide many examples of their work in committee, and vol. 3, p. 377 demonstrates that Anglesey drew up a toleration bill in 1680. Clarendon, *Life*, II, pp. 342–4 and Committee Minutes vol. 1, pp. 293–5, 298, 303 strongly suggest that Lord Robartes played a leading role in drafting and amending the highly controversial Indulgence Bill in 1663. For the drafting activities of Whitelock, see Ruth Spalding (ed.), *The diary of Bulstrode Whitelock 1605–75*, Records of Social and Economic History, NS, XIII (Oxford, 1990), p. 664.

[18] See table 3, p. 59, for a list of chairmen of the committee of the whole House.

[19] Committee Minutes 1, p. 370.

of Winchester, Ward of Salisbury and Dolben of Rochester were extremely talented, possessing a firm grasp of legislative procedure.[20] As the bishops had considerable understanding of ecclesiastical affairs it was only to be expected that they would play a leading role in the formulation and revision of religious legislation. Prelates dominated the committee proceedings on the Uniformity Bill in the spring of 1662, making a series of amendments and adding the controversial clause for the renunciation of the Solemn League and Covenant.[21] Some bills, notably those for infant baptism, preservation of the sabbath and against blasphemy and atheism were drafted and sponsored by the clerical members of the House. In 1674 the bishop of Chichester offered a committee proposals for a blasphemy bill and four years later Archbishop Sancroft chaired a committee considering a similar bill.[22]

A thorough understanding of parliamentary procedure was as essential a requirement for members of either chamber in the seventeenth century as it is for their modern counterparts. Unfamiliarity with procedure and precedents could impede the progress of business in parliament. In 1660 only a minority of peers had previous experience of the workings of the House of Lords. No more than sixty of those lords eligible to sit in the Convention Parliament had previously sat in the House of Lords at Westminster. In contrast 55 per cent of members of the Commons had sat in their chamber before 1660.[23] The events of the 1640s and 1650s provide the reasons why slightly over half of the restored House of Lords had no first-hand experience of proceedings in their chamber. After 1642 Royalist peers had ceased to sit at Westminster and seven years later the House of Lords itself was abolished. With the exception of a few former Parliamentarians, the vast majority of peers who had acquired titles between 1642 and 1660 had had no opportunity of entering the House of Lords.

But the unfamiliarity of the majority of peers with procedure does not appear to have substantially impaired their chamber's efficiency even in 1660. In fact two of the most industrious and capable committee chairmen in the Convention were new members, the earls of Dorset and Bridgewater.[24] Continuity with the early Stuart House was maintained by those peers who had previously sat in the chamber. Several had already had careers in the Lords spanning two or three decades: Lords Berkshire, Cleveland, Craven,

[20] Turberville, 'House of Lords under Charles II', pp. 405–6; R. Beddard, 'The character of a Restoration prelate: Dr John Dolben', *Notes and Queries*, NS, XVII, no. 11 (Nov. 1970), pp. 420–1.

[21] *LJ*, XI, 422; Committee Minutes 1, p. 169. A copy of the bill as it was delivered to the Lords is in Lord Wharton's papers in the Bodleian Library (Carte MSS. 81, fols. 102–5).

[22] Committee Minutes 3, pp. 70, 208, 212–13.

[23] Henning, *House of Commons*, I, p. 27. No fewer than twenty-two of the new peers had previously sat in the House of Commons.

[24] Dorset chaired at least six committees and Bridgewater four, totals which were only exceeded by the aged Lord Finch, who chaired seven.

Grey of Wark and Manchester were among those to have sat in the 1620s. One of the most active peers in the Convention, Lord Robartes, had acquired such an impressive array of procedural experience since taking his seat in the Short Parliament that he often supplied the defects of his less-learned colleagues. In 1661 he accurately instructed the House about the procedure to adopt in a tie-vote, arguing from an Elizabethan precedent.[25] Later, during a dispute over who should chair a committee of the whole House in 1679, he recalled 'that till 1642 there was no chairman of any committee and that the old earl of Manchester (who was Lord Privy Seal) was the first chairman of a committee'.[26]

Many peers understood legislative procedures from service in the House of Commons. Thirty per cent of those peers who had first entered the House in 1660 had previously sat in the Commons. Lord Holles, who entered the Lords in 1661, had been a member of almost every parliament since 1624. The newly ennobled Lord Delamer had served in four parliaments since 1646. For the reign as a whole 41 per cent of all peers who sat in the Lords had been MPs and almost half of these had been elected since 1660.

The peerage in Charles II's reign had more experience of parliament than their counterparts in the House of Commons. Unlike MPs, they were not subject to elections, and therefore there was greater continuity of experience and expertise in the Lords. In fact 85 per cent of the 345 MPs who obtained seats in by-elections between 1661 and 1678 were entirely new members, but during the same period 40 per cent of the 97 new members of the Lords had already served in the Commons.[27] The importance of serving in the Commons before elevation to the Lords was recognised by contemporaries: Lewis Stukeley wrote to Lord Wharton in 1673 suggesting that if Wharton's son should be elected to parliament 'he would be the fitter to serve in the Peers' house hereafter'.[28] The significance of the Commons for a political apprenticeship was not lost on the king, who recruited most of his ministerial talent from the lower chamber. By ennobling able commoners like Ashley, Anglesey, Finch and Danby Charles II denuded the Commons of some of its most experienced and industrious members. These and other 'men of business' played a leading role in the processing of legislation in the Lords.

III

Charles II's upper House generally acted with diligence and impartiality in its consideration of bills. Established procedures were usually adhered to.

[25] *LJ*, XI, 288.
[26] Manuscript Minutes 21, 26 May p.m. 1679.
[27] Henning, *House of Commons*, I, p. 27.
[28] Bodl., Rawlinson Letters, 104, fol. 89, Lewis Stukeley to Wharton, 29 March 1673.

Every bill that passed the House had the customary three readings, the first and second being informative exercises and not normally accompanied by debate.[29] Only in exceptional circumstances did the peers give a bill three readings in the same sitting. A bill for supplying the defects in a poll act received all three readings on 12 September 1660 because of the adjournment on the following day. Usually at least one day elapsed between each reading, with the House appointing a day in advance for the next reading. This gave every lord who was interested the opportunity of being present when a particular bill was read or debated. As in the early seventeenth century the second reading of a bill was generally a formality in which the Lord Chancellor read only the title of the bill and put the question for committing or engrossing. In Charles II's reign the vast majority of bills were committed. If no one objected to a bill the question was put for engrossing it on parchment, or as in the case of a bill from the lower House, for the third reading. Very occasionally the second reading stage was accompanied by debate and there are instances of the House refusing to commit bills it disapproved of.[30]

The crucial stage was when bills were scrutinised in committee. A bill was referred to one of two committees: a 'select' committee or a committee of the whole House (sometimes referred to as a 'grand committee' by contemporaries). As its name suggests a committee of the whole House was just that, consisting of all those lords present in the chamber. It was chaired by an experienced lord appointed by the House, the presiding officer, the Lord Chancellor (or Lord Keeper in the case of Lord Bridgeman) vacating the woolsack to sit in his place on the earls' bench to which his office entitled him.[31] The chairmanship of this important committee was monopolised by members of the privy council. Five particularly able privy councillors, the earls of Bridgewater, Manchester, Anglesey and Essex and Lord Robartes chaired the committee for almost 80 per cent of the bills and other matters debated there during the reign.[32] By the mid-1670s it was customary for most public bills to be referred to this grand committee; earlier in the reign only highly controversial bills were debated there. Parliamentary sessions were generally shorter in the 1670s and the more frequent recourse to committees

[29] An exception to the three-reading procedure occurred on 28 March 1673 when out of respect to the king the House passed his Bill for a Gracious Pardon after a single reading (*LJ*, XII, 577).
[30] The River Wye Bill, for example, was not committed after both counsels had been heard at the bar on 2 May 1664.
[31] There can be no doubt about the appointment of a chairman by the House, for on 27 February 1663 the clerk recorded that the peers voted Manchester into the chair of the committee of the whole House on the Bill of Ecclesiastical Affairs. On 20 March 1679 the House had difficulty in deciding who should chair the committee, but eventually appointed Bridgewater (*LJ*, XI, 485; Manuscript Minutes 21, 20 March 1679).
[32] See table 3.

Table 3 *Chairmen of committees of the whole House, 1660–1680*

Lord	Periods in Lords	Privy councillor	Number of committees[a]
Bridgewater	1660–86	PC	37
Manchester	1626–71	PC	18
Robartes	1640–85	PC	8
Anglesey	1661–86	PC	8
Essex	1660–83	PC	7
Ailesbury	1664–85	PC	3
Halifax	1668–95	PC	2
Huntingdon	1673–1701	–	2
Ormond	1660–88	PC	2
Shaftesbury	1661–83	PC	2
Northampton	1660–81	PC	2
Bishop of Rochester (Dolben)	1666–88	–	2
Bishop of Salisbury	1662–89	–	2
Buckingham	1660–87	PC	1
Clifford	1673	PC	1
Newport (viscount)	1660–1708	PC	1
Clarendon	1674–1709	PC	1

[a] This table does not indicate each occasion a lord chaired a committee on the same bill or issue.
Sources: Lords' *Journals* and Manuscript Minutes.

of the whole House was a way in which the government ensured that major pieces of legislation were dealt with efficiently and not left to overworked select committees. Such committees gave leading ministers the opportunity of influencing debate, which was not so easy when bills were committed to select committees that met at times when they had other governmental duties to perform. Unlike in formal debates, when a peer could only speak once on the same subject, a committee of the whole House was specifically designed to allow a lord to speak as often as he wished. This had the result that the most articulate and active peers, such as Danby, Shaftesbury, Finch and Halifax, were able to dominate proceedings in the 1670s. This was not necessarily a problem. From the surviving records of debates it seems that only a minority of lords present spoke in formal debates.[33] By lifting the rules

[33] More reports of debates have survived for the 1670s than for the 1660s. Fairly thorough notes exist for eleven debates between 1677 and 1680. These are: the debates on whether parliament was dissolved by the fifteen-month prerogation, 15/16 February 1677 (Carte MSS 79, fols. 31–2, 37–43), the legal case of *Lord Feversham* v. *Mr Watson and his wife*, 8 July 1678 (D. E. C. Yale (ed.), *Lord Nottingham's Chancery Cases*, 2 vols., Selden Society, 1954/1961, II, pp. 646–9), the debate on whether impeachments and writs of error continue from one parliament to the next, 19 March 1679 (Carte MSS 228, fols. 229–30), the impeachment of

governing formal debates the most active peers were better able to make their contribution by speaking on every clause of a bill if they so desired. It was in such a committee in 1674 that Shaftesbury, Halifax, Salisbury and Mordaunt proposed several of the clauses which were eventually incorporated in two bills for securing the Protestant religion.[34]

Committees of the whole House could be of considerable benefit to the government. They allowed a small group of Court speakers to answer objections to bills clause by clause, as happened with the 1675 Test Bill. The appointment of a privy councillor as chairman was also advantageous for the Court since he directed proceedings, interjected with his own views and formally reported on the committee's progress to the House. From the small sample of surviving debates in this committee it is impossible to determine the extent to which either the chairman or groups of articulate peers shaped legislation. However, all its decisions were subject to ratification by the House of Lords as a whole. In some instances peers entered the chamber as the chairman was reporting and could provide the votes necessary to overturn a decision taken in committee.

It is evident from the Manuscript Minutes that public bills were subject to very close scrutiny in the committee of the whole House. The Lords devoted thirteen days to the highly contentious Irish Cattle Bill, from 22 October to 21 November 1666. It was discussed line by line, and clauses were debated for many hours.[35] Four years later, in March 1670 the House adjourned into a committee for seven consecutive days to examine the Commons' Conventicle Bill clause by clause, postponing virtually all other business.[36] Major amendments to legislation were often drafted according to directions from the committee of the whole House by a subcommittee of four to six peers. On 22 March 1670 a subcommittee on the Conventicle Bill consisting of Ormond, Winchelsea, Frescheville and Arundel of Trerice and the bishops of Winchester and Salisbury prepared a clause 'to provide that no one man shall be liable to above £10 for any one offence for the poverty of any other person'.[37]

The vast majority of legislation (all private bills and 88 per cent of public bills) was considered by select committees. The plethora of bills and the

---

the earl of Danby, 21 March 1679 and the debate on his Bill of Banishment, 2 April 1679 (Add. MSS 28,046, fols. 49–56), the proceedings in committee of the whole House on whether bishops could vote in capital cases, 6, 7, 13 and 20 May 1679 (Carte MSS 81, fols. 561–8) and the debate on the Exclusion Bill, 15 November 1680 (Carte MSS 77, fols. 649–51).

[34] Committee Minutes 3, pp. 70–3; HLRO Main Papers 165, 10 February: heads considered by the House for bills to secure the Protestant religion; BL, Stowe MSS 204, fol. 114, Conway to Essex, 27 Jan. 1674.

[35] Manuscript Minutes 14, proceedings on the Irish Cattle Bill from 22 October to 21 November 1666; Bodl., Rawlinson MSS A.130, fols. 58v–63v; Clarendon, *Life*, III, pp. 145–7.

[36] Manuscript Minutes 16, 19–26 March 1670.

[37] Ibid., 22 March 1670.

limited interest in most private bills made it impracticable to commit the bulk of legislation to grand committees. Select committees met either at eight in the morning or after 3 p.m. when the House was not normally sitting. Meetings were held in rooms adjacent to the Parliament Chamber, the Little Room, the Painted Chamber and the Prince's Lodgings being the most regularly used venues. Before the functions of these committees can be delineated it is necessary to understand how they were appointed and who chaired them. In the early seventeenth century the House had generally appointed fixed proportions of peers from the earls', barons' and bishops' benches. This was no longer the situation after 1660 when the proportions between the benches fluctuated dramatically.[38] There were essentially two methods of appointing committees after the Restoration. Until the beginning of the 1670s committees consisted of every lord willing to be appointed by the Lord Chancellor or nominated by a fellow peer. Unless a bill was extremely controversial, the committee did not consist of every peer present in the House at the second reading.[39] Lords who were strongly opposed to a bill were not usually nominated because of their obvious partiality, though there were exceptions.[40] By the mid-1670s most select committees were named as in the eighteenth century, all those present in the chamber at the time of commitment being appointed.[41] One explanation for the gradual adoption of this practice was that small committees had often lacked the quorum of five necessary for them to function effectively.[42] Obviously the larger the number of appointments the greater the chance of committees achieving a quorum. Unnecessary delays caused by the chairman interrupting the business of the House by asking for further members to be added to his committee could thus be avoided.

There is no evidence to suggest that the appointment of committee members was manipulated for partisan or political purposes. An analysis of the appointments to public bill committees for the two sessions of 1675

[38] Foster, pp. 88–91; Davis, 'Committee and other procedures', p. 21. The old system of appointment had broken down with the exclusion of the bishops in 1642.

[39] The complex subject of the appointment of committees has been investigated by Richard Davis (ibid., pp. 20–35). In 1679 there was an attempt to fix the proportions of lords from the earls', barons' and bishops' benches with the House endorsing a report from the Committee for Privileges. However, with the exception of one committee, the proportion of one bishop to every four peers (two barons and two earls) was not adhered to by the House (*LJ*, XIII, 582–729).

[40] The earl of Southampton, for instance, did not serve on the committee for the Five Mile Bill in October 1665 because of his known opposition to the measure (Carte MSS 80, fol. 757, Lord Wharton's notes on the third-reading debate, 30 Oct. 1665). All but one of the 44 peers who had voted against committing the Roos Divorce Bill on 19 March 1670 were not appointed to the committee (*LJ*, XII, 316; Harris, *Sandwich*, II, pp. 323–4).

[41] Davis, 'Committee and other procedures', p. 22; J. C. Sainty, *The origin of the office of Chairman of Committees in the House of Lords* (HLRO, Memorandum 52, 1974), p. 2.

[42] Davis, ibid., p. 30.

Table 4 *Chairmen of select committees, 1660–1680*

Lord	Period in Lords	Number of committees
Dorset	1660–77	170
Bridgewater	1660–85	119
Anglesey	1661–85	77
Bolingbroke	1660–88	58
Ailesbury	1664–85	57
Shaftesbury	1661–83	42
Robartes	1640–85	41
Northampton	1660–81	41
Essex	1660–83	33
Richmond	1660–72	26
Portland	1640–63	26
Howard of Charlton	1640–79	23
Manchester	1626–71	16
Stafford	1640–80	15
Lucas	1660–71	14
Buckingham	1660–85	11
Dover	1640–77	11
Powis	1667–96	10
Wharton	1640–96	8
Derby	1660–72	8
Saye and Sele	1662–74	8
Clarendon	1674–1709	8
Berkeley (of Berkeley)	1660–98	7
Finch	1640–60	7
Carlisle	1661–85	6
Bishop of London (Compton)	1676–1713	5
Bishop of Durham (Cosin)	1661–72	5
Ormond	1660–88	5
Dorchester	1660–80	4
Bishop of Salisbury (Earle)	1663–65	4
Bishop of Salisbury (Ward)	1662–89	4
Worcester	1660–67	3
Lexington	1660–69	3
Halifax	1668–95	3
Berkeley (of Stratton)	1660–78	3
Mohun	1666–77	3
48 others		100
Total		984

This table only lists lords who chaired committees on three or more separate bills. It does not record each occasion on which the lord chaired the same committee.
Sources: Committee Minutes, Main Papers (loose committee sheets), Lords' *Journals*.

reveals that Court and Country peers were appointed in almost equal numbers.[43] Even if a lord was absent when a committee was named he could always be added at a later date, as was the case with the Uniformity Bill in 1662.[44] No limit was applied to subsequent additions: all the 46 peers present at the time of the commitment of the Durham Lead Mines Bill on 16 November 1667 were appointed to its committee and a further 22 were added two days later.[45] There was little to be gained from attempting to pack a select committee since the House could reverse any decision made there.

The ability of a committee to perform its tasks of scrutiny and revision depended less on the numbers appointed than on those who bothered to attend meetings. Although the Manuscript Committee Minutes rarely list peers who attended, they do record the figures for votes and these can be used as an approximate guide to attendance. Only committees dealing with the most interesting or controversial bills experienced attendance of more than half those originally appointed. A total of 43 lords were appointed to the committee for the Uniformity Bill, yet attendance ranged from thirteen to twenty-six.[46] Even relatively low levels of attendance did not necessarily hinder a committee's ability to process legislation. The crucial factor was the expertise of those who attended and, above all, the competence of the chairman. Committee chairmen performed an extremely important function: they were responsible for directing proceedings, advising other members on technical or difficult points and, when the parties in a private bill could not agree, endeavoured to effect a compromise. If interested parties wished to influence the committee's deliberations on a private bill they often applied first to the chairman. When the king desired that the Lords pass Sir Robert Paston's Yarmouth Fishing Bill in February 1665 he sent for the committee chairman, the earl of Dorset, and instructed him to inform those peers who were opposed that he favoured the bill in its existing form and would not prorogue parliament until it was passed. Accordingly the committee agreed to the measure without any amendments.[47]

Chairmen were appointed by the other committee members.[48] Earlier in the century the chairman had usually been the most senior lord on the committee (i.e. the peer first in order of precedence).[49] Reasons for selecting a

---

[43] From a sample of ten important committees 49 per cent of appointments consisted of Catholic and Country peers and 51 per cent were Court peers and bishops.

[44] *LJ*, XI, 366, 396, 400, 402, 412, 413.

[45] Ibid., XII, 138–9. Peers were added to a committee on the motion of any lord.

[46] Committee Minutes 1, pp. 176, 203, 206, 208–9, 211, 216; *LJ*, XI, 366, 396, 400, 402, 412, 413.

[47] The king's intervention here was probably a mark of his gratitude to Paston who had successfully moved the House of Commons in November 1664 to grant supply (Add. MSS 27,447, fol. 338, Sir Robert Paston to his wife, 23 Feb. 1665).

[48] Davis, 'Committee and other procedures', p. 35, note 45.

[49] Foster, p. 93.

particular chairman varied: availability and willingness to serve were certainly factors. More important though seems to have been the proven ability of the lord himself. Five peers, by no means the most senior in terms of precedence in the House, chaired the vast majority of committees: the earls of Dorset, Bridgewater, Anglesey, Bolingbroke and Ailesbury. There was some specialisation in particular types of bills. Bridgewater, a client of the earl of Clarendon, chaired almost every committee on religious legislation; the fifth earl of Dorset, social and economic bills and the earl of Anglesey, with his legal training and experience as Lord Privy Seal (1673–82), often presided over committees considering legislation of a legal nature. When bills affected a certain locality the peer with the requisite local knowledge was often appointed chairman.[50]

The fact that during Charles II's reign committees were generally chaired by a small group of experienced 'men of business' had three main effects: unnecessary delays due to inexperience were minimised, there was consistency in the handling of legislation and there was more likelihood that committees were thorough and impartial. Procedures were not sloppy or casual. Bills were examined paragraph by paragraph with an assistant clerk making detailed notes of proceedings, including the amendments. The committee summoned and heard all parties known to be concerned with a private bill on pre-arranged days. They either appeared in person or were represented by their legal counsel and testified on oath. A committee considering the Rivers Severn and Stour Navigation Bill spent several sessions in June 1661 simply hearing counsel for the owners of coal mines and watermen, whose livelihoods would be affected were the bill to become law.[51] If the committee found the objections of one party to be justified it could amend the bill in question. A committee chaired by Lord Bridgewater decided that to increase the amount of money involved in a land settlement in the earl of Cleveland's bill (1661) was warranted after hearing counsel for both parties. If either party refused to accept an amendment or several clauses in the original bill, the committee could appoint peers to try to reconcile the parties. On 9 July 1661 the earl of Dorset and Lords Lucas and Vaughan were instructed to speak to the parties involved in Sir Anthony Brown's Estate Bill. Four days later they reported to the committee that the parties had consented to a compromise financial settlement.[52]

---

[50] The earl of Northampton chaired the committee on a bill for rebuilding the town of Northampton in 1675, and the earl of Carlisle, a leading landowner in the northern counties, had chaired a committee on the Durham Enfranchisement Bill in 1673 (Committee Minutes 3, pp. 39, 129).

[51] A very thorough account of proceedings on this bill is in Bishop Henchman's Journal (Bodl., Rawlinson MSS A.130, fol. 13). Further details are furnished by the clerk's notes (Committee Minutes 1, pp. 14, 15, 18, 19, 22).

[52] Committee Minutes 1, pp. 51, 57, 58.

If a bill raised technical or legal issues the committee might obtain the advice of the judges from the law courts in neighbouring Westminster Hall. As in the decades before 1649 the judges continued to serve the House and its committees as assistants. Frequently they were employed to draft bills and prepare amendments. For instance on 26 October 1665 the Attorney General was ordered to peruse papers offered by the earl of Newport and Lord Wharton pertaining to the Plague Bill then under consideration and draft a proviso on the powers of JPs to shut up houses.[53] Earlier in June 1661 the committee for the earl of Derby's Estate Bill had asked the judges' opinion on whether the bill violated the Acts of Indemnity and Confirmation of Judicial Proceedings. The judges reported that it did not, a view endorsed by the committee itself.

On the whole, committees diligently scrutinised and amended legislation. On the vast majority of occasions the House of Lords endorsed the chairman's report of a committee's recommendations. But if it felt that a committee had not acted impartially, or objected to its decisions on technical, legal or political grounds it could order a bill to be recommitted, often adding further lords to the committee. The House ordered the recommitment of a bill against Quakers, Baptists and fanatics in 1661 because as it stood proposed it could be used to prosecute other nonconformists, especially Presbyterians and Catholics, which was considered to be beyond the scope of the bill.[54] A bill for the transportation of felons was also recommitted in April 1664 because Lord Ashley, the Chancellor of the Exchequer, convinced the House that the measure gave the judges excessive powers, for it would enable them to order the transportation of 'a man of a good estate' for petty larceny who should instead be fined.[55]

As in other periods, the House of Lords was not totally immune from external pressures. The most common source of influence on legislation was individuals intent upon promoting their own bills or protecting their interests when these were jeopardised by other people's bills. Both the short duration of parliamentary sessions and the plethora of bills meant that a private bill would not normally pass without a powerful sponsor in parliament. Private bills initiated in the Lords had to be introduced by a peer. Individual peers were of course approached by interested parties to guide bills through the Lords. The lawyer Bulstrode Whitelock waited in the lobby in November 1663 to request that several peers promote a bill which he had drafted on behalf of the earl of Portland. Eventually after visiting peers at their houses,

---

[53] Ibid., 2, p. 86. The functions of the legal assistants are discussed in detail by Mrs Foster (Foster, pp. 70–86).

[54] *LJ*, XI, 317; P. Seaward, 'Court and Parliament: the making of government policy, 1661–5' (Oxford University DPhil thesis, 1986), p. 204.

[55] BL, Verney MSS M/636, reel 19, Nathanial Hobart to Sir Ralph Verney, 3 April 1664; Committee Minutes 1, pp. 441–2.

he persuaded his brother-in-law Lord Willoughby to present it.[56] In the next session Lord Mohun, who owned estates in Cornwall, presented on behalf of the local inhabitants a bill for erecting a parish church at Falmouth.[57]

Obviously the success or failure of a bill could rest entirely upon the influence and industry of its sponsor. For this reason peers of considerable standing within the chamber, such as Lords Ashley, Robartes, Manchester, Southampton and Ailesbury, were singled out as potential sponsors. Aware of the significance of a 'patron' in the House, the countess of Rutland wrote to the earl of Ailesbury, in December 1666 acknowledging his 'most notable concern' in the bill to illegitimate her daughter-in-law's children, and implored him to continue his efforts on her behalf in committee.[58] Another of Ailesbury's correspondents, Lady Abergavenny, wrote during the same session desiring his 'charity in getting the committee to meet' to continue its proceedings on a bill for dealing with her late husband's estates.[59] To quicken the pace of such proceedings a patron might chair the committee himself. Lord Mohun chaired the committee for the Falmouth Church Bill. Sponsors were not above using unscrupulous practices to advance a bill through the committee stage. With regard to the controversial Yarmouth Fishing Bill, Sir Robert Paston dined thirteen members of the committee at the Quaker Tavern on 20 February 1665. At the same time his friend, and the bill's sponsor in the Lords, the earl of Lindsey (the Lord Great Chamberlain), 'took a great many home with him' for lunch. When the committee met at 3 p.m. the replete members unanimously passed the measure without alterations.[60]

The opponents of a private bill sought to influence members of the House to amend it, to impede its progress (especially if a prorogation was approaching) or to reject it altogether. Sir Edward Nicholas, a former Secretary of State, used his influence with his friend the earl of Clarendon in March 1663 to ensure that the Lords rejected Lady Dacre's Estate Bill, which attempted to recover land legally granted to Nicholas. When after Clarendon's fall in 1667 Lady Dacre had another bill drafted for the same purpose, Nicholas' son, Sir John, enlisted the assistance of several prominent men, including the earl of Northampton, Lord Ashley and Lord Keeper Bridgeman, to obstruct the progress of the bill when it was introduced in the House. Sir John Nicholas even went to the lengths of obtaining documentary evidence from his father to demonstrate the injustice of the proposed bill. It was perhaps

---

[56] Spalding, *Whitelock Diary*, pp. 664–5.
[57] Bodl., Rawlinson MSS A.130, fol. 7v.
[58] Wiltshire Record Office, Ailesbury Papers 1300/552, Countess of Rutland to Ailesbury, Dec. 1666.
[59] Ibid., 553, Lady Abergavenny to Ailesbury, no date but internal evidence indicates 1666/7.
[60] Add. MSS 27,447, fol. 338, Sir Robert Paston to his wife, 23 Feb. 1665. The king had also exerted pressure on the committee via the chairman, the earl of Dorset.

because of his diligence in fomenting opposition to the measure that its sponsors, the duke of Buckingham, the earl of Bristol, and Lord Howard of Charlton decided not to introduce the bill in the House of Lords.[61]

When individual members had a vested interest in a bill they recruited their friends and associates to exert influence on their behalf both in committee and on the floor of the House. In January 1667 Bishop Cosin of Durham wrote to six prelates and Lord Ashley, soliciting their support for his bill to lease his lead mines to Mr Wharton.[62] In the previous month Lord Delamer had written to his friend, the earl of Ailesbury, imploring him to attend and vote for the Irish Cattle Bill, in which the Cheshire landowner had a personal interest.[63] Peers with an obvious vested interest in a bill were not usually appointed to its committee, though this did not prevent them, like Bishop Cosin in 1667, from lobbying committee members.[64] Tactics were sometimes planned in consultation with the peer's agent. Shortly before the close of the first session of the Convention the earl of Bridgewater wrote to his agent, John Halsey, asking him to repair to Westminster to discuss the earl of Derby's Estate Bill. Earlier the same afternoon Derby had declared in committee a right to land owned by Bridgewater. Enclosed in the letter to Halsey were a copy of the bill together with a sheet of amendments made in committee. Although Bridgewater had persuaded the committee to allow his counsel to attend the following week to 'show cause why it should not pass ... as it is drawn', he still required his agent's advice on 'whether it be necessary to prevent the passing of this bill or no, and next, if it be necessary, then what course of action to take about it'.[65]

Often the House dealt more quickly with a nobleman's bill than with those belonging to commoners. One of the earl of Derby's estate bills was given its first two readings on 13 June 1660, probably out of sympathy for the earl's treatment during the Interregnum. A bill for restoring Lord Colepeper's estates received similar treatment in May 1662.[66] Where the rights of a peer and commoners were equally open to question in a measure, the peer's rights generally took precedence over the claims of his humbler opponents. Notwithstanding the fact that a committee heard the counsels representing all the parties in the Rivers Severn and Stour Navigation Bill in June 1661, the Committee Minutes strongly suggest that the claims of the earl of Bristol and Lord Windsor were treated more favourably than those of the other less influential parties: watermen and the proprietors of coal mines.[67]

[61] *LJ*, XI, 497; BL, Egerton MSS 2,539, fols. 135, 137, 139, 142, Sir John Nicholas to Sir Edward Nicholas, 12, 13, 14, 19 Nov. 1667.
[62] Ornsby (ed.), *Cosin Correspondence*, LV, pp. 165–6, Cosin to Mr Wharton, 7 Jan. 1667.
[63] Wiltshire RO, Ailesbury Papers 1300/548, Delamer to Ailesbury, 17 December 1666.
[64] *Cosin Correspondence*, vol. LV, pp. 165–6, Cosin to Wharton, 7 Jan. 1667.
[65] Hertfordshire RO, Ashridge Collection 1058, Bridgewater to Halsey, 31 Aug. 1660.
[66] *LJ*, XI, 59, 453.
[67] Committee Minutes 1, pp. 14, 15, 18, 22.

In the context of seventeenth-century parliaments there was nothing unique about the occasional bias and unscrupulousness of certain members of Charles II's House of Lords. There are many instances of MPs resorting to the same practices. Sir Edward Dering was employed to promote private bills in the Commons. One of the sponsors of Lady Roos' Bill dined forty MPs in January 1667 in order to hasten its passage through the House. M. W. McCahill has pointed out that similar practices still occurred in the Lords during the second half of the eighteenth century.[68]

IV

The legislative contribution of the House of Lords rested to a greater extent on the revision of bills from the Commons than on the initiation of its own. Even during the 1660s when parliament was fairly productive in terms of the quantity of bills passed, no more than half a dozen public acts began their life in the Lords each session. Since 70 per cent of all legislation started life in the Commons, MPs were frequently so inundated with bills that they could not always give each adequate scrutiny. Far fewer bills were introduced in the Lords and so the peers had more leisure to consider each in some detail. The chief function of the House of Lords was, as it is today, to smooth out the infelicities in the drafting of bills sent from the House of Commons.

The Lords played an extremely active role in clarifying and 'correcting' legislation. Approximately 64 per cent of all bills passing the House between 1660 and 1681 were amended there. Major public bills were subjected to rigorous scrutiny in committee. Without exception all the important bills comprising the Restoration settlement were revised in some way in the Lords. The 1661 Corporation Bill was so extensively altered to increase royal control over corporations in a committee dominated by government ministers and privy councillors that it was virtually unrecognisable when it was returned to the Commons.[69] Early in 1662 a bill to confirm three acts of the Convention was stripped bare of most of the Commons' amendments since these had entirely altered the original purpose of one of the three acts, the hotly debated Act for Confirming and Restoring Ministers.[70] Later in the reign bills which the peers partially disapproved of were sometimes drafted

[68] BL, Stowe MSS 774, fol. 42, earl of Winchilsea to Dering, 27 Aug. 1660; *Hist. MSS Comm.*, 24, 12th rept appendix, pt V (1889), MSS of the duke of Rutland, vol. II, p. 8; M. W. McCahill, *Order and equipoise: the peerage and the House of Lords, 1783–1806* (1978), pp. 102–6.

[69] *CJ*, VIII, 336–8; Seaward, pp. 152–6.

[70] E. Berwick (ed.), *The Rawdon Papers consisting of letters ... to and from Dr John Bramhall* (1819), pp. 136–8, Dr Pett to Archbishop Bramhall, 8 Feb. 1662; *LJ*, XI, 373; Seaward, pp. 173–4.

afresh before being returned to the Commons. In November 1669 the Lords rejected a Commons' bill concerning proceedings in parliament, substituting for it their own measure which did not entirely deprive them of their original jurisdiction.[71]

The number of bills amended in the House of Lords does not provide an accurate measure of the peers' legislative achievements. A large proportion of bills, particularly non-controversial private ones, received only a few minor alterations. Others which their lordships examined closely were either so well drafted, or had already been amended in the Commons, that they passed without amendment. A more satisfactory guide to the Lords' legislative contribution is the quality of their amendments. A common form of revision concerned the wording of bills. Sloppy or ambiguous phrases were altered. On 25 May 1661 the Lords replaced the Commons' phrase 'securing and preserving' in the title of the bill to safeguard the king's person with the phrase 'safety and preservation', which was considered less open to misinterpretation.[72] Redundant words were discarded. During its examination of the Conventicle Bill in 1664 the committee of the whole House decided to omit several words concerning evidence to satisfy JPs as they were unnecessary.[73]

Despite the obvious fact that peers were not answerable to electors, they were nevertheless not oblivious to blatant injustices in legislation. It was partly because peers were not elected that their consideration of legislation was not subject in the same way to pressures from constituents. A committee of the whole House, for example, decided on 19 December 1666 to strike out a clause in the Commons' Poll Bill, whereby aliens and nonconformists were to pay double, as there was strong feeling in the chamber that it was unreasonable to expect these people to shoulder excessively heavy burdens of taxation.[74] Five years later the House reduced the imposition on sugar in the Foreign Commodities Bill as it was regarded as prejudicial to plantation owners who had recently begun to refine their own sugar.[75]

Factors beyond the direct control of the House of Lords adversely affected the performance of its legislative duties. Not least of these was the interference of the king himself. Like his Stuart predecessors, Charles II kept sessions of parliament short. The average length of a session was eight to ten weeks, and the shortest, that of the Oxford Parliament, lasted a mere seven days in March 1681. Even during the longest session of the Cavalier Parliament – 14 February 1670 to 22 April 1671 – parliament only sat for a total of 28 weeks.

---

[71] Carte MSS 81, fols. 298, 300–1 (drafts of the two privilege of parliament bills); Committee Minutes 2, pp. 56–7, 58–9; Harris, *Sandwich*, II, pp. 307–9, 313–15.

[72] Committee Minutes 1, p. 8.

[73] Ibid., p. 455, 6 May 1664.

[74] Manuscript Minutes 14, 19 December 1666; *LJ*, XII, 72.

[75] Harris, *Sandwich*, II, pp. 333–7.

Less than a third of all bills introduced in parliament actually received the royal assent. A small proportion had been dropped by both Houses, or were withdrawn by their sponsors, and five bills received the royal veto.[76] But the vast majority failed because of insufficient parliamentary time.

The other main consequence of short sessions was that the Lords could not always scrutinise legislation as closely as it might have done with more time. The sheer volume of public bills in the lower House meant that it often had no alternative but to send up clusters of bills towards the end of a session. At times, even with additional afternoon and Saturday sittings, the peers were unable to give every bill a thorough examination. In the session of 23 May to 15 July 1678 all but three of the thirteen Commons' bills were received between 2 and 10 July. Although the House was only prevented from despatching one bill by the prorogation, the quality of scrutiny clearly suffered, as one bill passed all its stages in two days. Ten years earlier the House had protested that because a bill for raising taxes by duties on wines and spirits was of 'many paragraphs' and came 'from the House of Commons so near the time of the adjournment' the argument of shortness of time ought not to be used 'to precipitate the passing thereof' before it had been properly considered.[77]

Despite these obstacles to the performance of its legislative duties, the House made an extremely important contribution to the legislative process during the reign. Had it not been for the chamber's careful scrutiny of bills, the quality of many of the 151 public and 307 private acts of the reign would have been discernibly lower. In fact just under a third of these bills had been introduced in the House of Lords itself. Although the majority were private and local in nature, many individuals and groups would not have benefited at all had their bills been initiated in the Commons. The greater amount of legislation there impaired that chamber's ability to process bills. The peers passed a higher proportion of bills introduced in their House. This fact owed much to the committee system, and especially to the expertise of the 'men of business'. It is remarkable that the House of Lords was as effective as this, for unlike the Commons, it also had to devote time and energy to its judicial responsibilities.

---

[76] Bills receiving the royal veto were: Briscoe's Estate Bill (1662), the earl of Derby's Estate Bill (1662), the Pawnbrokers' Bill (1662), Sir Trevor Williams' Estate Bill (1677) and the Militia Bill (1678).

[77] *LJ*, XII, 242; D. J. Johnson (ed.), *The manuscripts of the House of Lords*, NS, XII, 1977, p. 5, 'Standing orders of the House of Lords'.

5

Justice

After the processing of legislation, the administration of justice was the most important and time-consuming function of the restored House of Lords. No fewer than 1,200 petitions and writs of error were presented to the House and its Committee for Petitions between 1660 and 1681. Over three-quarters of these were presented to the Convention Parliament and the majority concerned the restoration of ecclesiastical benefices.[1] Most cases involved private individuals, and were of little interest to the majority of peers. But several were highly controversial, providing heated debates, and in some cases resulted in protests being entered in the *Journal*. The peers valued their judicial powers so highly that when any were challenged by the Commons they vigorously asserted their exclusive right to the administration of justice in parliament. Yet the Lords' judicature for this period has until recently received only cursory treatment from historians.[2] Scholars have largely concentrated on the more controversial aspects, notably impeachments and judicial disputes with the Commons.[3] By ignoring the more mundane aspects of their judicial responsibilities, impeachments and judicial disputes cannot be viewed in perspective. The purpose of this chapter is to delineate the Lords' contribution to the redress of judicial grievances, and in so doing, it will focus on the two main categories of law suits: appeals from the court of Chancery and writs of error.

I

One of the most significant developments in seventeenth-century parliamentary history was that the House of Lords acquired a judicature. From the

---

[1] Hart, *Justice upon petition*, p. 222.

[2] The most detailed survey of the Lords' judicial functions is in Alan Horstman's PhD thesis, 'Justice and peers'. J. S. Hart's *Justice upon petition* has one chapter on the restored House of Lords, but apart from a discussion of the types of petitions presented to the Convention, concentrates on the most controversial aspects of the Lords' judicature.

[3] T. Beven, 'The appellate jurisdiction of the House of Lords', *Law Quarterly Review*, 17 (1901), 168–70; W. Holdsworth, *A history of English law* (17 vols., 7th edn, 1956–73), I, pp. 365–94; Pike, *Constitutional history of the House of Lords*, pp. 281–4.

1620s the House effectively became not only a court of law, but also the highest court of appeal in the land. In the sixteenth century the Lords had been concerned almost exclusively with legislation. The medieval judicial activities of the House, which fell into desuetude in the fifteenth century, had only involved the king's councillors. The king's small council, meeting in parliament after the majority of the barons had dispersed, had determined legal cases during the fourteenth and fifteenth centuries.[4] After 1621, however, every lord had judicial powers. These they continued to exercise until the abolition of the House of Lords. During the Civil War years the House extended the scope of its judicature, increasingly assuming the duties of the privy council, hearing original petitions, as well as appeals from almost every law court.[5] After the Restoration the House continued to exercise its pre-1649 judicial powers.

The significance of the restoration of the House of Lords was immediately evident to those concerned with the legal profession: from 25 April 1660 a higher court existed to question decisions made in the law courts in Westminster Hall, enabling litigants to appeal against their rulings. Although the House of Commons occasionally declared that it too was a law court, its powers were extremely restricted. Unlike the Lords, it could not examine witnesses under oath, nor could it impeach persons without the consent of the peers, because they conducted the trial and passed judgment. The lower chamber's judicial authority only extended to the preservation of its members' privileges. It could punish men for scandalous words against its members, vindicate MPs' and their servants' privileges in lawsuits during the duration of parliamentary privilege and could determine disputed parliamentary elections.

In contrast, the Lords' powers were more far-reaching, extending well beyond members of the nobility. The chamber provided a valuable service to those involved in litigation. In an age when litigation was progressively clogging-up the law courts, litigants regarded the House as another arena for their cases: an arena which could also provide a speedy and final settlement. The peers heard cases in error from the common law courts of King's Bench and Common Pleas, and determined appeals from the Chancery, the Courts of the Exchequer, Requests and the palatine Courts of Lancaster and Durham. The House also had an original jurisdiction, though this was rarely exercised from the late 1660s. Approximately 40 per cent of petitions between 1660 and 1667 were of this type and involved disputes over property which could not be remedied elsewhere.[6] The most famous first-instance case, that

[4] Horstman, 'Justice and peers', pp. 16–24, 107–46; C. Tite, *Impeachment and parliamentary judicature in early Stuart England* (1974), pp. 55–95, 218.
[5] Foster, pp. 182, 184–8; Horstman, 'Justice and peers', pp. 256–308.
[6] Hart, *Justice upon petition*, pp. 240–1.

of *Skinner v. The East India Company* (1667–70), resulted in a protracted dispute with the Commons. The case, which was exploited by lords and MPs disaffected to the court, did not, as some historians have claimed, result in the loss of the peers' original jurisdiction: two further first-instance cases were heard after 1670, though, as James Hart argues, the furore surrounding the affair did deter potential litigants.[7] Not all peers genuinely wanted an original jurisdiction, because they feared this might lead to an influx of petitions, the hearing of which would clog up the legislative and appellate functions of their House.[8]

As the reign progressed the House consolidated its other judicial powers and its members gained in legal expertise. Procedures became simpler and more efficient. The Lords was able to determine a greater proportion of cases from the late 1660s than at the beginning of the reign. Petitions from the Chancery comprised the largest single category of appeals: no fewer than 109 were presented to the House as compared with only 82 writs of error. Chancery appeals were complaints against the equity jurisdiction of the Lord Chancellor. The petition set down the facts of the case and asked the Lords to review the Lord Chancellor's decision. Sometimes the petitioner alleged malpractices in Chancery, perhaps claiming that the Lord Chancellor had overlooked certain facts, or had incorrectly decided which facts were relevant.

One of the most significant developments in the Lords' judicature during the Restoration period concerned this type of appeal. In an article on appellate jurisdiction James Hart demonstrated that the House of Lords had exercised its authority over equity appeals with considerable restraint in the early 1640s, setting aside Chancery decrees and instructing the Lord Keeper to rehear cases in that court.[9] It had not reversed Chancery decrees. After the dismissal of Lord Chancellor Clarendon in 1667, the peers began reversing several decrees, starting in 1668 with a judgment made against one Mr Grenville.[10] It is likely that the House was encouraged to do this by the duke of Buckingham and his adherents, who wished further to blacken the former Lord Chancellor's reputation by exposing his alleged malpractices in the Chancery. On 24 October, one of the duke's lieutenants, Lord Lucas, offered a petition from Robert Salvin, complaining of an injustice made against him by Clarendon.[11] The reversal of a decree was important, for it ensured that

---

[7] Horstman, 'Justice and peers', pp. 374, 417. John Kenyon takes the view that the issue of the Lords' original jurisdiction was left drawn (Kenyon, *The Stuart Constitution*, p. 414; Hart, *Justice upon petition*, p. 250).

[8] Both the *Journals* and the Committee for Petitions Minutes demonstrate that between 1660 and 1667 most original petitions were dismissed because relief could be found in lower courts.

[9] J. S. Hart, 'The House of Lords and the appellate jurisdiction in equity, 1640–1643', *Parliamentary History*, 2 (1983), 56–67.

[10] *LJ*, XII, 134, 206, 212; Committee for Petitions Minutes 3, 26 November, 10 December 1667.

[11] Bodl., Rawlinson MSS A. 130, fol. 91.

a petitioner could have a quicker remedy than had the House merely instructed the Lord Keeper, or Lord Chancellor, to re-hear the case, which was usually a slow and expensive process. Moreover, there was no guarantee that the Lord Chancellor would decide in the plaintiff's favour, especially if he was reviewing one of his own decisions.[12]

The peers' exercise of their appellate jurisdiction in equity cases was not without controversy. According to several historians this jurisdiction was genuinely questioned by the Commons. Scholars have cited the well-known case of *Shirley* v. *Fagg* of 1675 in support of their views. In this case and two others of the same year, one of which was also a Chancery appeal, the lower chamber opposed the Lords' proceedings, initially because the defendants were MPs, and therefore were entitled to parliamentary privilege. The Commons resolved 'that there lies no appeal to the judicature of the Lords in parliament from courts of equity'.[13] It is extremely doubtful if the Commons seriously wished to curtail the peers' appellate jurisdiction. The Lords had received and determined appeals from the Chancery earlier in the reign without the Commons raising an eyebrow. What the lower chamber really objected to in 1675 was that the Lords' proceedings encroached upon the immunity of its members from law suits during parliamentary privilege.[14] These disputes were in fact orchestrated by the Country parties in both chambers. Their aim was to divert the House of Lords from its consideration of the government's highly controversial Test Bill. Shaftesbury and his adherents encouraged the three appeals to be presented to the Lords in April when it was apparent that 'opposition' peers lacked the numerical strength to defeat the Test.[15] The eventual outcome of these bicameral disputes was that the Lords continued to exercise its appellate jurisdiction over Chancery decrees without opposition from the Commons.

One area of the Lords' judicature which was not exploited by discontented politicians was the right to hear writs of error. Writs of error were appeals from the common-law courts of King's Bench and Common Pleas. The House's jurisdiction over error cases had been recognised for many years: the *Journals* record five cases for the period 1514 to 1589, though it is unknown whether any of these was reversed or affirmed.[16] From 1621 to 1649 nearly 400 writs of error were brought into the House of Lords, many of which

---

[12] Horstman, 'Justice and peers', p. 433; Hart, 'Appellate jurisdiction in equity', p. 59. In the case of *Roberts* v. *Winn*, Clarendon refused to decree in favour of the former, despite a recommendation to do so from the Lords (Bodl., Rawlinson MSS A. 130, fol. 25, 29 Nov. 1664; Henning, *House of Commons*, III, pp. 338–9).

[13] *CJ*, IX, 347. The two other appeals were *Crisp* v. *Delmahoy* and *Stoughton* v. *Onslow* (*LJ*, XII, 663, 666, 668, 709).

[14] *CJ*, IX, 335, 337, 338, 347; *LJ*, XII, 691, 694.

[15] See chapter 7, pp. 134–6.

[16] Foster, pp. 179–83.

were determined by the peers.[17] After Chancery appeals these were by far the most numerous: 82 cases in error came before the House between 1660 and 1680. In contrast with other appeals – which began with a petition, normally presented by a peer – writs of error were delivered by a judge, usually the Lord Chief Justice, if they were from the King's Bench. The Lord Chief Justice brought up the record of the case, together with a transcript of the record.[18] These were compared in the House and then the record was returned to the court from whence it had come. The plaintiff was given a specific number of days to assign errors.[19] These were errors of law, not fact, which could be corrected in the King's Bench. For instance, the plaintiff might allege that on the basis of the record, judgment had been incorrectly given, that the verdict did not correspond with the original complaint or that the case was too weak in point of law to warrant an action.[20] After hearing counsel for both parties, the Lords would either reverse or affirm the judgment of the common-law court. Frequently writs of error were brought to delay the execution of a judgment made in a lower court. If this were the case the plaintiff proved dilatory at every stage of proceedings. This of course affected the Lords' ability to function as a court.

The Lords' appellate and error jurisdiction only involved civil cases: the peers also possessed a criminal jurisdiction. This was confined to impeachments and peerage trials. An impeachment was an action initiated by the House of Commons. As the representatives of the people, the Commons claimed a right to exhibit charges against a person – normally a government minister in this period – whose actions were considered harmful to the nation.[21] The Commons' jurisdiction ended with the accusation: the Lords acted as judge and jury. Although in most post-1660 impeachments the Commons alleged treason or misdemeanour, their action was usually politically inspired. In the cases of Lords Clarendon and Danby, they wanted to punish ministers whose policies they disliked.[22] Fears aroused by the Popish Plot led to the impeachment of five Catholic peers in 1678. For a variety of reasons a majority of peers usually took the side of the impeached. In the case of Clarendon, the House refused to imprison the former minister on a charge of general treason because it was feared that this would establish a

[17] Horstman, 'Justice and peers', p. 298.
[18] *LJ*, XII, 572, 575, 592, 611, 622, 671. Procedure in error is described fully by E. R. Foster (Foster, pp. 179–83).
[19] Usually the House allowed eight days to assign errors (*LJ*, XII, 627, 630, 635).
[20] F. Hargrave (ed.), *The jurisdiction of the Lords House or parliament ... by Lord Chief Justice Hale* (1796), p. 153; E. Coke, *The fourth part of the institutes of the laws of England: concerning the jurisdiction of courts* (1681), p. 22.
[21] Tite, *Impeachment and parliamentary judicature*, p. 23.
[22] Hutton, pp. 276–84; A. Browning, *Thomas Osborne, earl of Danby* (3 vols., Glasgow, 1944–51), I, pp. 300, 303, 324–5.

precedent for removing peers from the chamber on frivolous grounds.[23] The
Lords resisted pressure from the Commons to imprison Danby in December
1678 and again in the spring of 1679, because a majority did not accept that
the charges against the former Lord Treasurer amounted to treason.[24] Of the
thirteen impeachments presented to the House of Lords during the reign,
only one, that of Viscount Stafford, ran its entire course, leading to a trial
and a verdict. Impeachment was a remarkably ineffective weapon for the
Commons, since it required the cooperation of the Lords to be successful.

Earlier in this book we noted that a peer charged with treason, felony or
misprision of treason or felony could exercise his right to be tried by his
peers. If parliament was in session this involved a trial conducted by the
Lords and presided over by the Lord High Steward, a royal appointee,
usually the Lord Chancellor. During the intervals between parliamentary sessions a lord was tried by a court consisting of the Lord High Steward and a
jury of peers selected by the king. This happened in the cases of Lords
Morley (1666) and Cornwallis (1676). Only four peers, Lords Morley,
Cornwallis, Pembroke (1678) and Stafford (1680), were actually tried by their
peers during the reign. In each of the four trials the Lords acquitted themselves of their duties in an orderly and judicious manner. They were not
biased in favour of the noble defendants: they found Pembroke guilty of
manslaughter and Stafford guilty of treason on the basis of the evidence
before them.[25] That a majority of lords was able to act impartially in these
cases owed much to the judicial experience acquired by the House since 1660.

II

Writing in *The Jurisdiction of the Lords House* (c. 1675/6) the seventeenth-
century lawyer Matthew Hale argued that few lords were qualified to judge
legal cases in the reign of Charles II.[26] More recently Alan Horstman has
asserted that most peers were incapable of comprehending technical and legal
arguments, especially in error cases where a knowledge of the common law
was necessary.[27] This picture of the Lords' legal abilities is misleading. Hale's

[23] BL, Egerton MSS 2,539, fols. 141, 145, Sir John Nicholas to Sir Edward Nicholas, 19 and 27
November 1667; Bodl., Rawlinson MSS A. 130, fol. 95v.

[24] Browning, *Danby*, I, pp. 303–4; Leamy, 'The relations between Lords and Commons', pp.
172–6; Add. MSS 28,046, fols. 49–52, debate on the impeachment of Danby, 21 March 1679.

[25] Add. MSS 29,571, fols. 318–19, C. Hatton to Lord Hatton, 2 July 1676; BL, Stowe MSS 210,
fol. 6, Harbord to Essex, 1 July 1676. Lord Finch's detailed notes on Pembroke's trial have
been printed by D. Yale, *Lord Nottingham's Chancery cases*, II, pp. 622–30. For the trial of
Stafford see J. P. Kenyon, *The Popish Plot* (1972), p. 203; *LJ*, XIII, 689–90, 692, 694, 695,
697–706; *Hist. MSS Comm.*, 11th rept, appendix, pt II, MSS of the House of Lords 1678–88
(1887), pp. 31–44.

[26] Hargrave (ed.), *Jurisdiction of the Lords House*, p. 155.

[27] Horstman, 'Justice and peers', p. 435.

book is in places erroneous and far from impartial. Resenting the Lords' interference in the decisions of lower courts, this lawyer exaggerated the legal deficiencies of the nobility. Several peers were in fact trained lawyers themselves.[28] Horstman's views are derived from Hale and from Lord Chancellor Finch's account of a highly controversial and untypical legal debate concerning the second earl of Feversham's Chancery appeal in 1678. It is unwise to draw conclusions about the legal abilities of a majority of peers on the basis of the speeches of thirteen peers recorded as speaking in this debate.[29]

The legal ability of members of Charles II's upper House was better than previously thought. Many peers were in fact well versed in the law. No less than thirty-three peers had studied at an inn of court, acquiring there at least some legal knowledge. Of these, nine had qualified as barristers and three were benchers in Gray's Inn.[30] Others had accumulated considerable legal expertise by virtue of many years' presence in the House and on the Committee for Petitions: 44 per cent of the members of the Convention had sat in the House before 1649, and had already had direct experience of judicial procedures and precedents. From the Committee for Petitions Minutes it is apparent that several peers who chaired committee meetings on petitions and also spoke authoritatively on legal points in 1660 were those with previous legal experience. Lords Craven, Wharton, Portland, Robartes, Saye and Sele and Hunsdon had all taken an interest in judicial cases before the abolition of the House of Lords.[31] The marquis of Dorchester, a practising lawyer who had taken his seat in the Convention, regularly spoke in the Committee for Petitions.[32] Others acquired legal experience as the reign progressed: the fifth earl of Dorset, sitting first in 1660, quickly acquired an impressive knowledge of judicature, and was nominated to chair the Committee for Petitions more times per session than any other peer.[33]

Obviously not all lords were as familiar as this with legal processes in Restoration England. It is clear from the writings of Lord Holles that many younger lords had had little judicial experience before taking their seats.[34]

---

[28] Peers with a legal training are listed in Swatland, 'The House of Lords', pp. 349–56.

[29] Yale (ed.), *Lord Nottingham's Chancery cases*, II, pp. 646–9.

[30] The nine barristers were Lords Anglesey, Arundel of Trerice, Clifford, Crew (1661–79), Clarendon (1660–74), Finch (1640–60), Finch (1674–82), Holles (1680–90), Howard of Escrick (1678–94). The three benchers were Lords Shaftesbury, Dorchester and the fourth duke of Somerset.

[31] Committee for Petitions Minutes vol. 3: 12, 15, 17 May, 6 June, 2, 3 July, 22, 24 November 1660.

[32] For example, on 22 June, 2, 3 July 1660. Dorchester had in fact previously sat in the upper chamber in Oxford in 1645/6.

[33] Between 1661, when chairmen were regularly listed in the Committee for Petitions Minutes, to his death in 1677, Dorset chaired 63 per cent of committee meetings. See table 6.

[34] BL, Harleian MSS 6,810, fol. 127 ('The case stated concerning the judicature of the House of peers in the point of appeals', 1675/6).

One such peer, the earl of Bridgewater, wrote in 1664: 'I understand not the niceties of law nor the course and rules of the Chancery.'[35] Generally bishops were not well grounded in the common law prior to entering parliament. John Pearson, bishop of Chester, showed his ignorance of the law in one debate, talking 'scholastically' about some legal terms 'but understood not at all that sense in which the lawyers used those words'.[36] Yet, as Bishop Henchman suggests in his journal, it was possible to acquire an elementary understanding of legal practices simply by attending judicial debates. The bishop's detailed notes on several cases in the mid-1660s indicate that he perceived the essential legal issues involved.[37]

The fact that a majority of peers lacked a formal legal training was not an insuperable barrier to the effective functioning of this supreme court. Not every case required an understanding of the common law and legal precedents. Many error cases had already been heard before on appeal in the Exchequer, allowing the peers to discern whether the judges had been divided in their opinions. If they had been divided it really did not matter, except to the interested parties, how the peers ruled. This was often the situation in equity appeals, where, unlike in common-law courts, there was no series of precedents to be upset by the Lords' judgment. Several appeals resulting from the Stop of the Exchequer in 1672 (when repayments of government debts were suspended) came before the House later in the decade. The Stop of the Exchequer created a situation without legal precedent. Therefore the Lords were able to decide, on the merits of individual cases, who was to lose money as a result of the government's action: the bankers or their lenders.[38]

On difficult or technical cases the peers sought the advice of their legal assistants, the judges from Westminster Hall. Particularly in writs of error, the Lords relied heavily on the opinions of these men, often seeking their advice before reversing or affirming a decree. It is evident both from the *Journals* and from the writings of Lord Holles, a peer of impressive legal experience, that Matthew Hale was correct when he wrote that in the House the judges' opinions in cases of error were 'held so sacred, that the Lords have ever confirmed their judgments there unto', except in the few cases where they were parties to the former judgment and therefore might be biased.[39] Judges also assisted the peers in the scrutiny of petitions in committee, providing advice on specific legal points. Very early in the reign, on 17 May 1660, they were asked by Lord Craven to give their considered

[35] Hertfordshire Record Office, Ashridge Collection, 1079, Bridgewater to Halsey, 14 Feb. 1664.
[36] Yale (ed.), *Lord Nottingham's Chancery cases*, II, pp. 647–8.
[37] Rawlinson MSS A. 130, fols. 5v, 11v–12v, 13–15, 24v–26 (*Roberts* v. *Winn*), 102v (*Petit* v. *Hyde*), 105–105v, 109v (*Skinner* v. *The East India Company*).
[38] Horstman, 'Justice and peers', pp. 430, 432–3; *LJ*, XII, 592, 611, 626, XIII, 190, 276, 370.
[39] Hargrave (ed.), *Jurisdiction of the Lords House*, pp. 155, 158–9; BL, Harleian MSS 6,810, fol. 127; *LJ*, XI, 427, 559; XII, 208, 393, 630.

opinion on a petition from Trinity House as the possession of property rested upon the outcome of the case.[40] The judges' opinions were so highly regarded that the consideration of one petition in May 1661 was deferred until they could attend the Committee for Petitions.[41]

With advice from both their legal assistants and the handful of legally trained peers, the restored House of Lords was not as poorly qualified to carry out its duties as the supreme court as some writers have suggested. From the surviving evidence it is apparent that those peers with legal expertise, notably Anglesey, Ashley, Robartes and Finch, were prominent in the consideration of judicial matters, wielding considerable influence in the Committee for Petitions and on the floor of the House.[42] The members of the House of Lords in this period were certainly no worse qualified to judge cases than their early-Stuart predecessors. Because of the House of Lords' sudden acquisition of a judicature in 1621, it had taken the years up to 1649 to establish legal procedures in the chamber.[43] At least the restored House had the advantage of peers with several years of judicial experience and a wealth of legal precedents and established procedures to follow.

III

One essential yardstick with which to measure the calibre of a law court is the soundness of its procedures and judgments. Members of Charles II's high court considered these to be both fair and equitable. Writing in 1675 Lord Holles observed: 'In general it may [be] said of that House, that many among them are persons of honour and integrity that will not be biased, and [are] of experience to understand and judge a right of such matters as are brought before them.'[44] Three years later he asserted in debate that 'not only the honour of this House but the very peace of the kingdom depends upon the due and impartial administration of justice'.[45] Other peers, including Lords Finch, Shaftesbury, Huntingdon and Anglesey, have left evidence that they shared similar views about the administration of justice.[46] There are numerous examples of the House deliberately acting to preserve its impartiality.

[40] Committee for Petitions Minutes 3, 17 May 1660.
[41] Ibid., 24 May 1661.
[42] During one legal debate in 1678 'the earl of Shaftesbury and the Lord Privy Seal [Anglesey] had persuaded the House that the case was so clear they were ready to have pronounced the reversal'. Lord Chancellor Finch subsequently counselled the House against this course (Yale (ed.), *Lord Nottingham's Chancery cases*, II, pp. 655–6; *LJ*, XIII, 231).
[43] Foster, pp. 183–8; Horstman, 'Justice and peers', pp. 146–308.
[44] BL, Harleian MSS 6,810, fol. 127.
[45] Yale (ed.), *Lord Nottingham's Chancery cases*, II, p. 648.
[46] Committee for Petitions Minutes 3, 15 May, 3 July, 22 November 1660; Add. MSS 28,046, fol. 56, earl of Huntingdon's speech on Danby's Attainder Bill, 2 April 1679; Add. MSS 28,053, fol. 184, earl of Berkshire to Danby, 30 Aug. 1680; BL, Stowe MSS 215, fol. 120, earl of Essex to Shaftesbury, 4 May 1675; *LJ*, XI, 631, XII, 686–7, XIII, 275; Yale (ed.), *Lord Nottingham's Chancery cases*, II, pp. 629–30, 655–6.

Table 5 *Writs of error and Chancery appeals presented to the House of Lords*

Parliament/session	1	1a	1b	1c	2	2a	2b	2c	2d
Convention	1	–	–	–	5	–	–	2	–
Cavalier									
1661	1	1	–	1	–	–	–	–	–
1661/2	7	5	1	3	1	–	–	–	1
1663	2	1	–	1	2	–	–	–	2
1664	–	–	–	–	1	–	–	1	–
1664/5	1	–	–	–	2	–	–	1	1
1665	–	–	–	–	–	–	–	–	–
1666/7	1	–	–	–	1	–	–	–	–
1667/8	4	–	–	–	5	–	1(1)	1	–
1669	2	–	–	–	3	–	–	1	1
1670/1	10	7	–	4	20	–	2	5	11
1673	1	1	–	–	5	–	–	–	1
1673	1	1	–	–	2	–	–	–	–
1674	8	2	–	2	5	–	–	–	–
1675	6	1(1)	(1)	(1)	9	(1)	–	–	3(1)
1675	1	–	–	–	–	–	–	–	–
1677/8	14	8(1)	1	7	11	1(1)	2	1	–
1678	5	4	–	2	7	–	1(1)	(1)	1(5)
1678	1	–	–	–	–	–	–	–	–
1679 Parl.	1	(1)	–	–	10	(1)	–	–	1
1680/1 Parl.	15	2	–	2	20	3(5)	(3)	–	1
1681 Parl.	–	–	–	–	–	–	–	–	–
Totals	82	36	3	23	109	12	11	13	29

Key
1   Writ of error
1a   Affirm writ of error
1b   Reverse writ of error
1c   Writ of error for delay
2   Chancery appeal
2a   Affirm decision of Chancery
2b   Reverse decision of Chancery
2c   Instructions to the Lord Chancellor
2d   Chancery appeals dismissed
The numbers in brackets refer to cases received in an earlier session and are included in the totals.
Source: *Journals of the House of Lords.*

Peers expressed concern when members of their House had personal stakes in a suit. On 17 November 1675 the House was so worried about possible bias in an appeal which involved the admiralty commissioners – several of whom were peers – that it referred the matter to the Committee for

Privileges, asking the committee to ascertain whether these peers could participate in the legal proceedings.[47] In 1664 the peers had delayed hearing an appeal because Lord Chancellor Clarendon, who had made the original decree in the Chancery, was absent. A majority of lords wished to hear his views on the appeal before making any decision in the matter.[48] Concern was also expressed about the fitness of his successor, Lord Keeper Bridgeman, to guide the House in legal cases as he was partially deaf. On 28 April 1668 the Lords allowed him to vacate the woolsack and sit nearer the clerks' table when counsel and witnesses were being heard at the bar.[49]

When the peers considered petitions they did not proceed in an unruly or arbitrary manner. Particularly during the 1660s, most petitions were referred to the Committee for Petitions for scrutiny before the suit was heard on the floor of the House. This committee was a standing body, comprising all those present in the House at the beginning of a session, when it was appointed. Together with a subcommittee, with a quorum of five, its purpose was to vet petitions. It had orders to dismiss petitions which could find redress in lower courts, and retain those which could only be remedied in parliament.[50] Like legislative committees it was presided over by an elected chairman. Both the calibre and experience of the chairman were of the utmost importance if the committee was to function efficiently and without bias. A total of sixteen peers chaired meetings of the Committee for Petitions, or its subcommittee, between 1661 and 1677. Several were of outstanding legal ability, like Lords Robartes, Anglesey and Dorchester. One peer, the industrious fifth earl of Dorset, was in numerical terms the most prominent chairman, chairing 63 per cent of meetings from 1661.[51] Dorset's regular presence in the chair provided a consistency in the criteria which the committee followed in scrutinising successive petitions, which in turn diminished the possibility of ignorance and deliberate bias. If a vast number of lords had occupied the chair this might have been an indication that some, at least, wished to use this influential position to promote, or reject petitions in which they had a vested interest.

The Committee for Petitions adhered to well-tried procedures, which had been established between 1621 and 1649. These closely resembled private-bill procedures, and so peers who had previously served in the Commons were

[47] *LJ*, XII, 684, XIII, 27.
[48] Bodl., Rawlinson MSS A. 130, fol. 8 (*Roberts* v. *Winn*).
[49] Manuscript Minutes 15, 28 April 1668.
[50] HLRO, Committee for Petitions Book of Orders 1, p. 1, orders for 4, 20 June and 2 July 1660.
[51] See table 6. By the Restoration period the old system of the most senior peer in order of precedence taking the chair had been largely replaced by the committee choosing a chairman. There are numerous examples of the earl of Dorset chairing this committee, although a more senior peer was present (Committee for Petitions Minutes 3, 26 Oct. 1669, 8 and 22 November 1670 are three such instances).

Table 6 *Chairmen of the Committee for Petitions,*
1661–1677

Lord	Committees
Dorset	84
Richmond	15
Bolingbroke	10
Northampton	4
Dover (1666–77)	4
Derby (1651–72)	3
Buckingham	2
Lucas (1645–71)	2
Essex	2
Anglesey	1
Powis (1667–96)	1
Robartes	1
Chandos (1655–76)	1
Bristol	1
Dorchester	1
Winchester (1624–75)	1
Total	133

This table only indicates the number of times a peer chaired
the committee, not the number of petitions dealt with by
each chairman.
Source: Committee for Petitions Minute Book 3, 1660–94.

not entirely unfamiliar with those adopted by this committee. Once a
petition had been received and read, the committee asked the defendant to
respond in writing. After his reply had been received a date was allocated for
the hearing and interested parties were notified. The parties attended with
their counsel, having first been sworn at the bar of the House. The arguments
for the plaintiff and defendant were heard with an assistant clerk taking
copious notes. Following the withdrawal of the parties and their counsel,
committee members would discuss the case on the basis of the counsels'
arguments, the contents of the petition and any other papers presented to
them. Specific points of law were often referred to the judges for their
opinion. If the committee was divided on a petition, it conducted a formal
vote, with the clerk recording the result in the minute book. The committee
either dismissed the petition or recommended it to the House as fit to be
heard by all the peers. Of the twenty-three petitions received between
January 1662 and April 1664, four were dismissed, one was laid aside and
most of the remainder were ordered to be heard at the bar of the House.[52]

[52] Committee for Petitions Minutes 3, entries from 8 Jan. 1662 to 26 April 1664.

By the mid-1670s only a very few petitions which raised difficult legal questions were examined by the Committee for Petitions.[53] The precise reasons for this development are unclear. It is possible that the Lords gradually recognised that because counsel were heard in committee and again at the bar of the House – an extremely time-consuming process – it was much more efficient to hear them only at the bar. As the earl of Shaftesbury was aware, a double hearing inconvenienced the parties since it reduced the possibility of the Lords determining the case before a prorogation, which, until 1673, discontinued all cases before the House of Lords.[54] Also, because the parties had to pay heavy fees to their legal representatives, it was clearly more expensive to have them arguing both in the committee and on the floor of the House.[55] By the late 1660s the House had become more experienced in judicial matters, and on the basis of the petition and written answer from the defendant, was better qualified to decide whether a petitioner could find relief elsewhere, and therefore did not need to refer the petition to the Committee for Petitions.

Most of the judicial procedures followed in the House closely resembled those of the Committee for Petitions. As in committee, the petition was read and a copy was given to the defendant. The House demanded first that he put in his answer and once this had been received – sometimes it took several weeks for a defendant to reply – the plaintiff was entitled to respond in writing.[56] On completion of this process the Lords set aside time to hear the counsel for both parties argue at the bar on the basis of the facts of the case, if an appeal, or on the errors themselves, if a writ of error.[57] This procedure was entirely in accordance with contemporary legal practices of the law courts in Westminster Hall.

As in common-law courts, where a jury tried each suit, the peers themselves comprised the jury in this high court of parliament. But the peers were also the judges. After the parties and their counsel had withdrawn, the Lords debated the case on the basis of the legal facts, or on the validity of the errors. Sometimes debates were of several hours' duration, and, as Bishop Henchman's journal demonstrates, important issues were discussed in detail.[58] Decisions were often reached by a majority of votes, and there were

---

[53] Between 1673 and 1677 the committee in fact only met fourteen times.

[54] Carte MSS 228, fol. 229, earl of Shaftesbury's speech in the debate on whether impeachments and legal cases can continue from one parliament to another, 19 March 1679. In March 1673 the peers had decided that writs of error and appeals would not be discontinued by a prorogation.

[55] It could cost at least £5 a day to employ counsel. In 1664 Mr Winn had to pay over £10 each day just to retain his counsel (*LJ*, XIII, 378; Bodl., Rawlinson MSS A. 130, fol. 8).

[56] *LJ*, XII, 528, 536, 624, 628, 633, 634, 658, 662–4.

[57] Ibid., 228, 281, 608, 623; Horstman, 'Justice and peers', p. 430.

[58] On 5 and 7 May 1664 the House spent several hours debating whether to give directions to the Lord Chancellor when he reviewed the case of *Roberts* v. *Winn* (Bodl., Rawlinson MSS A. 130, fols. 14, 15).

occasions when peers entered a protest in the *Journal*. Anglesey, Shaftesbury, Carlisle, Widdrington, Vaughan and Denbigh, for example, signed a protest on 16 May 1675 following a majority decision not to affirm a judgment made by the House of Lords in May 1642. The dissenting peers considered the case to be too ancient for the House to take cognisance of, for most of the witnesses were dead, and a re-hearing might upset a judgment relating to an estate which had been in force for over thirty years.[59]

Generally a majority decision produced neither a protest nor an outcry from the judges in Westminster Hall. This was because the House did not arrive at its decisions lightly. It frequently sought the opinions of the judges.[60] The form of the Lords' judgments was not usually different from those of other courts. In an appeal from the Chancery the House might dismiss the petition, confirming the Lord Chancellor's decree.[61] Sometimes it instructed the Lord Chancellor to rehear a particular suit.[62] Alternatively the peers could simply reverse a decree, as happened frequently in the 1670s.[63] In error cases the Lords either affirmed or reversed the ruling made in the common law court.[64] If it was suspected that the plaintiff was merely abusing their judicature for the purpose of delaying the execution of a decree (this was very often the situation if he failed to assign errors), the House automatically affirmed the lower court's judgment.[65]

The *Journals* and Committee for Petitions Minutes demonstrate that the Lords closely adhered to these judicial procedures. Suits were determined in a careful and responsible manner. There was plenty of scope for both parties to present their arguments and evidence. The few surviving records of judicial debates suggest that the peers discussed the issues involved, and based their judgments on the legal facts of each case.[66] There was nothing about their procedure that could be described as either arbitrary or indiscriminative.

It is, however, occasionally possible to detect deliberate bias on the part of specific peers during legal proceedings. There is strong evidence of partiality on behalf of Robert Pitt, the plaintiff in an appeal from the Chancery in 1670. Pitt's petition was tendered to the House by the duke of Richmond, who used his influence to promote it vigorously at all stages.[67] He chaired the meeting of the Committee for Petitions which considered the petition on 22

---

[59] *LJ*, XII, 686–7.
[60] Ibid., 630; BL, Harleian MSS 6,810, fol. 127.
[61] See table 5 for the numbers of petitions dismissed by the House each session.
[62] *LJ*, XI, 265, 286, 539, XII, 275, 302; Bodl., Rawlinson MSS A. 130, fols. 15, 24v–26.
[63] *LJ*, XII, 147, 206, 212, 275, 392, 686–7, XIII, 120, 275, 283.
[64] Ibid., XIII, 159, 160, 166–8, 188, 231, 269, 281.
[65] Ibid., XI, 423, 532, XII, 378, 623, XIII, 152.
[66] Bodl., Rawlinson MSS A. 130, fols. 12v, 14, 15, 24v, 25, 28v; Yale (ed.), *Lord Nottingham's Chancery cases*, II, pp. 628, 646–9, 655–6, 661–4, 671–89.
[67] Add. MSS 21,948, fol. 456, Robert Pitt to Richmond, 28 Dec. 1672.

November. As soon as the committee decided to proceed with the suit, by appointing a day for the counsel to appear, Richmond vacated the chair and was replaced by the earl of Dorset.[68] Eventually the House reversed the Chancery decree. Pitt believed that Richmond was largely responsible for this, asserting that 'by your grace's interest in a good measure I had speedy relief and justice done me'.[69] As no accounts of debates on this case have survived, it is impossible to determine how influential Richmond was in persuading the House to reverse the decree.

As with private bills, there was considerable external pressure brought to bear on peers and their associates to promote petitions in the chamber. In June 1663 a Mr Benson, an interested party in a case involving Sir Christopher Clapham, frequented the company of Lady Pembroke's agent to discover the designs of his opponents. These involved the employment of Lords Thanet and Northampton to persuade the respected duke of Albemarle to present the petition.[70] In another case, one Edward Clerk, rector of Chevening, wrote to the sixth earl of Dorset in December 1680 complaining of a writ of error brought into the House on behalf of Sir Oliver Butler. He asserted that 'Sir Oliver Butler hath surreptitiously obtained a patent for erecting a market in Chatham ... which patent the city [of Rochester] hath overthrown in the high court of Chancery.'[71] Clerk argued that if Sir Oliver should succeed in prosecuting his writ of error, 'it will certainly ruin one of the most ancient and loyal cities of England', neighbouring Rochester. Dorset was implored 'to engage ... as many of [his] friends as are members of that noble house' to support the interests of the city of Rochester when the case was considered in the House.[72] The Lords asked the judges to examine the transcript of the case on 11 December, but urgent public matters intervened and parliament was dissolved on 10 January before the judges had reported.[73]

The lawyer Matthew Hale regarded the patronage of petitions in the upper House with contempt: it was a 'course that if it were used by the judges of Westminster Hall would be looked upon even by the parliament itself as indecent and carrying a probable imputation or temptation at least to partiality'.[74] This practice must be viewed in context. Unlike other law courts, the House of Lords was not solely concerned with legal matters. It spent a majority of its time on legislation. Because of the short duration of sessions, the Lords' heavy workload and the often protracted proceedings in legal

---

[68] Committee for Petitions Minutes 3, 22 Nov. 1670.
[69] Add. MSS 21,948, fol. 456, Pitt to Richmond, 28 Dec. 1672.
[70] Chatsworth House, Lismore MSS, vol. 33, no. 62, Richard Graham to the earl of Cork, 27 June 1663. Albemarle did not cooperate and Lord Thanet tendered the petition instead.
[71] Kent Archives Office, Sackville MSS U269/C12, fol. 65, Clerk to Dorset, 1 Dec. 1680.
[72] Ibid.; *LJ*, XIII, 701.
[73] *LJ*, XIII, 712, 734.
[74] Hargrave (ed.), *Jurisdiction of the Lords House*, p. 159.

cases, it was impossible for the House to determine all suits brought before it each session. Thus, if a petitioner wished to obtain swift relief it was necessary for him to engage peers to promote his suit in the chamber. Such lords were extremely useful in reminding the House to set a day aside to hear counsel at the bar.[75]

There is no conclusive evidence that the efforts of a sponsor persuaded a majority of lords to pervert the course of justice. Often the House, or the Committee for Petitions, decided in favour of the defendant, in spite of the efforts of the plaintiff's supporters. This happened with Sir John Reresby's Chancery appeal in 1671. Reresby tried to retrieve an estate in Derbyshire which had been mortgaged by his great-grandfather.[76] Shortly before his petition was due to be considered in committee, he asked his friend, Viscount Halifax, for his assistance. Apparently the viscount obtained the support of a few peers, but other matters prevented him from attending the committee in person. Halifax recognised the futility of Reresby's position: 'I should not have hoped to do much considering how many of the lords were possessed against you, but I would have struggled to have had your counsel heard before your petition had been dismissed.'[77] The baronet noted in his memoirs that the petition was dismissed on 31 January because the peers considered it was unjust to evict a man from an estate, which he had possessed for the previous fifty years.[78] This case was untypical: it had been brought in order to frighten the defendant into compensating Reresby privately for the loss of this estate. It is most unlikely that Reresby genuinely expected the peers to reverse the Chancery decree.[79]

Despite the increasing polarisation of political opinions within the peerage during the 1670s, judicial cases were rarely determined along party lines. Most litigation did not involve controversial political issues. In June 1678 the House dealt with an appeal against one George Porter and 'there was not a voice against him'.[80] Often peers holding opposing political views signed the same protest arising from a judicial case. Nine Court lords and nine Country lords signed a protest on 5 July 1678 against a majority decision to relieve a petitioner.[81] Party divisions were also blurred when each lord singly pro-

---

[75] Add. MSS 29,571, fol. 261, Christopher Hatton to Lord Hatton, 11 Jan. 1674; Bodl., Rawlinson MSS A. 130, fol. 8.

[76] A. Browning (ed.), *The memoirs of Sir John Reresby* (Glasgow, 1936), pp. 82–3; *LJ*, XII, 427.

[77] Leeds Archives Department, Mexborough MSS: Reresby Letters 3/12, Halifax to Reresby, 11 Feb. 1671.

[78] Committee for Petitions Minutes 3, 31 January 1671; Browning (ed.), *Reresby memoirs*, p. 83.

[79] Ibid. Reresby accepted £500 in 'compensation' from the purchasers of the estate.

[80] *Hist. MSS Comm.*, 58, MSS of the marquis of Bath, II (1907), pp. 164–5, Henry Savile to the earl of Rochester, 25 June 1678.

[81] *LJ*, XIII, 273. The arguments against giving relief were noted by Lord Finch. See Yale (ed.), *Lord Nottingham's Chancery cases*, II, pp. 687–9.

claimed his judgment at the end of a peerage trial. Thus, of the forty-two peers who found the seventh earl of Pembroke guilty of manslaughter in 1678, sixteen were Country peers and twenty-six were Catholics or Court lords.[82] Peers responded individually to this case on the basis of the evidence before the House, a point which is apparent from the Lord Chancellor's notes on the trial.[83] The Court party was again divided in December 1680 over the verdict in Viscount Stafford's treason trial. While thirty Court peers found him not guilty, a further seventeen joined with the 'opposition' in finding him guilty of treason, either on the basis of the evidence or because their perceptions of the truth were coloured by anxieties aroused by the popish plot.[84]

The House of Lords was not deliberately biased in its handling of judicial cases. Clearly, were the House perceived not to be impartial its credibility as the king's high court would have been severely damaged. The administration of justice was regarded by their lordships as an honour not to be abused, and it is in this context that an attempt by the House in 1678 to curb external pressure on its members should be seen. The House ordered that 'no person concerned in any cause as plaintiff or defendant do presume to attend any lord of parliament in relation to any cause otherwise than with their petitions to this high court, which can come no other way but by the hand of some lord'.[85] Rather than bias adversely affecting the Lords' administration of justice, other factors, such as short and infrequent parliamentary sessions had a far more marked impact upon their judicial proceedings.

IV

In terms of the number of suits determined, the House of Lords was more productive between 1660 and 1681 than it had been before 1649. It did not attain the degree of effectiveness characteristic of its successor during the two decades after the Glorious Revolution.[86] A decision was reached in slightly less than half of all error cases and in 60 per cent of Chancery appeals. Many suits were not determined in the session in which they were received. In contrast, for nine of the twenty-three sessions between 1689 and 1710 the House heard all cases during the session in which they were filed.[87] In Charles II's

---

[82] Ibid., p. 629; Swatland, 'The House of Lords', p. 129, note 133.
[83] Yale (ed.), *Lord Nottingham's Chancery cases*, II, pp. 627–9.
[84] BL, Egerton MSS 2,978, fols. 55–6, division on Viscount Stafford's guilt or innocence, 7 Dec. 1680; *Memoirs of Thomas, earl of Ailesbury* (2 vols., 1890), I, p. 50; Kenyon, *The Popish Plot*, p. 203. The evidence against Stafford was strong and incriminating and his defence was regarded by observers as weak (Haley, *Shaftesbury*, pp. 607–10).
[85] Committee for Privileges Minute Book 2, 13 June 1678.
[86] Horstman, 'Justice and peers', pp. 443–4; Hart, *Justice upon petition*, p. 242.
[87] Horstman, 'Justice and peers', pp. 443–4.

reign parliament was still an occasional institution, meeting infrequently and for short periods at a time. Between 1660 and 1681 there were five parliaments, meeting in total for three years and eleven months. The average duration of each session was eight weeks. Yet after 1689 parliament assembled annually and for several months at a stretch. When parliament eventually assembled in the reign of Charles II the peers were inundated with petitions which had accumulated during the long intervals between sessions. There were simply too many petitions and too much other parliamentary business for the House to process all judicial cases. Even in the longest session of the Cavalier Parliament, sitting on 184 occasions between 1670 and 1671, the House only dealt with seven of the ten writs of error received. But in the short session from 7 January to 24 February 1674, the Lords was only able to despatch two of the eight error cases brought before it. Non-judicial matters frequently took priority. From October 1678 to March 1681 the peers received 47 appeals, but could only hear 18 despite 215 sittings, because of their investigation of the popish plot, the impeachments of Danby and the five Catholic lords and their preoccupation with measures to secure the country from Popery.

Earlier in the reign peers had been well aware of the constraints of time and non-judicial business on their capability to determine legal cases. These problems were more serious before 1673, for, irrespective of how advanced the House was on a case, all suits were discontinued by a prorogation. This meant that if a plaintiff still wished to obtain justice after a prorogation he was obliged to re-introduce his petition in the next session where the peers would start on it afresh. To remedy this defect in their judicature, the peers decided on 29 March 1673 that writs of error and appeals could continue from one session to another in the same parliament.[88] This decision had a marked effect upon the Lords' ability to determine law suits. Although sessions were generally much shorter than they had been between 1660 and 1671, from 1673 the House was able to hear a greater proportion of cases.[89]

This reform did nothing to alleviate the other main threat to the Lords' judicial efficiency: time-wasting by litigants themselves. A significant number of plaintiffs deliberately abused the peers' judicature by lodging petitions as a method of delaying the execution of judgments against them in inferior courts.[90] Litigants were aware that the House usually ordered a stay of execution until it had determined the suit. This practice was of immense value to the plaintiff for it enabled him to retain land and money for a longer

---

[88] *LJ*, XII, 583.

[89] Between 1660 and 1671 the Lords heard 51 per cent of error cases received, but from 1673 to 1678 determined 57 per cent despite the average duration of a session being under half that of the 1660s.

[90] This had also been common practice before 1649 (Foster, p. 181).

period than would have been possible had the judgment of the lower court been immediately enforced. Some plaintiffs did everything in their power to impede the progress of their suits in parliament. Tactics included a failure to assign errors on time, or at all, and a feigned illness as a reason for not being present at the bar on the day fixed for the hearing.[91] In one case the plaintiff's excuse was an inability to obtain the necessary legal papers, which he claimed, were in the possession of a lawyer, who had recently, and most conveniently, left town.[92] Another plaintiff alleged that the solicitor holding his papers was indisposed.[93] The main consequence of these 'vexatious' suits, as the House described them, was a reduction in time available to hear genuine cases.[94]

Efforts were made to curb this destructive practice. On 9 December 1670 the Lords instructed the clerk to enter in the Roll of Standing Orders an order, made on 13 December 1661, for the dismissal of all writs of error in which the plaintiff had failed to assign errors within eight days of bringing the writ into the House. The *Journal* shows that on several occasions after 1670 writs were dismissed because the plaintiff had not assigned errors within this period.[95] Later in July 1678 the House made an order against 'frivolous' appeals from the Chancery, refusing in future to accept any petition unless it had been 'subscribed by some known practiser at law, as well as the petitioner'.[96] Those who prosecuted frivolous petitions were generally fined. This was often the case if the defendant and his counsel appeared at the bar at a pre-arranged time and the plaintiff failed to attend, offering no satisfactory excuse. In these circumstances the House dismissed the petition, fining the plaintiff and ordering him to pay the defendant's costs.[97] The July order was disregarded by sufficient litigants for the peers to take an even tougher line on 10 December: the plaintiff was instructed to provide the court which had decreed against him adequate security before the House would order a stay of execution. This order drastically reduced the number of vexatious suits and the *Journal* records only two petitions introduced for the purpose of delay between 1679 and 1681.[98]

In spite of the problems posed by short sessions and vexatious suits, the restored House of Lords provided a valuable service to those litigants who could not find redress in other law courts. Lower courts did make erroneous judgments and as the supreme court the Lords was able to provide remedies.

[91] *LJ*, XI, 286, 385, 532, XII, 623, 641, 675, XIII, 152, 159.
[92] Ibid., XII, 542 (*Cholmley et al. v. The Grocers' Company*).
[93] Ibid., XIII, 21 (*Dennies v. Frazer*).
[94] Ibid., XII, 378.
[95] *LJ*, XII, 623, 639, 679, XIII, 656.
[96] *LJ*, XIII, 285.
[97] Ibid., XI, 385, 532, XII, 378, 623, XIII, 160, 167, 278.
[98] Ibid., XIII, 411, 653, 710.

Numerous petitioners complaining of malpractices committed in the Chancery found relief there. Of course no Lord Chancellor was infallible, and Clarendon was certainly no exception. The House relieved one petitioner who had lost his suit in the Chancery, because Clarendon had forgotten that one of the referees appointed to adjudicate the case had already been objected to by the plaintiff. This referee had been hostile to the plaintiff and had held the casting vote.[99] Although only a tiny minority of the thousands of cases dealt with by ordinary courts ever came before the House of Lords, the existence of a high court both expanded the availability of litigation and gave a settlement that was final.

[99] Bodl., Rawlinson MSS A. 130, fol. 103; *LJ*, XII, 95, 147 (*Petit v. Hide*).

Part 3

KING, LORDS AND COMMONS

6

King and Lords

A prominent feature of parliamentary politics in the early modern period was the close relationship between the monarchy and the House of Lords. Approximately two-thirds of the peerage joined Charles I in the Civil War. Charles II strengthened the connection of interests between the nobility and the Crown by creating and promoting peers. In moments of crisis, the popish plot and succession crisis being the most well-known examples, the House of Lords proved to be a reliable ally of the Crown. Like his immediate predecessors, Charles II had a far tighter grip on the Lords than on the Commons. During the 1670s when the development of a substantial 'opposition' party reduced the government's influence over the Commons, the Lords usually proved amenable to the king's wishes. However the peers were certainly not the pawns of the monarchy. There were occasions when they resisted the royal will and forced the king to back down on a particular issue. The ways in which Charles II exerted his authority over the House of Lords provide the central theme of this chapter.

I

The vast majority of the king's parliamentary speeches and written communications, like those from Breda in April 1660, give the impression that he held the House of Lords in high esteem.[1] In his first letter to the Lords, which was read on 1 May 1660, Charles recognised both the authority and jurisdiction of the upper House.[2] As is often the case with politicians, and Charles was certainly no exception, such public pronouncements conceal the man's innermost thoughts. Charles' actions demonstrate that the Lords existed to serve his needs and those of his government. Of course he respected the authority and privileges of the House, but only providing these did not conflict with royal policy. Charles regarded the Lords as of greatest value when it was considering government policy or defending royal prerogatives. In spite of their different roles, the Commons was perceived by him to be the

---

[1] The king's parliamentary speeches are printed in the *Journals of the House of Lords*.
[2] *LJ*, XI, 6.

more important chamber, because it alone was able to initiate supply bills, though the Lords' concurrence was essential, and on most occasions a formality.[3] The Lords, on the other hand, blocked and amended bills which his majesty disapproved of and initiated key government measures. This was not achieved without some degree of management. Earlier in this book we saw that by paying close attention to its composition Charles laid the foundations for influencing proceedings in the Lords.[4] The addition of one or two royal creations a year did not in the short term enhance his control over the House. There was usually less need for the systematic management of the more dependable Lords than the potentially volatile Commons. But when occasion arose, there was a variety of methods which either the king or his leading ministers of the day employed to manage the House of Lords.

During the 1660s one of the most influential managers was his own brother and heir presumptive, the duke of York. Ever alert for opportunities to strengthen the power of the Crown, James was in some ways an ideal person to represent the king's interests in the chamber. Prior to public knowledge of his conversion to Catholicism in 1673, he was respected by his fellow peers. He had a personal following in the House, which consisted mainly of courtiers and military men such as the earl of Peterborough and Lords Berkeley of Stratton, Gerard and Belasyse.[5] He was generally prepared to further royal policies during the 1660s. It is likely that he was asked, by either Charles or Clarendon, to intervene in the acrimonious debate on the Bill to restore ecclesiastical jurisdiction on 26 July 1661. He stood up and informed the House that 'the Bill should pass on the morrow' and that the court was 'resolved to sit ... and talk it out' with the Catholic and Presbyterian peers who were impeding the progress of the measure.[6]

Two years later he made a strenuous effort to discredit the earl of Bristol as he sought the impeachment of the duke's father-in-law, the earl of Clarendon. Out of duty to his kinsman and loyalty to his brother, who abhorred such an attack on his minister, James spoke to his friends on 9 July instructing them to attend the Lords and oppose the impeachment, which was to be instigated the next day. From the earl of Salisbury's notes on the debate immediately following Bristol's accusations, it appears that one of the reasons for the peers' refusal to accept the earl's charges was the duke's

---

[3] Despite the recent revisionist approach to the House of Commons as exemplified in J. Miller's article, 'Charles II and his parliaments', *Transactions of the Royal Historical Society* (1982), 1–23, the chamber was a powerful force to be reckoned with. Though it did not seek to increase its authority at the expense of the Crown, it did frustrate royal policies, particularly those of a religious nature, far more frequently than the Lords. See both Seaward and Hutton, pp. 133–404.

[4] See chapter 3 above, pp. 31–2.

[5] HLRO, Proxy Books, 4 and 5, proxies held by the duke of York, 1662–75; Seaward, p. 23.

[6] Add. MSS 23,215, fol. 40, Sir John Finch to Lord Conway, 27 July 1661; *LJ*, XI, 320, 321.

vigorous defence of Clarendon in the House. York told the peers that Bristol was a 'sayer of sedition' for which he had been banished from the court and therefore his evidence should be disregarded.[7] The duke was instrumental in preventing Bristol from reviving his impeachment when parliament assembled on 21 March 1664, by advising the House to send a letter from the earl directly to the king, rather than to open it and therefore provide further ammunition for attacking Clarendon or disrupting the parliamentary session. Prior to the debate on the 22nd, when the House finally agreed to send the letter to the king, James had privately spoken to several lords, including Lord Lucas, one of Bristol's allies in the House.[8]

Yet the duke was not a consistent supporter of royal policies. His attitude towards the Irish Cattle Bill of 1666–7 illustrates this. Like his brother, James objected to the word 'nuisance' in the Bill because it prevented the use of the dispensing power: Charles was intending to allow some individuals licences to import cattle. The Lords replaced 'nuisance' with 'detriment and mischief' which in common law did not debar the exercise of the royal prerogative. The result of the peers' action was a dispute with the Commons in which neither House would back down. Charles and James backed the Lords.[9] Eventually a deterioration in the government's financial position forced the king to drop his objection to the word 'nuisance' in return for the Commons' despatching a poll bill. The duke of York was asked to convey the decision to the bishops and court lords, which he did on 13 January 1667, though most reluctantly. Along with almost all the bishops James withdrew from the chamber before the House of Lords voted to agree with the Commons on the Irish Cattle Bill.[10] The precise reasons for the duke's reluctance to implement his brother's wishes remain obscure. Perhaps, like Clarendon and those peers who protested at the House of Lords' decision to admit the word 'nuisance', he felt that to surrender to the Commons would establish a precedent for limiting royal prerogatives.[11]

Charles II's confidence in his brother's utility as a parliamentary manager was seriously undermined in the spring of 1670 when James incited opposition to the Roos Divorce Bill in the Lords in front of the king's eyes. Charles took a particularly keen interest in the Bill, even reviving the practice of personally attending debates, because he saw the Bill as a precedent for a

---

[7] Carte MSS 77, fol. 524, Salisbury to Huntingdon, 13 July 1663. See also Seaward, pp. 227–30, for more detail on the impeachment.

[8] Carte MSS 44, fol. 513, Broderick to Ormond, 26 March 1664; 76, fol. 7, Salisbury to Huntingdon, 22 March 1664; Add. MSS 38,015, fol. 77, Southwell to ?, 22 March 1664, Bodl., Rawlinson MSS A. 130, fols. 2, 5; *LJ*, XI, 584, 585.

[9] Carte MSS 217, fols. 342 and 344, Anglesey to Ormond, 16, 20 Oct. 1666; 46, fol. 387, Arlington to Ormond, 16 Oct. 1666; Hutton, pp. 254–5.

[10] Carte MSS 47, fol. 138, Anglesey to Ormond, 15 Jan. 1667; 215, fol. 318, Burlington to Ormond, 15 Jan. 1667.

[11] Seaward, pp. 290–1.

possible divorce from his barren wife.[12] As the heir presumptive it is not hard
to see why James was so hostile towards the bill. It was the need to diminish his brother's influence in the House that partly explains Charles' decision
to attend debates. According to Burnet the earl of Lauderdale advised the
king to attend to prevent 'all trouble from the Lords'.[13] The Bill was the
subject of a bitter row at court as well as in the Lords. Apart from York,
many of the bishops and privy councillors, including Manchester, attacked
the measure. At the same time Ashley, Buckingham, Anglesey and other ministers vigorously defended it.[14] Fearing his brother's influence would defeat it
at the third reading stage, the king attended to canvass votes so that the
balance of opinion remained in Lord Roos' favour.[15]

James' refusal to follow the royal line on the Roos Divorce Bill prompted
the king to become directly involved in the management of the House of
Lords. His revival, on 21 March 1670, of the custom, last exercised by Henry
VIII, of attending debates informally was in stark contrast with the ceremonial at the beginning and end of sessions when the king, attired in his robes,
addressed the assembled Houses from the throne in the upper House. Very
occasionally before 1670 he had entered the chamber and asked the House
to despatch pressing government business, but he did not linger to eavesdrop
on debates. On 27 July 1660 he had told the peers that he was anxious for
them to pass the Bill of Indemnity, expressing his opinion that only actual
regicides should be exempted from pardon.[16] By personally attending debates
during the 1670s Charles II was able to convey his views directly to peers and
force his critics either to speak openly or to remain silent.

There were other reasons why the king decided to attend debates in the
upper House regularly at this time. The extremely controversial second
Conventicle Bill was undergoing a rough passage through the chamber: when
the king entered the chamber on 21 March 1670 over eighty peers were
debating it in the committee of the whole House.[17] There was extensive
opposition to it from both Presbyterians and privy councillors. Manchester,
Ashley, Arlington and Carlisle were highly critical, and there was even the
possibility that the House would cast it out.[18] Charles was eager for the
Bill to pass with the addition of a proviso, inserted in committee, which
recognised his supremacy in ecclesiastical affairs. He wanted parliamentary

[12] Haley, *Shaftesbury*, p. 276; Hutton, *Charles II*, p. 271.
[13] Burnet, *History*, I, pp. 490–1; Manuscript Minutes, vol. 16, 21 March 1670.
[14] Burnet, *History*, I, p. 471; Harris, *Sandwich*, II, pp. 318–33. The Bill passed its three readings
by majorities of eight, fourteen and seven respectively.
[15] *Cal. SP Ven.*, 36, p. 180; H. M. Margoliouth (ed.), *The poems and letters of Andrew Marvell*
(2 vols., Oxford, 1971), II, pp. 316–17.
[16] *LJ*, XI, 108.
[17] Manuscript Minutes, vol. 16, 21 March 1670.
[18] *LJ*, XII, 326, 340; Lacey, *Dissent and parliamentary politics*, p. 60.

recognition of his power to exempt individual dissenters from the provisions of the act, and therefore make them dependent upon the monarchy for their freedom to worship. As with the Roos Bill, Charles made his views plain to peers, speaking to individuals, and even issuing warnings to the more independently minded.[19]

A third reason for attending at this time was that Charles wished to demonstrate his continuing respect for the peers after favouring the Commons in its protracted dispute with them over the case of *Skinner* v. *The East India Company* (1667–70). On 22 February the king had terminated this dispute, which had soured bicameral relations since 1668. To the displeasure of many peers, who believed they had right on their side, Charles had persuaded both Houses to expunge all proceedings on the dispute from their respective *Journals*. This prevented the case from being used as a precedent, and to many lords was seen as an endorsement of the Commons' argument that the Lords could not act as a court of first instance in civil cases. The House of Lords certainly received the king's revival of this ancient custom with 'much satisfaction', for they attended him in a body 'at the Banqueting House and gave him humble thanks for his favour therein'.[20]

Obviously not every peer was enthusiastic about the king's presence at debates. Some regarded his attendance as interference in the proceedings of their House and a restriction on freedom of speech, since lords might be reluctant to voice their true feelings on royal policy in front of the king. Those who criticised royal policies objected to his solicitation of votes. When he tried to influence proceedings on a contentious subsidy bill in February 1671 the earl of Clare, one of the Bill's opponents, 'stood up and made a smack against the king as being in the House of Lords and produced 20 precedents against it in diverse kings' reigns'.[21] Three years later on 24 January 1674 the same lord was so scathing in his condemnation of the king's practice that he was forced to ask the pardon of the king and the House for asserting 'the inconvenience of his going to the fireside when lords are drawn together' which 'he could not guess for what unless it were to receive orders how to give their votes'.[22] Bishop Burnet reported that other peers felt that the king's attendance placed a 'great restraint on the freedom of debate', with members afraid to criticise the government in the king's presence.[23] Charles

---

[19] Add. MSS 36,916, fol. 174, Starkey to Aston, 31 March 1670; PRO, S.P. 29/274, fol. 47 (proviso to Conventicle Bill); Burnet, *History*, I, pp. 493–4; Bodl., MSS Eng. Lett. c. 210, fol. 141, Henry Yelverton to Archdeacon Palmer, 21 March 1670.

[20] *Hist. MSS Comm.*, 55, Various Collections (1903), vol. II, MSS of Sir George Wombell, p. 134, Arlington to Fauconberg, 31 March 1670.

[21] Bodl., Tanner MSS 44, fol. 246, ? to Sancroft, ? Feb. 1671.

[22] Manuscript Minutes, vol. 18, 24 January 1674; Add. MSS 29,571, fol. 268, Christopher Hatton to Lord Hatton, 29 Jan. 1674.

[23] Burnet, *History*, I, pp. 492–3.

did not speak formally in debates, though he did whisper to lords individually in the chamber. When he sat, or stood, by the fire, government peers vacated their seats and noisily crowded round him, disturbing all order and decency in the House.[24] This resulted in the breakdown of the traditional seating arrangements: previously lords had sat according to their order of precedence within the peerage, which had been enshrined in a statute of 1539. Now barons, viscounts and earls were recorded as sitting on the same benches.[25]

Charles considered his presence to be a valuable contribution to the management of the upper House. Indeed he rather enjoyed attending debates, which he claimed were more amusing than watching a play.[26] From 1670 until his last parliament at Oxford in 1681 the king assiduously attended debates. He was present during forty-three of the forty-nine sittings of the spring session of 1675 and he sat by the fire for fifty-one of the fifty-nine sittings of the 1680–1 parliament.[27] He was never slow in expressing his views. He demonstrated his continued support for his Lord Treasurer's Test Bill in 1675 by remaining in the chamber late at night until the debates had finished.[28] His presence prevented Country peers from misrepresenting his opinions on a particular issue. On 28 November 1678 the Lords debated whether to concur with the Commons' address calling for the removal of the queen from Whitehall. It was alleged by the government's critics that Catherine was implicated in the plot to kill her husband. The Lords overwhelmingly rejected the address (only eleven peers voted to concur with the Commons) because 'the king carried himself most worthily, showing a detestation [of] what some thought might be acceptable to him'.[29] And of course Charles made his views plain to individual peers two years later as the Exclusion Bill was under consideration in the House.[30]

Throughout the reign Charles had both a powerful ally and a further channel of communication with the Lords in the person of the Lord Chancellor, or Lord Keeper of the Great Seal, who presided over the House on the woolsack. The Lord Chancellor was appointed by the king and acted

[24] Ibid., p. 493; Tanner MSS 44, fol. 246.
[25] The seating arrangements in the House can be deduced from the original presence lists in the Manuscript Minutes, which differ considerably from the lists in the printed *Journals*. The latter are arranged according to precedence within the nobility. See Clyve Jones, 'Seating problems in the House of Lords', 132–45.
[26] *Parl. Hist.*, VI, p. 447.
[27] Whenever the king attended his name was entered in the Journal at the top of the attendance lists (*LJ*, XII, 652–728; XIII, 610–742).
[28] C. E. Pike (ed.), *Selections from the correspondence of Arthur Capel earl of Essex, 1675–1677* (Camden Society, third series, vol. XXIV, 1913), p. 23, Francis Godolphin to Essex, 1 June 1675.
[29] *Hist. MSS Comm.*, 6th Rept, MSS of the duke of Ormond (1877), p. 723, Ossory to the duchess of Ormond, 30 Nov. 1678.
[30] Haley, *Shaftesbury*, p. 601.

and spoke for the government. He transmitted royal policy to parliament in a formal speech at the opening of a session. He adjourned and prorogued parliament at the king's behest. The king consulted with the Lord Chancellor and his other principal ministers on parliamentary affairs before and during a session.[31] It was particularly important for the Lord Chancellor to attend these management meetings because he directed the agenda in the House, and was thus in a good position to influence the order of business according to the king's expressed views, accelerating bills which the king favoured and retarding those which he disapproved of.[32]

The effectiveness of each of the occupants of the woolsack varied enormously according to his position at court, his relationship with the king, his personality, his parliamentary experience and the prevailing political climate. Excluding the earl of Manchester, who was temporary 'speaker' for the first 38 sittings of the Convention, there were four official 'speakers' for the reign. They were: Sir Edward Hyde, earl of Clarendon, Lord Chancellor from 1658 to 1667; Sir Orlando Bridgeman, Lord Keeper from 1667 to 1672; the earl of Shaftesbury, Lord Chancellor from 1672 to 1673; and Sir Heneage Finch, Lord Finch (1674), Lord Keeper to 1675 and Lord Chancellor until his death in 1682.

Of these Clarendon was the most influential in the House because he was also the chief minister. He was an able government servant, and an experienced parliamentary manager, using his position on the woolsack to promote the king's business. He played a leading role in guiding the legislation that constituted the Restoration Settlement through the Lords. His hand can be detected in the Ministers', Uniformity, Corporation and Conventicle Bills from the early years of the reign.[33] It was Clarendon who delivered the king's dispensing proviso to the Uniformity Bill in March 1662. When this controversial alteration was challenged by the earl of Bristol and other lords he vacated the woolsack and took his place at the head of the earls' bench so that under the rules of the House he could speak freely and defend royal policy.[34] Clarendon was indisposed for extended periods with gout, which undermined his standing in the House, though Charles did appoint substitutes, notably Lord Robartes, the Lord Privy Seal and Sir Orlando Bridgeman, the Lord Chief Justice, to occupy the woolsack and thereby maintain communication between the court and the Lords. In spite of his absences, Clarendon was still able to exert some influence on the House

---

[31] Macray (ed.), *Notes which passed*, pp. 18, 29, 55, 89; Clarendon, *Life*, I, pp. 313–14; II, p. 316; Hutton, *Charles II*, pp. 258–9, 296–7, 397.

[32] *Notes which passed*, p. 89.

[33] Seaward, pp. 153–4, 171–8; Committee Minutes 1, pp. 457–8, 10 May 1664; Bodl., Rawlinson MSS A. 130, fol. 15v.

[34] Add. MSS 22,919, fol. 203, Sir William Morrice to Sir George Downing, 21 March 1662; HLRO, Braye MSS, vol. 53, no. 17; *LJ*, XI, 411.

through his associates, the earls of Bridgewater, Portland and Manchester, who promoted royal policies on the floor of the House and at committees.[35] A combination of continued ill-health and growing unpopularity both at court and in parliament diminished his authority in the Lords, particularly during the last two years of his ministry. From 1666, proceedings in the House became increasingly dominated by the government's critics, most notably Buckingham and his faction. By the time of the lengthy debates on the Irish Cattle Bill (autumn 1666) the Lord Chancellor's influence had declined significantly. According to Lord Conway, the Chancellor 'could not make one convert' to the Irish interest in the chamber 'so strong is the current of the major part of the whole House'.[36]

Clarendon's immediate successor, Lord Chief Justice Bridgeman, who was given the lesser title of Lord Keeper, had far less authority in the House. He was not a peer, and therefore could not speak for the government in debates. Charles had appointed him because of both his familiarity with the speakership whilst deputising for Clarendon and his extensive legal expertise, which was a necessity when presiding over judicial cases. Bridgeman's ability to guide proceedings was also limited by his deafness. In 1668 he was forced to vacate the woolsack and sit near the clerks' table in order to hear counsel and witnesses at the bar.[37] Like Clarendon, he was frequently ill, though unlike his predecessor he was of minor political significance, neither closely linked to any faction nor intimate with Charles.[38] By the early 1670s his 'frequent sicknesses and not attending business was become a great grievance to the people'.[39] In November 1672 he was replaced by the earl of Shaftesbury.

Shaftesbury's brief spell on the woolsack was not a startling success. His only notable achievement was that his famous 'Delenda est Carthago' speech at the opening of parliament on 5 February 1673 helped to persuade the Commons to vote money for the war against the Dutch.[40] Although he was a skilful orator, he was unable to exercise much influence over the House. He did not enjoy a large personal following at this date and his period in office coincided with the explosion of anti-popish hysteria that followed the issue of the Declaration of Indulgence in 1672. To him fell the almost impossible task of defending the Declaration in parliament. Even his eloquence was insufficient to persuade the peers to support the Declaration in March 1673. His attempt to appeal to the monarchist sentiments of former-Royalist peers on 1 March proved ineffective, the Lords deciding by 60 votes to 27 to agree

---

[35] Seaward, pp. 93–4. See tables 3 and 4 for the number of committees chaired by these 'men of business'.
[36] Carte MSS 35, fol. 120, Conway to Ormond, 10 Nov. 1666.
[37] Manuscript Minutes, vol. 15, 28 April 1668.
[38] Haley, *Shaftesbury*, p. 306; Hutton, *Charles II*, p. 259.
[39] Add. MSS 21,948, fol. 427, J. Copleston to the duke of Richmond, 25 Nov. 1672.
[40] Haley, *Shaftesbury*, p. 316.

with the Commons that the king should proceed legislatively if he still wished to relieve dissenters.[41] During the last session he presided over, in the autumn of 1673, he had virtually deserted to the growing 'opposition' in the chamber, bitterly criticising the duke of York's marriage to Mary of Modena, vigorously beating the anti-popery drum and intriguing with the king's enemies in Scotland.[42] On 9 November he was dismissed and replaced by Sir Heneage Finch.

Finch was a competent government manager though he lacked Clarendon's influence and was in the shadow of Lord Treasurer Danby until that earl's dismissal in 1679.[43] His chief qualities were his legal and parliamentary expertise. He had been Solicitor General since 1660, and as an MP had chaired numerous committees, promoting government legislation.[44] Contemporaries admired his eloquence in debates and, as Burnet says, he justified 'the court in all debates in the House of Lords, which he did with the vehemence of a pleader rather than with the solemnity of a senator'.[45] And Finch's surviving speeches testify to his ability to marshal compelling arguments on behalf of the government. He strenuously promoted Danby's Test Bill in April and May 1675, argued vigorously against those who claimed in February 1677 that parliament was dissolved by a fifteen-month prorogation and defended Danby's foreign policy when it was criticised by Country peers the following year.[46] Although he was part of the inner circle of ministers who advised the king on parliamentary affairs, much of the management of the Lords was entrusted to Danby.[47] Only after the latter's dismissal in March 1679 was Finch's influence on proceedings in the House really significant. Acting on the king's orders, he persuaded the peers on 10 May 1679 to agree with the Commons and appoint a joint committee to consider the manner of the trials of the five Catholic lords imprisoned in the Tower.[48] Together with the Lord President, the earl of Radnor, Finch was involved in behind-the-scenes management of the House during the last two parliaments of the reign. In the Lords itself he tried to divert peers from issues which might produce conflict with the Commons, such as the possible release of Danby from the Tower or the impeachment of Fitzharris, and instead focused attention on private legal cases and less contentious legislation.[49]

[41] Ibid., p. 321; A. C. Swatland, 'Further recorded divisions in the House of Lords, 1660–81', *Parliamentary History*, 3 (1984), 180.

[42] Haley, *Shaftesbury*, pp. 335–9.

[43] Yale (ed.), *Lord Nottingham's Chancery cases*, I, pp. xxiii, xxvi.

[44] Ibid., p. xvii; Henning (ed.), *House of Commons*, III, pp. 620–2.

[45] Burnet, *History*, II, p. 43.

[46] Yale (ed.), *Lord Nottingham's Chancery cases*, II, pp. 982–98; Haley, *Shaftesbury*, pp. 374, 376–7.

[47] For Danby's management of the Lords, see chapter 12 of this book.

[48] Chatsworth House, Halifax Collection, E/7, Algernon Sidney to Henry Savile, 12 May 1679; Swatland, 'The House of Lords', pp. 149, 392.

[49] Carte MSS 79, fol. 164, proceedings of the Oxford Parliament, 21 March 1681; *Hist. MSS Comm.*, 14th Rept, Ormond MSS, VI, p. 8, Edward Cooke to Ormond, 26 March 1681.

Charles II also relied heavily upon his privy councillors to manage the House of Lords. The vast majority were peers. Privy councillors regularly attended and were responsible for steering government business through the House.[50] They chaired a high proportion of committees, drafted and amended legislation, and represented the House at conferences with the Commons. In fact six privy councillors, Clarendon, Anglesey, Manchester, Lords Robartes, Ashley and Finch, managed almost 90 per cent of conferences, and many of these involved government business.[51] Leading ministers and privy councillors were therefore the obvious men to keep the king well informed of developments in the chamber. During the tense debates on the impeachment of Clarendon in November 1667, two privy councillors in particular – Buckingham and Albemarle – reported daily to the king on events in their chamber, even supplying him with the names of peers who had opposed imprisoning the ex-Lord Chancellor.[52] Privy councillors communicated royal messages to the House. The earl of Manchester, the Lord Chamberlain, delivered the king's message on 13 July 1663 which categorically stated that 'several matters of fact' in the earl of Bristol's attempted impeachment of Clarendon were 'untrue' and were regarded by his majesty as a 'libel against his person and government'.[53]

The king expected ministers and privy councillors to defend and promote his interests in the Lords. Those who placed their own interests first or criticised royal policy risked the king's displeasure, and in some instances were removed from the privy council altogether.[54] At moments of potential danger for the government the king threatened privy councillors with dismissal. Fearing either the revival of Bristol's impeachment of Clarendon or a troublesome session, Charles declared in council at the end of February 1664 that he would remove any privy councillor who assisted Bristol in any way. In the interval before parliament met, Bristol wrote to privy councillors and ministers, seeking support in the House. But this was to no avail, for, like the earl of Anglesey who delivered his letter from the earl to the king, they heeded their master's threat and endorsed the duke of York's motion that Bristol's letter to the House should be delivered unopened to the king on 22 March.[55] Occasionally privy councillors disregarded the king's views on how they should conduct themselves in the Lords. In February 1663 Charles had urged them to promote his Indulgence Bill in the chamber. Those sympa-

[50] Swatland, 'Privy councillors', pp. 51–77.
[51] Conference managers are recorded in the Journals.
[52] BL, Egerton MSS 2,539, fol. 140, John Nicholas to Sir Edward Nicholas, 14 Nov. 1667; Hutton, p. 283; Bodl., Rawlinson MSS A. 130, fols. 95, 99, 100.
[53] LJ, XI, 559.
[54] In 1676 Charles removed Halifax and Holles from the council because of their criticism of government policy.
[55] Seaward, pp. 231–2.

thetic to dissenters, notably Lords Robartes, Manchester and Ashley, eagerly obeyed the king, but Clarendon and Southampton temporarily lost favour when they openly criticised the measure in debate.[56]

Divisions among privy councillors could delay legislation and reduce the king's control over the upper House. Often during the 1660s the privy council was divided between former Royalists and former Parliamentarians and this manifested itself in debates, particularly on religious issues.[57] As the decade progressed some privy councillors recruited followings of like-minded peers at court and in parliament. Leaders of rival factions included the dukes of Buckingham and Albemarle and Lord Arlington. Broadly speaking, their intention was to undermine their rivals and influence royal policy. The king's approach to politics encouraged factions to flourish: even his closest advisers frequently had difficulty in determining his actual views on a specific issue, for he tended to disguise his thoughts with dissimulation. It is no wonder then that his councillors were sometimes at variance with one another in the House, openly disagreeing over aspects of government business. Even when the king's opinions were well known, not all privy councillors proved amenable to royal influence. One of the reasons why the king failed to persuade the House to imprison his ex-Lord Chancellor in November 1667 was that a majority of privy councillors supported Clarendon, out of either friendship or justice.[58] The following year the protracted bicameral dispute over the case of *Skinner* v. *The East India Company*, which Charles was keen to resolve because it impeded supply bills, was exacerbated by a group of councillors headed by Buckingham.

During Danby's ministry these divisions became less frequent. With the death of ex-Parliamentarian members and their replacement with more compliant Anglican-Royalists, the council became more homogeneous. Several prominent privy councillors who sided with the government's critics in the mid-1670s, notably Buckingham, Shaftesbury, Halifax and Holles, were removed from the council board. From 1675 the government appeared to be pursuing more consistent and popular policies than previously. Danby's vigorous championing of the Church of England, his enforcement of the statutes against dissenters and Catholics and his anti-French foreign policy appealed to the vast majority of privy councillors. These policies, in conjunction with his systematic management of the Lords and the king's regular attendance at debates, tightened the government's grip on the Lords.

A further communications conduit between the king and parliament was

[56] Clarendon, *Life*, II, pp. 349–50; Hutton, pp. 196–7; J. R. Jones, *Charles II, royal politician* (1986), p. 62.
[57] Swatland, 'Privy councillors', pp. 69–70.
[58] C. Roberts, 'The impeachment of the earl of Clarendon', *Cambridge Historical Journal*, 13 (1957), 14–15; BL, Egerton MSS 2,539, fol. 145, John Nicholas to Sir Edward Nicholas, 27 Nov. 1667.

provided by individual peers who had no official connections with the court. The ex-Parliamentarian Horatio Townshend, created a baron in the coronation honours, had a considerable interest among Norfolk MPs and appears to have been used as a government manager in both Houses. In the Lords he was concerned with the promotion of legislation to settle the militia and in 1665 was actively involved in sponsoring a private bill which the king wanted to pass the Lords unamended.[59]

His fellow peer, Philip, Lord Wharton appears to have fulfilled a similar function in respect of religious legislation in the early 1660s. Traditionally depicted as a government critic, Wharton may well have been a manager for the court in the early 1660s.[60] As early as March 1660 this former political Presbyterian had made contact with the exiled court and was secretly aiding the unconditional recall of the king in exchange for a royal pardon.[61] There is no doubt that by June 1660 Wharton had friends at court, including the duke of York, who defended him in the Lords when the question of his involvement in an alleged anti-Royalist plot in 1648 was raised in the House.[62] Wharton's extensive contacts with dissenters (he was probably their spokesman in parliament) made him an essential person for the king to consult over the church settlement, and later in 1672 in connection with the Declaration of Indulgence.[63]

By the late summer of 1660 he was cooperating with the court in promoting religious legislation in both Houses. During September he was extremely active on behalf of the government in the Lords on the Bill for Restoring Ministers, chairing committee meetings, drafting and reporting amendments and, together with Hyde, managing a conference with the House of Commons. Had Wharton opposed the bill it is improbable that the peers would have appointed him to the committee and they certainly would not have nominated him to represent their views at a conference. The amendments Wharton helped to draft adhered closely to the current royal policy of giving security to existing incumbents, with exceptions to those Anglicans who had been forcibly ejected.[64] It is possible that his lists of members of the Commons (initially drawn up in the spring or summer of

---

[59] Seaward, pp. 81–2; *Hist. MSS Comm.*, 6th report (1877), Pt I, appendix, MSS of Sir H. Ingilby, p. 364, Paston to his wife, 14 Jan. 1665; Add. MSS 27,447, fol. 329, Paston to his wife, 4 Feb. [1665].

[60] This view of Wharton is developed at length by G. F. T. Jones in *Saw-pit Wharton*, pp. 151–221.

[61] Clarendon MSS 70, fols. 184–5, Lady Mordaunt to Hyde, 16 March 1660; *Cal. Cl. SP*, IV, p. 669, same to same, 20 April 1660.

[62] Carte MSS 81, fols. 736–8, Wharton's 'biographical' letter to Von Spaen, 18 Oct. 1685; G. F. T. Jones, *Saw-pit Wharton*, pp. 167–9.

[63] Ibid., p. 221; Lacey, *Dissent and parliamentary politics*, pp. 473–5; *Memoirs of the life of the most noble Thomas, late marquess of Wharton* (1715), p. 6.

[64] *LJ*, XI, 161–2, 165, 167, 168.

1660), with Presbyterian and moderate Anglican members being allotted to seven 'managers', was part of Wharton's attempt to influence proceedings in the Commons for the government on the same Bill.[65] The fact that by no means all the MPs listed were Presbyterians or their known sympathisers – there was a significant group of Anglicans and courtiers – might be an indication that Wharton was backed by the government in his scheme to manage the Commons. Whilst it is possible that these lists were for his own private use, it should be noted that the majority of surviving parliamentary lists were constructed by ministers for management purposes.[66]

Two years later he appears to have assisted the king on the committee for the Bill of Uniformity. Most of the nine amendments surviving among his papers accorded closely with the king's preferred settlement of the Church. Like Charles, he recognised that the main obstacles to Presbyterians conforming were ceremonies and episcopal re-ordination.[67] In his papers on the bill he records that Sheldon, bishop of London, gave him a copy of the 'alterations and additions' to the Book of Common Prayer, which no doubt proved useful as committee members reconciled the Uniformity Bill with the revised Prayer Book.[68] Would Sheldon have been so obliging had Wharton been an outright opponent of the bill? After 1663, when the court abandoned its attempts (at least until 1667) to encourage Presbyterians to conform to the Church of England, Wharton ceased to be employed as a parliamentary manager. Instead, he became a critic of the court. Together with other Presbyterian peers, he attacked the government's efforts to prosecute dissenters in the Conventicle and Five Mile Bills of 1664 and 1665 respectively.[69]

At the other end of the religious spectrum was the rigidly Anglican earl of Bridgewater. His capacity for hard work on committees and his Anglican connections brought him to Clarendon's notice and royal favour, though he did not become a privy councillor until 1667. He was one of the most prominent government managers in the 1660s, chairing virtually all committees on religious legislation during Clarendon's ministry, including that for the Uniformity Bill where he was 'as zealous … as any in the House'.[70] Until his

---

[65] These lists have been printed by G. F. T. Jones as an appendix to his article, 'The composition and leadership of the Presbyterian party in the Convention', *EHR*, 79 (1964), 332–54.

[66] Clarendon compiled a list of court dependants in 1664 in preparation for the repeal of the Triennial Act (J. R. Jones, 'Court dependants in 1664', *BIHR*, 34 (1961), 81–91). Sir Thomas Osborne drew up lists of MPs for his patron the duke of Buckingham in 1669 and management lists of both Houses when he was chief minister in the 1670s (Browning, *Danby*, III, pp. 33–122).

[67] Carte MSS 81, fols. 106, 109, 110–11, 112, 113, 114, 120, 121, 131.

[68] Carte MSS 81, fol. 117.

[69] Ibid., fols. 157, 170, 172, 182; C. Robbins, 'The Oxford session of the Long Parliament of Charles II, 9–31 October, 1665', *BIHR*, 64 (1948), 222–3.

[70] Seaward, pp. 93–4 and note 144; Bodl., MS Eng. Lett. c. 210, fol. 70, Henry Yelverton to Archdeacon Palmer, 29 Jan. 1662.

death in 1663, the earl of Portland provided another useful link between the
court and the Lords, chairing committees on major pieces of legislation, most
notably the King's Preservation Bill and the Corporation Bill in 1661.[71]

II

The existence of ministers, privy councillors and individual peers who strove
to assist the king in the House of Lords partly explains why Charles II was
normally more successful at managing the Lords than the Commons. His
regular attendance at debates from 1670 was of paramount importance, for
this enabled him to speak directly to lords when the House was sitting, rather
than rely on intermediaries. The degree to which he actually influenced
events in the Lords depended on several factors. First, there was the attitude
of his own ministers and privy councillors. Sometimes they were in disagreement with each other, or even openly hostile to royal policies. Secondly
there was the attitude of the majority of the House: occasionally the king
was out of step with the opinions of most peers, as in Clarendon's impeachment. If royal policies conflicted with the peers' privileges members almost
invariably placed their privileges first. Finally, his method of ruling, which
involved formulating policy with one or two confidants, and sometimes
simultaneously pursuing different lines of policy that had been conceived
with different ministers, confused his parliamentary managers, making them
uncertain which course they were to follow in the chamber.[72] Instead of
leading his ministers, he sought to set minister against minister and very
often did not bother to inform the whole of his privy council of his schemes
and policies.

The king's influence over the Lords was pronounced in the area of religion. Through his ministers Charles was able to persuade the House to
accept and revise religious legislation in the early 1660s. He was largely able
to accomplish this because the House was almost evenly split between those
who advocated a narrow Anglican Church settlement and, when this had
been achieved in 1662, preservation of the status quo; and those who, like
the king, preferred a more comprehensive Church and later wished to modify
some of the provisions of the Act of Uniformity.[73] By exerting pressure on
the Lords the king was usually able to tip the balance of opinion in his
favour. An example of this concerned the struggle over the 1662 Bill to
confirm three Acts of the Convention, including the controversial Act for
Confirming and Restoring Ministers. The Commons had so extensively
altered this measure that it would have resulted in the wholesale eviction of

[71] Ibid., p. 93 and note 143.
[72] Hutton, Charles II, p. 454.
[73] The involvement of the Lords in the Church Settlement is explored in chapter 9.

Presbyterian ministers from their livings and the establishment of a narrow Anglican ministry, something the king was anxious to avoid. The Lords was evenly divided in its attitude towards the Bill when it was received from the Commons in January 1662: a point underlined by a tied vote of forty on each side of the 29th.[74] Charles exerted pressure upon the Lords during the following few days and his Chancellor obtained the support of seven bishops, the duke of York and the Catholics. Together with Presbyterian and government peers they persuaded the House to discard the Commons' amendments, thereby confirming the 1660 Act without change.[75]

For the remainder of the reign there were further instances of the king successfully influencing religious legislation. In 1663 Charles used the Lords to suppress Commons' bills against conventicles and papists, and in the same session probably instructed his privy councillors to ameliorate the severity of an additional Uniformity Bill.[76] It has already been mentioned that one of the reasons for the king's attendance at debates in March 1670 was to facilitate the passage of the Conventicle Bill. Unlike the 1663 bill, Charles was eager for this to pass because ministers had inserted a proviso in committee recognising his prerogative in ecclesiastical affairs which could enable him to dispense dissenters from the bill's provisions. Burnet argues that Charles II sought to make dissenters dependent on him alone for their freedom of worship.[77] The proceedings on the Conventicle Bill were both protracted and at times acrimonious, and votes were close, with Presbyterians and their sympathisers speaking against it. The king spoke personally to such men, and through his efforts and those of his privy councillors the bill was passed. Not every lord was prepared to obey the king. When asked by the king not to oppose the bill, John Wilkins, bishop of Chester answered that 'he thought it an ill thing both in conscience and policy' and was 'bound to oppose it'. Wilkins refused to act upon the king's advice and refrain from attending the House whilst the Conventicle Bill was depending.[78] Even the king's personal attendance was no guarantee of success: in 1673 the House refused to endorse the Declaration of Indulgence and two years later the government's Non-resisting Test Bill ran aground on the rocks of a bicameral privilege dispute in front of the king's eyes.

In the field of financial legislation the king successfully applied pressure on the House via his privy councillors. Peers received a poll bill on 8 March 1678 suspiciously because it infringed their highly esteemed privilege of

---

[74] Bodl., MS Eng. Lett. c. 210, fol. 69, Henry Yelverton to Archdeacon Palmer, 29 Jan. 1662; Seaward, p. 173.
[75] Berwick (ed.), *The Rawdon papers*, pp. 136–8, Dr Pett to Archbishop Bramhall, 8 Feb. 1662; *LJ*, XI, 376, 377.
[76] Seaward, pp. 187–9.
[77] Burnet, *History*, I, p. 493; Hutton, *Charles II*, pp. 266, 270.
[78] Burnet, ibid., pp. 493–4.

taxing themselves. All the proposed tax commissioners were to be members of the Commons. In the face of deteriorating government finances Charles was intent on the peers passing the Bill quickly and without amendment. His views were communicated by privy councillors to members of the Court party, and on 12 March the measure passed without alteration, thereby avoiding a potentially destructive privilege dispute with the Commons.[79] The Commons did not accept that the Lords had the right to alter financial bills, and previously several financial measures including a foreign commodities bill in 1671 had foundered, despite royal pressure on parliament, amid disputes over financial privileges. Usually, though, the influence of the Crown was sufficient to persuade the Lords to back down. In April 1677 the peers agreed to pass a supply bill unamended only because the Lord Chancellor and Lord Treasurer had spoken persuasively to members of the House. The Bill, which was intended to raise £600,000 for the construction of warships, had been deliberately delayed in the chamber by 'opposition' peers hoping to exploit for political purposes the Lords' traditional jealousy of the Commons' financial privileges. In this instance the contentious issues concerned the Lords' rights to amend money bills and participate in scrutinising the king's accounts after the money had been spent.[80]

Also on many occasions the Lords vigorously defended the king's prerogative powers when these were threatened by the Commons or groups in the Lords itself. The peers defended the use of the royal dispensing power from criticism by the Commons during the proceedings on the Irish Cattle Bill in the autumn of 1666. Despite both the lobby of Irish landowning peers in the House and the king's known antipathy towards the Bill, a slight majority of peers approved of the intention of the Bill, which was the prohibition of the import of cattle from Ireland; a trade, they believed, which had suppressed their own land values through unfair competition.[81] Yet a combination of the Lords' deep respect for royal prerogatives and the king's influence on the House through Clarendon, Butler, Berkeley, Anglesey and the duke of York ensured that the word 'nuisance', which debarred the use of the dispensing power, was rejected in favour of a milder phrase that did not impinge upon the royal prerogative.[82] Thus Charles would be able to dilute the effect of the statute, by dispensing individual importers from its provisions.

When the king's power to prorogue parliament for more than a year was

---

[79] *Hist. MSS Comm.*, Ormonde MSS, IV, pp. 413–14, Sir Robert Southwell to Ormond, 9 and 12 March 1678.

[80] Add. MSS 29,571, fol. 388, Christopher Hatton to Lord Hatton, 19 April 1677; BL, Egerton MSS 3,345, fols. 56–7, report on a free conference on the supply bill, 11 April 1677.

[81] Carte MSS 46, fol. 385, Arlington to Ormond, 13 Oct. 1666; Edie, 'The Irish Cattle Bills', pp. 14, 26–9.

[82] Carte MSS 217, fol. 348, Anglesey to Ormond, 27 Oct. 1666; Swatland, 'Privy councillors', p. 68.

disputed by 'opposition' peers on 15 February 1677, Charles and Danby employed both privy councillors and Court peers to defend this power in a protracted debate. The government decisively defeated this assault on the royal prerogative, in the course of which four leading 'opposition' peers were sent to the Tower for contempt.[83] The most famous occasion when the Lords rallied to the aid of the royal prerogative occurred on 15 November 1680 when the king's right to name his successor was challenged in the Exclusion Bill. A variety of factors, including the king's extensive solicitation of votes, ensured that the Bill was overwhelmingly rejected after its first reading.[84]

However, there are several well-documented occasions when neither the king nor his ministers could persuade a majority of peers to comply with royal policies. Peers were sometimes uncertain as to where the king stood on a particular issue, and this was especially the case in the early 1660s when he was inexperienced in the management of parliament.[85] Confusion as to the king's intentions was manifest in the Lords' reaction to the earl of Derby's estate bills. Between 1660 and 1662 the earl of Derby introduced four bills into parliament in an attempt to reclaim lands conveyed during the Interregnum. Both the Acts of Indemnity and Judicial Proceedings confirmed all voluntary conveyances made between 1642 and 1660. Yet the Royalist majority in the Lords believed that the king wished to make Derby a special case, because on 27 June 1660 Lord Gerard had transmitted a message to the committee considering the earl's first bill, in which Charles had desired 'the committee's favour and justice to the earl of Derby who hath been a great sufferer'.[86] Shortly after this Charles changed his mind and encouraged his ministers to oppose this and Derby's subsequent bills. Had any of them become law a precedent would have been established for other Cavaliers to reverse Interregnum conveyances, and thereby alienate the king's former enemies, who were in possession of Royalists' lands, at a time when the government felt insecure.[87] Confusion about the king's exact opinions and a general desire in the Lords to give the Stanley family special treatment resulted in the peers passing a fourth bill in February 1662, which the king had no alternative but to veto.[88]

---

[83] Haley, *Shaftesbury*, pp. 409, 416–19; Carte MSS 79, fols. 31–2, 37–43, Lord Wharton's notes on debates in the Lords, 15/16 Feb. 1677.

[84] See chapter 12 of this book, pp. 256–8.

[85] This is a point overlooked by scholars. The king's first-hand experience of the Lords had been as a boy in 1640–2, when he had sat near the throne as Prince of Wales. Hyde too had previously sat in parliament as an MP in 1642 and tended to retain rather anachronistic views on parliamentary management (J. R. Jones, *Charles II, royal politician*, p. 65).

[86] HLRO, Committee for Petitions Minute Book 3, 27 June 1660.

[87] *LJ*, XI, 378–9; Carte MSS 77, fol. 520, list of opponents of Derby's Bill which passed the Lords on 6 Feb. 1662; Seaward, pp. 196–8, 201–3.

[88] *LJ*, XI, 379.

Even when the king's views were abundantly clear there was no guarantee that the House would comply with them. On 12 November 1667 Clarendon was impeached by the Commons on a charge of treason. Charles enthusiastically backed the impeachment, optimistic that the Lords would commit him to the Tower to await trial by a carefully chosen body of compliant peers.[89] The king's aim was to use him as a scapegoat for his government's mishandling of the second Anglo-Dutch war. The current rising star at court, the duke of Buckingham, had persuaded him that Clarendon's impeachment would conciliate the Commons and induce it to consider requests for supply. Charles made his views plain to peers, speaking to many individually, and even threatening not to translate bishops to higher sees unless they voted as he directed.[90] Several privy councillors, notably Buckingham and Albemarle, exerted their influence too, but to no avail: the vast majority of peers steadfastly refused to imprison Clarendon, voting by sixty to twelve against commitment on 29 November.[91] Most peers refused to obey the king because they believed that imprisonment on a general and unsubstantiated charge of treason would establish a precedent for the indiscriminate imprisonment of innocent lords, without specific written charges being produced by the Commons.[92] The personal safety of peers was regarded as more important than the short-term expediency of Charles II and his government.

When the royal will ran counter to the peers' privileges, the House normally placed its members' interests first. This was frequently the situation during jurisdictional disputes with the Commons. From April 1668 to February 1670 relations between the two chambers were embittered by the dispute resulting from *Skinner* v. *The East India Company*. Before parliament assembled in October 1669 the king had decided that the dispute had to be resolved if government business were to be conducted in parliament.[93] Charles employed his brother and one of the original instigators of the dispute, the duke of Buckingham, to sponsor a bill to smooth over the differences between the Houses. The bill, introduced in the Commons, was for abolishing the peers' original jurisdiction. But the government had dramatically misjudged the mood of the peers, for it was greeted with 'universal indignation' upon its first reading in the Lords on 11 November.[94] Most lords

[89] Roberts, 'Impeachment of Clarendon', pp. 10–11.
[90] Carte MSS 35, fol. 764, Conway to Ormond, 15 Oct. 1667; BL, Egerton MSS 2,539, fols. 139–40, John Nicholas to Sir Edward Nicholas, 14 Nov. 1667; Pepys, VIII, p. 532; *The Bulstrode papers: the collection of autograph letters and historical documents formed by Alfred Morrison* (1897), pp. 13, 15, 17.
[91] PRO, 31/3/117, fol. 39, Ruvigney to Louis XIV, 2 Dec. 1667.
[92] BL, Egerton MSS 2,539, fols. 141, 145, John Nicholas to Sir Edward Nicholas, 19 and 27 Nov. 1667; Bodl., Rawlinson MSS A. 130, fol. 95.
[93] Add. MSS 36,916, fol. 100, Starkey to Aston, 16 May 1668; PRO, 31/3/123, fol. 20, Colbert to Lionne, 24 Oct. 1669.
[94] *Cal. SP Ven.*, 36, p. 131, Piero Mocenigo to the Doge and Senate, 22 Nov. 1669; HLRO, Committee for Privileges Minute Book 2, pp. 56–8; Harris, *Sandwich*, II, pp. 307–9.

regarded it as 'destructive to the constitution of this government and infamous for us to pass [a bill] giving away most considerable privileges left unto us by our ancestors and by the laws of the land'.[95] Peers considered they had an exclusive right to initiate any bill concerning their judicature. Although the duke of Buckingham 'spoke showing reasons why he would have the bill retained and made such as might be fitting to pass', it was decisively rejected by every peer except two of the king's companions, the earl of Bristol and Lord Berkeley of Berkeley.[96]

Charles II's attempts to exert pressure on the House of Lords produced mixed results. Often his efforts proved successful. The House processed the majority of legislation in which the king had an interest according to his wishes. But on several well-documented occasions the Lords pursued an independent line, rejecting royal policy. The peers certainly cannot be described as the monarch's 'servile creatures' during this period. Charles II was generally only able to have a decisive impact upon events in the House when the peers themselves were evenly divided, royal authority tipping the scales of opinion in the king's favour.

III

Two main assumptions have coloured historians' views of the constitutional role of the restored House of Lords.[97] The first was that a system of government existed in England described as 'mixed monarchy', involving the king and his two Houses of parliament. Each partner was of equal standing in the parliamentary trinity. No partner could enact laws or break existing ones without the consent of the other two. According to C. C. Western, during the period before 1642 the first two Stuarts had regarded themselves as above their two Houses of parliament. Charles I's 'Answer to the Nineteen Propositions' of 1642 represented the replacement of this view with that of 'mixed monarchy'.[98] The second assumption was that after 1660 the House of Lords even-handedly maintained this system as the balance weight of the constitution, repelling the advances of the other two branches.[99] Did the peers themselves accept this theory of mixed monarchy, and, if so, was the House of Lords really an impartial mediator, or balance, in this system of government?

[95] Ibid., p. 307.
[96] Ibid., pp. 308–9.
[97] In particular see B. Kemp, *King and Commons 1660–1832* (1957), pp. 1–7; C. C. Western, *English constitutional theory and the House of Lords, 1556–1832* (1965), pp. 1–5, 88–110; C. C. Western and J. R. Greenberg, *Subjects and sovereigns* (Cambridge, 1981).
[98] Western, *English constitutional theory*, p. 5.
[99] Ibid., p. 3.

There is no evidence to show that lords accepted a theory of government in which the powers of the three partners were equal. Very few peers appear to have even addressed this subject in their correspondence. One who did was the fifth earl of Dorset. He wrote that legislative power was 'in the Lords and Commons jointly by the fundamental constitution of this realm'.[100] But he did not assert that each element had equal powers: he merely recognised that each had a role to play in the enactment of legislation, a view which was prevalent in the sixteenth and seventeenth centuries.[101] Although the earl suggested that broken laws could be redressed by parliament, he recognised that if the king refused to call one every three years (as prescribed by the Triennial Act) there was no remedy for royal breaches of statute law, because none could force the king to summon parliament.[102] The earls of Peterborough and Ailesbury rejected all notions of 'mixed governments', arguing that since the monarch's powers were derived from God, he had authority to suspend acts of parliament.[103] The actions of the House itself strongly indicate that most peers accepted the view propounded by the earl of Shaftesbury when as Lord Chancellor in 1673 he argued that the 'two Houses' were 'equal with his majesty in legislature, whereas the sanction of laws is in the king alone'. A majority of lords recognised the king's prerogative of dispensing individuals from acts of parliament and his use of the royal veto.[104]

The peer who came closest to assigning the House a balancing function was the second marquis of Worcester. Writing in 1666/7, he referred to: 'your lordships, who are as well by divine providence as human policy allotted to be as it were the medium between the king and the people; that is to impose yourselves as mediators if the king's supreme authority should become severe which cannot be feared from so gracious a prince, as also to be curbers of the peoples' rustic stubbornness, if they should prove insolent'.[105] The significance of this statement should not be exaggerated: it was part of a speech designed to win the backing of the Lords for his scheme to raise a troop of horse composed entirely of nobles to guard the king.[106] There is no evidence that the speech was ever delivered in the House.

[100] Kent Archives Office, Sackville MSS U269/036, fol. 81, 'Certain queries concerning the ancient and legal government and parliament of England...', n.d., but c. mid-1660s.
[101] Elton, Tudor Constitution, pp. 236–7.
[102] Sackville MSS U269/036, fol. 81.
[103] PRO, S.P. 29/81, fol. 180, earl of Peterborough to Charles II, 14 Oct. 1663; Thomas Bruce, earl of Ailesbury, Memoirs, written by himself (Publications of the Roxborough Club, 2 vols., 1890), I, p. 11; Carte MSS 77, fol. 650, earl of Huntingdon's notes on the debate on the Exclusion Bill, 15 Nov. 1680.
[104] Haley, Shaftesbury, p. 321. The House had defended the dispensing power in the Bill of Uniformity and the Irish Cattle Bill.
[105] Hist. MSS Comm., 12th rept appendix, pt IX (1891), MSS of the duke of Beaufort, p. 57, draft of a speech by the marquis of Worcester (1666–7).
[106] Ibid., pp. 57–8.

The actions of the House do not indicate that the peers regarded themselves as a balance in the constitution. It was exceptional for the Lords to side with the Commons against the Crown. The American scholars Western and Greenberg claim that the only notable occasion when the Lords maintained this constitutional balance, siding with the Commons, concerned the King's Declaration of Indulgence in March 1673.[107] Charles II infringed the legislative powers of the two Houses with his Declaration which suspended several acts of parliament, and the House of Lords assisted the Commons to redress the 'balance' in 1673 by refusing to endorse the king's action. The Lords' attitude was not prompted primarily by opposition to the use of the suspending power. Obviously legalistically minded peers did question the king's exercise of his prerogative to suspend acts of parliament, but the Lords' attitude did not reflect a general desire to ensure that legislative power remained equally with the king, Lords and Commons, as Western and Greenberg assert.[108] The Lords' main objection to the Declaration of Indulgence was the encouragement it gave to papists. It allowed Catholics to worship freely in their own homes, a small concession: but one of major significance in the context of anxieties about a popish conspiracy. Like the majority of seventeenth-century Englishmen, the aristocracy possessed an anti-Catholic phobia.[109] This phobia was strongly reinforced by recent events: the duke of York's widely suspected conversion to Catholicism, the increasing favour shown to papists at court and their employment in the administration, and the king's alliance with the foremost Catholic monarch, Louis XIV of France, against the Protestant Dutch in the war of 1672–4.[110] These developments confirmed men's fears about the existence of a popish conspiracy at Court, a conspiracy, it was believed, designed to subvert Englishmen's birth-rights and liberties, through the imposition of popery and arbitrary government. The House did not express disapproval of the exercise of the royal prerogative to suspend laws against Protestant dissenters, only if this power was extended to Catholics. When a bill to relieve Protestant nonconformists came up from the Commons later in March the peers decided the king had power by proclamation to suspend the penal laws against such persons and the authority to license teachers and preachers.[111]

The Lords had a deep respect for all royal powers and was often willing to strengthen them. In July 1661 the peers proposed a dramatic extension of royal control over municipal corporations in their amendments to the Corporation Bill. The House omitted a large chunk of the Commons' bill,

[107] Western and Greenberg, *Subjects and sovereigns*, pp. 172–3.
[108] Ibid.
[109] See chapter 10 of this book, pp. 191–2.
[110] J. Miller, *Popery and politics in England 1660–88* (Cambridge, 1973), pp. 1, 101, 109–20.
[111] Manuscript Minutes vol. 17, 25 March 1673.

including the appointment of commissioners, and instead inserted clauses for all corporations to renew their charters by a given date, for the king to appoint recorders, town clerks and mayors and for county JPs to exercise their powers in towns within their jurisdiction. Had the Commons accepted such drastic alterations, municipal independence would have been severely curtailed.[112] Many, particularly former Royalists, were keen to remove the limitations placed upon the Crown in 1641–2. As early as January 1662 the Lords voted to repeal the Triennial Act, two years before the Commons' measure reached the statute book.[113] At the same time a committee chaired by Lord Lucas proposed the re-establishment of the court of Star Chamber, though with reduced powers.[114] None of the Lords' attempts to repeal the acts of the Long Parliament in 1662 and again in 1663 came to fruition, except the repeal of Strafford's attainder. This was probably a reflection of the court's lack of commitment to schemes that risked antagonising former enemies. The heated debates over the bill to establish a court at York in January 1662, in which the House was split between the earl of Northumberland and ex-Parliamentarians on one side and the duke of Buckingham and Royalists on the other, revealed how easy it was to revive Civil War divisions.[115] Later, in 1677, when 'opposition' leaders claimed parliament was dissolved by the fifteen-month prorogation, an overwhelming majority of peers defended the royal prerogative. Court speakers, like the earl of Anglesey and Lord Finch, claimed that the king's authority to prorogue was not restricted by medieval statutes, as 'opposition' leaders argued, but was unlimited.[116] Later still in 1679, the House vigorously upheld the royal right to pardon when Charles II's power to pardon the earl of Danby for all his alleged crimes was questioned by the Commons and Country peers.[117]

Several factors account for the Lords' desire both to defend and, in some instances, to extend monarchical powers. For one thing, many lords owed their titles and offices to Charles II, and therefore tended to identify their interests with those of their sovereign.[118] Another was the effort of Charles II and his ministers to influence proceedings in the chamber. But of greatest significance was the conservative outlook of most peers, whose memories of the events of the 1640s and 1650s repelled them from constitutional innovation. Just as peers resisted all attempts to erode their own privileges, so they believed that any reduction in the powers of the Crown would have danger-

---

[112] Seaward, pp. 153–4.
[113] *LJ*, XI, 369–70; Committee Minutes 1, pp. 118–19.
[114] Seaward, pp. 133–4.
[115] PRO, 31/3/110, fols. 56–8, D'Estrades to Louis, 28 Jan./6 Feb. 1662; HLRO, Braye MSS, vol. 53, no. 16.
[116] Haley, *Shaftesbury*, pp. 409, 416–18; Carte MSS 79, fols. 31–2, 37–43; Yale (ed.), *Lord Nottingham's Chancery cases*, II, pp. 982–8.
[117] Browning, *Danby*, I, pp. 325–37.
[118] See chapter 3, p. 31.

ous consequences for both the monarchy and their own standing in government and society. Royalist peers considered that any reduction in the king's prerogatives might lessen his ability to quell possible rebellions and disorders. Therefore the peers were the king's natural allies. In 1668 Lord Howard of Charlton reported from the Committee for Privileges that the English nobles were 'the best, safest, and most natural fence of monarchy against the popular distempers of this last age'.[119] One reason why the earl of Chesterfield spoke against the Exclusion Bill and its encroachment on the king's right to determine the succession, was that he feared another republic, for 'the blood of the last king has left an eternal stain upon this kingdom'.[120]

In constitutional terms the peers were not mediators between the king and the Commons, as their descendants viewed themselves in the eighteenth century. They were not mediators in the true sense, since they normally favoured the Crown. In periods of political tension the House of Lords usually rallied to aid the king and his prerogatives. Few peers seriously wanted to limit the king's authority, since this might weaken the existing form of government, and perhaps usher in another republic. Nevertheless, the Lords was not an entirely safe House from the viewpoint of the king. It did resist the royal will on several occasions, though far less frequently than the more independently minded House of Commons.

[119] *LJ*, XII, 197.
[120] Add. MSS 19,253, fols. 197–8, Chesterfield's speech on the Exclusion Bill.

Lords and Commons

Scholars of the early modern period are increasingly studying parliament as a trinity comprising the king, the Lords and the Commons. Some recent works on the reign of Charles II emphasise the role played by all three in the enactment of legislation.[1] Connections between the Houses have received less attention from historians. The only work to focus on the relations between the Lords and the Commons is A. R. Leamy's unpublished MA thesis.[2] There was a multitude of links between peers and MPs, including the obvious ties of kinship and friendship, patronage and clientage as well as those of a local, electoral, religious and political nature. An analysis of bicameral links provides new insights into our understanding of later Stuart parliamentary politics. The first part of this chapter will briefly consider these connections, whilst the second will investigate that phenomenon of post-Restoration parliamentary politics: bicameral privilege disputes.

I

The bulk of parliamentary business was transacted on the floor of both Houses and in their respective committee rooms. Neither chamber operated in isolation from the other. At the opening of a session MPs assembled in the Lords' chamber to listen to the king's and Lord Chancellor's speeches. Normally at the close of a session MPs returned to witness the king declaring his assent to public and private bills. These formal occasions did not provide opportunities for members to exchange views: peers sat in their places and MPs crowded into the restricted space at the bar. But they did emphasise the tripartite nature of parliament.

By far the most frequently used method of communication during a session was the verbal or written message. The content of messages ranged from the need to expedite a bill to arranging a conference for the exchange of infor-

---

[1] In particular see Hutton and Seaward.
[2] A. R. Leamy, 'The relations between Lords and Commons in the reign of Charles II' (University of Leeds MA thesis, 1966).

mation. If the message came from the Commons it was delivered by an MP at the bar to the Lord Chancellor. Thus on 28 January 1662 the MP Lord Falkland delivered a message from his House desiring the peers to despatch the Uniformity Bill.[3] Messages from the upper House were generally conveyed to the Commons by one or two of their legal assistants. Often when the Houses were engaged on business of the utmost importance messages became almost a daily occurrence. During the last session of the Cavalier Parliament (1678) hardly a day elapsed without one or other House sending a message on an aspect of the popish plot. On the first day of the session (21 October 1678) the Lords penned an address to the king for a fast day after hearing of the plot against his life. The address was delivered to the Commons for their concurrence by the Lord Chief Justice of the court of Common Pleas and Mr Justice Jones, who quickly returned with a favourable answer.[4]

Messages preceded conferences. Conferences were used to hasten the despatch of business that required the agreement of both Houses. They were usually concerned with legislation in this period, though other issues, such as privilege and judicature, also provided grounds for them. Conference procedure had become established by the late sixteenth century and was generally adhered to. Either chamber could request a conference by sending a message to the other, giving the subject of the meeting. If the conference concerned a bill the chamber in possession of the written papers initiated the request. The upper House set the time and place of the meeting. Conferences were normally held in the Painted Chamber, an elongated room adjoining the lobby of the House of Lords. The Lords decided how many peers would represent them as the 'conference committee' and the Commons usually selected twice that number. Conference committees varied considerably in size from two or three senior peers to a group of sixteen to twenty, though the norm was between eight and twelve members.[5] The Lords chose those whom they considered fittest to represent them. Sometimes these were the sponsors of a particular bill or those skilled in oration. Privy councillors were almost invariably appointed conference managers, and on most occasions reported to the House on the course and outcome of a conference.[6]

There were essentially two categories of conferences: those to inform (formal conferences) and those for debate (free conferences).[7] The first involved the managers of one or other chamber delivering papers or verbally communicating the reasons for their House's position on a specific issue, such

[3] *LJ*, XI, 372.
[4] Ibid., XIII, 297.
[5] Normally the *Journals of the House of Lords* list peers appointed to manage conferences.
[6] See Swatland, 'Privy councillors', pp. 75–7.
[7] For more discussion on conferences in the seventeenth century see Foster, pp. 126–33.

as why a bill was amended in a particular way, to the representatives of the other chamber who listened. The second category, termed 'free' conferences by the Lords, was where one House submitted a proposition and the other replied verbally with objections, amendments or a rejection. Often a debate ensued as both sets of managers forwarded their arguments and counter-arguments.[8] The Lords made careful preparations for conferences. The conference managers on the Irish Cattle Bill – Lords Robartes, Manchester, Bridgewater, Anglesey, Buckingham, Lucas and Ashley – were instructed by the House on 17 December 1666 to prepare reasons to be communicated at a free conference why the Lords would not admit the word 'nuisance', which the Commons had inserted in the bill.[9] Sometimes the managers scoured the parliamentary records for precedents as Lord Holles did when the House sought to justify its proceedings in the case of *Skinner* v. *The East India Company* (May 1668). This industrious peer found no less than 45 precedents, dating back to the reign of Richard II from his perusal of the 'ancient records'.[10] The order of speakers and what each would say might be pre-arranged if the subject of the conference was considered important enough. Prior to the aforementioned conference on Skinner's case, the committee agreed that the duke of Buckingham should make the introduction, Lord Howard argue for the Lords' processing Skinner's petition and Lords Robartes, Holles and Anglesey answer what the House of Commons offered at the conference.[11]

By tradition the managers of the House that had requested a conference spoke first.[12] Only those members chosen as the committee were entitled to speak, though other lords and MPs could attend and lend moral support. Normal procedure was for the peers to enter as a body and sit with their hats on at the table whilst MPs stood bareheaded before them, a practice which served to underline the peers' social superiority. The Lords' managers generally spoke as planned, according to the sense of the House. Very occasionally a peer spoke on his own initiative. Lord Chancellor Finch's speech on the upper House's alteration of a supply bill in April 1677 aroused the anger of his fellow managers because he intimated that the House would eventually comply with the Commons, when the peers had only recently voted to adhere to their amendments.[13] Such actions served to weaken the peers' position for they suggested that the Lords itself was not of one mind on a specific issue.

This impression was also provided on the rare occasions when lords fell

[8] *LJ*, XII, 496–500, 508–12; XIII, 509–10.
[9] Manuscript Minutes 14: 17 Dec. 1666; *LJ*, XII, 48–9.
[10] *Hist. MSS Comm.*, 8th Rept, Appendix, MSS of the House of Lords (1881), pp. 169–70.
[11] Ibid., p. 171.
[12] Foster, p. 132.
[13] Add. MSS 29,571, fol. 388, Christopher Hatton to Lord Hatton, 19 April 1677.

out among themselves before the representatives of the Commons. During a conference on the Canary Trading Company's patent in December 1666, two of the Lords' managers, the imperious duke of Buckingham and the quick-tempered marquis of Dorchester, very nearly came to blows over a petty incident at the conference table. Apart from being pulled by the nose and losing his hat, only the marquis's pride was hurt before Manchester and other peers interposed. The House was so incensed by this embarrassing scuffle that both peers were sent to the Tower to cool off.[14] Exchanges between the two sets of managers at free conferences were sometimes very heated and did not necessarily produce agreement. On one occasion the rival managers stormed out of the Painted Chamber, leaving a disputed bill to gather dust on the table.[15]

One of the conference managers, usually a privy councillor, reported proceedings to the House. Reports were drafted either by the reporter, who had taken notes during the conference, or by a group of managers, as occurred on the 1670 Conventicle Bill.[16] Reports were often the subject of debate with the peers voting to agree with the Commons' suggestions, reject some of them or adhere to their own propositions.[17] The outcome of the Lords' debate was often communicated to the lower House at a further conference. On average there were approximately ten conferences each session between 1660 and 1681.[18] Obviously they became very frequent when there was a serious disagreement between the Houses. The 1679 parliament witnessed fifteen conferences on a range of issues, including Danby's attainder and the trials of the five impeached Catholic lords.

In exceptional circumstances joint committees, normally comprising twelve peers and twenty-four commoners, were appointed.[19] They had been used extensively during the Civil War period when parliament had assumed an executive function.[20] Only three such committees sat during Charles II's reign, one in 1661 to investigate an alleged plot against the Crown, another in May 1679 to discuss the procedure for the trials of the peers imprisoned in the Tower, and the last, in November 1680, to arrange Lord Stafford's trial. Joint committees differed from conference committees in that they tended to have fewer members and met in the Inner Court of Wards for a duration of several days to discuss business in detail. The ceremonial surrounding conferences was dispensed with. Peers and MPs sat together and the latter retained their hats.[21] The chairman was always a lord: Lord

[14] Bodl., Rawlinson MSS A. 130, fols. 71v, 72v; Pepys, VII, pp. 414–15; *LJ*, XII, 52–3.
[15] PRO, SP. 29/40/19, T. Baines to Lord Conway, 3 Aug. 1661.
[16] *LJ*, XII, 374.
[17] Ibid., 334; XIII, 505, 510, 514, 594.
[18] For the details of these conferences see the *Journals of the House of Lords*.
[19] However, only six peers were chosen in November 1680 (HLRO, Joint Committee Minute Book, 1679–95, 27 November 1680).
[20] Foster, pp. 116–25.
[21] This was certainly the situation in 1661 (Foster, p. 126).

Chancellor Finch and the earl of Shaftesbury in 1679.[22] As with other committees the chairman reported to the House on the committee's deliberations and its decisions were subject to ratification by both Houses.

Joint committees could fulfil a useful political purpose for the government. That of May 1679, appointed to consider 'propositions and circumstances in reference to the trials of the lords in the Tower', made no discernible progress on this issue, despite having met frequently.[23] The clerk's minutes strongly suggest that Lord Chancellor Finch, the government's most senior representative on the committee, deliberately spun out proceedings by focusing attention on the highly contentious subject of the rights of bishops to participate in the trials of the five Catholic peers and that of the earl of Danby.[24] The court's intention was to divert the Commons from passing the Exclusion Bill.[25] The joint committee's deliberations necessitated lengthy debates in both chambers as representatives could not table proposals without the agreement of their respective Houses. In these circumstances the Exclusion Bill had not even begun its committee stage in the Commons by the prorogation on 27 May.[26] In contrast the joint committee on Viscount Stafford's trial, meeting between 27 and 29 November 1680, after the defeat of the second Exclusion Bill in the Lords, quickly reached agreement on the bishops' rights and the procedures to be adopted during the trial in Westminster Hall.[27]

Besides these formal methods of contact between the two chambers there were local connections between peers and MPs. One of the most significant was still a lord's patronage of elections. Despite the abolition of the House of Lords and the temporary changes in the franchise during the Interregnum, the peerage exercised a considerable influence over parliamentary elections after the Restoration. No fewer than ninety MPs were to varying degrees beholden to lords for their seats at the general election of 1661. A similar number was elected at by-elections to the Cavalier Parliament partly as a result of the influence of peers.[28] Thus members of the upper House helped to determine the composition of approximately a quarter of the Cavalier Commons. This was all the more remarkable when one considers the increasing influence both of the gentry and of political and religious issues in parliamentary elections after 1640.[29]

[22] Joint Committee Minute Book, 1679–95, 12, 13, 14, 15, 16, 17, 19, 21, 22, 23, 24 May 1679.
[23] LJ, XIII, 567.
[24] Joint Committee Minutes, 1679–95, 14, 19, 23 May 1679.
[25] Chatsworth House, Halifax Collection, E/7, Algernon Sidney to Henry Savile, 12 May 1679; Haley, Shaftesbury, pp. 523–5.
[26] CJ, IX, 626, 634.
[27] Joint Committee Minutes, 1679–95, 27, 29 November 1680; LJ, XIII, 690, 692, 694, 695–6.
[28] The figures for the peers' electoral influence are derived from Henning (ed.), House of Commons, I, pp. 125–522.
[29] J. K. Gruenfelder, Influence in early Stuart elections, 1604–1640 (Columbus, Ohio, 1981), pp. 217–18.

As the principal landowners peers were able to nominate candidates, and in contested elections construct an 'interest'.[30] Constructing an 'interest', or a majority among the electorate, involved a mixture of natural ties, patronage and outright bribery. In a period when the cost of elections was spiralling dramatically, wealthy noblemen were in a strong position to create a majority interest in a constituency. Lord Berkeley, a prominent Gloucestershire landowner, built up a sufficient interest among his tenants, kinsmen and local gentry for the county to return Matthew Hale to the Convention.[31] Often a lord's nominee was automatically endorsed by the voters without a contest. Writing in 1681 the second earl of Clarendon recalled: 'The borough of Christchurch is my borough, the manor is my own and one or both of the burgesses have been always elected on the recommendation of the Lords of the place.'[32] Even during the elections to the 'Exclusion' Parliaments the patronage of the local landowner was still an important factor. The earls of Bedford, Pembroke and Carlisle, all manorial lords, continued to act as borough patrons throughout the second half of the seventeenth century. Other leading landowners who enjoyed electoral influence included the earls of Winchester (Hampshire), Lindsey (Lincolnshire) and Dorset (Sussex), Lords Robartes (Cornwall) and Townshend (Norfolk) and the dukes of Newcastle (Nottinghamshire and Derbyshire).[33]

An equally common foundation for patronage relationships between peers and MPs was the possession of local offices. Sometimes peers were high stewards and recorders in local boroughs, offices which gave them a say in the choice of parliamentary candidates. The earl of Bolingbroke, recorder of Bedford Corporation, persuaded the borough to elect his brother, Paulet St John, in a by-election in 1663.[34] Throughout the 1660s and 1670s the earl of Bath placed relatives in the West Country boroughs of which he was recorder.[35] During the period covered by this book lord lieutenants began to exercise a strong electoral influence. Most lord lieutenants were noblemen. Their influence was derived from their control over the militia and their close links with the gentry, who often served them as deputy lieutenants or militia officers. The marquis of Worcester was a powerful parliamentary patron in the three counties of which he was lord lieutenant, Gloucestershire, Herefordshire and Monmouthshire. During the elections to the three 'Exclusion' Parliaments the second duke of Albemarle employed his interest

---

[30] M. A. Kishlansky, *Parliamentary selection: social and political choice in early modern England* (Cambridge, 1986), pp. 228–30.
[31] Henning (ed.), *House of Commons*, I, pp. 236–7; BL, Verney MSS M/636/17, Denton to Verney, 29 March 1660.
[32] *Cal. SP Dom.* 1680–1, p. 165.
[33] Henning (ed.), *House of Commons*, I, pp. 153–81, 245, 283, 299, 301, 319, 330, 349–51, 422.
[34] Ibid., p. 126.
[35] Kishlansky, *Parliamentary selection*, p. 155.

for the court in Devon, where he was lord lieutenant.[36] Acting on behalf of his father, the earl of Rutland, Lord Roos despatched letters to specific electors in the Leicester by-election of 1677, urging that 'all and every of you who have any commission from my father in the militia or have any other dependence upon him and me ... that you give your votes for Mr Grey'.[37]

Involvement in parliamentary elections brought its rewards for members of the nobility. A lord's prestige and local standing was reinforced if his nominee were elected. The ability to influence an election was an indicator of social and political status in the seventeenth century. Patron–client relationships were reinforced at the county level. One of Lord Powis' correspondents observed in February 1661 that if Sir Henry Herbert 'be chosen by your lordship's favour [it] is a greater testimony of his ability and obligation than he will ever acknowledge'.[38] Having friends and clients in the Commons could also enhance a peer's standing in the eyes of the king, particularly if these MPs voted for the court. 'His majesty thinks that no man deserves more value than he who has so many friends in the House of Commons, and who are to be relied upon when things of importance shall lie at stake', wrote Sir Robert Southwell of the earl of Danby in 1678.[39]

It became increasingly common in this period for the eldest sons of peers to occupy parliamentary places, especially the more prestigious county seats. Between 1661 and 1681 at least one of the knights of the shire for both Leicestershire and Hampshire was always the titled son of a nobleman. The heirs of aristocrats regularly held seats in Bedfordshire, Buckinghamshire, Derbyshire, Lancashire, Monmouthshire, Rutland and Shropshire.[40] For the country as a whole during these twenty years no more than 10 per cent of MPs were the sons of peers.[41] There were many reasons why lords encouraged their heirs to enter parliament. These included family tradition and duty, boosting one's influence in the Commons and education: service in the Commons made the heirs of peers better equipped to sit eventually in the upper House.[42]

During the elections to Charles II's last three parliaments (elected in 1679 and 1681) party-political considerations increasingly lay behind peers' interventions. With the development of organised Court and Country parties in both Houses during the mid-1670s, ideology had an impact on parliamentary elections. Throughout the decade the king directed 'government' peers to

---

[36] Ibid.; Henning (ed.), *House of Commons*, I, p. 74.
[37] *Hist. MSS Comm.*, 12th Rept, Appendix, pt V, MSS of the duke of Rutland, II, p. 35.
[38] PRO, 30/53/7, Powis-Herbert MSS, fol. 76, ? to Lord Powis, 23 February 1661.
[39] Carte MSS 38, fol. 678, Sir Robert Southwell to Ormond, 10 Dec. 1678.
[40] Kishlansky, *Parliamentary selection*, pp. 139–40.
[41] Henning (ed.), *House of Commons*, I, pp. 19–24.
[42] Bodl., Rawlinson Letters, 104, fol. 89, Lewis Stukeley to Lord Wharton, 29 March 1673; *Cal. SP Dom.*, 1666–7, p. 196; Henning, ibid., 151, 154, 214, 242, 296.

construct interests in constituencies and return the Court candidate.[43] In March 1679 he urged the former Country peer, Lord Townshend, to use his influence with his father-in-law, Sir Joseph Ash, to make Sir John King burgess for a Wiltshire borough.[44] During the same general election the duke of Newcastle was informed that 'the king … desires you will promote as much as you can the choice of good members in those places which are influenced by your grace'.[45] 'Opposition' peers were just as active in this and the two subsequent elections of the reign. Lords Grey of Wark and Chandos canvassed on behalf of 'opposition' candidates in Essex, whilst at Eye Lord Cornwallis refused to sell alcohol to Court supporters.[46]

It is important not to exaggerate the degree of peerage influence in elections. There were plenty of occasions when electors spurned a lord's candidate.[47] Esteemed a 'creature of the court' by the Presbyterians and 'factious people' in Lincoln, the duke of Newcastle failed to secure the election of Court candidates in March 1679.[48] Another Court peer, Lord Norreys, was thought to have lost his influence 'for sticking so highly for my Lord Treasurer in so much that at Oxford the people hooted him out of town crying "no Lord Treasurer, no Papist"'.[49] During the elections to the Oxford Parliament peers intervened in approximately a fifth of all seats, but were only successful in a half of these (sixty-two seats).[50] During the elections to the 'Exclusion' Parliaments the electoral influence of the nobility declined as national political issues became significant in determining the selection of MPs.[51] Court candidates were often rejected by electors because of the court's alleged associations with Popery and arbitrary government. The corporation of Great Yarmouth vetoed one of the earl of Yarmouth's candidates in 1679 stigmatising the earl as a 'friend to the duke of York's interest'.[52] Nevertheless the electoral influence of the nobility in Restoration England helped to foster close ties between peers and MPs, which in turn reinforced the institutional authority and prestige of the upper House.

Besides the direct ties of blood and patronage peers and MPs were of course connected through marriage and friendship. The vast majority of MPs from

[43] Kishlansky, *Parliamentary selection*, pp. 153–5; *Hist. MSS Comm.*, 10 Rept, Appendix pt IV, MSS of Captain Stewart, pp. 117–18, Newsletter 25 November 1670.
[44] Add. MSS 25,124, fols. 23, 24.
[45] *Hist. MSS Comm.*, 13th Rept, App. pt II, MSS of the duke of Portland, II, p. 153, Danby to Newcastle, 24 Jan. 1679.
[46] Henning (ed.), *House of Commons*, I, 229–31; BL, Verney MSS M/636/33, Sir Framlingham Gaudy to Sir Ralph Verney, 28 Aug. 1679.
[47] Ibid., pp. 218, 232, 247–8, 274, 292, 346.
[48] Leeds Public Library, Mexborough MSS, Reresby Letters 13/1, Newcastle to Reresby, 2 March 1679.
[49] BL, Verney MSS M/636/32, Edward Verney to John Verney, 20 Feb. 1679.
[50] Henning (ed.), *House of Commons*, I, pp. 125–521.
[51] Kishlansky, *Parliamentary selection*, p. 172.
[52] *Cal. SP Dom.*, 1679–80, p. 66.

noble families married within their own class and no fewer than 10 per cent of all MPs were married to the daughters of peers.[53] Often peers and MPs from the same locality were friends. Sir Robert Paston (later earl of Yarmouth), a Norfolk deputy lieutenant, was on the most amicable terms with his lord lieutenant, Lord Townshend, describing him in 1665 as 'the best friend I have in the world'.[54] After Paston had successfully steered his Yarmouth Fishing Bill through the Commons he applied to Townshend and the earl of Lindsey, another friend, for their assistance in the Lords. Both peers did their utmost to promote the measure in the House and at committee, helping to ensure it passed without amendment.[55] Conversely peers employed their friends in the Commons to advance bills in which they had a vested interest. Thus the earl of Strafford asked his friend Sir Gervase Holles to speed Lord Clare's estate bill through the House in 1667 by attending the relevant committee.[56] Seven years previously the earl of Winchilsea had written to his kinsman, Sir Edward Dering, desiring him 'to get the act for settling of my estate in the north ... to be passed your House with all the speed you can, and also to entreat you to use your endeavours with your friends in the House for my lord marquess of Hertford's business, and to be tomorrow in the afternoon at the committee at 2 of the clock, where you will find occasions enough to assist my lord'.[57] Dering's efforts on behalf of the two peers were successful: both estate bills received the royal assent on 13 September 1660.

Lords and MPs sharing similar religious views frequently associated with each other during parliamentary sessions. Both Lord Wharton and the earl of Manchester had strong ties with Presbyterians in the Commons in 1660, and according to one historian Wharton had a substantial following there in 1660 and 1661.[58] Another Presbyterian, John, Baron Crew, corresponded regularly with his close friend and agent, John Swinfen, the MP for Tamworth. In his letters to this 'rigid Presbyterian'[59] Crew reflected on an assortment of religious subjects including the ugliness of sin, God's mercy, salvation and personal Bible study.[60] Rigidly Anglican lords, such as the earls of Bridgewater and Northampton, also had like-minded associates in the Commons.[61]

[53] Henning (ed.), House of Commons, I, pp. 20–4.
[54] Add. MSS 27,447, fol. 329, Paston to wife, 4 Feb. 1665.
[55] Ibid., fols. 327, 329, 330, 334, 336, 338, Paston to wife, 13 Dec. 1664, 5, 9, 21, 23 Feb. 1665.
[56] Hist. MSS Comm., 58, MSS of the marquis of Bath, vol. II, p. 151, earl of Strafford to Gervase Holles, 27 July 1667.
[57] BL, Stowe MSS 744, fol. 42, Winchilsea to Dering, 27 Aug. 1660.
[58] G. F. T. Jones, Saw-pit Wharton, pp. 174–86.
[59] 'The Gentry of Staffordshire, 1662–3', R. M. Kidson (ed.), Collections for a History of Staffordshire (Stafford Co. RO, 4th ser., Shrewsbury, 1958), II, p. 29.
[60] Bedfordshire RO, Lucas Collection, letters from Lord Crew to John Swinfen, L30/20/2 (19 Sept: 1671), /3 (30 Dec. 1671), /5 (16 Feb. 1672), /8 (30 July 1672), /9 (8 Oct. 1672).
[61] Seaward, pp. 66, 93, 97.

Sometimes lords and MPs coordinated tactics in their respective chambers. Anglicans opposed to any alteration of the Restoration Church settlement colluded to frustrate a government scheme to broaden the Church in 1668. In February Archbishop Sheldon warned his Anglican friends in the Commons of the king's intention of introducing a comprehension bill in that House at the same time as one of the bill's sponsors, the duke of Buckingham, was rumoured to be canvassing support from Presbyterian MPs.[62] According to the bishop of Coventry and Lichfield, Sheldon's will ultimately prevailed and Anglican MPs quickly suppressed the measure before it was even presented to the House.[63]

The most dramatic manifestations of collusion between members of both Houses involved factions and later political parties. From the mid-1660s Buckingham, Bristol, Arlington and Ormond had factions of varying sizes in the Commons.[64] Whilst describing the activities of the duke of Buckingham in 1666, the earl of Clarendon noted that 'there was a correspondence ... begun and warmly pursued between some discontented members of the house of peers, who thought their parts not valued ... and some members of the house of commons who made themselves remarkable by opposing all things which were proposed in that house for the king's service'.[65] At this time Buckingham's adherents included the Yorkshire MPs, Sir Thomas Gower and Sir Thomas Osborne, and discontented politicians, such as Sir Richard Temple, Sir Robert Howard and possibly the independently minded members William Garraway and Sir Edward Seymour.[66] There is evidence that Buckingham and his associates met privately to coordinate tactics in parliament. Writing to his eldest son in 1669, Ormond reported that 'frequent consultations' were held at Lord Orrery's house where Buckingham, the bishop of Chester and Sir Thomas Osborne 'make the cabal'.[67] The duke operated through his faction in the Commons to attack his enemies at court, most notably Clarendon, Ormond and Mordaunt.[68] His associates promoted the controversial Irish Cattle Bill to undermine Clarendon and Ormond, the Lord Lieutenant of Ireland, in the autumn of 1666, and drove on the impeachments of Mordaunt and Clarendon the following year.[69] These MPs also sponsored

[62] Ibid., p. 97; Bodl., Tanner MSS 45, fol. 278, Hacket to Sheldon, 15 Feb. 1668.
[63] Bodl., Tanner MSS 45, fol. 288, Hacket to Sheldon, 4 March 1668.
[64] Seaward, pp. 219, 223–7, 230, 298–301, 313; Pepys, VIII, p. 93; Carte MSS 35, fol. 246, Broderick to Ormond, 12 Jan 1667.
[65] Clarendon, *Life*, III, pp. 132–3.
[66] Henning (ed.), *House of Commons*, II, pp. 390–2, 425–7; III, pp. 185–7; B. Yardley, 'The political career of George Villiers, 2nd duke of Buckingham, 1628–87' (Oxford University DPhil thesis, 1989), pp. 89–91.
[67] Carte MSS 50, fol. 58, Ormond to Ossory, 31 July 1669.
[68] Yardley, 'George Villiers', pp. 66, 90, 96, 132.
[69] Ibid., pp. 88–98, 119–26, 129–32; Clarendon, *Life*, III, pp. 135–6.

legislation, such as the 1668 Comprehension and Triennial Bills, with the duke's prior approval.[70]

From the middle of the next decade very close links were fostered between Country party members in both Houses. Most leaders of the Country party were peers, and Shaftesbury and Buckingham were the most prominent.[71] Their lieutenants in the Commons included William Cavendish, William Russell, Sir Robert Howard, Sir Thomas Meres, William Garraway and Colonel Birch. These men appear to have had almost identical aims as Country lords: relief for peaceable Protestant dissenters, stringent measures against papists and the dissolution of the Cavalier Parliament itself.[72] Peers and MPs attended secret meetings to formulate their strategy in parliament.[73] A vivid illustration of coordinated bicameral tactics occurred on 15 February 1677. At the same moment as Country peers challenged the legality of a fifteen-month prorogation of parliament in their chamber, leading opposition MPs attempted to persuade their House to debate the long prorogation.[74] Many of the same MPs had cooperated in 1675 with their leaders in the Lords to exploit a bicameral privilege dispute with the intention of distracting the upper House from passing the government's unpopular Test Bill.[75]

Leaders of the Court party also did not confine their activities to their own chamber. By virtue of the extensive patronage opportunities available to Lord Treasurers, the earl of Danby constructed a considerable party in the Commons. Although estimates of the number of his adherents have varied, he was able to rely on a hard core of 120 to 150 MPs in 1677–8.[76] Many of these were excisemen, government officeholders and the king's household servants. Others were conservative country gentlemen who approved of Danby's orthodox Anglican policies.[77] Danby conveyed the government's intentions to these men in letters, at secret meetings, or via Court peers who had friends and relatives in the Commons.[78] He employed Viscount Conway to urge

---

[70] Carte MSS 36, fol. 167, Broderick to Ormond, 18 Feb. 1668; 46, fols. 600–1, Arlington to Ormond, 18 Feb. 1668; BL, Egerton MSS 2,539, fol. 155, John to Sir Edward Nicholas, 19 Feb. 1668, fol. 168, same to same, 12 March 1668.

[71] Haley, *Shaftesbury*, pp. 352–3, 357, 360–1; Yardley, 'George Villiers', p. 222.

[72] Haley, ibid., pp. 335–7, 339, 351–3; Lacey, *Dissent and parliamentary politics*, pp. 379–80; BL, Stowe MSS 203, fols. 113–14, Sir William Temple to Essex, 25 Oct. 1673; Longleat House, Thynne MSS XVI, fol. 104, Coventry to Thynne, 31 March 1673.

[73] PRO, 31/3, 130, fol. 47, Ruvigny to Louis XIV, 22 Jan. 1674; O. Airy (ed.), *The Essex papers* (Camden Soc., NS 47, 1890), I, p. 168, Conway to Essex, 27 Jan. 1674; *Cal. SP Dom.*, 1675–6, p. 562.

[74] Stowe MSS 211, fol. 139, C. Wyche to Essex, 20 Feb. 1677; Add. MSS 28,091, fol. 29, report on debate in the House of Commons, 15 Feb. 1677; Grey, IV, pp. 64–95.

[75] See below, pp. 135–6.

[76] Browning, *Danby*, III, pp. 112–20; K. H. D. Haley, 'Shaftesbury's lists of the lay peers and members of the Commons, 1677–8', *BIHR*, 43 (1970), 88–90.

[77] Browning, *Danby*, III, pp. 44–56, 61–71.

[78] Ibid., pp. 82–4, 96–111.

those members who resided in Ireland to attend and support the Court in 1675.[79] Government managers in the Commons were employed by the Lord Treasurer and Lord Chancellor to argue the government line on bicameral privilege disputes. When his Test Bill was threatened by a series of disputes between the Houses in May and June 1675, Danby exerted his influence via the Speaker, Sir Edward Seymour, to compose the differences between them. Seymour dined with four of the lawyers in one of the controversial appeals, giving them 'very good advice to obviate and prevent any further disputes between both Houses', and succeeded in persuading them not to appear on their client's behalf at the bar of the House of Lords, which the earl believed might have intensified the dispute still further.[80]

II

English parliamentary history from 1660 to 1714 was punctuated by a series of bitter disputes between the two Houses. These were not simply disagreements over legislation, which were a feature of many parliaments since their establishment in the thirteenth century. Most concerned rather the privileges of both chambers. Some involved religious and constitutional issues. A few bicameral disputes were protracted, spanning several weeks, or almost two years in the case of one from the late 1660s.[81] Barely a session elapsed in the reign without at least one bicameral conflict arising. Precisely why Charles II's parliaments were afflicted in this way has never been satisfactorily explained.

The most frequent types of dispute involved the Lords' financial and judicial powers. There were essentially two financial issues at stake, neither of which had been productive of disputes earlier in the century.[82] First was whether the House of Lords could initiate a bill which imposed a tax on the population. Second was the 'right' of the Lords to amend money bills. A majority of peers accepted that giving money to the king in the form of an aid should begin below because the Commons theoretically knew how much the people could reasonably pay in taxation.[83] But the upper House did not accept that the Commons had the sole right to introduce bills which in the main were not financial, yet imposed local charges. The peers believed the Commons' attitude would prevent their chamber from initiating measures which, though they imposed taxes, were also for the public good, such as

[79] Stowe MSS 207, fol. 172, Danby to Essex, 15 Feb. 1675.
[80] C. E. Pike (ed.), *Selections from the correspondence of Arthur Capel earl of Essex, 1675–1677* (Camden Soc., 3rd ser., 24, 1913), pp. 24–7, Lord Aungier to Essex, 5 June 1675.
[81] The dispute surrounding *Skinner* v. *The East India Company* lasted from April 1668 to February 1670.
[82] Add. MSS 6,416, fol. 25.
[83] Committee for Privileges Minute Book 2, p. 13, 27 Feb. 1665; Clarendon, *Life*, III, p. 14.

highway repair and poor-relief bills. Therefore the peers clashed with the
Commons in 1661 when they introduced a bill for the repair of highways,
paid for by a tax on local communities.[84]

The upper House also tried to exercise its 'right' to alter financial bills
after 1660. Peers argued that bills which gave money to the king were 'as
much the gift and present of the house of peers as they are from the house
of commons, and are no more valid without their consent than without the
consent of the other, and they may alter any clause in them that they do not
think for the good of the people'.[85] In June 1678 the Lords amended a bill
for paying off the army, lengthening the period of disbandment, which they
felt was too short, thereby provoking a dispute with the Commons.[86]
Throughout the reign lords were afraid that the Commons would deliberately tack a financial clause to public bills, thus making them immune from
emendation in the upper chamber.[87]

By far the most acrimonious and prolonged disputes concerned three
aspects of the Lords' judicature. These have been discussed earlier and will
only receive brief mention here.[88] The first was whether the upper House
could act as a court of first instance in civil cases. The second concerned the
Lords' right to determine appeals from equity, and the third involved the procedures which the peers used in impeachments, especially their refusal on
several occasions to imprison a person charged with treason. The Commons
did not normally object to the Lords' functioning as a law court, but resented
encroachments upon its members' parliamentary privileges when the Lords
exercised its original jurisdiction in 1668 and heard three appeals in 1675.[89]
MPs were the defendants in all four cases and were entitled to immunity
from lawsuits when parliament was sitting. At the same time peers were
extremely sensitive about their judicature, resisting any attempt by the
Commons to restrict the exercise of their powers, even when MPs' privileges
were involved.[90]

Several theories have been propounded to account for why judicature and
finance became the subject of a multitude of bicameral disputes after 1660.
One scholar writing in the 1960s argued that a desire on the part of the

[84] Committee for Privileges Minute Book 2, pp. 11–14; *LJ*, XI, 467–9. A further reason for the
Lords' acceptance of this Bill was that it had originated from the Privy Council and had the
king's approbation. See PRO, PC2/55, fol. 124.

[85] Clarendon, *Life*, III, p. 14.

[86] Manuscript Minutes 20, 19 June 1678; *Hist. MSS Comm.*, 12th Rept, Appendix pt IX, MSS
of the duke of Beaufort (1891), p. 69, Worcester to the marchioness, 22 June 1678.

[87] Kenyon, *Stuart constitution*, p. 413. The Commons did accept minor amendments to money
bills in the early 1660s.

[88] See chapter 5, pp. 72–4.

[89] The cases were: *Skinner* v. *The East India Company* (1668–70), *Shirley* v. *Fagg*, *Crisp* v.
Delmahoy and *Stoughton* v. *Onslow* (all 1675).

[90] *LJ*, XII, 680–1, 691, 694, 700.

House of Commons to increase its authority underlay many of the conflicts.[91] This theory was in accordance with the then fashionable view of parliament in the seventeenth century, in which the Commons was viewed as intent upon winning the initiative in parliamentary affairs at the expense of the king and the House of Lords.[92]

This view of a power-hungry lower chamber has been discredited by historians.[93] In 1982 John Miller argued that between 1660 and 1681 the House of Commons was not an aggressive body in search of parliamentary sovereignty.[94] There is no satisfactory evidence that MPs genuinely wished to expand their chamber's powers at the expense of the House of Lords. The overriding consideration of most members was the redress of national and local grievances which directly affected themselves and their constituents, such as fears about popery and arbitrary government.

A more plausible explanation for bicameral disputes concerned contemporary attitudes to the history of parliament itself. Members of both Houses had a far better knowledge of the early history of parliament than their predecessors had before the Civil War.[95] With the publication after 1650 of works by Scobell, Elsynge and Sheridan on the history of parliament and the circulation in manuscript of treatises by Matthew Hale and William Petyt on the judicature of the House of Lords, contemporary attitudes to parliamentary history began to alter.[96] Lacking a strong sense of chronology, Englishmen in the early seventeenth century had usually regarded the medieval precedents, from which they thought the powers of early Stuart parliaments were derived, as all of equal importance. But Hale's and Petyt's treatises demonstrated that many medieval judicial precedents were no longer applicable, having been invalidated by subsequent statutes. The East India Company's defence in Skinner's suit (1668–70) was based on the entire history of the upper House: a history which indicated that many of the Lords' judicial actions in the 1620s and 1640s had actually violated earlier statutes. The Company, and later the Commons, referred to four cases from Edward I's reign to show that the Lords lacked an original jurisdiction.[97] To

[91] Leamy, 'Relations between Lords and Commons', pp. 30, 100, 207–8.
[92] This view underlies much of the analysis in Western and Greenberg's *Subjects and sovereigns*.
[93] See C. Russell, *Parliaments and English politics, 1621–1629* (Oxford, 1979) and J. H. Hexter, 'Historical perspectives: the early Stuarts and parliament: old hat and nouvelle vague', *Parliamentary History*, 1 (1982), pp. 181–215.
[94] Miller, 'Charles II and his parliaments', 1–23.
[95] Horstman, 'Justice and peers', pp. 24–32, 365.
[96] Ibid., p. 411; H. Scobell, *Memorials of proceedings in parliament in passing bills* (1656); H. Elsynge, *The manner of holding parliaments in England* (1675); T. Sheridan, *A discourse on the rise and power of parliament* (1677); *The jurisdiction of the Lords House of parliament by Lord Chief Justice Hale* (1796); Inner Temple Library, Petyt MSS 538, vol. 16, pp. 141–57.
[97] Horstman, 'Justice and peers', pp. 25–6, 365–6; Add. MSS 25,116, fols. 6, 11–18, proceedings in parliament in the case of Thomas Skinner against the East India Company, 1667–9; *Hist. MSS Comm.*, 8th Rept, Appendix, MSS of the House of Lords, pp. 167–8, proceedings on Skinner's case.

members of the House of Commons, history justified limiting the Lords' judicature in 1668–70.

A clearer understanding of medieval parliaments did not necessarily benefit the House of Commons. For almost fifty years before the publication of Sir Robert Filmer's *Patriarcha* in 1680 antiquaries had discovered that the Commons had not always existed since time immemorial, but had been summoned to parliament at a specific date in the thirteenth century. Although this view was not widespread until the publication of the *Patriarcha*, Filmer's treatise had been circulating in manuscript since 1641.[98] It is likely that peers had read the manuscript, for in his 'Letter upon Parties' of 1669 the earl of Sandwich recorded that many lords were already aware that there had been no House of Commons before Henry III's reign (1216–72).[99] This view of the House of Commons seems to have inspired some peers to propose reducing its exclusive financial powers.[100] Fearful for the future the Commons fought hard to preserve its powers over taxation.

Memories of the abolition of the House of Lords had left peers insecure and vulnerable, and all the more determined that their House would never suffer the same fate again. The peers' greatest fear was of becoming redundant in the government and of exciting thereby the renewed pretext for abolition once again. There was a widespread feeling among peers throughout the reign that if they were prevented from exercising their judicial and legislative powers the House of Lords would cease to play a useful role in government. As late as 1679 the earl of Northampton argued in a debate that 'if you part with one privilege and another you may at last lose all'.[101] In 1667 the earl of Dorset had observed that if the peers frequently waived privileges in financial matters this would establish a precedent which in turn would irrevocably weaken their House.[102] Members of the restored House of Lords had good reason for asserting what they considered to be their just rights and privileges.

This deep concern for privilege manifested itself in the dispute over the case of *Skinner* v. *The East India Company* in which the peers believed their judicature to be under attack from the Commons. In 1666 Thomas Skinner, a merchant, petitioned the king, protesting at the East India Company's seizure of his goods and island (Barella in Sumatra), which he had purchased from the king of Djambi during the Interregnum.[103] The Company's action had in fact occurred in 1659 after Skinner had taken advantage of a general

98 Horstman, 'Justice and peers', p. 411.
99 Harris, *Life of Sandwich*, II, p. 314.
100 Horstman, 'Justice and peers', p. 411.
101 Add. MSS 28,046, fols. 55–6, Northampton's speech in the debate on Danby's Attainder Bill, 2 April 1679.
102 Kent Archives Office, Sackville MSS U269/036, fol. 81, Dorset's protest against lords being taxed by the Commons, 1666/7.
103 Add. MSS 25,116, fols. 3–5.

liberty and freedom to trade in the East Indies, which overrode the East India Company's monopoly. Skinner claimed damages of more than £17,000 but the Company only offered £1,500 as compensation for the seizure of his ship and merchandise. The privy council had tried to mediate but failed, and so at Skinner's request Charles II referred the matter to the Lords in January 1667 because it was doubtful whether common-law courts had jurisdiction over crimes allegedly committed by Englishmen outside the realm.[104] The Lords proceeded upon the suit, but was prevented from reaching a decision because parliament was prorogued in February. Determined to see justice done, Skinner revived the suit in the following session. In its answer to his petition the Company denied that the Lords could hear the case at all since it was not an appeal but an original complaint. After hearing counsel for both parties on 7 March 1668 the upper House decided in Skinner's favour, awarding him a total of £5,000 in damages on 29 April.[105]

Meanwhile on 17 April the Company's directors had petitioned the Commons. They denied that the peers had any jurisdiction in the case and pointed out that a proportion of damages would fall upon MPs who were also members of the East India Company. This they claimed would infringe these MPs' parliamentary privileges. The Commons took the side of the Company, passing several hastily conceived resolutions against the Lords' jurisdiction.[106] The peers responded with counter-resolutions defending their privileges, and also imprisoned one of the Commons' own members, Sir Samuel Barnardiston, the deputy governor of the Company. The dispute dragged on through the sessions of 1668 and 1669 until Charles II directly intervened in February 1670, ordering both Houses to expunge all traces of it from their respective Journals.[107]

However, this dispute like many others during the reign was fomented by factions and interest groups in parliament. The duke of Buckingham and his associates in both chambers played leading roles.[108] His friend in the Commons, Sir John Vaughan, drafted the Company's petition to the lower House in which it was alleged that the Lords' proceedings in the case were illegal and constituted a 'breach of privilege of the House of Commons'.[109]

---

[104] Ibid., fols. 3–6; Manuscript Minutes 14: 19 Jan. 1667. The best account of the dispute is in Hart, *Justice upon petition*, pp. 242–50.

[105] Add. MSS 25,116, fols. 6, 9; Manuscript Minutes 15: 17, 30 March, 7, 11, 13, 18, 20 April 1668.

[106] Add. MSS 25,116, fols. 115–24.

[107] Manuscript Minutes 15: 8, 9 May; *Hist. MSS Comm.*, 8th Rept, Appendix, MSS of the House of Lords, p. 174.

[108] Add. MSS 25,116, fols. 26, 115. In his account of Skinner's case James Hart ignores the key role played by Buckingham and the Presbyterians in manipulating the dispute for religious and political purposes (Hart, *Justice upon petition*, pp. 245–50).

[109] Harris, *Life of Sandwich*, II, p. 312; Grey, *Debates*, I, p. 192; BL, Stowe MSS 304, fols. 89–94, Sir Richard Temple's discourse on the failure of the 1668 session of parliament; BL, Egerton MSS 2,539, fol. 193, John to Sir Edward Nicholas, 12 May 1668; C. Robbins (ed.), *The diary of John Milward* (Cambridge, 1938), pp. 286–91.

Sir Robert Howard, Sir Richard Temple and the 'Presbyterians' Sir John
Maynard and William Prynne angrily condemned the peers' judicature in
debates. These and more of the duke's allies sat on the committee appointed
to consider the Company's petition, whilst several also managed conferences
during the dispute. Yet in the upper House Buckingham and his adherents
proved the most vociferous champions of their chamber's privileges. The
duke chaired several important committee meetings and vigorously asserted
the Lords' judicial rights in the House and at conferences.[110] His friends – in
particular, the earls of Essex and Northampton and Lords Howard of
Charlton and Lucas – were also prominent in encouraging the House to
defend its privileges.[111]

Contemporaries suspected that there was more to the dispute than simply
privilege. Sir John Nicholas wrote on 12 May 1668 that 'the undertakers
[members of Buckingham's faction who had promised to procure money for
the king from the Commons] in ours and the d[uke] of Bucks [sic] and some
of the Presbyterians in the Lords' House are most passionate in it, which
makes it be looked on by sober men as a design to break this parl[iament]'.[112]
Sir William Morrice believed that Skinner was patronised by a 'great lord',
presumably Buckingham.[113] An anonymous correspondent of the duke of
Northumberland asserted that the dispute was deliberately spun out to frustrate the passage of controversial legislation.[114]

No single factor explains the behaviour of Buckingham and his associates
during the dispute: religion, politics and self-interest all played a part. The
dispute was orchestrated initially to scupper a conventicle bill. The 1664
Conventicle Act expired in May 1668 and the Anglican majority in the
Commons was intent upon passing a replacement.[115] Despite stiff opposition
from Presbyterians and moderate Anglicans in the Commons such a bill
passed the House on 28 April and was presented to the Lords the same day.
Buckingham, who was worried about the plight of Protestant dissenters and,
at the same time, keen to increase his own popularity and standing in parliament with the friends of nonconformists (who formed a sizeable minority),
was concerned that the Lords might eventually consent to the Bill, especially
since the controversial Five Mile Bill had passed the House in 1665.[116] Earlier

---

[110] Add. MSS 25,116, fols. 22–3, 40–1, 115, 119, 130–1, 140; *Hist. MSS Comm.*, 8th Rept,
Appendix, MSS of the House of Lords, pp. 168–9. Committee for Privileges Minute Book 2,
pp. 44, 45.

[111] Committee for Privileges Minutes 2, pp. 46, 49–55; Add. MSS 25,116, fols. 34, 38, 40, 56.

[112] BL, Egerton MSS 2,539, fol. 193, John to Sir Edward Nicholas, 12 May 1668.

[113] *Hist. MSS Comm.*, 71, MSS of Allan George Finch Esq., vol. I (1913), p. 505, Sir William
Morrice to the earl of Winchilsea, 15 May 1668.

[114] Alnwick Castle, MSS of the duke of Northumberland: Letters and Papers 1664–84,
fols. 132–3, ? to Northumberland, 11 May 1668.

[115] Milward, *Diary*, 238, 282–3.

[116] Yardley, 'George Villiers', pp. 144–52.

in the 1668 session the duke and his supporters had backed the court's abortive Comprehension Bill, which had been introduced in the Commons in February, but not proceeded with. Skinner's suit was therefore latched upon by the duke's allies as a means of distracting the peers from the Conventicle Bill.[117]

The dispute was also a reflection of a rift at court and in the privy council. Buckingham and Presbyterian councillors, notably Anglesey, Ashley, Holles and Robartes, believing a new House of Commons would be sympathetic to relieving Protestant dissenters, were anxious for the king to dissolve the Cavalier Parliament.[118] Most of the disgraced earl of Clarendon's friends at court, described by Sir Richard Temple as 'Clarendonians', advised Charles to retain the existing Commons, arguing that it would grant adequate supply provided he adhered firmly to the Restoration Church settlement.[119] Distrustful of either faction, the king refused to make any decision about the future of the existing parliament during 1668. Angered by the king's inertia the 'Anti-Clarendonians', as they were termed by contemporaries, transferred their efforts into parliament and whipped up the conflict over Skinner's case to such a pitch that virtually all parliamentary business stagnated as the two chambers concentrated all their energies on vindicating their respective privileges. The king, they believed, would have no option but to dissolve parliament if he wanted future sessions to be harmonious.[120]

Those who incited the dispute also sought power and influence at court and in the administration. In the autumn of 1667 Buckingham and his adherents had agreed to manage parliament for the king and obtain a generous supply from the Commons. In return Charles had apparently promised to give them preferment at court and offices in the administration. However, their attempts at management proved fruitless and it was the Clarendonians who eventually obtained supply in the spring of 1668, with the result that few of the duke's ambitious friends obtained offices.[121] Incensed by their own failure, Anti-Clarendonians endeavoured to make themselves indispensable to Charles by transforming Skinner's suit into a bicameral dispute in April 1668,

---

[117] Ibid., pp. 148–9; J. Spurr, 'The Church of England, comprehension and the Toleration Act of 1689', *EHR*, 104 (Oct. 1989), 933–4; MSS of the duke of Northumberland: Letters and Papers 1664–84, fols. 132–3, ? to Northumberland, 11 May 1668; BL, Egerton MSS 2,539, fols. 214, 215, John to Sir Edward Nicholas, 5/7 May 1668.

[118] Egerton MSS 2,539, fols. 193, 214, same to same, 5/12 May 1668; Add. MSS 36,916, fol. 103, Starkey to Aston, 6 June 1668.

[119] Pepys, VIII, p. 558, IX, pp. 360–1; C. Roberts, 'Sir Richard Temple's discourse on the parliament of 1667–1668', *HLQ*, 20 (1957), pp. 140, 142, 144; Add. MSS 36,916, fols. 118–19, 122, Starkey to Aston, 18 Nov., 22 Dec. 1668.

[120] Roberts, 'Sir Richard Temple's discourse', p. 137.

[121] Ibid., pp. 137, 140–1; C. Roberts, *The growth of responsible government in Stuart England* (Cambridge, 1966), pp. 174–5; Hutton, *Charles II*, pp. 256–7; Yardley, 'George Villiers', pp. 151–2.

hoping thereby to demonstrate that parliament could only be managed with their cooperation. And of course their cooperation was dependent upon royal patronage. It is significant that Charles blamed the Anti-Clarendonians for the acrimonious relations between the Houses in the sessions of 1668 and 1669.[122]

Similar factional manoeuvrings were at the heart of other privilege disputes. Turberville cited the controversy over the rate of imposition on sugar in the Foreign Commodities Bill in April 1671 as nothing more than an example of MPs questioning the Lords' 'right' to amend money bills.[123] The earl of Sandwich's detailed commentary on the dispute shows that it resulted rather from a division within the privy council between Buckingham and his rival Secretary Arlington. Arlington and his 'Court' group, which controlled the Commons, tried to discredit Buckingham and his 'Country' followers with the king by blaming them for the loss of the bill. Arlington's adherents in the Commons were forward in pressing their House's rights, whilst Buckingham and a majority of peers took the opposite view, arguing in favour of their own amendments. The duke and his allies, Lords Holles and Anglesey, persuaded their House that if the Commons' claims were allowed the Lords' right of emendation might disappear altogether, re-awakening memories of 1649.[124] The Commons' demands shook 'the very foundation of parliament', wrote Lord Holles, 'and utterly over throw the being of this house, rendering it altogether useless to the general good of the nation'. The peers would be reduced to 'so many parish clerks', he predicted, 'only to say amen to what the House of Commons hath resolved'.[125] Sandwich was convinced that the dispute could have been resolved without the loss of the bill had it not been for the animosity between Buckingham and Arlington.[126]

Bicameral conflicts from 1675 to 1681 were symptomatic of the emergence of coherent political parties in both Houses. Conflicts developed largely because the Country party 'controlled' the lower chamber and the Court party, the upper House. Yet members of either House were never completely united in defence of their respective privileges. Court party members in both Houses usually united with each other, and Country lords and MPs acted in collusion. In short, disputes were horizontal within each House, as well as vertical between both Houses.

These features were evident in disputes over the Lords' appellate jurisdiction. In April 1675 three appeals in which the defendants were members of the Commons were brought before the Lords. Two, *Shirley* v. *Fagg* and

[122] Roberts, 'Sir Richard Temple's discourse', pp. 137–44.
[123] Turberville, 'House of Lords under Charles II', pp. 65–6.
[124] Harris, *Life of Sandwich*, II, pp. 333–7.
[125] D. Holles, *The case stated of the jurisdiction of the House of Lords in the point of impositions* (1676), pp. 4, 48. This tract was written in 1671.
[126] Harris, *Sandwich*, II, p. 334.

Crispe v. *Delmahoy*, were from the Chancery, and one, *Stoughton* v. *Onslow*, came from the Court of Exchequer. The Lords had exercised an appellate jurisdiction on numerous occasions earlier in the reign, but because these particular appeals directly concerned MPs the Commons became involved, reminding the Lords to have regard for its members' privileges.[127]

Country party members in each House exploited these appeals as a method of setting the two chambers at loggerheads, and thereby of completely wrecking the session. 'It was easy to get those causes set on foot and to procure the members to stand upon privilege', reflected Lord Guildford later in the reign.[128] It is likely that the three plaintiffs had been persuaded to present their appeals by either Shaftesbury or his lieutenants. Shirley's appeal was almost certainly prearranged by these discontented men. He had previously petitioned the House in 1669, but had not renewed his petition in any of the four subsequent sessions. In fact Shaftesbury told Bishop Burnet that he had orchestrated Shirley's appeal for political purposes in 1675.[129]

Members of Shaftesbury's party were prominent in the disputes at every stage. Country peers, including Lords Holles, Buckingham, Salisbury, Bedford, Denbigh, Bridgewater, Dorset, Newport, Mohun, Stamford and Grey of Rolleston, were among the staunchest defenders of the Lords' judicature in debates and during conferences with the Commons.[130] Those who most fervently insisted on the privileges of the Commons were also Shaftesbury's adherents: Sir Thomas Meres, Sir Thomas Littleton, Sir Thomas Lee, Henry Powle, John Swinfen, Sir Thomas Clarges and Henry Sacheverell.[131] Ministers and Court party members, notably Danby (Lord Treasurer), Finch (Lord Keeper), Anglesey (Lord Privy Seal), Albemarle (second duke), the earl of Sussex, Sir Edward Seymour, Sir Edmund Jennings, Francis Gwyn and Sir Edward Dering made several concerted attempts to resolve the disputes through a compromise, as they jeopardised government legislation, in particular the Lord Treasurer's Test Bill.[132]

There were two main reasons for the orchestration of bicameral conflicts over the Lords' appellate jurisdiction. The first was to prevent Danby's Test Bill from passing the House of Lords.[133] Country lords, who were generally sympathetic to the plight of dissenting Protestants under the penal laws,

---

[127] *LJ*, XII, 680, 694.
[128] Add. MSS 32,518, fol. 147, Lord Guildford's notes on parliament.
[129] Burnet, *History*, II, p. 85.
[130] *LJ*, XII, 681, 706; *Bulstrode Papers*, pp. 292–3; 'A letter from a person of quality to his friend in the country', *Parl. Hist.*, IV, pp. 791–800.
[131] Grey, *Debates*, III, pp. 112–15, 139–47, 149–56, 167–74, 176–7, 181–236, 241–89; Haley, *Shaftesbury*, pp. 353, 360, 382–4.
[132] Leamy, 'Relations between Lords and Commons', pp. 114–20; Henning, *House of Commons*, II, pp. 456, 647; *Bulstrode Papers*, pp. 318, 321; Add. MSS 18,730, fol. 4.
[133] Burnet, *History*, II, pp. 85–6; *Hist. MSS Comm.*, ser. 72, Laing MSS, I (1914), p. 403, George to James Scot, 17 June 1675.

objected to the Test because it sought to prevent any change to the Church settlement. 'Opposition' peers were outnumbered in the House and alone could not defeat this measure. They regarded a privilege dispute as the best method of distracting the privilege-conscious House from the Test Bill. Their tactics worked, for sufficient Court lords, including the marquis of Worcester and Lord Colepeper, voted with the 'opposition' in defence of their judicature. Worcester wrote that he and other peers were unable to stand impassively while their House received 'greater affronts than ever were offered it except in the time of the late rebellion'.[134] These peers may also have shared the fears expressed so succinctly by one of Lord Hatton's correspondents, who observed 'doubtless if you lose your judicature your part in the legislature will follow and the consequence of that must inevitably be the total ruin of our government'.[135]

The second reason for fomenting the bicameral conflict was to dissolve parliament itself, and in the process discredit the earl of Danby as a parliamentary manager. There is evidence that both Shaftesbury and Buckingham still hankered after high office at this time and saw Danby as a barrier to achieving it. Country peers were anxious for a new House of Commons that contained more men whose religious views were similar to their own.[136] By concentrating members' energies on judicial disputes instead of on government business, 'opposition' leaders hoped that the resulting deadlock would force Charles to dissolve the Cavalier Parliament and dispense with his Lord Treasurer. Danby had been entrusted with the task of persuading parliament to grant supply as well as to pass the Test Bill. Contemporaries, including the Venetian Resident, perceived that the dissension between the Houses had been incited so as to 'force him [i.e. the king] to dissolve them speedily'.[137]

Other disputes from this decade were in part a consequence of the actions of the king and his ministers. A dispute arose in June 1678 over a bill granting the king a supply to enable him to disband his armed forces because he had instructed the Lords to amend the measure. On 19 June the Lord Treasurer, on the king's command, informed the peers that the state of affairs abroad necessitated a longer time for disbandment.[138] Charles II wanted the Lords to prolong the time-scale for disbanding because of French deception at the Nijmegen peace conference, which was interpreted by the allies as a means of continuing the war. On 21 June the Court majority in

---

[134] *Hist. MSS Comm.*, 12th Rept, Appendix pt IX, MSS of the duke of Beaufort (1891), p. 65, Worcester to the marchioness, 5 June 1675; *LJ*, XII, 681.

[135] Add. MSS 29,555, fol. 271, R. Langham to Hatton, 27 Nov. 1675.

[136] Haley, *Shaftesbury*, pp. 513–15; Hertfordshire RO, Cowper Papers, D/EP/F42, Shaftesbury to Sir William Cowper, 8 Sept. 1678; Yardley, 'George Villiers', pp. 221, 240.

[137] *Cal. SP Ven.*, 38, p. 423, Paolo Sarotti to Doge and Senate, 11/21 June 1675; Burnet, *History*, II, p. 86.

[138] Manuscript Minutes 20: 19 June 1678.

the House accordingly revised the Bill. Members of the Country party in both chambers felt that the 'crisis' at Nijmegen had been manufactured by the court as an excuse for keeping the forces in being longer, thereby allowing the king to intimidate parliament with military force if it refused further supplies.[139] A bicameral conflict erupted as frightened commoners and Country peers seized upon the House of Lords' alleged inability to amend money bills as a means of ensuring that the forces were disbanded swiftly.

Fear of royal intentions underlay a later dispute over a subsequent disbanding bill in December 1678. On 16 December the Commons sent up a bill for disbanding all forces raised since 29 September 1677. The popish plot crisis was at its height and MPs feared that Charles and his brother might utilise the money raised by the bill to maintain a standing army with which to establish popery in England. Therefore they inserted a clause for the tax to be paid into the Chamber of London, outside the government's control, instead of the Exchequer. Charles interpreted this infringement of his royal prerogative with alarm. Royal pressure was exerted on the Lords and on 19 December the peers voted by a majority of thirteen to amend the bill making the Exchequer the repository of the money.[140] This action immediately embroiled the peers in a serious conflict with the Commons in the course of which the bill was lost. The Commons challenged the peers' right to amend any aspect of a money bill – a right which the king and his ministers vigorously defended.[141]

Charles II did not always side with his peers in bicameral disputes. Indeed, by studying bicameral conflicts it is possible to modify the traditional view of politics in this period which sees tension and conflict between Charles and his House of Commons. Disputes between the two chambers were more frequent than those between the king and the Commons, with bicameral disputes occurring in every session of the reign except those of 1664–5 and 1674. In three major bicameral conflicts and several lesser ones the king allied himself with the House of Commons.

The first instance of this concerned the impeachment of the earl of Clarendon in November 1667. Samuel Pepys recorded in his diary that 'the present sort of government is looked upon as a sort of government that we never had yet; that is to say, a king and House of Commons against the House of Lords; for so it indeed is, though neither of the two first care a fig for one another'.[142] The king openly supported the Commons in its dispute with the Lords over the peers' refusal to imprison his former Lord

[139] Haley, *Shaftesbury*, pp. 448–51.
[140] *LJ*, XIII, 419; Dr Williams' Library, Morrice MSS, Entering Book P, p. 102, 20 Dec. 1678; PRO, 31/3/141, fol. 107, Barrillon to Louis, 19/29 Dec. 1678.
[141] *CJ*, IX, 561, 563, 565; Haley, *Shaftesbury*, p. 491.
[142] Pepys, VIII, p. 584.

Chancellor. Charles wanted Clarendon to be a scapegoat for the government's mishandling of the war against the Dutch. Despite Charles' canvass of individual peers, the House of Lords refused to commit Clarendon on a general charge of treason, fearing that this would establish a precedent for the indiscriminate imprisonment of peers before specific written charges had been delivered by the Commons.[143] The resulting bitter dispute with the Commons was only terminated by Clarendon's flight to France on 29 November after he discovered that Charles was considering a trial outside parliament in a court packed with his enemies.[144]

Royal financial insolvency, however, determined the king's stance in the disputes over Skinner's suit and the Lords' appellate judicature in 1675. These disputes embittered relations between the Houses to such an extent that financial bills were not despatched. In the autumn session of 1669 a hearth-tax bill slumbered in the Commons as angry MPs concentrated on their judicial conflict with the Lords.[145] Relations with the Lords were so soured in the two sessions of 1675 that the Commons, already highly suspicious of the court's connections with popery, refused to pass a single supply bill.[146]

The king's best hope of obtaining money was to instruct his ministers in the Lords not to challenge the Commons' privileges as he exerted pressure on peers not to insist on exercising controversial privileges. In 1669 Charles employed the dukes of Buckingham and York to promote a bill aimed at curtailing the Lords' judicial privileges in an attempt to resolve the dispute over *Skinner* v. *The East India Company*. Trying desperately to restore harmony in parliament in 1675, the king relied on his ministers to moderate the actions of his two Houses. When their efforts proved to be of no avail, king and ministers sided with the Commons.[147] Charles II's refusal to gratify the Lords by dismissing Sir John Robinson, Lieutenant of the Tower of London, for imprisoning on the order of the Commons four of the legal counsel in one of the disputed appeals, was regarded by some contemporaries as a vindication of the Commons' position in the conflict.[148]

The most immediate effect of these and other disputes between the Houses

---

[143] BL, Egerton MSS 2,539, fols. 141, 145, John to Sir Edward Nicholas, 19/27 Nov. 1667; Bodl., Rawlinson MSS A. 130, fol. 95; Pepys, VIII, p. 544. Many peers regarded Clarendon's flight as an admission of guilt (Bodl., Rawlinson MSS A. 130, fol. 109; Hutton, *Charles II*, p. 253; Add. MSS 36,916, fol. 35, Starkey to Aston, 5 Dec. 1667).

[144] Add. MSS 25,116, fols. 125–71.

[145] Grey, *Debates*, III, pp. 104, 156–66, 296, 302–11, 317–26, 354–6, 399; VI, pp. 10–54.

[146] *Cal. SP Ven.*, 36, pp. 130–4, Piero Mocenigo to Doge and Senate, 12/22, 19/29 Nov. 1669; Harris, *Sandwich*, II, pp. 307–9.

[147] Leamy, 'Relations between Lords and Commons', p. 120; *Cal. SP Ven.*, 38, p. 423, Paoli Sarotti to Doge and Senate, 11/21 June 1675.

[148] Leamy, 'Relations between Lords and Commons', pp. 90–1, 96, 119–20, 126, 174–5, 197, 200–1; Browning, *Danby*, I, p. 166; *Cal. SP Dom.*, 1675–6, pp. 413–14, newsletter to Sir Francis Radcliffe, 23 Nov. 1675.

was the disruption of normal parliamentary business. The most severe led to a stalemate in which neither House was prepared to compromise, leaving the king with no alternative but to terminate the session. On no less than eight occasions – 1668, 1669, 1671, 1675 (twice), 1678, 1679 and 1681 – a bicameral conflict was a significant factor in persuading the king to terminate a parliamentary session. In the autumn session of 1669 tempers were so inflamed that not a single bill was ready for the royal assent at the prorogation on 11 December. Only one piece of legislation had actually passed the Lords during the entire seven-week session. Judicial and legislative business was also seriously delayed in the upper chamber in the two sessions of 1675 as peers channelled their energies into vindicating their privileges. Only two of the seventeen bills initiated in the Lords were ready for the royal assent on 9 June when parliament was prorogued. Of the seven writs of error received by the House during these two sessions only one was in fact determined in the session in which it had been brought into the Lords.

Factions and parties were often the main beneficiaries of the bicameral conflicts they had fomented. Although the instigators of the disputes over Skinner's and Shirley's cases failed to achieve one of their objectives, the dissolution of the Cavalier Parliament, they did achieve two short-term aims. Hostility between the Houses prevented the passage of a conventicle bill for two years after the 1664 Act had expired in May 1668. An attempt by rigid Anglicans to rush through a replacement in 1668 failed because of the amount of parliamentary time devoted to Skinner's suit. Many nonconformists were thereby able to worship unhindered until parliament passed the second Conventicle Bill in 1670. Five years later the furore which resulted from the conflict with the Commons over the Lords' appellate jurisdiction achieved precisely what Country and Catholic peers had been unable to achieve by force of argument on the floor of the House: the loss of the government's Test Bill. The Bill never surfaced from the committee of the whole House to receive a third reading. It was debated for the last time on 31 May and from then until the prorogation on 9 June the peers devoted all their efforts to the defence of their judicature.[149]

From the perspective of the majority in either House the honours of war in the various privilege disputes of the reign divided out fairly evenly. Most of the Lords' defeats occurred in the area of finance. Their attempts to initiate measures to impose a tax upon a section of the population in 1661 and 1662 failed because of opposition from the Commons. Likewise efforts to amend money bills were usually ineffective for the same reason. The Commons asserted its exclusive right to alter rates of taxation. Several financial bills were lost because neither chamber would compromise. More often

---

[149] Manuscript Minutes 19: 31 May–9 June 1675.

though, government ministers persuaded the Lords to abandon amendments, convincing a majority of peers that the urgent needs of the state ought to assume priority over parliamentary privileges. However, the House of Lords did not accept the principle of the non-alteration of money bills until 1911. It made further attempts to revise such bills after 1685, and in the eighteenth century the Commons did accept changes to money bills that corrected verbal or literal infelicities.[150]

The peers were on firmer ground when their judicature was involved in a bicameral dispute. They threw out every Commons' bill which in any way tried to curb their judicial powers, asserting 'it to be their indisputable privilege that no law concerning their own privileges or matters of judicature should begin anywhere else than in the House of peers'.[151] None of the Lords' judicial powers was reduced as a consequence of bicameral disputes. The House did not lose its original jurisdiction as a result of the conflict over *Skinner* v. *The East India Company* as some historians have alleged. The outcome of the dispute was a stalemate in which the king ordered both chambers to erase all references to it from their Journals in February 1670.[152] The upper House continued to exercise an appellate jurisdiction in equity suits despite the events of 1675. The Commons singularly failed to persuade the peers to impeach either Clarendon or Danby. Although Danby was despatched to the Tower in 1679 the Lords refused to bring him to trial despite pressure to do so from the Lords.[153]

There are several reasons why the Lords repelled the challenges of the Commons in judicial disputes. First, the historical precedents, which both chambers used to support their arguments at conferences, generally substantiated those of the House of Lords. In *Shirley* v. *Fagg*, for example, the peers were able to demonstrate by reference to their archive in the Jewel Tower that they had exercised an equity jurisdiction since the 1620s.[154] Secondly, peers did not feel that by defending their judicial powers they were jeopardising government tax bills, and could not be so easily accused of impoverishing the king. Obviously such bills did suffer in prolonged judicial disputes, lying dormant in the Commons. Indeed when the Commons eventually sent up a money bill the peers would normally pass it.

Thirdly, as in the disputes surrounding the impeachments of Danby and the five Catholic lords in 1678–9, the king sometimes intervened on the side of the Lords. Charles II employed his ministers to urge the House to stand firm. If necessary he terminated a dispute by proroguing or even dissolving

[150] McCahill, *Order and equipoise*, p. 44.
[151] Quoted by Harris, *Sandwich*, II, p. 308.
[152] See chapter 5, pp. 72–3.
[153] Leamy, 'Relations between Lords and Commons', pp. 156–60, 171–6; Browning, *Danby*, I, p. 317.
[154] *LJ*, XII, 682, 700–29; Committee for Privileges Minute Book 2, p. 116.

parliament as he did in 1679 and 1681. At the Oxford Parliament of 1681 the king backed the peers in their dispute with the Commons over the impeachment of Fitzharris. Before the Lords had rejected the impeachment of this informer, the king personally intervened, influencing lords in the casting of their votes. The dissolution on 28 March 1681 ensured that Fitzharris' fate would be sealed by common-law courts. This thwarted the designs of the 'opposition', who had hoped that a parliamentary trial would reveal evidence of the government's alleged involvement in the popish plot, out of which they could make political capital. Such evidence could be more easily suppressed in a common-law trial.[155]

In the two decades before the abortive impeachment of Fitzharris, the House of Lords had been in frequent conflict with the House of Commons, and had proved a tough and resolute opponent. Members did not watch impassively as the lower chamber questioned their fundamental rights and privileges. It is perhaps remarkable that the House of Lords possessed the determination and muscle to contest almost every inch of disputed ground with the Commons so soon after its restoration. This was not the response of an impotent institution.

[155] Burnet, *History*, II, 285; Leamy, 'Relations between Lords and Commons', pp. 199–205.

Part 4

RELIGION

8

Religious composition

Religious issues were of the utmost importance to the overwhelming majority of lords: bills concerned with the Church of England or nonconformists brought them flocking to Westminster. Particularly controversial pieces of legislation, such as the 1662 Uniformity Bill and the Conventicle Bill of 1664, witnessed attendances in excess of eighty lords per sitting. A considerable variety of religious views existed within the nobility, with few peers being either sceptics or unbelievers. The vast majority of lords conformed to the rites and ceremonies of the established church, but a tiny minority consisting of Protestant nonconformists and Catholics did not.

Categorising peers according to their religious beliefs is fraught with difficulties. Only a handful of peers have left records of their opinions in letters, commonplace books and diaries. For many the only surviving evidence of their religious views is parliamentary speeches, division lists and protests. Even here the evidence is sparse: there was no noble equivalent of a Grey or a Milward diligently scribbling down speeches. Several complete division lists survive from the 1670s, whilst none on religious subjects exists for the 1660s.[1] Of course political actions did not necessarily accord with a lord's private religious beliefs. Despite his ultra-Anglican views, the earl of Bridgewater voted with his Country party friends for an amendment favourable to Protestant dissenters in a 1679 bill for removing papists from London.[2] Others holding court posts, like the duke of Ormond and the king's own brother, the duke of York, had been persuaded by Clarendon to support amendments to religious bills in 1662, despite having private reservations.[3] Additional indicators of lords' religious views include clerical patronage, relationships with dissenters in the localities and attendance at Church.

---

[1] For division lists in the House of Lords see R. W. Davis, 'Recorded divisions in the House of Lords, 1661–80', *Parl. Hist.*, 1 (1982), 168–71 and Swatland, 'Further recorded divisions', pp. 179–82.

[2] *LJ*, XIII, 549.

[3] Berwick (ed.), *Rawdon papers*, pp. 136–8, Dr Pett to Archbishop Bramhall, 8 Feb. 1662; *Hist. MSS Comm.*, 78, Rawdon–Hastings MSS, IV (1947), p. 129, Dr Edward Lake to John Bramhall, 5 April 1662.

I

Despite these problems of evidence it is still possible to categorise over three-quarters of the House of Lords on the basis of religious views. Three broad groupings of Catholics, Presbyterians and rigid Anglicans existed in the chamber.[4] The smallest group, the Catholics, was far greater in proportion than its counterpart in the Commons. No more than 2 per cent of the lower House consisted of Catholic or suspected Catholic MPs under Charles II, whereas they comprised 15 per cent of the Lords temporal.[5] Electors were unlikely to return known papists to the Commons. The Commons expelled those who refused to take the sacrament and conform to the Church of England.[6] Immune from electoral pressure, the Lords up to the anti-popish hysteria of 1672–4 adopted a more relaxed and pragmatic attitude to Catholic members, even punishing JPs who had indicted recusant peers during parliamentary privilege.[7] Catholic noblemen had enthusiastically served the Royalist cause in the 1640s and were thus deemed as deserving of parliamentary privilege as their Protestant brethren. All were entirely loyal to the king and, like the earl of Bristol, recognised the distinction between being a Catholic of the 'Church of Rome' and of the 'Court of Rome'.[8]

The widespread anti-popish phobia of the 1670s had a direct effect on the position of Catholic peers both in the administration and in the Lords. The 1673 Test Act, which had been rushed through the House with little opposition even from Catholic peers, incapacitated all persons refusing to take the Anglican sacrament and make a declaration against transubstantiation from holding either civil or military office.[9] Since few Catholic peers held offices, the impact of the Act on them as a group was limited.[10] Four Catholic lords, including the duke of York, held offices but these were surrendered in 1673.[11] However, Catholic peers' parliamentary privileges remained intact until the enactment of the 1678 Test Act. Drafted in the midst of the popish plot hysteria, this measure excluded persons from parliament who refused to make the declaration against transubstantiation and the invocation of the saints. Apart from the duke of York, who was exempted by a special proviso, and Lords St Albans, Rivers and Morley, who subscribed to the tests,

[4] See Appendix 1 for the religious designations of peers.
[5] Henning, *House of Commons*, I, p. 13.
[6] Ibid., p. 12.
[7] *LJ*, XI, 534; XII, 98–9.
[8] BL, Stowe MSS 182, fol. 90, Bristol's speech to the House of Commons, 1 July 1663.
[9] Haley, *Shaftesbury*, pp. 322–3.
[10] Miller, *Popery and politics*, pp. 65–6.
[11] At the beginning of 1673 these Catholic peers held government posts: Clifford (Lord Treasurer), Belasyse (lord lieutenant of the East Riding and governor of Hull), Bristol (governor of Deal Castle) and the duke of York (various civil and military offices).

Catholic peers ceased to sit in the House of Lords from 20 November 1678.[12]

The Catholics had rarely been a united group in the chamber. There is evidence from the Proxy Books that Catholic peers associated together: Lord Arundel of Wardour, for instance, was chosen on several occasions by Lords Cardigan, Langdale and Stourton to receive their proxies during their absences from parliament.[13] But there are nearly as many instances recorded of Protestant lords holding the proxies of Catholics.[14] On a variety of legislation, ranging from the Uniformity Bill to the government's 1675 Test, Catholic peers were divided.[15] During the mid-1670s several, notably Petre, Berkshire, Audley and Belasyse, voted with the Country party in the House against the government, whilst others, such as Bristol and St Albans, generally supported the Court party.[16]

It is not difficult to account for this lack of unity among Catholic lords. They did not possess strong and respected leaders. The most active Catholics, the earl of Bristol, Viscount Stafford and Lord Arundel of Wardour, were second- or even third-rate politicians, enjoying little influence in the chamber. None enjoyed followings like Shaftesbury and Danby. During the reign the Catholic aristocracy lost some of its most senior members. A lunatic held the once-prestigious dukedom of Norfolk up to 1677. The marquisates of Winchester and Worcester and the earldom of Shrewsbury all succumbed to Protestantism.

At the beginning of the reign Catholic peers were reasonably united. Their prime aim was to secure religious toleration for the English Catholic community. They intended to achieve this by modifying the Oath of Allegiance and repealing the penal laws. Despite enjoying the sympathy of the king and the support of the queen mother, their efforts were in vain.[17] From 1662 divisions within the Catholic group between those who favoured legislation and those who regarded the royal prerogative as the more realistic method of achieving toleration became manifest. In that year the earl of Bristol discarded his antipathy towards Protestant dissenters and started to court their support for a general toleration. At various occasions after this date the earl and other Catholics allied themselves with disaffected Protestants in the hope that their combined strength would force a toleration bill through parliament. At no time during the reign did the Anglican House of Commons contemplate giving relief to Catholics. After the cancellation of the

---

[12] *LJ* XIII, 396. Lords Rivers and St Albans were certainly Catholic sympathisers, though there is no clear evidence that they were practising Catholics in 1678.
[13] HLRO, Proxy Book 4 (5/12 March 1662); 5 (22 Nov. 1664, 21 Sept. 1666, 25 July and 14 Oct. 1667, 12 Nov. 1670); 6 (10 March 1677).
[14] Ibid., vols. 4–6.
[15] See chapter 10, pp. 187–94.
[16] For the voting behaviour of Catholic peers, see Swatland, 'The House of Lords', pp. 383–400.
[17] Their attempts to establish toleration are discussed further in chapter 10, pp. 187–9.

Declaration of Indulgence in 1673 most Catholic peers abandoned any remaining hopes of achieving toleration in Charles II's lifetime and contented themselves with resisting the additional constraints parliament endeavoured to impose on the Catholic community.

II

Useful though the Catholics were in supporting those seeking to ease restrictions on nonconformists, their influence in the Lords never approached that of the Presbyterians. This is not surprising as it was exceptional for more than twelve Catholics to be present during any one sitting, and in fact only thirty-seven took their seats between 1660 and 1678. In contrast approximately a hundred Presbyterians and probable Presbyterians (38 per cent of temporal lords eligible to sit between 1660 and 1681) entered the chamber during the reign.[18] Most historians have overlooked the existence of these peers.[19] Contemporaries, however, recognised them as an active force within the House. Writing to Lord Conway in July 1661, Sir John Finch mentioned 'the Presbiterian lords' participating in a debate on the bill to restore ecclesiastical jurisdiction.[20] In April 1662 Dr Edward Lake wrote about the support which the 'Presbiterian party in the House' gave to Lord Chancellor Clarendon as he sought to modify the Uniformity Bill.[21] Peers themselves commented on the existence of Presbyterian lords. In his memoirs Clarendon mentions 'the Presbyterian party', which 'was not without an interest in both houses of parliament', and also identifies leading Presbyterian peers, notably, the earls of Manchester and Northumberland.[22] The earl of Cardigan wrote about the presence of the 'Presbyterian lords' at the trial of his fellow Catholic peer, Lord Morley, in 1665.[23] Writing to Lord Bruce, probably in 1664 when the Conventicle Bill was undergoing a stormy passage through parliament, Lord Delamer (formally Sir George Booth) implored the Anglican lord and his associates to be 'merciful to us Presbiterians and at least give us leave to play innocently at bowls'.[24]

---

[18] Forty Catholic and possible Catholic peers were eligible to sit in the House, but the two Lords Vaux and the duke of Norfolk (1627–77), did not sit during the Restoration period, preferring to reside abroad. Presbyterians and probable Presbyterians are listed in Appendix 1.

[19] The only historian to focus on them as a group is Richard Davis in 'The "Presbyterian" opposition', pp. 1–35.

[20] Add. MSS 23,215, fol. 40, Sir John Finch to Lord Conway, 27 July 1661.

[21] *Hist. MSS Comm.*, 78, Rawdon–Hastings MSS, IV, 129, Lake to Bramhall, 5 April 1662.

[22] Clarendon, *Life*, II, p. 99.

[23] West Sussex RO, Winterton MSS 129, Cardigan to Edward Turner, 7 Nov. 1665.

[24] Wiltshire RO, Ailesbury papers, 1300/653, Delamer to Lord Bruce, undated, but internal evidence suggests a date of 1664.

There can be no doubt about the existence of a 'Presbyterian' group or faction in the restored House of Lords, but what was meant by the term 'Presbyterian' when applied to members of the nobility? It is only by examining the context in which contemporaries used the term that we can establish what constituted a Presbyterian lord in the Restoration period. Early in the Convention Parliament those old Parliamentarian lords of 1648 who wished to restrict membership of the House of Lords and place limitations on the king's powers were sometimes described as 'Presbyterians'.[25] However, their political objectives were quickly abandoned by early May 1660 and the 'Presbyterian' epithet was thereafter applied to mean something altogether different. Sir John Finch employed the term on 27 July 1661 to denote those peers who spoke against the bill to restore ecclesiastical jurisdiction in the hope of curbing the powers of the bishops.[26] Dr Lake used it to describe those lords who voted on 4 April 1662 to add Clarendon's famous proviso to the Bill of Uniformity, in order to retain moderate Presbyterian ministers in the Church by dispensing them from wearing the surplice and signing with the cross in baptism.[27] Clarendon refers to an attempt by the Presbyterian earl of Northumberland in the House of Lords in 1662 to confirm the 1604 Book of Common Prayer (instead of the revised Prayer Book of 1662) along with the Elizabethan Act of Uniformity, which was far less prescriptive in terms of rites and ceremonies than the new Bill of Uniformity, and therefore was more acceptable to moderate Presbyterian ministers.[28]

When used in a religious context contemporaries used 'Presbyterian' in 1661 to mean peers who favoured restraints on the powers of the bishops and from 1662 lords who advocated a comprehensive Church, that included moderate Presbyterian ministers. As we shall see in subsequent chapters, this second objective remained dear to most Presbyterian peers for the rest of the reign. Peers who held these objectives included Albemarle, Manchester, Northumberland, Bedford and Holles.[29] There was, however, a third characteristic which distinguished Presbyterians from other lords and this was a desire to procure toleration for those peaceable Protestant dissenters who wished to worship outside the Church of England. It manifested itself first in the Lords during the debates on the government's Indulgence Bill, which was

[25] *Cal. Cl. SP*, IV, 682, Lady Bristol to Hyde, 27 April 1660; 683, Warwick to Hyde, 27 April.
[26] Add. MSS 23,215, fol. 40. Clarendon alludes to Presbyterian peers' concern over bishops' powers in 1661 in his *Life*, II, pp. 99–101.
[27] Rawdon–Hastings MSS, IV, 129.
[28] Clarendon, *Life*, II, pp. 128–9. Clarendon says that Northumberland was 'known to be of the Presbyterian party'.
[29] Joan Thirsk (ed.), *The Restoration* (1976), p. 41; Lacey, *Dissent and parliamentary politics*, pp. 463–4, 466–8; *Cal. Cl. SP*, IV, 654, Baker to Hyde, 13 April 1660; Clarendon, *Life*, II, pp. 128–9, 367; Green, *The re-Establishment of the Church of England*, p. 19.

introduced by Lord Robartes on 23 February 1663 and promoted by Ashley and Manchester.[30] Other peers known to have favoured toleration during the reign included Wharton, Anglesey, Buckingham, Salisbury, Pembroke, Delamer, Denbigh and Saye and Sele (1582–1662).[31] 'Presbyterian' is used in this study, as it was by most contemporaries from 1662, to denote those peers who were sympathetic to the cause of peaceable Protestant dissenters.[32]

Presbyterian peers held a variety of strongly Protestant views and opinions. Most revealing are the earl of Anglesey's two diaries preserved in the British Library. In these the former Parliamentarian portrayed himself as an advocate of modified episcopacy and someone anxious to purify the Church of what he regarded as popish ceremonial practices.[33] In a tract published anonymously, he urged that 'an episcopal Calvinist is the highest son or father of the Church of England'.[34] John, Lord Crew's letters to his friend and agent John Swinfen provide a window into the mind of a Presbyterian peer. Writing during the 1670s, Crew explored a range of subjects including the ugliness of sin, God's mercy and wisdom, and the importance of daily Bible study (particularly of the Old Testament) in attaining salvation.[35] Several others, most notably Bedford, Saye and Sele (1582–1662), Wharton and Clare (1633–89), have left evidence that they too shared similar Calvinist views.[36]

Almost all Presbyterian lords conformed to the rites and ceremonies of the established Church, although a few also attended nonconformist services in their own houses. Lords Holles, Anglesey, Delamer and Bedford heard readings from the Book of Common Prayer in their parish church on Sunday

---

[30] Clarendon, *Life*, II, pp. 342–50; Seaward, pp. 181–3; Haley, *Shaftesbury*, pp. 164–6.

[31] Probably only a minority of Presbyterian peers advocated toleration at this time, but by the mid-1670s, when it was apparent that the government had abandoned its policy of broadening the Church, a greater proportion of Presbyterian lords supported toleration. Seaward, pp. 30, 31, 181, 189; Lacey, *Dissent and parliamentary politics*, pp. 459–63, 464–6, 472–5; Burnet, *History*, I, 454; A. G. Matthews (ed.), *Calamy revised: being a revision of Edmund Calamy's account of the ministers and others ejected and silenced, 1660–62* (Oxford, 1934), pp. 177, 328, 342.

[32] The label 'Presbyterian' was applied as a result of parliamentary behaviour. All the contemporary writers cited in this section of the chapter used the label in a parliamentary context. I have only found one example of it applied as a result of non-parliamentary behaviour, by the Staffordshire gentry to Lord Paget (1609–78). See R. M. Kidson (ed.), 'The gentry of Staffordshire, 1662–63', in *Collections for a history of Staffordshire*, II, p. 40. My definition of a Presbyterian peer is necessarily broad, incorporating those who sought a comprehensive church and those who wanted toleration for peaceable nonconformists, but is based firmly on contemporary usage. It accords closely with that offered by Richard Davis: a peer presumed to be favourable to protestant dissenters ('The "Presbyterian" opposition', p. 6).

[33] Add. MSS 40,860, fols. 5–7, 43, 52, 59, 60 *passim*; 18,730, fols. 23, 26, 36, 42.

[34] *The truth unvailed in behalf of the Church of England* (1676), pp. 28, 33–9.

[35] Bedfordshire RO, Lucas Collection: Letters from Lord Crew to John Swinfen, L30/20/2, 19 Sept. 1671, /3, 30 Dec. 1671, /5, 10 Feb. 1672, /8, 30 July 1672, /9, 8 Oct. 1672, /10, 31 Dec. 1672.

[36] Lacey, *Dissent and parliamentary politics*, pp. 463–4, 472–5; Add. MSS 30,013, fol. 28, Lord Paget to John Swinfen, 26 Nov. 1681; Ward, 'The English peerage', p. 250.

mornings and in the afternoon enjoyed the sermons of their own resident nonconformist chaplains.[37] Other peers known to have kept Presbyterian chaplains in their households during the 1660s and 1670s were the duke of Albemarle, Viscount Saye and Sele (died 1662) and Lord Wharton.[38] Ejected Presbyterian ministers were protected by Presbyterian peers. Warwick, Denbigh and Devonshire were their patrons in Essex, Warwickshire and Derbyshire respectively. The earl of Bedford made substantial donations to nonconformists in 1661 and 1664.[39]

Very few peers belonged to nonconformist sects. One who did, Lord Wharton, was in fact arrested in 1675 whilst attending an illegal service conducted by the dissenting minister, Dr Thomas Manton.[40] From his letters it is apparent that the baron was in close contact with nonconformist ministers, including the Presbyterian Samuel Hieron and the congregationalists Lewis Stukely and Thomas Gilbert.[41] The fifth earl of Pembroke, the earl of Newport and Lord Herbert of Cherbury (1633–78) had considerable sympathy with Quakerism. Pembroke and Newport had attended Quaker meetings immediately prior to the Restoration. As a practising Friend Pembroke presented a Quaker petition to the Lords in May 1661 and chaired the committee appointed to examine it.[42] William Howard, third baron Howard of Escrick, had reputedly been an Anabaptist preacher in the 1650s, but it is not clear whether he still held Baptist beliefs when he succeeded to his title in 1678.[43]

Very few Presbyterian lords wanted to include the more extreme sects, particularly Quakers and Baptists, in a general toleration. Venner's attempted rebellion of 1661 underlined the threat they presented to public order. Two Presbyterians, the earl of Northumberland and Viscount Fauconberg, perceived that the greatest challenge to law and order came from Quaker and Baptist leaders, and in their capacities as lord lieutenants had such men imprisoned. Yet both favoured some degree of toleration for peaceable nonconformists.[44] The Interregnum admiral, Edward Montagu, created earl

[37] Lacey, ibid., pp. 460, 463–4, 466–8.
[38] Ibid., pp. 472–5; Matthews (ed.), *Calamy revised*, pp. 103, 156, 270, 325, 355.
[39] *Calamy revised*, pp. 55, 328, 342; Hutton, *Charles II*, pp. 163–4; Lacey, *Dissent and parliamentary politics*, pp. 463–4.
[40] *Hist. MSS Comm.*, 45, MSS of the duke of Buccleuch and Queensberry, vol. 1 (1899), 321, William Montagu to Lord Montagu, 4 March 1675.
[41] Lacey, *Dissent and parliamentary politics*, pp. 473–5.
[42] Friends House Library, A. R. Barclay MSS I, fol. 40, Edward Burrough to Francis Howgill, 24 Sept. 1658. Pembroke was still a Quaker in 1665. See *Hist. MSS Comm.*, 78, Rawdon–Hastings MSS, II (1930), pp. 150–1, J. Jaques to Lord Huntingdon, 27 April 1665. Lord Herbert had close connections with Quakers on the English–Welsh border (*DNB* 26, p. 180). For the Quaker petition see HLRO, Main Papers, 6 June 1661 and Committee Minutes 1, p. 12.
[43] *GEC*, VI, pp. 586–7.
[44] For Northumberland see West Sussex RO, Wiston MSS 5426/2, Northumberland to the deputy lieutenants of Sussex, 3 Sept. 1661, /3 same to same, 5 Sept. 1661, and for Fauconberg see Durham University Library, Mickleton and Spearman MSS 31, fol. 55r, Fauconberg to Bishop Cosin, 18 Aug. 1665.

of Sandwich in 1660, found the sects abhorrent, preferring 'uniformity and form of prayer'. Nevertheless, he disliked religious persecution, and, like most other Presbyterian lords, advocated the establishment of a comprehensive Church after the Restoration.[45]

There was a close correlation between Civil War Parliamentarians and post-1660 Presbyterian lords. In spite of the upheavals of the 1640s and 1650s, the vast majority of former Parliamentarians – there were over forty who sat in the Lords in 1661 – were Presbyterians. They included the earls of Manchester, Bedford, Scarsdale, Stamford, Salisbury, Clare, Leicester, Denbigh, Warwick, Anglesey, Carlisle, Pembroke and Northumberland; viscounts Fauconberg, Hereford and Saye and Sele, and barons Ashley, Crew, Delamer, Eure, Holles, Howard of Escrick, Hunsdon, Paget, Robartes, Townshend, North and Wharton.[46] Most peers and MPs who had espoused the Parliamentarian cause after 1642 had become alienated from the Church of England by the Laudian innovations of the 1630s, and identified the Parliamentarian cause with their desire for church reform. With the restoration of the monarchy they, like Charles II, were not opposed to episcopacy, but had no desire to revive a Laudian-style church establishment. Wharton, in particular, was so stirred by memories of Laud that when he entered the House of Lords on 25 April 1660, 'looking on the bench where the archbishop did sit, ... his blood did rise to see where that cursed man did sit'.[47]

Former Parliamentarians were not the only Protestant lords to express concern over the plight of dissenters after 1660. Almost thirty lords who had had no close connection with the Parliamentarian cause favoured a broad Church which embraced some nonconformist ministers.[48] Some, like Buckingham, Berkeley, Burlington and Lucas had in fact borne arms for the Royalists. Others such as Rochester, Essex, Cornwallis, Chesterfield, Lovelace and Halifax were closely related to Royalist soldiers. By all these peers a policy of clemency and moderation to peaceable dissenters was deemed preferable to one of severity and persecution. Southampton and Lucas criticised the Five Mile Bill of 1665 because it enjoined ejected ministers to take an oath repudiating any alteration of the Act of Uniformity, even through peaceful means. It was feared that this would leave dissenters humiliated and with no option but to resort to violence to achieve their aims.[49]

There is no simple explanation of why peers should have sympathised with dissenting Protestants in the years after 1660. For some the answer lies with their education and the religious practices of their parents. A high propor-

[45] Pepys, I, pp. 125–6; Harris, *Life of Sandwich*, II, pp. 199, 291; *LJ*, XI, 570, 572.
[46] These peers are listed in Appendix 1.
[47] Bodl., Clarendon MSS 72, fol. 59, J. Butts to Hyde, 27 April 1660. For the impact of the Laudian innovations on these peers see Adamson, 'Peerage in politics', pp. 29–30.
[48] See Appendix 1.
[49] C. Robbins, 'The Oxford session', pp. 221–2.

tion of old parliamentarian peers had been educated in pre-Laudian Cambridge. Some, such as Denbigh, Manchester and Montagu, belonged to those colleges which had been centres of Puritan teaching like Emmanuel and Sidney Sussex.[50] The earl of Lincoln (1600–67) had been tutored by the pious Puritan Preston. Several peers of a similar religious outlook had finished off their formal education at an inn of court, where again reformed religious views often prevailed.

Parents' religious views had in some cases a considerable impact on their sons. William Russell, earl of Bedford, almost certainly derived his Puritan outlook from his father, the fourth earl, who was a staunch Calvinist.[51] The aforementioned earl of Lincoln was the son of a Calvinist matriarch, Elizabeth Clinton. Such 'Puritan' family traditions often survived the political and religious vicissitudes of the Civil War and Interregnum only to manifest themselves in the actions of former Parliamentarians and their sons in the Restoration period. The heirs of Parliamentarians, like Lords Holles (1627–90), Grey of Wark (1655–1701), Paget (1637–1713), and Salisbury (1648–83), all gravitated towards the 'Puritan' tradition of their families.[52]

A further explanation, and one that may account for the flexible attitude of peers without Puritan ancestries, concerns the religious climate of the 1650s. The religious atmosphere during this decade was more relaxed than it had been during either the 1630s or 1640s. It is possible that the development under Cromwell of a more comprehensive church, with *de facto* toleration for most Christians who were unable to accommodate themselves within it, demonstrated that toleration for religious minorities did not necessarily jeopardise law and order.[53] Clearly much depended on an individual's temperament. To many ardently Anglican-Royalist peers the political and religious upheavals of that decade served to reinforce their desire for religious conformity and for severe penalties against those who dissented from the established church.[54]

There was a tendency for Royalists who had resided in England during the 1650s, in particular Southampton, Essex, Dorset, Strafford and Lucas, to be more flexible in religious matters than many of those who had fled abroad after the Civil War to join Charles II's court in exile.[55] This may help to

---

[50] Seaward, 'Court and parliament', pp. 43–4.
[51] N. Tyacke, 'Puritanism, Arminianism and counter-revolution', in C. Russell (ed.), *The origins of the English Civil War* (1978), p. 136. For the Lords the term 'Puritan' was almost synonymous with 'Presbyterian'.
[52] Swatland, 'The House of Lords', p. 187 and Appendix II B.
[53] C. Cross, 'The church in England 1646–1660', in G. E. Aylmer (ed.), *The Interregnum: the quest for settlement 1646–1660* (1979 edn), p. 99; Ward, 'The English peerage', p. 254. Ward argues that a strong sense of religious toleration existed throughout the peerage during this decade and gained in intensity as the Restoration approached.
[54] G. R. Cragg, *From Puritanism to the age of reason* (Cambridge, 1966), pp. 1, 156–66.
[55] This is borne out by I. Ward's recent study of the peerage in the 1650s (Ward, 'The English peerage', pp. 208–54).

explain why the young earl of Dorset (1622–77) wrote after the Restoration that 'no religion that is true can enjoin persecution of any person merely for being of another or different opinion, just because it is unreasonable for any man to be punished for what he cannot help'. Religious persecution, he continued, was against 'our Saviour's doctrine ... that we should love one another and do nothing that we would not have done to ourselves'.[56] The second earl of Strafford also urged a sympathetic approach to dissenters, arguing in 1670 that were concessions offered, many nonconformists would return to the Church of England. These concessions involved dispensing ministers from using the cross in baptism, the ring in marriage, wearing a surplice and other 'lesser matters' incorporated in the 1674 Comprehension Bill.[57]

In the Lords, Presbyterian peers and their sympathisers were an influential minority throughout the reign. During the early 1660s the king relied upon them to amend religious legislation, such as the Ministers' and Uniformity Bills, according to his expressed wishes. It is likely that because of their known sympathy towards Protestant dissenters the king and his leading ministers, several of whom were Presbyterians themselves, chose the upper House for the attempted modification of the church settlement after 1662. During the 1670s Presbyterian peers played an important role in criticising government policies as members of the Country party.[58]

III

The staunchest defenders of the church settlement were rigidly Anglican members of the House. At most this element comprised 45 per cent of the total membership of the House for the period 1660 to 1681: a lower percentage than in the Cavalier Commons.[59] There was a close connection between former Royalists and rigid Anglicans; often they were one and the same person.[60] To many Royalist peers the Cavalier cause had seemed the best guarantor of the continued existence of the Church of England in the 1640s. In 1660 they regarded its re-establishment as the surest bulwark against sectarianism and republicanism. Like their counterparts in the Commons, their innate conservatism served to strengthen their desire for religious unity and

---

[56] Kent Archives Office, Sackville MSS U269/C20, fol. 86, Dorset's notes on religion, undated, but *c.* 1672–3.

[57] *Hist. MSS Comm.*, 58 Bath MSS II, p. 152, Strafford to Gervase Holles, 1 May 1670, pp. 155–6, same to same, 13 Oct. 1673.

[58] This subject is explored in chapter 11 of this book.

[59] Henning, *House of Commons*, I, p. 13. It is difficult to make a meaningful comparison with the Commons because Henning has only two categories of Anglicans: 'Anglicans' and 'Probable Anglicans'. For the five parliaments of the reign they comprised 68 per cent of the total membership.

[60] See Appendix 1.

social harmony.[61] Many had a profound affection for a church which they had known since childhood. The views of the duke of Newcastle were typical of many rigid Anglicans. He traced the origins of the Civil War to religious fanaticism. Episcopacy was the only form of church government compatible with monarchy, which popery and Presbyterianism, he believed, sought to destroy. The duke advocated the re-establishment of the Church of England in 1660 so that the king's subjects would have 'an easy and sweet government' in comparison with the 'other two most tyrannical governments either of popery or Presbytery'.[62]

There is surprisingly little evidence of the views of rigid Anglican peers on the character of the church at the Restoration. That they demanded the restoration of a church governed by bishops and urged Charles II to settle religion 'as it was in the time of his royal grandfather and father of ever blessed memory' is not open to question.[63] It is possible that some, most notably Bishop Sheldon, did initially contemplate making minor concessions to enable Presbyterians to conform, but after the passing of the Act of Uniformity refused any further negotiations with nonconformists.[64] They were opposed to any form of liberty of worship for Presbyterians and members of the sects. Among the most extreme Anglicans were those who protested on 25 July 1663 against an amendment inserted in an 'Act for the relief of such persons as by sickness or other impediment were disabled from subscribing the Declaration in the Act of Uniformity'. These peers, who included the duke of York, and Lords Northampton, Peterborough, Derby, Mordaunt and Gerard, particularly objected to the amendment stating 'that the declaration and subscription of assent and consent' to the Prayer Book in the Act of Uniformity 'shall be understood only as to the practice and obedience to the said Act and not otherwise'. Dissenters had vehemently criticised the assent and consent clause in the 1662 Act because it implied that they considered everything in the Book of Common Prayer to be perfect.[65] The incorporation of the words 'practice and obedience' was an attempt to overcome dissenters' scruples by making conformity a question of outward obedience, with no recognition of inner conviction. York and Northampton together with several bishops openly displayed their intolerance of nonconformists during the debate on the controversial Five Mile Bill on 30 October 1665. They regarded dissenting preachers as seditious influences in towns and

[61] Cragg, *Puritanism to the age of reason*, pp. 1–4, 157–66, 191–4.
[62] C. H. Firth (ed.), *Memoirs of William Cavendish duke of Newcastle and Margaret his wife* (1907), p. xxiii.
[63] R. A. Beddard, 'The Restoration Church', in J. R. Jones (ed.), *The restored monarchy 1660–1688* (1979), p. 161; *Mercurius Publicus*, no. 24 (7–14 June 1660): petition of the Somerset nobility and gentry.
[64] Thirsk (ed.), *The Restoration*, p. 65.
[65] Committee Minutes 1, p. 436 (25 July 1663); Clarendon, *Life*, I, pp. 556–7; *LJ*, XI, 573.

cities, undermining the work of the established clergy with their preaching in public places.[66]

Staunchly Anglican peers sought to impose severe penalties upon dissenters, and especially members of the sects, whom they regarded as posing the greatest threat to internal security. They were the principal supporters of those measures directed against nonconformists, known collectively today as the 'Clarendon Code'.[67] The earl of Northampton often 'boldly spoke in parliament' against Quakers and Baptists, and his enforcement of the Corporation Act in Coventry in 1662 was thorough indeed, purging the borough of those he termed the king's 'implacable enemies'.[68] By far the most zealous and industrious rigid Anglican in the chamber was the earl of Bridgewater. Bridgewater chaired almost every committee considering religious legislation from 1660 to 1680.[69] With regard to the Uniformity Bill, a contemporary noted that the earl was as 'zealous ... as any in the house'.[70]

In contrast with Presbyterian peers, between 1662 and 1674 rigid Anglicans rarely supported government and episcopal attempts to modify the Church settlement and establish a more comprehensive Church.[71] They were among the king's most vociferous critics when his measures to relieve Catholics were debated in the chamber. Staunchly Anglican peers condemned the Declarations of Indulgence of 1662 and 1672 respectively.[72] Yet after 1675, when Charles II openly endorsed the conservative Anglican policies associated with the earl of Danby's ministry, these peers not only regularly supported the government in debates, but also provided the Lord Treasurer with the nucleus of his Court party.[73]

IV

Among the government's most ardent adherents in the House after 1675 were the bishops, or at least those holding uncompromisingly Anglican opinions. To some extent the differences of opinion that existed within the Protestant peerage were mirrored by the bench of bishops. Seeking to establish an episcopate which reflected the range of opinions that existed within the church as it stood at the outset of his reign, the king appointed bishops from diverse religious backgrounds. These included Laudians such as Juxon and Wren, uncompromising Anglicans, notably Sheldon and Henchman, Calvinists, in

---

[66] Carte MSS 80, fols, 757–9: Wharton's notes on the debate, 30 Oct. 1665.
[67] See chapter 9, pp. 164, 165–6, 169–70.
[68] Clarendon MSS 77, fol. 236, Northampton to the king, 18 Aug. 1662.
[69] For Bridgewater's chairmanship of committees see Committee Minutes vols. 1–3 (1661–81).
[70] Bodl., English Letters, C 210, fols. 69–70, Sir Henry Yelverton to Archdeacon Palmer, 29 Jan. 1662.
[71] See chapters 9 and 10 of this study.
[72] See below, pp. 173–4, 189, 236, 241
[73] This feature is discussed in depth in chapter 12, pp. 246–59.

particular Reynolds and Gauden, and Commonwealth conformists, such as Edward Rainbow and Ralph Brideoake.[74] The result of this Erastian policy was that approximately a quarter of the prelates who sat in the House during the reign preferred a broader church than that established in 1662.[75]

Several members of this minority group of prelates have revealed their views both in their writings and in their actions on the floor of the House. It is evident from the published works of Bishops Sanderson, Gauden and Croft that they regarded a united Protestant church as essential for maintaining peace and stability in the nation as a whole.[76] To them the prosecution of all categories of nonconformists would never create religious unity. Recognising that liturgical differences kept Protestants apart they proposed minor liturgical and ceremonial changes as a means of bringing dissenters back into the established church.[77] Although a majority of bishops feared such concessions would create a schism, at least seven, including Morley of Winchester, Ward of Salisbury, Pearson of Chester, Wood of Coventry, Fuller of Lincoln and Dolben of Rochester, promoted a Comprehension Bill in the House in 1674.[78] The bill tried to eliminate some of the Presbyterian ministers' main objections to the Act of Uniformity by providing for the repeal of the assent and consent clause and the declaration renouncing the Covenant.[79] The following year Bishop Herbert Croft went even further in his anonymously published pamphlet, *The naked truth*, in which he suggested that the liturgy and ceremonies should be optional, and Presbyterian ordination should be recognised as legitimate in the Church of England.[80] Apart from Bishop Gauden, who favoured freedom of worship for most nonconformists, prelates of the Restoration period did not, however, advocate toleration.[81]

Prior to 1675 when the privy council ordered all JPs vigorously to execute the penal laws against dissenters, the king's ministers had marshalled the votes of sympathetic bishops to assist them in establishing a broad Church of England. At least four – Reynolds, Gauden, Morley and Sanderson – aided Clarendon in the revision of the controversial Ministers' Bill in favour of Presbyterian clerics early in 1662.[82] Later that year the same bishops rallied

---

[74] Green, *The re-establishment of the Church of England*, p. 90; J. Spurr, *The Restoration Church of England 1646–1689* (Yale, 1991), pp. 315–16.

[75] See Appendix 2.

[76] These works are summarised in Cragg, *From Puritanism to the age of reason*, pp. 61–75.

[77] Ibid., pp. 28, 198, 214–15.

[78] BL, Tanner MSS 44, fol. 249, J. Lowland to Sancroft, 21 Feb. 1674 (misdated 1671); 42, fol. 89, J. Tillotson to Sancroft, 23 Feb. 1674; Add. MSS 23,136, fol. 98, Robert Moray to Lauderdale, 21 Feb. 1674.

[79] HLRO, Main Papers, 170, fols. 68–9, draft of Comprehension Bill.

[80] See John Spurr, 'Anglican apologetic and the Restoration Church' (University of Oxford DPhil thesis, 1985), pp. 114–21 for a discussion of Croft's ideas.

[81] BL, Sloane MSS 4164, fol. 341, Gauden to the earl of Bristol, 1 May 1662.

[82] See chapter 9, pp. 161–2.

to the royal banner when the earl of Bristol challenged the legality of the
king's proviso to exempt individual ministers from wearing the surplice and
signing with the cross in baptisms during an emotive debate on the
Uniformity Bill.[83] Staunchly Anglican Cosin of Durham was so firmly
opposed to such concessions that he spoke in support of the Catholic earl's
criticisms of the amendment.[84]

For much of the early 1660s Cosin and his fiercely Anglican colleagues on
the bishops' bench vehemently criticised those royal policies which they
believed undermined the church settlement. In December 1662 Sheldon of
London urged his fellow prelates to attend the forthcoming session and block
Court attempts to transform the Declaration of Indulgence into an act of parliament.[85] They also spearheaded subsequent parliamentary campaigns
against dissenters, promoting legislation in the House and at committees.
Archbishop Frewen of York was a leading advocate of the two Conventicle
Bills of 1663 and 1664, and it is evident from Bishop Henchman's journal
that bishops of a similar stamp were amongst those lords most anxious for
the upper House to pass the 1664 measure unamended.[86] The following year
at Oxford two of their number, including Archbishop Sheldon, led the proponents of the Five Mile Bill during an acrimonious debate in the House. It
is apparent from Lord Wharton's notes that they regarded dissenting
preachers as a major threat to law and order in corporations.[87]

Differences of opinion on religious subjects were a recurring feature of the
restored House of Lords, especially during the early 1660s when parliament
was formulating the series of measures that constituted the church settlement.
Yet without exception all subsequent major pieces of religious legislation
provoked bitter debates in the Lords. This feature of Restoration parliamentary politics owed much to the religious composition of the House itself
and is examined in the next two chapters.

[83] Add. MSS 22,919, fol. 203, Morrice to Downing, 21 March 1662.
[84] Ibid.
[85] Tanner MSS 48, fol. 69, Sheldon to Frewen, 6 December 1662; G. Ornsby (ed.), *The correspondence of John Cosin*, p. 101, Sheldon to Cosin, 26 Dec. 1662.
[86] Ibid., p. 106, Frewen to Cosin, 10 May 1663; Bodl., Rawlinson MSS A. 130, fol. 17, 13 May
1664.
[87] Carte MSS 80, fols. 757–9.

9

Church settlement

When in his Declaration of Breda (April 1660) Charles II appealed to his English subjects for unity he knew that religious differences were among the chief causes of disunion.[1] The recently restored upper House, like the court, was not united on religious issues during the summer and autumn of 1660, though divisions between Presbyterians, 'rigid' Anglicans and Catholic lords did not become manifest until 1662.[2] There were those peers who thought that religious unity could best be achieved by compelling obedience to a restored Anglican church, and others, including Presbyterians in both Houses, the king and most of his influential advisers, who preferred a relaxation of the laws against dissenters and accordingly proposed concessions on church ceremonial and the liturgy to encourage moderate dissenters to conform to a broad national church. The king's preferred religious settlement ultimately failed because of opposition from both intolerant country gentlemen and many of his own courtiers and government officials who dominated the Cavalier House of Commons.[3] The Lords was usually more receptive to the king's religious policies in the early 1660s than the House of Commons. This feature, together with its role in the making of the church settlement, provide the main focus for this chapter.

I

When the king set foot on English soil on 26 May 1660, that great pillar of the monarchy, the Anglican church, no longer existed. It had been replaced first by a Presbyterian model and later under Cromwell by a broadly based national church, with toleration for peaceable nonconformist Protestant groups. Yet a strong attachment to Anglican practice persisted through all levels of society despite efforts by the Interregnum regimes to suppress it.

[1] Kenyon, *Stuart constitution*, pp. 357–8.
[2] Divisions between rigid Anglicans and Presbyterians were particularly noticeable during the proceedings on the Bill to confirm the 1660 Ministers' Act and the Bill of Uniformity.
[3] Seaward, p. 163.

159

I. Ward has shown that Anglican peers such as Hatton, Hertford, Devonshire and Dorset retained Anglican chaplains in their households and regularly received communion in private.[4]

As the Restoration approached, a strong feeling of conciliation pervaded the peerage, with few lords openly taking rigid positions on the character of a future national church.[5] A majority of the Convention House of Lords, like Charles II himself, favoured the establishment of a traditional Church of England that accommodated moderate Presbyterians. A flexible attitude towards religious issues was one of the characteristics of the Convention Lords. This is not to deny that there were religious disagreements within the House in 1660; there were differences of opinion during the debates on the Ministers' Bill, for example, but the differences that did exist were normally eclipsed by a general desire for compromise and conciliation.[6]

This last feature is illustrated by the peers' response to the problem of the parish clergy. Many Anglican clerics had been ejected from their livings in the 1640s for Royalism or 'scandalous' behaviour. The vast majority of those holding livings in 1660 were either Presbyterians or Anglicans who had conformed during the 1650s. Naturally when the restoration of Charles Stuart was almost certain the ejected clergy hoped to regain their livings. Recognising the seriousness of the problem, the Commons prepared a bill in the second week of May for confirming the 'rights' of existing incumbents, but it had not passed that House by the time the king returned. Charles II was placed in an almost impossible situation. Were he to brush aside the claims of ejected Anglican clergymen he risked angering his Anglican supporters, while the removal of existing incumbents might alienate those Presbyterian politicians who had helped to make a Stuart restoration possible. After lengthy discussions with his ministers and moderate Presbyterians Charles II chose a middle course: all those who had entered into livings whose lawful incumbents were dead should continue in them, whilst financial provision should be made for ejected ministers still alive. Fearful of unrest in the provinces, the king issued a proclamation on 1 July that no incumbent was to be removed except 'by due course of law' or order of parliament.[7]

During the early summer ejected or 'sequestered' clerics petitioned the House of Lords for part of the revenue of their former livings, prompting the peers to make two orders on 22 and 23 June. The profits of the livings of ejected clergy were to be secured by churchwardens or overseers of the poor until the title of each living was determined, and sequestered ministers

[4] Ward, 'The English peerage', pp. 208–17.
[5] Ibid., p. 254.
[6] Green, *Re-establishment of the Church of England*, pp. 7, 8, 30–2.
[7] Ibid., p. 41.

were to be paid the fifth of the revenue due to them for their maintenance.[8]

The Commons' Bill for Confirming and Restoring Ministers reached the Lords in early September and was promptly referred to a large committee whose composition reflected the breadth of religious views existing in the House.[9] Chaired by the congregational peer, Lord Wharton, it made several amendments favourable to sequestered ministers, the most significant being the removal of a clause for vetting them prior to the title of a living being decided.[10] If Cavalier-Anglican peers sought a more extensive purge the mood of the House was certainly against it. Presbyterian peers wanted to retain a greater number of Cromwellian clerics than the majority in either House would allow.[11] The measure which received the royal assent represented a compromise between the wishes of rigid Anglicans in both chambers and the desires of moderate Presbyterian members and, as I. M. Green argues, closely resembled royal policy.[12] It unconditionally confirmed all incumbents who had served in cures on 25 December 1659. Those who held livings claimed by sequestered ministers, or where the lawful patron had made a presentation but his nominee had been refused admission by the Triers 'without lawful cause', had to surrender them. The statute also provided for the ejection of the tiny minority of ministers who had petitioned for the execution of Charles I, opposed the Restoration or were Baptists.[13]

The revelations of Presbyterian and Republican plots early in 1661 and the election of a predominantly Anglican House of Commons led to marked hostility, especially in the Commons, towards the Presbyterian clergy confirmed in their livings by the Convention. This hostility became apparent during the autumn and winter when the Commons extensively altered the Ministers' Act prior to its inclusion in a bill for confirming three Acts passed by the Convention. The Commons' revisions would have imposed stiffer tests of conformity than those required by the Bill of Uniformity in its early stages.[14] Ministers not episcopally ordained were to be ejected and any holding a sequestered living was to compensate his predecessor with a fifth of its profits. But the most far-reaching amendment was that all incumbents were to make a declaration against the Covenant and acknowledge the illegality

[8] *LJ*, XI, 72–3; HLRO, Main Papers 31 Aug.–8 Sept. 1660, fol. 43, petition of Christopher Stone; Huntingdon RO, Manchester Collection, DDM 32/9/8, 11, 14, 19, petitions of Thomas Warren, Roger Flint, Edward Perkins and Richard Golty, 1660.

[9] The figures were: 14 Presbyterians, 15 Anglican-Royalists and 5 Catholics.

[10] *LJ*, XI, 167–8.

[11] Green, *Re-establishment of the Church of England*, p. 40; Bodl. Dep. F. 9, Seymour Bowman's parliamentary diary, 1660, fols. 78, 103–8, 135–6.

[12] Ibid., p. 40.

[13] *Statutes*, V, 12 Car. II, c. 17, 242–6.

[14] *CJ*, VIII, 275, 278, 322, 324–5, 330–1, 332; Carte MSS 81, fols. 152–5, Lord Wharton's copy of the Uniformity Bill as it was sent from the Commons.

of resistance to Charles II.[15] Notwithstanding strong criticism from both Presbyterian and government MPs, the Bill eventually passed the Commons on 8 January 1662.

Such was the threat posed by the measure to the king's policy of comprehending moderate Presbyterian clerics within the church (the measure would have resulted in their complete ejection) that the most senior government manager in the Lords, Lord Chancellor Clarendon, used all his skills of persuasion to muster a majority against the Commons' amendments. Since the readmission of the twenty-six bishops in the previous November, orthodox Anglican lords were in a distinct majority and without careful management there was a very real possibility that the Lords would pass the bill with the Commons' provisos intact. Opinion in the Lords was in fact so evenly balanced that the vote on whether the committee of the whole House 'shall be restrained to the confirming of the said act without the provisos, only with a liberty to speak to the point of ordination' was tied with forty on each side on 29 January, thus defeating the motion.[16] Alarmed by this vote Clarendon persuaded seven bishops, the duke of York, the earl of Bristol and all the Catholic lords to vote against the Commons' amendments.[17] Accordingly on 3 February the committee voted to confirm the 1660 Act without any alterations. Inflamed by the Lords' decision, the Commons requested a conference, but this did not take place, for it seems that Clarendon, acting on royal instructions, had promised the lower House that many of their amendments would be inserted in the Uniformity Bill as it progressed through the House of Lords.[18]

II

The second major religious problem confronting the Lords was episcopacy. Two main issues were involved: the restoration of the bishops to the House of Lords and what powers they should have. The bishops had been excluded from the Lords at the beginning of 1642 and episcopacy itself was abolished the following year. Charles II delayed appointing bishops to the fourteen vacant sees until the autumn of 1660, hoping to persuade moderate Presbyterians, like Reynolds, Baxter and Calamy, to become bishops, presumably as the first step towards establishing a diverse bench of bishops that

---

[15] *Hist. MSS Comm.*, Hastings MSS, IV, pp. 124–5, Parker to Bramhall, 14 Dec. 1661; Committee Minutes 1, pp. 163–5, 169; Seaward, p. 173.

[16] *LJ*, XI, 364, 373; Bodl., MSS Eng. Lett. c. 210, fol. 69, Sir Henry Yelverton to Archdeacon Palmer, 29 Jan. 1662.

[17] Berwick (ed.), *The Rawdon papers*, pp. 136–8, Dr Pett to Archbishop Bramhall, 8 Feb. 1662; *The Mather Papers* (Collections of the Massachusetts Historical Society, 4th series, VIII, 1868), p. 194, Hooke to Davenport, 31 March 1662.

[18] Committee Minutes 1, p. 152, 27 Feb. 1662; Seaward, p. 174.

reflected many of the religious opinions that existed among the clergy.[19] Charles and Hyde intended the bishops to exercise their duties of ordination and correction, not in the manner of Laudian prelates, but with the voluntary cooperation of the senior parish clergy in their dioceses. They hoped this modified style of church government would meet the objections of moderate Presbyterians to episcopacy and would also prove acceptable to a majority of Anglicans. Among the Presbyterians in the upper House were many like Manchester, Robartes, Northumberland, Wharton, Leicester and Saye and Sele, who preferred a modified form of episcopacy with strict limits on the bishops' powers.[20]

The desire of these peers to contain the authority of any new episcopal bench is evident in their reactions to the Bills for repealing both the act excluding the bishops from the Lords and the 1641 act abolishing the coercive powers of the church courts. Neither measure received any notable check in the°Commons in the summer of 1661. However, aristocratic opposition to the government-sponsored bill repealing the act for excluding the bishops from the Lords was anticipated before the measure had passed the Commons. Edward Gower predicted that 'the Lords will scarse pass it with so little difficulty; some do not stick to say they will oppose it there'.[21] Once in the Lords it was indeed attacked by Presbyterian and Catholic peers, with almost thirty of the former attending the House at the third reading on 18 June.[22] In the vanguard of the bill's Catholic critics was the earl of Bristol, who reputedly informed the king that its enactment would 'deprive Catholics of all those graces and indulgence which he [the king] intended for them' since they were sure to be contradicted and opposed if the bishops returned to the Lords.[23] The presence of twenty-six bishops, the Presbyterians knew, would further consolidate the position of rigid Anglicans in the chamber and jeopardise their aim of establishing a broad Church of England. However, according to Clarendon, when they realised that the bill would 'unavoidably pass, they either gave their consents, as many of them did, or gave their negative without noise'.[24]

Presbyterian opposition in the Lords was more concerted in July during the debates on the measure restoring the jurisdiction of church courts. Despite the passage of time since the abuses of the High Commission and the other Church courts, a strong feeling of anti-clericalism lingered in the House, with former parliamentarian peers being the most anxious for either

[19] Green, *Re-establishment of the Church of England*, p. 57.
[20] Ibid., p. 19; Hutton, pp. 144–5; *Cal. Cl. SP*, IV, 654, J. Baker to Hyde, 13 April 1660.
[21] *Hist. MSS Comm.*, 5th rept (1876) pt I, Appendix, MSS of the duke of Sutherland, Edward Gower to Sir R. Leveson, 30 May 1661.
[22] *LJ*, XI, 283.
[23] Clarendon, *Life*, II, pp. 101–2.
[24] Ibid., p. 100.

curbs on their powers or the confirmation of their abolition.[25] The scale of opposition in the Lords is indicated by the length of time it took to pass the House, ten days as opposed to four for the earlier bill; during that time the bill was vigorously debated and recommitted. As a means of preventing future extensions of ecclesiastical jurisdiction, the bill's opponents proposed that all writs in church courts should be in the king's name.[26] Following Lord Lucas' report on 25 July the bill was savagely assaulted by Presbyterians, which prompted the duke of York on behalf of the Court to inform them 'that the bill should pass on the morrow and that they were resolved to sit it and talk it out' with them.[27] The bill eventually passed on 27 July with a proviso that denied the legality of the canons of the 1640 Convocation and stated that the act 'was not to abridge or diminish the king's supremacy in ecclesiastical matters and affairs'.[28]

Rigid Anglicans were present in good numbers when these two bills were in the Lords, casting their votes for them at every stage. No fewer than thirty attended on 18 June and thirty-three on 27 July for the respective third-reading debates.[29] To them episcopacy was an integral part of local government with bishops using their powers to prosecute sectaries. The re-establishment of episcopacy also prepared the way for the complete restoration of the liturgy, rites and ceremonies of the Church of England, a process legitimised by the votes of the bishops in parliament. This was the belief of the Royalist earl of Northampton, who asserted in 1662 that sectaries intended the 'monarchy's eternal destruction and the Church's fall'.[30] His colleague, the duke of Newcastle, also regarded bishops as essential to maintain order in their dioceses and keep the government informed about the activities of schismatics and papists.[31] The defenders of episcopacy also argued, as the earl of Dorset did, that the exclusion of the bishops from the House of Lords had been contrary to the fundamental laws and therefore any legislation passed in their absence was technically illegal.[32] Perhaps it was with this in mind that the earl of Winchilsea, upon learning of the bishops' re-admission, despatched letters from Constantinople, where he was ambassador, to the archbishop of Canterbury and the bishop of London, requesting that their graces accept a 'voluntary subscription as my own vote and assent

---

[25] Seaward, p. 168; Add. MSS 23,215, fol. 40, John Finch to Lord Conway, 27 July 1661.
[26] Committee Minutes 1, p. 69, 23 July 1661.
[27] Add. MSS 23,215, fol. 40.
[28] *LJ*, XI, 323; *Statutes*, V, 316, 13 Car. II, c. 12, para. V.
[29] *LJ*, XI, 283, 323.
[30] Bodl., Clarendon MSS 77, fol. 236, Northampton to the king, 18 Aug. 1662.
[31] Firth (ed.), *Memoirs of William Cavendish*, p. xxiii.
[32] Kent Archives Office, Sackville MSS, U269/O36, Dorset's speech, undated, but 1661; Seaward, p. 165.

for their admission, whose presence will hallow the House of peers, which have been by so many acts prophaned and unblessed since their expulsion'.[33]

III

Not long after their re-admission to the upper House on 20 November 1661 the bishops were to play a key role in shaping the Uniformity of Worship Bill and revising the Book of Common Prayer. The original bill, which was drafted by the Anglican MP John Kelyng and a committee of lawyers, was not entirely in accordance with the king's religious policy. The bill sent up to the Lords in July essentially endorsed such legal stipulations for uniformity as existed before 1642. It confirmed all previous laws on uniformity and the Prayer Book without making the concessions to moderate Presbyterians hoped for by the king. The use of the 1604 Prayer Book by all ministers was prescribed and they were to declare publicly before Michaelmas 1661 their 'unfeigned assent and consent' to everything in the Book or suffer deprivation.

The bill was not given its first reading in the upper House until 14 January 1662, because the revised Prayer Book was not completed before mid-December. It was quickly committed on 17 January to a substantial committee that including later additions numbered forty-six. Of these, twenty-one were Presbyterians and their sympathisers, twenty-one were uncompromisingly Anglican and three were Catholic. Those most active on the committee were ardent Anglicans, like Bridgewater, Portland, Bolingbroke, who took the chair, and several of the eleven episcopal committee members, notably Morley of Worcester, Cosin of Durham, Croft of Hereford and Gauden of Exeter who assisted in the drafting of amendments.[34]

The Uniformity Bill was altered by the staunch Anglican members of the committee during February and March. Whilst some time was devoted to making the bill compatible with the revised Prayer Book (received by the Lords on 25 February), most attention was given to making the measure more severe. As promised by the government during the disagreement with the Commons over the bill to confirm the Ministers' Act, some of the Commons' amendments to that statute were incorporated in the bill. Of these the most important was that all incumbents had publicly to abjure the Covenant.[35] With this and other additions the bill that was reported to the House on 13 March bore little resemblance to that originally envisaged by

---

[33] *Hist. MSS Comm.*, 71, MSS of A. G. Finch, 4 vols. (1913–65), I, pp. 147–8, Winchilsea to Juxon and Sheldon, 22 Aug. 1661.
[34] *LJ*, XI, 366, 383, 396, 400, 402, 406, 412, 413, 421, 423, 424, 425; Committee Minutes 1, pp. 117, 119, 133, 137, 147, 152–3, 157–8, 163–5, 169–70, 176, 203, 206–8, 216.
[35] Committee Minutes 1, pp. 157–8, 163–5, 169–70.

Charles and Clarendon. As it stood, the Uniformity Bill would have created a narrower and more exclusive Church than the pre-Civil War institution, with all ministers, including the moderate Presbyterians whom the king wanted to retain in the Church, being forced to make several public declarations on the liturgy or face ejection from their livings.[36] From the Committee Minutes it is apparent that the government made little effort to modify the bill in committee, presumably because the king had already decided to mitigate its severity by offering amendments to the House before the third reading.[37]

Presbyterian peers were not so reticent in voicing their criticisms. They objected to at least three aspects of the bill. First, the requirement added by the bishop of Durham on 24 March, that all incumbents had to be ordained by a bishop, was unacceptable because Presbyterian ministers did not wish to undergo re-ordination when they had already been ordained by presbyters. When the bill was being debated in the House Lord Wharton 'complained seriously and openly ... judging it unjust that pastors ordained by a Presbyter, or from foreign parts, should be prevented from performing the ministerial office or obtaining church preferment unless re-ordained, while it would be possible for those who had been Romish priests, without re-ordination, by a single profession of our faith, to enjoy that liberty'.[38] In fact a proviso was initially agreed in committee for avoiding re-ordination. This was later dropped and another added requiring subscription to the Thirty-Sixth Article on episcopal ordination during the re-commitment of the Bill on 24 March.[39]

The second unpalatable requirement concerned the assent and consent to all the Thirty-Nine Articles and the prayers, rites and ceremonies contained in the revised Book of Common Prayer. Many moderate Presbyterians would have conformed to a pre-Laudian style church since the Elizabethan Act of Uniformity had required subscription and assent only to those articles which concerned 'the confession of the true Christian faith and the doctrine of the sacraments'.[40] They did not necessarily object to the liturgy, rather to certain rites and ceremonies, which by their very nature were considered indifferent for salvation. It was perhaps for these reasons that when the revised Prayer Book was presented to the Lords on 25 February the Presbyterian earl of Northumberland moved that 'the old [1604] Book of Common Prayer might be confirmed without alteration or addition, and then the same Act of Uniformity that had been in the time of queen Elizabeth, would be likewise applied'.[41]

---

[36] Seaward, p. 175.
[37] Committee Minutes 1, pp. 165, 169, clause for avoiding re-ordination.
[38] Carte 81, fols. 736–8, Wharton to Von Spaen, 18 Oct. 1685.
[39] Committee Minutes 1, pp. 169, 211.
[40] Carte MSS 81, fol. 109; Lacey, *Dissent and parliamentary politics*, pp. 21–2.
[41] Clarendon, *Life*, II, p. 128.

A third objection to the Uniformity Bill was that ministers were compelled to renounce the Solemn League and Covenant. Old Convenanting Presbyterian peers deemed this clause repugnant because, as a solemn oath taken in the presence of God, the Covenant was inviolable.[42] According to the bishop of Winchester, speaking in a debate on the Five Mile Bill in 1665, many who would have conformed to the doctrine and practices of the Church of England regarded the renunciation of the Covenant as the main reason who they were forced into nonconformity.[43] Those among the peers who had taken the Covenant disliked the clause because they feared it would be inserted in 'all others acts which related to the function of any other offices, and so would in a short time be required of themselves'.[44]

The battle to soften the provisions of the Uniformity Bill began in earnest on 17 March. It was on that day that the opening shots were fired when Clarendon presented a royal proviso to the House of Lords. Written in the Lord Chancellor's own hand, the proviso mentioned the king's obligation to implement the promise made at Breda for a 'liberty to tender consciences' and expressed his desire for such an 'indulgence as may consist with the good and peace of the kingdom'.[45] The proposed concessions were modest: perhaps the king was testing the mood of the House before more far-reaching amendments were offered. The proviso authorised the king to dispense with the act in order to retain any minister who had held a living on 29 May 1660 by exempting him from the requirements of wearing the surplice and signing with the cross in baptism, provided the minister employed another clergyman to conduct the Anglican baptismal ceremony. Exempted ministers were not to write or preach against the 'Liturgy, rites or ceremonies established in the Church of England'.[46]

The reading of the proviso 'passed smoothly', because it had been presented towards the end of the sitting and took rigid Anglican peers by surprise.[47] The following day, with an exceptionally high turn-out of ninety-seven lords, the House debated the proviso and almost immediately the Catholic earl of Bristol condemned it. Initially Bristol tried to inflame passions by exploiting the peers' anxieties about privilege, asserting it was 'the highest breach of privilege ever offered the House for the king to take notice of anything done in that House and send them a proviso'.[48] The earl's ploy succeeded in distracting the peers from the proviso until a motion to

[42] R. Thomas, 'The rise of the reconcilers', in *The English Presbyterians*, ed. C. G. Bolem, J. Goring, H. L. Short and R. Thomas (1968), p. 82.
[43] Carte MSS 80, fols. 758–9.
[44] Clarendon, *Life*, II, p. 135.
[45] Clarendon MSS 76, fol. 162, draft proviso.
[46] Ibid.
[47] The entry in the Lords' Journal indicates that the proviso was tendered after the House had considered the committee's alterations to the Uniformity Bill (*LJ*, XI, 409).
[48] Add. MSS 22,919, fol. 203, Morrice to Downing, 2 Mar. 1662.

enter a protest in the Journal protecting the privilege of the House 'upon the occasion of this proviso from the king' was defeated.[49] Next he claimed the proviso was not from the king at all and therefore did not represent royal policy. However, Ormond, Clarendon and the duke of York contradicted him, and a stormy debate ensued.[50]

Later that day the Lords referred the king's proviso together with the Uniformity Bill back to the committee. Several peers whom one would have expected to support the proviso, notably the king's cousin, the duke of Richmond, Lords Herbert of Cherbury and Newport were added to the committee at this time, presumably to diminish the influence of the staunchly Anglican contingent.[51] When the committee met at 3 p.m. on 20 March no fewer than twenty-six lords were present. After the proviso was read a motion was put, to adjourn until the following day, which was carried by sixteen votes to ten.[52] If the ten lords who voted against the motion were opposed to the proviso the government certainly had some cause to be alarmed. The next meeting was delayed until 22 March to provide the king and his senior ministers with sufficient time to persuade the proviso's critics not to attend future sessions.[53] That the government was successful in this is indicated by the reduced numbers voting on 22, 24 and 26 March: maximum attendance, which can be deduced from the recorded number of 'Contents' and 'Not-contents' in the committee Minute Book, was probably never more than twenty-two.[54] The votes of the proviso's opponents did not exceed seven whilst the 'Contents' ranged from twelve to eighteen.[55]

The committee's deliberations were still far from harmonious. The clause dispensing ministers from wearing the surplice and using the cross in baptism aroused such passions that it only passed by twelve votes to seven on the 22nd. It is likely that at this stage the government made a deal with leading Anglican clerics, particularly Bishop Cosin of Durham who had savaged the proviso on the floor of the House. In return for their not opposing the proviso, Clarendon may have agreed to allow the earlier clause for avoiding re-ordination to be exchanged for a stiff proviso requiring subscription to the Thirty-Sixth Article on episcopal ordination. It is significant that Cosin introduced this proviso two days later and it was accepted by twelve votes to one.[56] Only minor alterations were made to the royal proviso to make it

[49] *LJ*, XI, 410.
[50] Ibid. 411; Add. MSS 22,919, fol. 203.
[51] *LJ*, XI, 411, 412, 413.
[52] Committee Minutes 1, p. 203, 20 Mar. 1662.
[53] Ibid., p. 206.
[54] The Committee Minutes do not provide formal attendance lists, but they often give the numbers of 'Contents' and 'Not-contents' when a vote occurred (Committee Minutes 1, pp. 203, 206, 208, 211, 216).
[55] Ibid.
[56] Ibid., p. 211, 24 March. 1662; Carte MSS 81, fols. 110–11, endorsed, 'Proviso in the Bill of Uniformity as to the 36th Article of the 39 Articles touching ordination'.

compatible with the bill, and on 26 March the committee agreed by sixteen votes to two to report to the House.[57] The earl of Bridgewater made his report on 4 April and an angry debate followed over the dispensation from wearing the surplice and using the cross, and attention was focused on whether the words used in the proviso to describe them – 'though indifferent in their own nature' – should stand.[58] The House agreed in the affirmative and after further debate the proviso was incorporated in the bill.

A second and more far-reaching alteration was proposed by the Lord Chancellor the same day. Clarendon and other lords urged that the renunciation of the Covenant should also be dispensed with by royal licence or indeed expunged from the bill altogether.[59] A committee of bishops was appointed to consider whether there was anything good in the Covenant which ought not to be renounced. Reporting to the House on 5 April, the bishops found nothing of benefit in it. However, Clarendon and the Presbyterian peers continued to argue that it should not be renounced, but after a heated debate were defeated by thirty-nine votes to twenty-six.[60] Seeing that the feeling of the House was against expunging this clause, Bishop Morley of Worcester offered an amendment on 7 April to dilute the declaration so that no obligation existed from the Covenant itself, but this too was unacceptable.[61] Two days later the House accepted a final government-sponsored amendment enabling Charles II to allow ministers ejected under the act to receive a fifth of the profits of their livings until they died.[62] With the addition of this amendment the Uniformity Bill was read for the third time and returned to the Commons.

During the protracted proceedings on the Uniformity Bill in the upper House religious groupings became more conspicuous. Debates were frequently angry and votes both in the House and in committee were at times close.[63] The efforts of the staunchly Anglican members, particularly prelates, to make the bill more severe are documented in contemporary letters.[64] The Committee Minutes record their amendments and propositions, but rarely refer to individual peers by name and never record speeches.[65] Led by Bishop Cosin, they were extremely critical of the king's dispensing proviso,

---

[57] Committee Minutes 1, p. 216.
[58] *LJ*, XI, 421.
[59] *Hist. MSS Comm.*, Hastings MSS, IV, pp. 129–30, Lake to Bramhall, dated 4 April 1662, but was probably written on the 5th when the division it refers to is recorded in the Journal (*LJ*, XI, 421–2).
[60] *Hist. MSS Comm.*, Hastings MSS, IV, p. 130.
[61] Clarendon, *Life*, II, pp. 136–8; *LJ*, XI, 423, 424.
[62] *LJ*, XI, 424–5; HLRO, Main Papers, 10–22 Mar., parchment copy of the 'fifths' proviso.
[63] Committee Minutes 1, pp. 176, 203, 206, 208; *Hist. MSS Comm.*, Hastings MSS, IV, p. 130.
[64] Ibid., pp. 129–30; Add. MSS 22,919, fol. 203; *Mather Papers*, p. 194, Hooke to Davenport, 31 Mar. 1662.
[65] Committee Minutes 1, pp. 152, 169–70, 176, 211.

condemning it in the debate on 18 March as 'destructive to the Bill itself'.[66] Cosin reputedly attacked the king's actual power to dispense individual ministers from wearing the surplice and using the cross in baptism.[67] The existence of a group of Presbyterian peers eager to ameliorate the bill's harshness was noted by contemporaries, even if individuals are rarely mentioned by name.[68] They were not of one mind on the king's modifications to the bill. From some rare scribbled notes on the debate on the royal proviso in the Braye MSS it seems that some considered the proposed indulgence 'not large enough'.[69] Presbyterians together with a few government peers, such as the duke of Ormond, the earl of Southampton, and the moderate bishops, Gauden, Reynolds, Morley, Croft and Sheldon, were the chief supporters of the king's modifications.[70] At least one contemporary noticed an 'alliance' between the government and the Presbyterians, a feature that was to recur in 1663 during the court's attempts to alter the Church settlement.

The king's influence on the House via the earl of Clarendon and other ministers helps to explain why the Lords, unlike the Commons, was prepared to make the bill more acceptable to moderate Presbyterians. The existence of twenty-five to thirty Presbyterian peers was obviously significant, but without a lead from the court they were too weak to secure concessions from the Anglican majority. It was only after the king had declared his position with the introduction of his dispensing proviso that 'support' for modifications to the bill increased: some of those peers who depended on the king for office and favours rallied to the aid of his chief minister in the chamber.[71]

There was nevertheless a limit to the extent of royal influence on the upper House. Clarendon was unable to secure sufficient support to expunge or revise the clause requiring the renunciation of the Covenant because of the passions it aroused. The Covenant awakened memories of the 1640s, since it had originally been 'entered into to fight against the king and to destroy the church', and many Anglican lords fervently believed that, far from being dead, this obligation upon people was very much alive.[72] In August the former Royalist earl of Northampton associated religious dissent with the Covenant, writing that Presbyterians and sectaries were the king's only 'implacable enemies' and 'it is the Covenant they adore'.[73] The recent risings and rumours of republican plots merely intensified these views. Therefore

---

[66] Add. MSS 22,919, fol. 203; HLRO, Braye MSS, vol. 53, no. 17, 18 Mar. 1662.

[67] Add. MSS 22,919, fol. 203.

[68] See *Hist. MSS Comm.*, Hastings MSS, IV, pp. 129–30 and also Clarendon, *Life*, II, pp. 128–9.

[69] Braye MSS, vol. 53, no. 17.

[70] Add. MSS 22,919, fol. 203; *Hist. MSS Comm.*, Hastings MSS, IV, pp. 129–30.

[71] Peers supporting the king's amendments included Ormond and Southampton, and possibly Herbert of Cherbury and Newport, who were added to the Uniformity committee on 20 and 21 March respectively.

[72] Clarendon, *Life*, II, pp. 137–8.

[73] Clarendon, MSS 77, fol. 236, Northampton to king, 18 Aug. 1662.

because the Covenant 'was still the idol to which the Presbyterians sacrificed' a majority of Lords wanted ministers to declare that it was no longer binding before they could be 'trusted with the charge and cure of the souls of the king's subjects'.[74] Bishops and courtiers who had previously voted for the royal proviso deserted the king on the question of the Covenant for these reasons. One would expect that most of the twenty-six peers who supported the Lord Chancellor in the division on 5 April were drawn from the ranks of the twenty-eight Presbyterians who attended the sitting.[75]

Having misjudged the mood of the House towards the Covenant, Clarendon must have expected substantial opposition to the dispensing proviso and fifths amendment in the lower House. MPs spent a considerable portion of April on the bill, and although some divisions were close, these amendments were struck out, whilst others unfavourable to Presbyterians were accepted.[76] The terms of the renunciation of the Covenant were made even more severe by the addition of a phrase requiring incumbents to forswear 'to endeavour any change or alteration of government, either in church or state'.[77] Following a conference on 30 April the Lords voted on 8 May to accept the Commons' alterations. Surprisingly, no lord registered his dissent by entering a protest in the Journal despite the fact that the final Bill was far harsher than the king desired: it would expel many of the more moderate Presbyterians from the Church. Faced with the Commons' intransigence, a divided House of Lords, the indisposition of his principal manager in the Lords, Clarendon, and the pressing need to settle the Church, the king decided to accept the Uniformity Bill as it was returned from the Commons.[78] It is significant that the numbers attending on 8 May were considerably lower than earlier in the session and are an indication of the government's decision not to mobilise votes against the measure.[79] Both the earl of Anglesey in a letter, and Clarendon in his speech to parliament at the end of the session, indicated that the king had decided to execute the Act with 'great moderation', by means of the royal prerogative.[80]

The passage of the Bill of Uniformity marked the end of the Lords' involvement in the main phase of the church settlement – further measures were subsequently passed against dissenters – but the government-led campaign to retain moderate Presbyterians in the Church of England had barely

[74] Clarendon, *Life*, II, p. 138.
[75] *LJ*, XI, 421.
[76] *CJ*, VIII, 403, 404, 405, 406, 407–8, 408–11, 412–13, 414, 415; PRO, SP 29/448/18, J. Wandesford to R. Norton, 21 April 1662.
[77] *CJ*, VIII, 410–11.
[78] *LJ*, XI, 450–1; Carte MSS 31, fol. 485, Sir Edward Nicholas to Ormond, 4 May 1662; Seaward, p. 178.
[79] Only 65 lords attended on 8 May as compared with over 80 earlier in the session.
[80] *Parl. Hist.*, IV, p. 252; West Sussex RO, Orrery Papers 13217/3, Anglesey to Orrery, 20 May 1662.

begun. Between 1660 and 1662 the Lords had essentially followed royal policy on the settlement of the church and, with few exceptions, had tempered the severity of religious legislation formulated in the Commons. Its more conciliatory attitude towards moderate Presbyterians was a reflection both of the opinions of the sizeable contingent of Presbyterian lords and of government management. Presbyterian peers formed a substantial minority, whose votes proved crucial in the government's battle to amend both the bill to confirm the 1660 Ministers' Act and the Uniformity Bill. Their services were required again in 1663 when Charles and his ministers chose the House of Lords to modify the Church settlement.

10

Religious nonconformity

The Act of Uniformity created a church that was more exclusive than either the king or many in his upper House desired. Ministers who refused to accept the conditions imposed by the Act were ejected from their living. Despite vociferous complaints in the Lords, further measures were enacted against nonconformists in an attempt to prevent them from worshipping freely. Initially the king employed legislation to lessen the severity of the church settlement in the hope that moderate dissenters might be enticed back into the established church. At the same time he sought to provide a limited toleration for those peaceable dissenters who would not conform, and on at least two occasions tried to accomplish this with his prerogative powers. The first part of this chapter is concerned with the Lords' involvement in these endeavours and its reaction to legislation against moderate dissenters especially during the 1660s. The second is concerned with the peers' changing attitude towards Catholics.

I

The first parliamentary assault on the church settlement occurred on 23 February 1663 when Lord Robartes introduced on behalf of the government a Bill of Indulgence in the Lords. This measure followed closely on the heels of the king's Declaration of Indulgence, which had been issued on 26 December. The Declaration had announced his intention of seeking parliament's approval to 'exercise with more universal satisfaction that power of dispensing which we conceive to be inherent in us', and also secure limited relief for loyal Catholics.[1] The purpose of the bill was to enable Charles II to dispense with the Act of Uniformity and any other laws enjoining conformity to the Church of England. Dissenting Protestants of an 'unoffensive and peaceable disposition' were to be granted licences to worship freely.[2] The

---

[1] Kenyon, *Stuart Constitution*, pp. 403–6.
[2] *Hist. MSS Comm.*, 7th Rept, Appendix pt I, MSS of the House of Lords (1879), p. 167; HLRO, Main Papers, 23 Feb. 1663: draft Bill of Ecclesiastical Affairs (Indulgence Bill).

intention was to lure moderate presbyterian ministers back into the Church. The bill stated that the use of the Book of Common Prayer and subscription to the doctrinal articles were to be the only tests of conformity. Catholics were not specifically mentioned in the bill, but they hoped to benefit from it in some measure.[3]

It is difficult to gauge the Lords' reaction to the bill as detailed accounts of debates in the committee of the whole House do not exist. Clarendon's assertion in his memoirs that the bill was never committed because so few spoke in favour of it is incorrect.[4] From the Lords' *Journal* it is clear that it was given a second reading on 25 February and referred to the committee of the whole House, chaired by the earl of Manchester.[5] The main supporters of the bill were Catholics, and Presbyterian peers, notably the privy councillors Manchester, Robartes and Ashley.[6] There was certainly substantial opposition to aspects of the indulgence in the chamber. Many bishops and rigid Anglicans condemned it because it would jeopardise the church settlement. On 27 February the clerk recorded that lords did not believe that the indulgence would ever 'bring any in from their errors to the Church'.[7] Peers were also alarmed by the clause allowing the king to dispense individuals from any statute, including the Corporation Act, that required conformity to the Church of England.[8] Feelings were so strong on this point that on 5 March they restricted the bill to the Act of Uniformity.[9]

Even some of those who held flexible views on the composition of the Church recognised the measure's constitutional implications. Clarendon felt it would strengthen and make permanent the royal prerogative in ecclesiastical matters, and in so doing enable the king to control the church as he pleased. Such an extension of the royal prerogative would jeopardise the legal basis of the church, which was ecclesiastical and statute law.[10] Lord Dorset, by no means an inflexible Anglican, voted for the bill's commitment, yet was fearful that Covenanting Presbyterians would be given ecclesiastical promotions. He observed during a debate that each was still obliged by the Covenant to 'endeavour ... to the best of his power the ruin of that government [episcopacy] under which himself [i.e. the minister] is placed a member by the king'.[11] The earl of Southampton, the Lord Treasurer, who was later to demonstrate his sympathy towards moderate dissenters during

---

[3] Seaward, p. 182.
[4] Clarendon, *Life*, II, p. 348.
[5] *LJ*, XI, 484, 485.
[6] Charles II, *Life*, II, p. 348.
[7] Committee Minutes 1, p. 293, 27 Feb.
[8] Clarendon, *Life*, II, p. 345; Seaward, pp. 182–3.
[9] Committee Minutes 1, p. 294, 5 March.
[10] Seaward, pp. 182–4.
[11] Kent Archives Office, Sackville MSS, U269/036, fol. 82: undated speech by the earl of Dorset, Feb./Mar. 1663.

a debate on the Five Mile Bill, is reputed by Clarendon to have spoken against the Indulgence Bill 'as unfit to be received ... being a design against the Protestant religion, and in favour of the papists'.[12]

The bill's progress was painfully slow, an indication of the anxieties it aroused. It was debated in committee on 27 and 28 February and later on 5, 6, 12 and 13 March, but little was actually achieved apart from restricting it to the Act of Uniformity.[13] After a lengthy debate on 13 March it was referred to a subcommittee to be amended according to the satisfaction of the committee of the whole House. The subcommittee, which met three times, the last being on 26 March, did not complete its task, because the government decided to suppress the bill.[14]

The bill's promoters had misjudged the mood of the Lords. Whilst many peers had been prepared in 1662 to revise the Bill of Uniformity in favour of moderate Presbyterians, they were not willing to consent to the far more drastic provisions of the Indulgence Bill. 'Great pains were taken' by the Court 'to persuade particular men to approve it', but the extent to which ministers could pressurise peers to vote against their consciences was more limited than in 1662.[15] The Indulgence Bill had so completely divided the privy council that some senior ministers who had managed the Lords in 1662 either condemned the bill in the House, like Southampton, or tried to remain neutral, like Clarendon.[16] Clarendon in fact was absent from the Lords until 12 March, and when he did attend he could not conceal his misgivings.[17] Other influential members, including Archbishop Sheldon and the duke of York were openly hostile.[18] The government's decision to drop the measure was also influenced by events in the lower chamber. After debating the king's opening speech, the Commons decided to reject the royal scheme to dispense dissenters from the penalties of the penal laws.[19] A severe bill against Catholics was drafted, and on 17 March the Commons resolved to petition the king to issue a proclamation expelling Catholic priests. By mid-March it was apparent that the Commons would never accept even a watered-down bill of indulgence and therefore the bill was quietly dropped in the subcommittee of the whole House.[20]

Later in the same year the government made another attempt to make the Act of Uniformity acceptable to moderate Presbyterians. In July the Lords

[12] Clarendon, *Life*, II, p. 345.
[13] Committee Minutes 1, pp. 293, 294.
[14] Ibid., pp. 295–6, 298, 303.
[15] Clarendon, *Life*, II, p. 345.
[16] Ibid., p. 345; Seaward, pp. 182–4.
[17] *Cal. SP Ven.*, p. 238, Giavarina to Doge and Senate, 19/29 March 1663; PRO, PRO 31/3/111, Comminges to Lionne, 12/22 March 1663; Hutton, p. 197.
[18] Clarendon, *Life*, II, p. 348.
[19] CJ, VIII, 440; Carte MSS 47, fol. 397, H. Coventry to Ormond, 28 Feb. 1663.
[20] Committee Minutes 1, p. 303; Seaward, p. 184.

received from the Commons a bill allowing a late subscription for ministers who by accident, illness or duties abroad had been prevented from subscribing to the doctrine and practices of the Church of England as required by the Act of Uniformity. On 24 July the bill was referred to a committee composed largely of those sympathetic to an indulgence: government ministers (Southampton, Sandwich, Anglesey, Ashley and Manchester), Presbyterians (notably Saye and Sele, Wharton and Eure) and court bishops (Morley and Earle).[21] The next day they inserted a clause 'that the declaration and subscription of assent and consent in the said Act [of Uniformity] ... shall be understood only as to the practice and obedience to the said Act and not otherwise'.[22] For many nonconformists the assent and consent requirement was unpalatable because it implied that they believed everything in the Prayer Book to be perfect. The addition of the phrase 'practice and obedience' was the government's ploy to make the assent and consent requirement acceptable to nonconformists. Assent to the Prayer Book was to be a question of outward obedience, with no acknowledgement of any inner conviction. The Lords accepted the revised bill, but fourteen peers, mostly zealous Anglicans, such as Bridgewater, Northampton, Derby, Colepeper and Gerard, protested against the amendment as 'destructive to the Church of England as now established'.[23] The next day, however, the Commons rejected the amendment.

Whilst the House of Lords was prepared to support such royal schemes to entice moderate and peaceable Presbyterians back into the church, it had very little sympathy for the plight of sectaries. During the 1660s few lords seriously contemplated toleration for dissenters, and certainly not for those regarded as holding extreme views, like Quakers and Baptists.[24] Even some former-Parliamentarian peers, such as Northumberland and Fauconberg, regarded sectaries as a threat to order and stability, and Presbyterians in both Houses eagerly participated in passing legislation against them.[25]

At the outset of the reign dissenters viewed the Lords as more sympathetic to their cause than the Commons. In the summer of 1661 Quakers and Baptists petitioned the Lords for liberty to worship freely. The earl of Pembroke, a Quaker himself, and a few other lords were sympathetic enough to consider the possibility of a 'promissory' oath for Quakers when they

---

[21] *LJ*, XI, 570, 572.

[22] Ibid., 573; Committee Minutes 1, p. 436.

[23] *LJ*, XI, 573.

[24] Peers favouring toleration included Lords Wharton, Ashley, Robartes, Bristol and Buckingham (Lacey, *Dissent and parliamentary politics*, pp. 470–5; Haley, *Shaftesbury*, pp. 28–9, 66–7, 164–5; Yardley, 'George Villiers', pp. 79, 149; Seaward, pp. 170–1).

[25] Seaward, p. 171; West Sussex RO, Wiston MSS 5426/2/3, Northumberland to deputy lieutenants of Sussex, 3/5 Sept. 1661; Durham University Library, Mickleton and Spearman MSS 31, fol. 55r, Fauconberg to Cosin, 18 Aug. 1665.

discussed a Quaker petition in committee on 30 May.[26] But the majority of the House was opposed to all concessions, preferring instead the suppression of Quakers. Coming in the wake of Venner's rebellion (January 1661), these petitions served to remind peers that additional legislation was required to suppress dissenters. A bill to punish Quakers and radicals who refused oaths was received from the Commons in July, but progressed very slowly. It was committed four times and finally passed both Houses on 2 May 1662.[27] Peers had serious reservations about several aspects of the bill, in particular whether Quaker peers and other nonconformists could be prosecuted under it. Provisos were added protecting the right of lords to be tried by their peers and the bill was restricted solely to those (i.e. Quakers) who refused oaths and believed that 'the taking of the oath in any case whatsoever, although before a lawful magistrate, is altogether unlawful and contrary to the word of God'.[28] The Commons rejected most of these amendments and the completed bill applied to anybody who refused the Oath of Allegiance and attended a conventicle.[29]

Both the Committee Minutes and the Lords' *Journal* give few clues as to which peers backed their chamber's amendments. Pembroke was certainly one of the Quakers' principal allies, presenting a paper from them to the committee on 12 December.[30] Bishop Gauden was sympathetic to their cause, arguing in the House on 20 March 1662 for the execution of the bill to be delayed by several months.[31] There is no evidence that Clarendon was active on behalf of the king in moderating the bill. He harboured a profound dislike of Quaker principles, describing Quakers as 'a sort of people upon whom tenderness and lenity do not at all prevail'.[32] Charles favoured absolving Quakers from oaths and certainly did not want the bill to extend to Catholics.[33] Lord Privy Seal Robartes, who managed two conferences with the Commons in February and March 1662, may have been the driving force behind the Lords' alterations.[34]

The following year the government frustrated a Commons' bill against conventicles in the Lords. Worried about the frequent assemblies of Quakers, Baptists and other dissenters, the Commons had passed a bill against all dissenters (including Presbyterians) apprehended attending illegal places of worship. The penalties were severe. Transportation was prescribed for

[26] Committee Minutes 1, p. 12; HLRO, Main Papers, 6 June 1661, Quakers' petition.
[27] *LJ*, XI, 318, 338, 340, 353, 365, 372, 388, 389, 390–1, 395, 397.
[28] Committee Minutes 1, p. 88; *LJ*, XI, 318, 338, 340, 353, 365, 372.
[29] Hutton, p. 169; *CJ*, VIII, 353, 355, 356, 367, 376.
[30] Committee Minutes 1, p. 88.
[31] John Gauden, *A discourse concerning publick oaths* (20 March 1662).
[32] Quoted by Hutton, p. 169.
[33] Ibid., pp. 169–70.
[34] *LJ*, XI, 388–9, 395, 397.

anyone who attended an unlawful conventicle and refused within a month to take the oaths and declaration in the Act of Uniformity. After its first and second reading on 3 and 11 July respectively, the bill was debated once in the committee of the whole House on the 22nd, but was never reported as fit to pass. The controversy surrounding Bristol's abortive impeachment of Clarendon distracted the peers from the bill and may have provided the government with a smokescreen to suppress it.[35] It was certainly not a government-sponsored measure. Its failure to distinguish between sectaries and presbyterians was contrary to existing royal policy.[36]

Both royal policy and the attitude of the Lords towards Presbyterians were transformed by the discovery of the Yorkshire Plot in the autumn of 1663. Not only were the risings the most dangerous since the Restoration, but they involved Presbyterians as well as other radicals. The involvement of Presbyterians demonstrated to the king and peers that many of these men were irreconcilable to the regime and needed to be dealt with severely. Any plans the king still had of moderating the religious laws were swiftly abandoned.[37] One of Secretary Williamson's correspondents reported in January 1664 that many peers who had previously advocated the dissenters' cause at court 'fail them and prove enemies' now.[38] In the aftermath of the Yorkshire Plot members of both Houses were extremely concerned that conventicles might provide a focus for hatching plots against the church and the monarchy. In an attempt to allay these fears the Commons passed a bill in April to suppress conventicles. Though similar to the earlier Conventicle Bill, there were differences, such as the addition of a scale of penalties for the first to third offence and the omission of a clause requiring all officeholders to take the oaths and declaration in the Act of Uniformity. On 28 April one of the bill's chief backers in the Commons, Lord Fanshaw, presented it to the House of Lords.

There it aroused serious and protracted debates, notably in the committee of the whole House. Attempts were made, particularly by Presbyterian lords, to amend it in a manner favourable to dissenters. Lord Ashley tried to soften its impact on those wrongly convicted with a proviso 'for reparation without just cause', but this was not allowed.[39] On 7 May a subcommittee that included the Presbyterians Anglesey, Manchester, Ashley and Paget, worded the penalty for the first offence in such a way as to give the accused, not the JP, the option of paying a £5 fine or going to prison.[40] Other amendments included: the imposition of a stiff fine as an alternative to mandatory trans-

[35] Seaward, p. 188.
[36] Ibid., pp. 186–8.
[37] Ibid., p. 190.
[38] PRO, SP 29/90/10, Sir Brian Broughton to Joseph Williamson, 16 Jan. 1664.
[39] Committee Minutes 1, p. 458, 7 May 1664.
[40] Ibid., pp. 457–8.

portation for a third offence, the enlargement of the numbers allowed at a conventicle and two provisos protecting peers' privileges. The first of these provisos was probably also intended to provide greater legal security for any lord wishing to worship in private non-Anglican services because it would have authorised only lord lieutenants to search peers' houses. The second, offered by Lord Bolingbroke, permitted those lords indicted for a third and subsequent offence to be tried solely by their peers.[41] Only in one respect did the House make the bill more severe. Their annoyance at the Quakers' refusal to take a lawful oath in a court of law encouraged the peers to accept an amendment offered by Lord Chancellor Clarendon on 6 May. Clarendon's clause prescribed transportation for anyone who refused an oath in a court of law.[42] Six days later the amended bill was returned to the House of Commons.

MPs accepted many of the Lords' amendments, but threw out those concerned with oaths and privilege. Eventually after several conferences a compromise was agreed on the subject of peers' privileges. On the issue of searching peers' houses both chambers agreed that this could only be done if either a lord lieutenant, deputy lieutenant or two JPs were present.[43] The Lord Chancellor's proviso proved by far the most contentious amendment. It was regarded by MPs as 'a thing foreign to the Bill which was intended only to suppress conventicles' because it brought anyone (even if they had never attended a conventicle) who refused a lawful oath in any court within the scope of the bill.[44] The Commons proposed a compromise involving the transportation of those who refused an oath and had twice been convicted for attending a conventicle, but this was rejected by the Lords. After adding a short preamble to the bill on the 16th that Quakers were the most dangerous conventiclers, the Commons backed down and the Conventicle Bill received the royal assent the next day.[45]

The passage of the Conventicle Bill underlined both the government's change in religious policy and the gradual decline in support for moderate dissenters in the Lords. A significant number of Presbyterian peers were still sympathetic to dissenters, and indeed some spoke in their favour during the debate on the Five Mile Bill in 1665, but as a whole the upper House was far more willing to pass legislation against them than it had been earlier in the 1660s. As in the Commons there was significantly more support for measures against the sects and less for the persecution of moderate Presbyterian

[41] Ibid., p. 458; HLRO, Main Papers, 10 May 1664, Bolingbroke's proviso.
[42] Bodl., Rawlinson MSS A. 130, fol. 14v.
[43] *Statutes*, V, 519–20; *LJ*, XI, 614, 616, 617–18; *CJ*, VIII, 562–3, 564; Pepys, V, 147–8; HLRO, Main Papers, 6 May 1664, for the peers' amendments.
[44] *CJ*, VIII, 564–5; Bodl., Rawlinson MSS A. 130, fols. 16v, 18v.
[45] Ibid., fol. 19; HLRO, Main Papers, 6 May for the Lords' preamble; *CJ*, VIII, 564–5; *LJ*, XI, 617–18, 619.

ministers.[46] The peers had accepted the king's dispensing proviso in the Bill of Uniformity and endorsed their committee's emendation of the Additional Uniformity Bill in 1663. On both occasions their intention was to encourage moderate Presbyterians to conform. Disturbed by the principles and disrespectful behaviour of Quakers they passed the Quaker Bill and accepted Clarendon's oath in the 1664 Conventicle Bill.

Oaths were a contentious issue the following year during proceedings on the Five Mile Bill. All ejected ministers who refused to swear an oath promising not to make any change or alteration in church or state would be compelled to reside at least five miles away from towns and corporations. The war against the Dutch, a substantial minority of whom were Calvinists, had aroused fears that dissenters were in league with the enemy and therefore posed a greater security hazard to the government than in peacetime. Fearful of unrest in the capital, parliament meeting at Oxford decided to take firm action against nonconformist ministers preaching to congregations whose incumbents had left to escape the ravages of the plague. Although it seems the original bill was not directly a government measure, it did enjoy the backing of ministers and privy councillors, such as the duke of York and the archbishop of Canterbury.[47] After a swift passage through the Commons, it had its first and second readings in the Lords on consecutive days and was committed on 27 October 1665 to a committee chaired by the ultra-Anglican earl of Bridgewater. Few of the bill's critics sat on the committee and votes for the Contents ranged from ten to fourteen and from two to five for the Not Contents.[48]

The most serious opposition emerged immediately after Bridgewater's report on the 30th. Lord Wharton's notes of speeches delivered in the House demonstrate that the bill aroused a passionate debate. Archbishop Sheldon and his colleague George Morley, bishop of Winchester, were among the bill's most committed advocates, emphasising the danger nonconformist preachers posed to towns and cities. Lords Lucas, Manchester and Southampton countered this by urging the recommitment of the bill 'upon the oath and also that the committee might consider of some ways how those ministers that are laid aside might be made use of'.[49] Southampton suggested the insertion of a clause enabling those dissenting ministers who accepted the Book of Common Prayer to be licensed by bishops to preach in public.[50] Lucas and Southampton objected to the oath because it appeared to prevent even peaceful attempts to alter any laws relating to either church or state.

[46] Seaward, 'Court and parliament', p. 233.
[47] Seaward, pp. 192–3; Hutton, p. 235.
[48] Committee Minutes 2, p. 89.
[49] Carte MSS 80, fol. 757.
[50] Ibid.

Wharton himself confined his speech to the loyalty of Presbyterian ministers, whom he described as 'sober, loyal and peaceable persons'.[51] Although other Presbyterians spoke in favour of the bill's recommitment, the majority of peers voted to pass it, thereby completing the series of legislation known as the 'Clarendon Code'.

Towards the end of the 1660s fear of dissenters began to recede and once again the Lords displayed sympathy for the cause of moderate Presbyterians. Following peace with the United Provinces in 1667 people recognised that dissenters were no longer the security risk they had believed them to be during wartime.[52] The king's attitude was also changing. After the dismissal of Clarendon in the summer of 1667 those politicians who favoured relief for moderate dissenters were in the ascendancy at court. Buckingham, Bishop Wilkins of Chester, Lord Ashley and particularly Arlington, who dominated government policy between 1667 and 1670, persuaded Charles to endorse schemes for comprehending Presbyterians within the Church. Between October 1667 and February 1668 two government-backed comprehension bills were drafted though, for various reasons, neither was presented to parliament.[53] The Lords readily responded to this change in government policy, blocking a Commons' conventicle bill in 1668. The 1664 Conventicle Bill was due to expire in May 1668 and the Commons had passed an even more severe replacement. There was a marked reluctance on the part of the court and the Lords for the replacement bill to pass and, following a speech by a privy councillor, the earl of Anglesey, on 2 May, it was laid aside without a day being appointed for the second reading.[54] The Lords' stance here together with the protracted bicameral dispute over Skinner's case prevented the enactment of a new conventicle bill until 1670.

The 1670 measure aroused the peers' passions to an extent not witnessed on a religious issue since 1662. The battle to modify it took place in the committee of the whole House during March 1670. Exceptional attendances of over a hundred are recorded in the *Journal* and even the king revived the ancient practice of attending debates.[55] The bill's most severe critics were Presbyterians and they comprised fifteen of the seventeen peers who protested after its third reading on 26 March.[56] Privy councillors were certainly not united, for at least three (Manchester, Anglesey and Holles) voted against it on the 26th. Between 15 and 24 March the peers increased the number of people not belonging to the same household that constituted an illegal

[51] Ibid., fol. 758.
[52] A. M. Coleby, *Central government and the localities: Hampshire 1649–1689* (Cambridge, 1987), p. 111.
[53] See Spurr, 'The Church of England', pp. 933–4.
[54] Add. MSS 36,916, fol. 95, Starkey to Aston, 2 May 1668.
[55] Manuscript Minutes vol. 16: 14, 15, 16, 19, 21, 22, 23, 24, 25, 26, 28 March 1670.
[56] *LJ*, XII, 326.

conventicle, from five to ten, added a clause protecting their own houses against search by one JP, threw out a clause making conventicles riots and accepted a government proviso preserving the king's right to dispense with ecclesiastical laws.[57] After a series of conferences with the Commons the completed bill represented a compromise between the views of both chambers, with the Lords dropping several amendments, such as that increasing the number of persons at a conventicle and the Commons accepting the proviso about the royal supremacy in ecclesiastical affairs.[58]

There were several reasons why the stiffest opposition to the Conventicle Bill manifested itself in the Lords. The most important was that a higher proportion of the Lords consisted of Presbyterians who were sympathetic to dissenters, and it was largely these peers who signed the two protests against the bill.[59] Several still retained nonconformist ministers in their households, and if five or more of their neighbours were present at their non-Anglican services, they were liable for prosecution.[60] Like the 1664 Act, it was viewed by many as unjust. The provision which allowed 'notorious evidence and circumstance of the fact' to be used as proof of guilt, and provided that the recording of the 'crime' by a JP would be 'taken and adjudged a full and perfect conviction', provoked heated debate in the committee of the whole House on 16 March.[61] Wharton noted that 'the exorbitant power given to a single Justice of the Peace or town officer [is] greater than [that which] the judges and all the Justices of Peace in England together now have or ever had' since the testimony of one JP was sufficient to imprison anyone apprehended at a conventicle.[62] A desire to protect their personal privileges lay behind the proviso, which the Commons eventually accepted, that the search of a noble's house could only be authorised by a royal warrant, and only then in the presence of a lord lieutenant, his deputy or two JPs.[63]

Three years later the Lords again displayed a more lenient stance than the Commons towards peaceable nonconforming Protestants. Following the withdrawal of the king's Declaration of Indulgence in March 1673, the Commons passed a bill granting limited relief to Protestant dissenters.[64] In reality there was little enthusiasm in the lower House for the bill, but under intense court pressure MPs committed themselves to securing some degree of toleration for Protestant dissenters in their address against the Declaration.

---

[57] Manuscript Minutes, vol. 16, 14–25 March 1670; Margoliouth (ed.), *Marvell, poems and letters*, II, p. 104.
[58] *LJ*, XII, 335–6, 340.
[59] *LJ*, XII, 326.
[60] Lacey, *Dissent and parliamentary politics*, pp. 459–75.
[61] *Statutes*, V, 648–50; HLRO, Main Papers, 16 March 1670.
[62] Carte MSS 77, fol. 592, Wharton's observations on the Conventicle Bill.
[63] Margoliouth (ed.), *Marvell, poems and letters*, II, p. 104; *Statutes*, V, 649–50.
[64] *CJ*, IX, 254, 271.

The peers on the other hand broadened the scope of the bill by leaving out a clause for the repudiation of the Covenant and recognised that the king could use his royal prerogative to suspend penal laws against Protestant dissenters and license teachers and preachers.[65] These alterations were too extreme for the Commons and both chambers were still in dispute at the prorogation on 29 March.

The following year a group of bishops initiated a comprehension bill in the Lords. This important bill has been overlooked by historians, perhaps because of the mis-dating of a key letter in the Tanner MSS. Only recently has an account of a debate on the bill come to light in the Lauderdale papers.[66] In an attempt to remove some of the Presbyterian ministers' chief criticism of the Act of Uniformity, the bill provided for two things: first the repeal of the assent and consent clause and second the omission of that part of the declaration relating to the Covenant.[67] The House had certainly shifted its ground since 1662 when it had refused to remove this second requirement from the Uniformity Bill despite pressure to do so from the court. A majority of the House backed the bill and the motion to commit was carried by a majority of almost twenty votes on 19 February 1674. George Morley, bishop of Winchester, was its chief sponsor, and he enjoyed the support of a further six, including Ward of Salisbury, Pearson of Chester, Wood of Coventry, Fuller of Lincoln and Dolben of Rochester.[68] At least eleven bishops were opposed to the measure, believing that comprehension would create a schism within the church. Temporal advocates of the Comprehension Bill included Danby, Shaftesbury and his Presbyterian associates Holles, Carlisle, Fauconberg, Clare and Salisbury.[69] There is no clear evidence to connect Charles with this Bill, though it was entirely in keeping with his avowed policy of broadening the church, a policy he did not formally abandon until early 1675 when the privy council ordered the enforcement of the penal laws. Had this potentially far-reaching measure not died with the prorogation on 24 February, many ministers who had been ejected in 1662 might have reentered the Church of England.

The apparent high degree of support from the House of Lords for a broader church reflected a gradual softening of attitudes in the country towards Protestant dissenters. By the mid-1670s it had become clear to many

---

[65] Manuscript Minutes, vol. 18, 22, 24 Mar. 1673.

[66] Bodl., Tanner MSS 44, fol. 249, John Lowland to Sancroft, 21 Feb. 1674 (mis-dated 1671); Add. MSS 23,136, fol. 98, Sir Robert Moray to Lauderdale, 21 Feb. 1674.

[67] Main Papers 170, fols. 68–9, 13 Feb. 1674, draft Comprehension Bill.

[68] Bodl., Tanner MSS 42, fol. 89, Tillotson to Sancroft, 23 Feb. 1674; 44, fol. 249; Add. MSS 23,136, fol. 98.

[69] *Parl. Hist.*, IV, 'A letter from a person of quality to his friend in the country', p. xliv; M. Sylvester (ed.), *Reliquiae Baxterianae: or Mr Richard Baxter's narrative of the most memorable passages of his life and times* (1696), III, p. 109.

members of the political nation that the prosecution of nonconformists would not produce religious uniformity. Therefore it was considered reasonable to offer Presbyterians concessions to entice them back into a broadly based Church of England.[70] Such a church was thought to be the best counterbalance to the threat of popery. The period from 1672 to 1674 was characterised by extreme anti-popish paranoia of a ferocity not seen in England since the early 1640s. The discovery of the heir presumptive's conversion to Catholicism, and his marriage to a Catholic princess in 1673, had unleashed the spectre of a popish monarch. Some who earlier in the reign had been averse to making concessions to nonconformists changed their minds. The bishop of Winchester had been prepared to make only minor concessions to Presbyterians in April 1673, and would never 'have consented nor ever will consent to that which they call a comprehension'.[71] Yet during the ensuing ten months, which saw the duke of York's second marriage, his opinions had altered so much that he was commanding the vanguard of noble adherents to the Comprehension Bill, crying out the 'danger of Popery' in the Lords.[72]

From 1675 to 1678 the government pursued orthodox Anglican policies and only Country peers espoused the dissenters' cause with any commitment. The furthest they got was when one of their most prominent figures, Buckingham, sought permission of the House to introduce a toleration bill in November 1675. The bill was never read because of the prorogation on 22 November.[73] The popish plot revelations of the years 1678–9 and the consequential heightened anxieties over the succession led to a rapid reappraisal of attitudes towards Protestant dissenters, who were increasingly regarded by Anglicans as allies in their struggle against popery.[74]

At the same time the government encouraged parliament to consider ways of relieving Protestant dissenters. The king was not committed to an indulgence, but as in earlier years gave the impression he genuinely sought one. The Compton Census of Catholics and dissenters in England and Wales of 1676 had demonstrated that there were far fewer nonconformists than the king had previously thought. Therefore they did not pose a significant threat to either the Church or the government, and Charles never again seriously contemplated an indulgence in England.[75] Intent upon pacifying the mounting opposition to his brother's position as heir presumptive, Charles publicised

[70] Cragg, *From Puritanism to the age of reason*, p. 208.
[71] Bodl., Tanner MSS 42, fol. 7, Morley to Sheldon, 7 April 1673.
[72] Add. MSS 23,136, fol. 98; Bodl., Tanner MSS 42, fol. 89; 44, fol. 249.
[73] The proposed bill is discussed by Bruce Yardley in 'George Villiers', pp. 225–7. A copy of the bill is in Carte MSS 77, fols. 595–6.
[74] H. Horwitz, 'Protestant reconciliation in the Exclusion Crisis', *Journal of Ecclesiastical History*, 15 (1964), 202–3.
[75] Hutton, *Charles II*, p. 334.

his willingness to assent to any comprehension or toleration bills that parliament might present to him.[76]

During the autumn of 1680 a comprehension bill was sponsored in the Commons by the members of the Court party, in particular Daniel Finch and Sir Thomas Clarges.[77] In the same session the Lords discussed three bills favourable to Protestant dissenters, and each was backed by senior ministers and privy councillors. The Country party turncoat, the earl of Halifax, having firmly fixed his colours to the royal flagpole, was responsible for reintroducing in the chamber on 23 October an unsuccessful bill from the 1679 parliament for banishing Catholics from London, with an additional clause to exempt nonconforming Protestants from the penalties of the recusancy statutes.[78] After lengthy consideration in the committee of the whole House the bill passed on 10 November, but was eventually substituted for another banishing papists by the Commons.[79]

In late November the Commons sent up a bill to repeal the Elizabethan Sectaries Act of 1593 which had only occasionally been invoked in Charles II's reign. This was supported in 1680, and at the subsequent Oxford Parliament, by Halifax and Lord Chancellor Finch, who presented it again on 21 March 1681. It was vigorously opposed by several members of the episcopal bench, but passed the House on 15 December with only minor amendments to which the Commons quickly agreed.[80] Yet the bill did not reach the statute book because the king ordered the clerk to 'lose' it so that it was not presented to him for his assent on 10 January 1681. Despite his professed willingness to accept bills favourable to Protestant nonconformists, the fate of this bill demonstrated that the king really had no intention of relieving such persons.[81]

By far the most vociferous champions of the cause of Protestant dissenters were 'opposition' lords. Strenuous efforts were made to exempt Protestant dissenters from several of the penal laws in an attempt to construct an anti-Catholic alliance. They had every reason to doubt the sincerity of the king's promise to relieve Protestant dissenters even before the episode over the bill to repeal the Sectaries Act, since the government was still employing Elizabethan and Jacobean Acts, which had originally been intended only against Catholics, to indict Protestants. On 8 November 1680 they proposed

---

[76] J. R. Jones, *Charles II, royal politician*, pp. 132–3, 160.
[77] Horwitz, 'Protestant reconciliation', pp. 207–8.
[78] Chatsworth House, Halifax Collection, E/19, Algernon Sidney to Henry Savile, 31 Oct. 1680; *LJ*, XIII, 616.
[79] *CJ*, IX, 677.
[80] Hutton, p. 397; Carte MSS 77, fol. 164, proceedings at the Oxford Parliament, 21/22 March 1681.
[81] Ibid., p. 397; Lacey, *Dissent and parliamentary politics*, p. 144; Horwitz, 'Protestant reconciliation', p. 214.

framing an address from the House of Lords to the king recommending that recusancy laws were not enforced against Protestant dissenters.[82] A lengthy debate ensued and a committee was appointed to prepare the address. Chaired by the duke of Buckingham on 26 November and the earl of Shaftesbury on 8 December, it heard evidence from Quakers and other non-conformists that they were being prosecuted under Elizabethan statutes, originally intended for papists.[83] The relevant statutes were perused and eventually the committee recommended that the Lords should proceed by legislation. This was endorsed by the House and the earl of Anglesey was instructed to prepare the bill.[84] To remedy 'the disuniting [of] the Protestant interest at a time when papists are designing and practising the ruin of our religion', the bill proposed that dissenters prosecuted under the recusancy laws should be discharged and pardoned if they subscribed to the declaration in the 1678 Test Act. At the insistence of government peers and bishops, the bill was amended (by a majority of three votes) so that dissenters had to subscribe to the Oath of Allegiance.[85] Forbidden by their scruples to swear oaths, Quakers were thereby denied any benefit from the Act. When it received a third reading on 3 January 'opposition' peers were in a slight minority and it was probably the votes of government ministers, such as Finch, Radnor and Halifax, which ensured its passage.[86] Nevertheless it reached the Commons too late for consideration as that House was still engaged on its own projects to relieve dissenters when the king suddenly prorogued parliament seven days later.

The House of Commons had often been a major obstacle to the Lords' attempts to modify the church settlement. It was rarely as indulgent in religious matters as the Lords. Even when under government pressure it had passed a toleration bill in 1673, the measure was of so limited a nature that the peers added a proviso authorising the king to dispense with the penal provisions of acts of parliament against Protestant dissenters.[87] In spite of the influx of new MPs during the general elections of 1679 and 1681, there were still fewer Presbyterians than there had been in 1660.[88] There was little agreement among Presbyterian MPs on the provisions of the 1680 Comprehension and Toleration Bills, and both measures received only lukewarm support.[89]

[82] *LJ*, XIII, 654.
[83] Committee Minutes 3, p. 375.
[84] Committee Minutes 3, pp. 374–7, proceedings on the bill for distinguishing Protestant dissenters from Popish recusants, Dec. 1680; *LJ*, XIII, 709.
[85] *Hist. MSS Comm.*, 11th Rept, Appendix II, House of Lords MSS, pp. 202–5.
[86] Dr Williams' Library, Morrice MSS P, p. 286. Thirty-two 'Whigs' were present as opposed to 35 Court peers. *LJ*, XIII, 728; Swatland, 'The House of Lords', p. 226.
[87] For the Lords' proviso see Manuscript Minutes, vol. 17, 25 Mar. 1673.
[88] Henning (ed.), *House of Commons*, I, p. 13.
[89] Horwitz, 'Protestant reconciliation', p. 212.

There were essentially three reasons for the Lords' willingness to make concessions to peaceable nonconformists. First there was the higher percentage of Presbyterians and their sympathisers than in the Commons; second there was the susceptibility of the Lords to royal influence; and third there was the obvious fact that, unlike MPs, peers did not face electoral pressure. However, few peers contemplated an unlimited toleration, or the complete dismantling of the church settlement. Many hoped limited concessions on ceremonial, the assent and consent clause in the Act of Uniformity and the Covenant would entice moderate Presbyterians back into the Church of England. Radical Protestant sects were, however, regarded by most lords as beyond the pale, posing a serious threat to law and order and the established church.

II

Between 1660 and 1671 the upper House was significantly more sympathetic towards Catholics than the Commons. Peers even considered schemes to lift the legal restrictions on Catholics. There is no single explanation for their attitude towards English Catholics during these years. The relatively small size of the House, coupled with a far higher proportion of Catholic members than the Commons, ensured that lords had extensive first-hand knowledge of Catholics, not just as neighbours but as colleagues, who performed their duties like any other peer. Protestant and Catholic lords often served on the same committee. Colleagues in war as well as in peace, many had served the Royalist cause during the Civil War.

Government pressure on the Lords may also have shaped opinions there. Virtually all attempts to lessen the severity of laws against Catholics either originated with the king or enjoyed his approbation. Without firm royal support, any endeavour to assist Catholics was almost certainly doomed to fail, as the earl of Bristol discovered when he tried to persuade the peers to add a proviso to the Bill of Uniformity for exempting Catholics from the recusancy laws.[90]

The principal aim of Catholic peers was to modify the oaths of allegiance and supremacy and repeal the penal laws, and hence secure freedom of worship for their co-religionists.[91] The first attempt to revise the 1606 Oath of Allegiance occurred in the committee for privileges on 14 June 1660. Catholics objected to the oath because subscription implied the repudiation of all papal authority in England. Most were prepared to promise loyalty to the king, but were unwilling to swear an oath that described the papal authority to depose princes as an 'heretical and damnable doctrine'.[92] Instead

[90] Seaward, p. 176.
[91] Ibid., pp. 168–9.
[92] Miller, *Popery and politics*, pp. 31–3; Kenyon, *Stuart constitution*, pp. 458–9.

of examining how the oath should be imposed on peers, members of the committee decided to question both its validity and phraseology. Several lords desired to know the views of the House on the imposition of an oath which would 'exclude and entrench upon their birth right'.[93] Lord Strafford, a man who spoke on behalf of nonconformists later in the reign, moved that 'an oath may be framed not touching upon doctrine but subjection' to the monarchy. Staunch Anglicans, however, defeated this move. The earl of Portland, a close associate of the Lord Chancellor, urged that 'the oath of fealty may be taken by us all'.[94] To what extent Catholic peers were involved in these proceedings is impossible to determine as only two Protestant peers are mentioned by name in the minutes. Six Catholics were members of the committee for privileges at this time, and of these Lords Petre and Berkshire are known to have attended meetings in previous weeks.[95]

A more sustained effort to alter the oath of allegiance and relieve Catholics from the penal laws was made the following year. On 10 June 1661 Catholics petitioned the Lords to repeal the penal laws and requested a modified allegiance oath. In their petition they reminded the House of their unswerving loyalty to the king and drew attention to the economic effects on the country of their disablement from the professions and trades.[96] Among the signatories were Lords Bristol and Arundel of Wardour (Master of the queen mother's horse), who were the leaders of the Catholic contingent in the chamber. Bristol proposed a new oath which would bind Catholics to the king and yet contained no reference to doctrine.[97] Lord Arundel went further by appealing to opinion outside parliament for the repeal of the penal laws in his widely circulated document: 'A letter from a person of quality to a principal peer of the realm now sitting in parliament'.[98]

The upper House was sufficiently persuaded by the strength of the Catholics' case to appoint a committee under the chairmanship of the earl of Portland to consider the repeal of those penal laws which carried the death penalty. It is probable that the king was throwing his weight behind this development, for the committee included leading government figures: the dukes of York and Ormond, the earls of Southampton and Manchester and Lord Robartes.[99] During its six meetings the committee perused all the relevant Elizabethan and Jacobean statutes and made some far-reaching

---

[93] Committee for Privileges Minute Book 1 (1660–4), p. 16, 14 June 1660.
[94] Ibid.
[95] Ibid., pp. 4, 12, 38.
[96] HLRO, Main Papers, 10 June 1661, recusants' petition for repealing the penal laws.
[97] BL, Harleian MSS 1579, fols. 114–20, speeches by the earl of Bristol.
[98] J–H–, *A letter from a person of quality to a principal peer of the realm, now sitting in parliament. Occasioned by the present debate upon the penal laws*, 17 June 1661 (no date or place of publication); Seaward, p. 169.
[99] *LJ*, XI, 291–2; Committee Minutes 1, p. 44, 1 July 1661.

recommendations which were incorporated in a draft bill.[100] Catholics were still to be excluded from office, but were exempted from all other penalties for their refusal to subscribe to the oaths. With the exception of Jesuits, priests would be able to practise their religion provided they registered with the Secretary of State. All Catholics were to take an oath of allegiance and were not to be compelled to leave the country for non-attendance at church. The committee was still concerned about the threat posed by seditious Catholics and, therefore, recommended that several laws against papists remained in force.[101] The draft bill was in fact never presented to the House. Parliament was adjourned on 30 July and no further proceedings are recorded in the minutes for the autumn session. It seems the government had decided to suppress the bill, though the reasons for this remain obscure.[102]

In December 1662 the king made what proved to be his last endeavour for several years to relieve Catholics with the issue of a declaration of indulgence to Catholics and Protestant nonconformists. In the Declaration the king promised some relief for loyal Catholics, presumably so that they could worship in private.[103] Yet when the bill to transform the Declaration's proposals into law was introduced in the Lords in February 1663, it did not extend to Catholics. Perhaps this was because the king recognised that he had misjudged the extent of hostility towards Catholics in the country when he had issued the Declaration. Incensed by the Declaration and worried by the growing influence of Catholics at court, especially priests, the Commons drew up an address asking Charles to issue a proclamation expelling all priests from the realm. The sentiments in the address ran counter to royal policy and, as so often in the reign, the king chose the Lords to give voice to his views. On 23 March the Lords appointed a committee that included the most influential ministers to consider the Commons' address.[104] At its meeting on the 24th the Lord Chancellor tendered a revised version of the address, which simply asked the king to facilitate the departure of all priests he found to be disloyal or who behaved in an unacceptable manner.[105] The House of Lords agreed to the new petition, but the Commons rejected it almost in its entirety. Eventually the Lords assented to the Commons' petition.[106] The fact that only three lords dissented suggests that the House was now being actively encouraged to concur with the Commons by the court. Charles II had decided to issue a bland proclamation which would allow English and foreign priests to retain their posts.

[100] Committee Minutes 1, pp. 44, 45, 62–3, 64.
[101] Seaward, pp. 169–70.
[102] Possible reasons for the suppression of the bill are discussed by P. Seaward, ibid., p. 170.
[103] Kenyon, *Stuart constitution*, pp. 403–6.
[104] *LJ*, XI, 495, 497.
[105] Committee Minutes 1, p. 302, 24 Mar. 1663; HLRO, Main Papers, 24 Mar. 1663.
[106] *LJ*, XI, 500, 501, 502; BL, M636/19, Denton to Sir Ralph Verney, 29 Mar. 1663.

During the following eight years the peers did not significantly change their views about English Catholics. There was never the same hostility towards Catholics in the Lords as existed in the Commons. For instance on 2 March 1671 the committee scrutinising a Commons' petition for the more effectual enforcement of the laws against Catholics questioned 'facts' in it, asserting that 'we know not of any convents ... at St James ... but what are allowed by the articles of marriage'.[107] In contrast with the Commons there was still a strong desire to exempt loyal Catholics from the penalties of the penal laws.[108] Later in March the House received a severe Commons' bill for tightening up procedures for the conviction of Papists and for the enforcement of existing laws against them. This bill was too extreme for both the king and many peers because it did not distinguish between loyal and disloyal Catholics. On 13 April the committee of the whole House decided that a subcommittee was to prepare a test or oath 'which being taken may obtain a mitigation of the penalties of the law following conviction to such recusants, intended in his majesty's answer to both Houses ... as shall take the same, and thereby assure their obedience and faithfulness to the king and that they are not dangerous to the peace of the kingdom'.[109] Not surprisingly, several members of the subcommittee were either privy councillors (Ormond, Manchester, Bridgewater, Anglesey and Ashley) or men close to the king like the bishop of Chester, Lord Berkeley of Berkeley and the earl of Essex. The membership of the subcommittee coupled with the committee's reference to the king's answer to parliament's anti-Catholic petition (13 March), in which he had promised to draw a distinction between those recently converted to Catholicism and those older papists who had 'faithfully served his father and himself in the late wars', indicate that the House of Lords believed it was following royal policy.[110] But the subcommittee never in fact met. Perhaps the court had decided to suppress the bill, realising that the Commons would never agree to such a drastic amendment, or perhaps the House was too preoccupied by its dispute with the Commons over the Foreign Commodities Bill until the prorogation on 22 April?[111]

The next three years witnessed a profound change in peers' attitudes towards Catholics. Catholics were increasingly perceived to be a greater threat to the church and the government than Protestant dissenters. There was never quite the same intensity of anti-Catholic feeling in the Lords as there was in the Commons, but nevertheless the vast majority of peers shared the general concern about a popish conspiracy against Protestantism and

---

[107] Committee Minutes 2, p. 422, 2 Mar. 1671.
[108] *Cosin correspondence*, II, p. 276, Cosin to Stapylton, 11 April 1671.
[109] Committee Minutes 2, p. 451.
[110] *LJ*, XII, 454.
[111] *Cal. SP Ven.*, vol. 37, p. 32, Girolamo Alberti to Doge and Senate, 3 April 1671.

Englishmen's liberties. Presbyterian peers were among the most zealous anti-papists in the Lords. So concerned was the earl of Denbigh that he compiled a set of proposals for countering the Catholic threat and restoring the reputation of the monarchy following the issue of the 1672 Declaration of Indulgence.[112]

Whilst the English anti-Catholic tradition stretched back to the Reformation, the anti-popish mania which swept the nation in the 1670s was in part a consequence of the court's religious policies and the growing power of Louis XIV's France on the continent. But of fundamental importance was the duke of York's conversion and later marriage to a foreign Catholic princess in 1673. Following his refusal to take Anglican communion at Easter 1673 and the surrender of his offices under the Test Act, it was evident to contemporaries that the heir presumptive was a Catholic. This unleashed the spectre of a popish monarch after the death of Charles II. Fearful for the survival of the Church of England under a Catholic ruler, Denbigh wanted the duke to assert publicly that he would defend the 'Protestant religion now here established'.[113] In 1670 the king had signed the Treaty of Dover with France, the foremost Catholic state in Europe. From 1672 to 1674 England and France were engaged in an expensive war against the Dutch, which Denbigh regarded as being contrary to the national interest and for the 'grandeur of France'.[114] During 1673 Charles had raised an army ostensibly to fight the Dutch, but its protracted presence on Blackheath aroused suspicion about the government's motives. Many in both Houses strongly suspected that the king harboured a secret design to use the army to establish popery and arbitrary government.[115]

The first indication of a change in attitude towards Catholics was the Lords' cool response to the Declaration of Indulgence. Facing outright opposition from the Commons to the Declaration, on 1 March 1673 Charles II sought the advice of his House of Lords. Both the king and Lord Chancellor Shaftesbury expected the peers to endorse the Declaration. Yet three days later, after a vigorous debate, they did not explicitly approve the measure, but resolved by 60 votes to 27 that 'the king's answer to the House of Commons in referring the points now controverted to a parliamentary way by bill is good and gracious'.[116] A committee was instructed to frame a bill of advice to the king, and both Clifford and Anglesey presented proposals.

---

[112] Warwickshire RO, Denbigh MSS, CR/2017/R13, 'The steps of descent whereby of late this monarchy hath much declined and lessened itself', undated but written in 1673 and amended in early 1674.

[113] Ibid.

[114] Ibid.

[115] Miller, *Popery and politics*, pp. 119, 130–1.

[116] C. H. Josten (ed.), *Elias Ashmole ... his autobiographical and historical works ... correspondence and other contemporary sources* (5 vols., Oxford, 1966), IV, p. 1312.

Lord Treasurer Clifford's proposals were intended to remove objections about the exercise of the royal prerogative by giving the king 'power (if it be not in him already) to suspend penal statutes in matters ecclesiastical out of time of parliament', provided those laws to be dispensed with were named.[117] On the other hand Anglesey's paper proposed that the king could not suspend or dispense with such laws except with the 'advice and consent' of parliament and only for a period of five years.[118] But the committee made little progress on either set of proposals, as the King cancelled the Declaration on 8 March. Whilst peers were concerned about the king's exercise of his prerogative to suspend and dispense with all penal statutes in his Declaration, their prime objective was the encouragement it had given to papists. Indeed, later in March, during proceedings on a bill to ease Protestant dissenters, the House did not disapprove of the king's power to suspend penal laws against Protestants, provided this power did not extend to Catholics.[119]

In contrast with previous sessions, the Lords was now agreeable to imposing further constraints on Catholics. The Test Bill, which was targeted at Catholics holding commissions in the armed forces and occupying places at court, passed with uncharacteristic haste for such an important measure in seven days in March.[120] It was intended to incapacitate from holding civil or military office all persons who refused to take the Anglican sacrament and make a declaration against transubstantiation. Several minor amendments were made, the most significant being a clause to exempt the queen's and the duke of York's household servants from its provisions. What opposition there was came from Clifford, a secret Catholic, the duke himself and several bishops close to the court. Clifford delivered a speech in which he castigated the Commons both for encroaching on the peers' privileges and for interfering in religious matters.[121] His aim was to foment a bicameral privilege dispute in which the bill would be lost. Almost all Catholic lords 'readily concurred' when the House passed the Test, 'declaring there should be no occasion given on their side to keep up any fears and jealousies between the king and his people'.[122] Very few Catholic lords were directly affected by the bill. Few held offices and, as the earl of Bristol observed in a speech in support of it, the measure was modest for it did not prevent Catholics from worshipping in private or banish them from court. Bristol and his Catholic colleagues latched on to the Test Bill as a means of demonstrating both their

---

[117] Committee Minutes 3, p. 16, 6 Mar. 1673.
[118] Ibid., p. 22, 17 Mar. 1673; *Hist. MSS Comm.*, 9th Rept, Appendix, House of Lords MSS, p. 25, Anglesey's draft proposals.
[119] Manuscript Minutes vol. 17, 25 Mar. 1673.
[120] *LJ*, XII, 554–84.
[121] Josten (ed.), *Elias Ashmole*, IV, p. 1312.
[122] *Parl. Hist.*, IV, p. 565.

continued loyalty to the king and their willingness to compose 'the disturbed minds of the people' about popery.[123]

Following York's failure to take communion in April, the surrender of his offices in June and his marriage to a Catholic in the autumn, anti-Catholic feeling reached a new peak in the country. When parliament assembled on 7 January 1674 England, allied to France, was still engaged in an increasingly unpopular war against the Dutch. Despite a recent proclamation, English and Irish Catholic priests continued to be employed at court. The average daily attendance for the session was eighty-seven, by far the highest since 1664. The session marked a turning point in the history of the House of Lords because it witnessed the birth of a trend that endured until Charles II's last parliament, of 'opposition' peers promoting legislation against the duke of York and Catholics in general. Disaffected Protestant peers, who formed the nucleus of the Country party in 1675, met regularly at Lord Holles' London house to formulate parliamentary tactics during the winter of 1673 and the spring of 1674.[124]

Not only did they try to dominate the debates on religious issues during the session, but they also endeavoured to arouse anti-Catholic sentiment still further by resorting to the scaremongering tactics usually associated with Shaftesbury and his adherents during the popish plot and succession crisis. When the Lords debated religion on 8 January Shaftesbury made an impassioned speech in which he warned of an imminent armed uprising by 16,000 Catholics in the neighbourhood of London.[125] This piece of hyperbole was sufficient to send a wave of panic through the House. The Lords voted almost unanimously on Lord Mordaunt's motion to address the king to issue a proclamation banishing all papists to at least ten miles from the capital.[126] Bristol and the Catholic peers cast their votes with the majority: only the duke of York and his two clients, Anglesey and Northampton, voted against the motion.[127] Four days later Shaftesbury proposed that every member, including the duke of York, should take the Oath of Allegiance before entering the House.[128] The House rapidly endorsed this motion and for the first time in the reign all peers were obliged to take the oath. Of the Catholic lords, Berkshire, Cardigan, Audley, Stourton, Bristol, Belasyse, Norwich, Stafford and the duke of York took the Oath of Allegiance, whilst the remaining half dozen avoided it by non-attendance.[129]

[123] Ibid., p. 566.
[124] PRO, 31/3/130, fol. 47, Ruvigny to Madame Pomponne, 22 Jan. 1674; Airy (ed.), *Essex papers*, I, p. 168, Conway to Essex, 27 Jan. 1674.
[125] PRO, 31/3/130, fol. 31, Ruvigny to Pomponne, 11 Jan. 1674.
[126] *Cal. SP Ven.*, vol. 38, pp. 201–2, Girolamo Alberti to Doge and Senate, 16 Jan. 1674; BL, Stowe MSS 204, fol. 23, Conway to Essex, 10 Jan. 1674.
[127] BL, Stowe MSS 204, fol. 25, Lord Aungier to Essex, 10 Jan. 1674.
[128] *Cal. SP Ven.*, vol. 38, pp. 201–2, Alberti to Doge and Senate, 16 Jan. 1674.
[129] *LJ*, XII, 606–7, 610–11, 620, 639, 641, 674.

Both the address to the king and the motion on the Oath of Allegiance were intended by Shaftesbury and his adherents as first steps in imposing restrictions on the duke of York and his children. Two of the four motions made by these peers in a debate on 26 January for securing the Protestant religion directly impinged on the duke and his family. Salisbury proposed that the duke's children should be educated as Protestants and his associate, Carlisle, advocated that none of the royal family ·should marry a Catholic without the assent of parliament.[130] Shaftesbury, Halifax and Salisbury subsequently framed a bill incorporating these proposals along with others for disarming papists and removing all English Catholic priests from court.[131] The bill also stipulated that James's daughters, Mary and Anne, 'be delivered over for education in a separate house and family ... and there confirmed in those good and wholesome principles of the Protestant religion as they have been already instructed in'.[132] Suspected or practising Catholics were required to subscribe annually to an oath denying papal supremacy, to declare the 'doctrine of transubstantiation is false and erroneous' and to swear that not receiving the Anglican sacrament is 'directly contrary to the institution of Christ'.[133] This far-reaching measure did not pass the House as the king abruptly terminated the session on 24 February. Almost identical bills were introduced in the next two sessions, but they too suffered the same fate: neither the king nor his brother was prepared to countenance restrictions on their authority and interference in their domestic arrangements.

Another source of anti-Catholic legislation was paradoxically the court itself. Under the guiding hand of the earl of Danby, the government sought to give the impression that it genuinely desired to take action against papists and so allay recurrent fears about the survival of the established religion. These fears ebbed and flowed, receding somewhat after the ending of the Dutch War in 1674 and surging forward again in 1676 with rumours of Catholic plots in Herefordshire and Yorkshire. Two government-sponsored bills were introduced in the Lords on 1 March 1677. The first, entitled an 'Act for further securing the Protestant religion by education of the children of the royal family and providing for the continuance of a Protestant clergy', actually provided for the accession of a Catholic monarch.[134] On the demise of Charles II his successor had to comply with the provisions of the Test Act. Failure to do so would result in the removal of ecclesiastical patronage from royal control, which would be vested in the archbishops of Canterbury and York for the clergy in their respective provinces, and in the Lord Chancellor

---

[130] Stowe MSS 204, fol. 114, Conway to Essex, 27 Jan. 1674.
[131] Committee Minutes 3, pp. 70–1, 16 Feb. 1674.
[132] *Hist. MSS Comm.*, 9th Rept, Appendix, House of Lords MSS, pp. 45–6.
[133] Ibid.
[134] HLRO, Main Papers, 352, 1 March 1677, for the draft bill.

when presentations to benefices lay in the king's gift. Danby's intention was to protect the Church of England from interference from an English Catholic monarch. In an attempt to appease the government's critics, three further clauses were inserted: the first provided for the education of a Catholic monarch's children in the Protestant religion; the second barred English Catholic priests and Jesuits from attending the present queen or a future queen and the third imposed the Test Act on all Englishmen serving in the royal household after Queen Catherine's death.[135]

The main opposition to this bill came from the one person who had most to lose by its enactment – the duke of York. Along with his close associates, Oxford, Peterborough, Huntingdon and Anglesey, and the Catholic Lords Berkshire, Stafford, Petre and Norwich, James entered his dissent in the Journal after its third reading on 15 March.[136] Two Country peers, Grey of Rolleston and Lovelace, also dissented, but for very different reasons. They regarded it as an inadequate restraint on the powers of a Catholic monarch, especially as it could be repealed after Charles II's death. Not surprisingly the bill met with a very icy reception in the Commons. MPs objected to both the extensive ecclesiastical patronage it conferred on the bishops and its diminution of the royal supremacy. Several believed it would pave the way for popish bishops and clerics. The opposition was such that it never emerged from committee.[137]

The second government bill, 'for the preservation of the Protestant religion and the more effectual conviction and prosecution of popish recusants', was rejected by the Commons after its first reading because it appeared to tolerate Catholics.[138] Harking back to the earlier government initiative in the Lords in 1671, it proposed a distinction between loyal and disloyal Catholic laymen. To this end those Catholics who registered themselves annually, paid a fine amounting to 5 per cent of their yearly income, and took the Oath of Supremacy were exempted from the penalties of the penal laws. The full force of the law was confined to those who concealed their religion and were detected.[139] The passage of this and its sister bill demonstrates that a majority of peers were not hostile to all Catholics, only to those dangerous papists who posed a threat to the stability of the church and state. Many peers, however, were still profoundly concerned by the constitutional and religious implications of the heir presumptive's conversion.[140]

---

135 Ibid.
136 *LJ*, XIII, 74–5.
137 Grey, *Debates*, IV, 285–94.
138 Ibid., 335–8; *CJ*, IX, 414.
139 HLRO, Main Papers, 353, 21 Feb. 1677; *Hist. MSS Comm.*, 9th Rept, Appendix II, pp. 82–3; *LJ*, XIII, 48–51, 62.
140 Miller, *Popery and politics*, pp. 143–4, 145, 153.

Eighteen months later in October 1678 Titus Oates' revelations about a Jesuit plot to assassinate the king and forcibly establish a Catholic government in England aroused passions against papists to an unprecedented degree in both houses of parliament. Upon officially learning of the popish plot, the Lords requested a day of fasting and repentance. As in January 1674 the peers prepared an address asking the king for a proclamation to remove all papists from London. A committee was constituted to investigate the plot, and it set to work by interrogating Edmund Coleman, secretary to the duchess of York. The House did not protest when it was informed on 25 October that the Commons was in the process of arresting five Catholic peers (Petre, Belasyse, Stafford, Powis and Arundel of Wardour) for alleged treasonable complicity in the popish plot. Even if some peers were privately sceptical about the existence of the plot, the House unanimously endorsed the Commons' resolution on 1 November, 'that there hath been, and still is, a damnable and hellish plot, continued and carried on by popish recusants for the assassinating and murdering the king and subverting the government, and rooting out and destroying the Protestant religion'.[141]

There was of course no single view in either chamber regarding Catholics at this time, or indeed at any time during the years from 1678 to 1681 when the king dissolved his last parliament. Those most ardently anti-Catholic were still Country peers, who, as one contemporary observed, desired a 'thorough cleansing and reformation as to the business of popery'.[142] The earl of Essex in particular 'appeared ... really possessed with fear and concern ... of what the plot may every hour produce'.[143] His associate the earl of Salisbury was often deep in thought about the 'dangers the nation was in of popery'.[144] Country peers were in complete agreement with the Commons' harsh measures against popery, and were always the most forward in pressing their House to adopt the most extreme measures possible. Distrustful of the court, especially of the authoritarian duke of York, they were the chief proponents of a range of anti-Catholic legislation that included bills to clear London of papists, the Habeas Corpus Bill of 1679, and the Exclusion and Association Bills of 1680. On the other hand the bulk of the Court party and most bishops, who constituted the majority of the Lords, adopted a more cautious approach to the problem, reluctant to offend the king and his Catholic brother. They were certainly anxious to protect the Church of England, but few were prepared to support measures that encroached on royal prerogatives like a Commons' address to remove the queen from court (November 1678) and the Exclusion Bill.

---

[141] *LJ*, XIII, 333.
[142] Carte MSS 38, fol. 678, Southwell to Ormond, 10 December 1678.
[143] Ibid.
[144] PRO, 30/24, Shaftesbury Papers, 6B, fol. 417, undated letter to Madam, *c.* 1680s.

Such differences of opinion manifested themselves during the long and bitter proceedings on the second Test Bill. Entitled 'An Act for the more effectual preserving [of] the king's person and government, by disabling Papists from sitting in either House of Parliament', it had been rushed through the Commons in a week, and was presented to the Lords on 28 October 1678.[145] In spite of a succession of reminders from the Commons, it received a more leisurely treatment there, not passing the House until 20 November. It required every MP and peer to subscribe to a declaration against transubstantiation and the invocation of the saints and take the Oath of Allegiance. Refusal to comply brought exclusion from parliament. Although the promoters of the Test intended to drive all Catholics from both parliament and the court (it forbade anyone coming into the king's presence unless he had first taken the oaths and subscribed to the anti-Catholic declaration), the duke of York was the real target. As long as James and his Catholic adherents sat in parliament to obstruct their every move, Country peers believed, it would prove impossible to enact far-reaching anti-Catholic legislation.[146]

From the committee of the whole House's first deliberations on 7 November to Bridgewater's final report on the 20th, Catholics and their sympathisers struggled to moderate the bill. Extensive use was made of its infringement of a peer's right to sit and vote in parliament. On 7 November Catholics reminded the House of the order it had passed during the furore accompanying Danby's Test three years earlier, that no oath should be allowed to take away a peer's seat in parliament.[147] When it was decided that all lords must take the Oath of Allegiance and Supremacy to retain their places, it was proposed that excluded peers might still vote by proxy, but this suggestion was quickly brushed aside.[148] Five days later the committee decided by a majority of ten votes to retain both the oaths and declaration, and on the 14th agreed by a substantial majority that the penalty for refusing the Oath of Allegiance should be expulsion from parliament.[149]

Opinion was more sharply divided the next day when the committee debated the declaration against transubstantiation and the invocation of the saints. By a majority of five votes the Catholics, aided by three bishops and many Court lords, secured an amendment allowing peers to keep their seats even if they refused this declaration.[150] There is no single explanation for why Court peers and bishops voted for this alteration. They objected to estab-

---

[145] *LJ*, XIII, 305.
[146] Haley, *Shaftesbury*, pp. 480–1.
[147] Ibid., pp. 376, 481.
[148] Manuscript Minutes, vol. 20, 7 Nov. 1678.
[149] BL, M636/32, John Verney to Sir Ralph Verney, 14 Nov. 1678.
[150] Dr Williams' Library, Morrice MSS, Entering Book P, p. 55; Carte MSS 81, fol. 380, division list on Test Bill, 15 Nov. 1678; Manuscript Minutes, vol. 20, 15 Nov. 1678.

lishing a precedent whereby peers could lose their parliamentary rights simply because of their religious beliefs.[151] Perhaps they did not feel their Catholic brethren, whom they had worked with for many years, posed a threat to the king or the Church of England. Some may have been exposed to royal influence: it is likely that the king backed this amendment. Catholic peers were a useful source of government support in the Lords, and Charles certainly did not want his brother incapacitated from either parliament or the court by an act of parliament. The issue of the declaration split the Court party in the Lords: nine peers who normally voted with the government, including Lord Chancellor Finch and six bishops, sided with the Country party on the 15th.[152]

However, five days later, when Bridgewater reported the amendments, the House reversed the committee's decision on the declaration. Aware of the closeness of the vote on the 15th, it seems that the government had decided to abandon the amendment and replace it with another exempting only the duke of York from the bill. Accordingly James asked the House to accept a special proviso for this purpose and delivered a very persuasive speech in which he declared, that he had no desire to subvert the government.[153] The House agreed to the proviso and the Test Bill passed by a majority reported by contemporaries as six, twelve and twenty.[154] Eventually, after an extremely close vote in the Commons over the duke's proviso, and conferences with the Lords over their amendments concerning the queen's and the duchess of York's household servants, the Test Bill received the royal assent on 30 November.[155]

The Lords' acceptance of the duke's proviso, which was viewed by Country peers as so destructive to the bill, underlined the vital role the House continued to play in defending the interests of the monarchy. In its attitude to both Protestant dissenters and Catholics, Charles II's House of Lords was usually more tolerant than the Commons and more willing to consider royal schemes for their relief. Even during the popish plot the Lords never adopted such a tough stance towards popery as the Commons. Despite the government's firmer control over the Lords, it was not a rubber stamp for the king's religious policies. This was particularly the case when divisions within the privy council spilled over into the House. The painfully slow progress of the 1663 Indulgence Bill in the Lords was partly a consequence of several senior

---

[151] Chatsworth House, Devonshire Collection, 1/C, newsletter to Devonshire, 16 Nov. 1678; *Hist. MSS Comm.*, 14th Rept, Appendix VII, Ormond MSS, IV (1906), p. 474, Southwell to Ormond, 16 Nov. 1678.
[152] Carte MSS 81, fol. 380.
[153] Haley, *Shaftesbury*, p. 481.
[154] Ibid.
[155] *CJ*, IX, 543; Grey, *Debates*, VI, 240–60; Carte MSS 38, fols. 664–9; Southwell to Ormond, 21 Nov. 1678; *LJ*, XIII, 365–6, 373, 374, 378–9, 384.

ministers being at loggerheads. The development of an organised 'opposition' in the 1670s also threatened government legislation, as the earl of Danby discovered when his Test failed to pass the upper House in 1675. Prior to 1675 the government was a prime initiator of legislation to broaden the Church: after this date the initiative transferred to the Country party in both Houses.

Part 5

POLITICS

11

Factions, Country peers and the 'Whig' party

The development of political parties was one of the most significant features of Charles II's reign. The Court and Country parties of the 1670s have been regarded as the ancestors of the late seventeenth-century Tory and Whig parties. Most historians have almost exclusively focused on the emergence of parties in the House of Commons during Danby's ministry and the succession crisis period of 1679–81.[1] Yet from 1675 proceedings in the Lords were increasingly influenced by the 'Court' and 'Country' parties. The purpose of this and the next chapter is to place the traditional Commons-centred view of party in perspective by analysing the development of factions and parties in the upper House from the Restoration to the Oxford Parliament.

What constituted a political party in the second half of the seventeenth century and how was it distinct from a faction? The terms 'party' and 'faction' had almost identical meanings in the seventeenth century.[2] Both words were employed in a derogatory sense to describe a group of men intent upon using mischievous and even unscrupulous methods to achieve private and self-interested ends.[3] Throughout this study the term 'faction' is used to denote a fluid group whose aims were essentially of a private or self-interested nature. The two small groups of lords and MPs nominally led by the earl of Bristol and the duke of Buckingham in the 1660s can best be described as 'factions', for they possessed a fluid membership and sought personal gain through the acquisition of court offices.[4] The term 'party' on the other hand

---

[1] See J. R. Jones, 'Parties and parliament', in J. R. Jones (ed.), *The restored monarchy, 1660–1688* (1979), pp. 48–70 and *The First Whigs; the politics of the Exclusion Crisis, 1678–1683* (1961). Jonathan Scott in *Algernon Sidney and the Restoration Crisis, 1677–1683* (Cambridge, 1991) denies the existence of coherent, organised parties in the Commons, whilst Tim Harris takes a more balanced view in the first major study of party politics over the later Stuart period as a whole, but the emphasis is still on the House of Commons (*Politics under the later Stuarts: party conflict in a divided society* (1993)). The best survey of the historiography of political parties is in the first chapter of Mark Knights' *Politics and opinion in crisis, 1678–81.*

[2] J. R. Jones, 'Parties and parliament', p. 49.

[3] J. H. Murray (ed.), *A new English dictionary on historical principles*, 10 vols. (Oxford, 1888–1927), IV, p. 12.

[4] Unlike the later Country party, neither faction had a reform programme.

is used to describe an organised group with a fairly consistent membership and voting behaviour, possessing several common objectives and adhering to publicly professed political principles.[5]

I

For the first fifteen years of the reign an 'opposition' party did not exist in either House. There were, however, groups of men who criticised royal policies and government ministers. They were neither effectively organised nor consistent in their behaviour. As in the period before the Civil War, lords who disliked specific royal policies continued the practice of criticising the king's advisors rather than the king himself. It is impossible to pinpoint all the government's critics in any one session between 1660 and 1675 because of the paucity of division lists and reports of debates.[6]

From protests, dissents,[7] proxy lists and letters it is possible to discern four main groups of government critics during the 1660s. Often their personnel and ideas re-appeared in the later Country party. There was a small group led by the Catholic earl of Bristol during the years 1661 to 1663, a diverse faction headed by the flamboyant duke of Buckingham in 1666/7, a larger group of ex-Parliamentarians and finally various disgruntled former Royalists who criticised aspects of the Restoration settlement.[8] The picture is complicated both because Bristol and Buckingham drew support from ex-Parliamentarians and former Royalists and because at times these lords supported royal policies. Former Parliamentarians backed Clarendon's religious policies during the early 1660s, and only later drifted into 'opposition' when the government sponsored legislation against moderate dissenters.[9]

Short parliamentary sessions meant that the principal arenas for factional and political jousting were the court and the privy council. The king's appointment of a privy council composed of both former Royalists and former Parliamentarians, holding ·opposing religious views, guaranteed disagreement on policy, which sometimes spilled over into the Lords.[10] In September 1662 there were deep divisions between orthodox Anglicans and

---

[5] J. R. Jones, 'Parties and parliament', p. 58; Tim Harris, *Politics under the later Stuarts*, pp. 5–6. There is no exclusive definition of 'party'. It was necessarily a vague and flexible concept.

[6] The only known surviving division list for this period which gives all the names of those voting is on the question of who was entitled to hold the office of Lord Great Chamberlain (Carte MSS 109, fols. 313–17, 11 July 1661).

[7] Only the names of those lords who attended the day after a vote and bothered to sign the Journal are given in protests and dissents. Therefore they are not necessarily an accurate guide to the strength of 'opposition' in the House.

[8] Former Royalist peers are discussed in the first section of the next chapter.

[9] See below, pp. 209–10.

[10] Seaward, p. 27; Swatland, 'Privy councillors', pp. 69–70.

Presbyterians in the council over the enforcement of the Act of Uniformity.[11] This disunity manifested itself in the Lords in February and March 1663 when Anglican privy councillors clashed with their Presbyterian colleagues Anglesey, Robartes and Manchester, over the king's bill to dispense ministers from the provisions of the Uniformity Act.[12] Unresolved conciliar disagreements over the Irish Cattle Bill and the impeachment of Clarendon also flowed over into the chamber. Ministers who opposed government policy on the floor of the House rarely became permanent critics in the 1660s. Even Lord Ashley (later earl of Shaftesbury), the Chancellor of the Exchequer, who criticised aspects of royal policy during this decade, did not lead an 'opposition' group until the mid-1670s when the political climate was dominated by anxieties about popery.[13]

A strong desire for offices and rewards also underpinned factional struggles at court and in parliament. Many of those who followed the lead of Bristol and Buckingham did so because they had not received in 1660 those offices and financial rewards which they considered their due for their adherence to the Royalist cause during the 1640s and 1650s. At the Restoration there were simply not enough offices, pensions and gifts at the Crown's disposal to satisfy every ex-Cavalier. One contemporary commented that 'the poor Cavalier, or loyal suffering party, who hoped for a heaven upon earth in this king's reign fell into a worse state than that they were in before'.[14] Many such men had incurred considerable debts in the Royalist cause, and with little success petitioned the king for reparation during the 1660s.[15] As the old Cavalier, Lord Lucas, realised when he vigorously complained about a supply bill in 1671, one method of drawing the king's attention to the plight of his fellow sufferers was to obstruct government business in the upper chamber.[16]

Ex-Royalists' frustration was further compounded when the king honoured his former enemies with titles, offices of state, land and pensions in 1660/1. The Parliamentarian commander, the earl of Manchester, became Lord Chamberlain; his associate, Viscount Saye and Sele, held the office of Lord Privy Seal; Lord Ashley was made Chancellor of the Exchequer; and other senior ex-Parliamentarians, such as the duke of Albemarle and the earl of Sandwich, acquired an array of civil and military posts. Their influence in government aroused bitter jealousy on the part of some ex-Cavaliers, who in

[11] Carte MSS 32, fol. 3, O'Neale to Ormond, 2 Sept. 1662.
[12] Haley, *Shaftesbury*, pp. 164–6; Committee Minutes 1, pp. 295, 298.
[13] Ibid., p. 345.
[14] *A detection of the Court and the state of England* (3rd edn, 1697), p. 425.
[15] *Cal. SP Dom.*, 1663–4, p. 6, earl of Norwich to Charles II, 8 Jan. 1663; 1665–6, p. 138, earl of Berkshire to the king, undated petition; p. 330, petition of the marquis of Worcester, c. March 1666; *Memoirs of Thomas, earl of Ailesbury*, 2 vols. (1890), pp. 6–7.
[16] Stowe MSS 182, fols. 96–7, Lord Lucas' speech to the House of Lords, 12 Feb. 1671.

1663 tried to persuade Charles that 'he ought not to hear or listen to the advice of those old dotards or councillors that were heretofore his enemies'.[17]

The target of most resentment was the man regarded as the architect of government policy, Clarendon. The Lord Chancellor's censorious and imperious manner, his influence with the king and his domination of government business won him few friends and much animosity. Bristol and Buckingham loathed him, believing him responsible for preventing them from obtaining high offices at the Restoration. Between 1661 and 1663 Bristol mounted an offensive both at court and in parliament to undermine him. In part he was motivated by revenge – Clarendon had agitated for his removal from office in 1659 following his conversion to Catholicism – but he also saw the Chancellor as a barrier to achieving toleration for English Catholics.[18] It is difficult to be sure who were Bristol's allies in the Lords during this period. In 1662 when he was advocating schemes for a liberty of conscience for Catholics and Protestant dissenters he was associated with Bishop Gauden and possibly with Lord Ashley. In 1663 when he launched his inept impeachment of Clarendon in the Lords he drew support from discontented former Cavaliers, notably Northampton, Lucas, Derby and Gerard.[19]

In several respects Bristol's tactics anticipated those of the Country party. His revival of impeachment as a method of attacking an unpopular minister, though a dismal failure in 1663, was adopted by Buckingham in 1667 and by members of the Country party, most successfully against Danby in 1678/9. Like Buckingham, he sought popularity both inside and outside parliament. He deliberately mingled with London citizens immediately before his impeachment of Clarendon in July 1663.[20] To broaden the basis of his parliamentary following, he allied himself with the Chancellor's critics in the House of Commons, such as Thomas Tompkins, Sir Richard Temple and Sir Charles Hussey, and achieved some popularity there with backbench MPs by voicing widely held criticisms of the government. In a speech to the Commons on 1 July he condemned the corruption and misdemeanours of the king's ministers and hinted at a connection between Clarendon and popery.[21] This was the first occasion in Restoration England that a peer addressed the Commons, and might have been seen as a direct challenge to the king's control over the Lords in so much as he was asserting views in two Houses instead of one.

Following his failure to impeach Clarendon, Bristol went into hiding, and relative tranquillity was restored to the Lords until Buckingham established

[17] Pepys, IV, p. 137, 15 May 1663.
[18] Seaward, p. 217.
[19] Ibid., pp. 219, 230 n. 75.
[20] Yardley, 'George Villiers', pp. 79–81.
[21] Seaward, pp. 223, 227.

himself as the leading government critic during the autumn of 1666.[22] This was in the midst of an unpopular, indecisive and expensive war against the Dutch. Trade had suffered and rents had fallen on English estates. At the same time extravagance at court and corruption in the administration were rife. It was in a climate of mounting anti-court feeling that the duke launched his attack on the administration with a 'wild motion' that those officials who had embezzled public money during the war should be executed as traitors.[23] Calculated to appeal to the government's critics, this was a first step towards creating a faction in parliament. Buckingham's desire for popularity inside and outside parliament was to be the hallmark of his political 'career'. He intended to use his parliamentary following to obstruct government business, particularly supply bills, and to push through controversial measures, like the Irish Cattle Bill, and in so doing advertise his own ability to manage parliament for the king.[24]

His vigorous support for the Irish Cattle Bill during the autumn of 1666 enabled him to establish a small, but vocal following among discontented peers. Initiated in the Commons at the beginning of the session, the bill provided for the banning of imports of cattle from Ireland: a trade which was regarded by many as unfair competition for English beef farmers, and was seen as responsible for falling rents on native estates. On the other hand those peers who owned Irish estates, like Conway, Anglesey, Burlington and Butler, or who fattened and later sold the imported cattle in England, such as Berkeley of Berkeley, Cardigan and Bridgewater, mounted a ferocious opposition to the bill in the Lords. Charles and Clarendon were anxious for the Lords to reject, or, at the very least, amend it because any prohibition of Irish cattle imports would deprive the treasury of a useful source of customs duties.[25]

The bill's principal advocates were members of the king's privy council, particularly Southampton, Robartes, Carlisle, Dorchester, Manchester, Arlington and Northumberland. Their motives were various, and there is no evidence to connect them with Buckingham.[26] Only three peers can in fact be identified as working closely with him during the session: Lucas, Ashley and Northampton.[27] Lucas was an aggrieved ex-Cavalier, whose dislike of Clarendon had prompted him to move in the Lords at the beginning of the Oxford session (1665) that it was 'improper and derogatory' for the House

---

[22] Yardley, 'George Villiers', pp. 87–94.

[23] *Cal. SP Dom.*, 1666–7, pp. 185–6, Clifford to Arlington, 6 Oct. 1666; Pepys, VII, p. 309, 5 Oct. 1666.

[24] Yardley, 'George Villiers', pp. 91, 94, 333.

[25] Ibid., pp. 88–9; Seaward, p. 269.

[26] Seaward, pp. 268–9.

[27] Carte MSS 35, fol. 126, Conway to Ormond, 13 Nov., fols. 197–8, same to same, 29 Dec. 1666.

to thank the Lord Chancellor for his opening speech in the same manner as they had thanked the king for his.[28] Northampton's support of the Cattle Bill was also an anti-Clarendon gesture. This former Royalist soldier had been a close associate of Bristol in 1663 and had spoken on his behalf in the House in 1664.[29] Ashley's motives were a mixture of intense anti-Irish sentiment, hatred of Ormond, the lord lieutenant of Ireland, whose position in Ireland would be undermined by the passage of the bill, and economic self-interest. Other peers associated with Buckingham at this time included the Catholic earls of Berkshire, Shrewsbury and Bristol, Lord Gerard of Brandon, whose proxy the duke held after 27 November, and the northern peer, Lord Darcy.[30]

In several respects Buckingham's faction had features that were similar to the later Country party. Both the duke's faction and the Country leadership in the Lords had adherents in the Commons. Although Shaftesbury, one of the Country party leaders, had the greater number, Buckingham was able to muster a small group of Yorkshire members, such as Sir Henry Belasyse, Sir Thomas Gower and Sir Thomas Osborne, and other articulate government critics from the 1664/5 sessions, most notably Sir Richard Temple, Edward Seymour, William Garraway and Sir Robert Howard.[31] Clarendon noted in his autobiography that these MPs made themselves 'remarkable by opposing all things which were proposed in that house for the king's service, or which were like to be grateful to him'.[32] Both Buckingham and later Shaftesbury coordinated the parliamentary activities of their followers at meetings held in their private houses. At these the duke was highly critical of ministers' fitness to govern and of Charles' neglect of business, and 'then reported all the license and debauchery of the court in the most lively colours'.[33]

Several of the parliamentary tactics adopted by Shaftesbury, Buckingham and other Country party leaders in the 1670s had been used in the session of 1666/7. Both men succeeded in getting themselves appointed as chairmen of committees and managers of inter-House conferences so that they could influence proceedings. In contrast with his political inactivity during the years 1660 to 1665, Buckingham chaired a subcommittee appointed to draft a proviso on the Irish Cattle Bill in November 1666 and managed conferences on this and supply bills.[34] Impeachment was used in both periods to destroy government servants and highlight corruption in the administration. Just as

---

[28] Bodl., Rawlinson MSS A. 130, fol. 53v.

[29] Ibid., fols. 3–4; Carte MSS 81, fols. 224–34.

[30] Haley, *Shaftesbury*, pp. 187–9; Seaward, p. 269; Proxy Book 5, proxies entered between Sept. and Dec. 1666; Carte MSS 35, fol. 240, Conway to Ormond, 5 Jan. 1667; 217, fols. 352–3, Anglesey to Ormond, 10 Nov. 1666; fol. 354, same to same, 20 Nov. 1666.

[31] Seaward, pp. 300–1; Yardley, 'George Villiers', pp. 90–1; Clarendon, *Life*, II, pp. 132–3.

[32] Clarendon, *Life*, II, p. 133.

[33] Ibid.

[34] *LJ*, XII, 12, 30, 33, 37, 48–50, 58, 74; Yardley, 'George Villiers', p. 93.

in 1678 Country peers welcomed the Commons' impeachment of five Catholic peers who were not themselves prominent figures, so in the 1660s Buckingham's adherents in the Commons were involved in the attempt to impeach Viscount Mordaunt, the governor of Windsor Castle, ostensibly for corrupt practices, but in reality for his friendship with Clarendon. In the Lords, Buckingham pressed for a speedy trial. Eager to suppress the impeachment, the government used a variety of delaying tactics, including fomenting a privilege dispute with the Commons until the prorogation in early February 1667.[35] The impeachment may have been, as some contemporaries believed, a trial run for Clarendon's own impeachment.[36]

In other respects, however, the Country party was distinct from Buckingham's faction. Shaftesbury and his lieutenants had a definite reform programme that included relief for Protestant dissenters, firm measures against papists, and regular parliaments. During his short period as an 'opposition' leader in the session of 1666–7, Buckingham had few tangible policies, and those he did advocate, such as the prohibition of the import of Irish cattle and the reduction of corruption at court, were essentially negative, employed to win him popularity and government office. Unlike Shaftesbury, neither Buckingham nor his associates managed proxies. Also, in terms of personnel Buckingham's faction was far more of a hotch-potch of discontented former Cavaliers, Catholics and the occasional ex-Parliamentarian than the Country party, which was exclusively Protestant and had a substantial Presbyterian element.

There were over forty Presbyterians sitting in the House in 1661, and the majority had had close associations with the Parliamentarian cause in the Civil War. Presbyterian peers had sought a conditional restoration with statutory limitations on the powers of the Crown in April 1660. They had wanted parliament to control the militia and to appoint all major officers of state. Although leading Civil War Presbyterians had been 'neutralised' by court offices and rewards, others still hankered after restrictions on the Crown in the mid-1660s. In the summer of 1667 Northumberland, Leicester and Holles met in Guildford to discuss impeaching Clarendon, disbanding the king's guards and the redress of other unspecified grievances. Northumberland alleged that the troops ostensibly raised to defend England from coastal attack could be used to establish rule by a standing army. Earlier he had criticised the government in the Lords, resisting the re-establishment of the council of the North and the Bill of Uniformity in 1662.[37]

[35] Seaward, pp. 286–7; Yardley, 'George Villiers', pp. 96–7.
[36] Bodl., Rawlinson MSS A. 130, fols. 75v, 80; Carte MSS 35, fols. 148, 191–2, Conway to Ormond, 27 Nov., 29 Dec. 1666.
[37] H. C. Foxcroft (ed.), *A supplement to Burnet's history of my own time* (Oxford, 1903), pp. 77–8; PRO, PRO 31/3/110, D'Estrades to Louis XIV, 28 Jan./6 Feb. 1662; Clarendon, *Life*, I, p. 553; J. S. Clarke, *The life of James the Second, king of England, etc., collected out of memoirs writ of his own hand*, 2 vols. (1816), II, pp. 426–7.

Most criticism was vented against the church settlement. Until the government's abandonment in the spring of 1663 of its policy of establishing a broad church, Presbyterians provided Charles and Clarendon with the support necessary to modify bills sent from the Commons to settle the church. After this date most condemned legislation against Protestant dissenters, such as the Conventicle Bills of 1663, 1664 and 1670, and the Five Mile Bill of 1665.

They were much less unified than has been portrayed by one historian.[38] Those who were strong exponents of toleration, such as Ashley and Wharton, supported Bristol's impeachment of Clarendon in July 1663, whilst a few, notably Grey of Wark and Townshend, were sympathetic to Clarendon.[39] Four years later, during the protracted debates in the Lords on whether to commit Clarendon to the Tower following his impeachment, Presbyterians were even more divided. Some remained neutral, such as Wharton and Manchester; others, notably Holles, Anglesey and Denbigh, defended the ex-Lord Chancellor whilst a small group that included Pembroke, Saye and Sele, Albemarle, Carlisle and Dover protested when the House refused to imprison him.[40] Denbigh was a close friend of Clarendon whilst Holles and Anglesey objected to the imprisonment of a peer on a general, unsubstantiated charge of treason. Those Presbyterians who backed the impeachment may have done so for religious reasons since they had been critical of the orthodox Anglican policies associated with Clarendon since 1663.[41]

All the groups and factions that appeared in the House during the 1660s were transitory. As issues changed so existing factions fragmented and others appeared. The most serious opposition to government policy manifested itself during the session of 1666–7 when England was fighting an unpopular war against the United Provinces and France. After the war and the fall of the earl of Clarendon it is more difficult to detect 'opposition' groups in the House. This is largely because there was no single chief minister to dominate government policy and provide a focus for discontent, as Clarendon had done.[42] Also, from the autumn of 1667 Clarendon's leading critic in the House, Buckingham, was involved in the formulation of government policy and, for the most part, sought to manage parliament for the king.

The main feature of the five years after Clarendon's fall was rivalry between privy councillors. The Francophile Buckingham and the Hispanophile Arlington clashed over foreign policy before Arlington eventually acqui-

---

[38] See Richard Davis, 'The "Presbyterian" opposition', pp. 1–35.

[39] Carte MSS 81, fols. 2, 224; Seaward, pp. 229–30.

[40] *LJ*, XII, 142.

[41] Davis, 'The "Presbyterian" opposition', p. 9.

[42] See John Miller, *Charles II* (1991), pp. 142–219 and Ronald Hutton, *Charles II: King of England, Scotland and Ireland* (Oxford, 1989), pp. 254–86 for an analysis of government policy during the years 1667–72.

esced in the declaration of war against the Dutch in 1672. However, neither was in total agreement on foreign policy during these years. The same two ministers were united in their anxiety that Ormond be deprived of his lord lieutenancy of Ireland – which happened in 1669. Buckingham also laboured to undermine the position of his long-time enemy the duke of York as head of the navy, and succeeded in having his client Osborne made joint Treasurer of the navy together with Arlington's client, Littleton. All this was essentially 'court' faction, but 'court' faction rarely lacked a parliamentary dimension. Thus in 1670 Buckingham and Ashley supported a private divorce bill (that of Lord Roos), which many saw as a possible precedent should Charles II decide to remarry, and hence disinherit the heir presumptive, York. In 1671 the supporters of Buckingham and Arlington continued a privy council disagreement over amendments to a foreign commodities bill in both Houses.[43]

II

During the sessions of 1674 and 1675 contemporaries commented on an organised 'opposition' in the Lords, which they variously described as 'Malcontent', 'Confederate', and most commonly, the 'Country Party'.[44] The term 'Country' had been coined in the 1620s by those members of both Houses who believed they represented the interests of the country against a corrupt and unpatriotic court faction, dominated by the first duke of Buckingham. From the mid-1670s Country lords were a distinct group of noblemen (in the main former Parliamentarians and discontented ex-Royalists), advocating policies that were remarkably similar to those usually associated with the Whigs after 1680. Their policies, which included securing a Protestant succession to the throne, protecting subjects' rights and liberties, easing restrictions on Protestant dissenters and the adoption of a Protestant foreign policy, were designed to reduce the danger from popery and arbitrary government.

The Country party was neither another court faction nor a short-lived group of discontented lords. Most of the thirty-two lords that can be identified in 1675 had no close association with the court. Only eight held government or court offices and of these five were removed from office by 1677. Country peers comprised a party in the sense that they had specific policies, which they publicised beyond Westminster, and were highly consistent in their voting habits. They had acknowledged leaders, the earl of Shaftesbury, the duke of Buckingham and Lords Salisbury, Holles and Wharton, and also

[43] Harris, *Life of Sandwich*, II, pp. 333–7.
[44] Burnet, *History*, II, p. 82; *Cal. SP Ven.*, 38, pp. 228, 391, 416, Alberti to Doge and Senate, 20 Feb., 9 April, 4 June 1674; Add. MSS 29,571, fol. 312, C. Hatton to Lord Hatton, 22 June 1676.

a rudimentary organisation that extended beyond the confines of the House of Lords. However, they did not constitute a formal opposition in the modern sense of waiting to form the next administration. Whilst there is evidence that Shaftesbury and Buckingham sought senior positions in the government after their dismissals in 1673 and 1674 respectively, most of their followers preferred to redress national grievances rather than shoulder the burdens of the executive.[45]

The emergence of the Country party was a consequence of both extreme anxieties about popery, in particular the danger posed to the church by a Catholic heir to the throne, and the authoritarian policies associated with Lord Treasurer Danby. From 1673/4 many in both Houses genuinely believed in a popish conspiracy in which the court, assisted by France, intended to impose Catholicism and an absolutist form of government based on the French model on England.[46] The existence of such a conspiracy appeared to be confirmed by recent events: the alliance with France against the United Provinces, the issuing of the Declaration of Indulgence (neither of which had been undertaken with parliamentary approval), the failure of the duke of York to take Anglican communion at Easter 1673 and the surrender of his offices under the Test Act, giving credence to rumours of his conversion to Catholicism, and finally his marriage to the Catholic Mary Beatrice in the autumn of that year. Together these last two events aroused anxiety about the succession to the throne and, according to Sir Edward Dering, 'gave no unreasonable foundation to fear that the king having no children, when the duke should come to the crown the Protestant religion would be at least oppressed, if not extirpated'.[47]

When parliament assembled on 7 January 1674 those keenest to counter the alleged popish conspiracy were ex-Parliamentarians and Presbyterian lords. Foremost among them was the skilled orator and experienced politician, the earl of Shaftesbury. Shaftesbury had been dismissed as Lord Chancellor on 9 November 1673 for alleged intrigues against York. After thirteen years as a minister he was now at liberty to criticise the court in the Lords and to establish a following of like-minded peers. The former Cromwellian councillor opened the debate on religion, alleging that an uprising of 16,000 Catholics was imminent in the vicinity of London. Fearing the slaughter of Protestants, the House addressed the king to issue a proclamation for the removal of all Catholics from a ten-mile radius of the capital.[48] It soon became evident that the duke was Shaftesbury's real target. On 24

---

[45] Haley, *Shaftesbury*, p. 515; Hertfordshire RO, Cowper Papers, D/EP/F24, Shaftesbury to Sir William Cowper, 8 Sept. 1678.

[46] Miller, *Popery and politics*, pp. 121–53.

[47] M. F. Bond (ed.), *The diaries and papers of Sir Edward Dering* (1976), p. 126.

[48] BL, Stowe MSS 204, fol. 23, Conway to Essex, 10 Jan. 1674.

January his associate, the earl of Salisbury, moved 'that the duke of York's children should be bred up in the Protestant religion'. The earl of Carlisle, who had sat in the Barebones Parliament, had the duke in mind when he urged that 'none of the royal family should be married to papists except it were by consent of parliament'.[49] Even exclusion was openly debated. On 10 February when the peers were discussing a clause in the bill to secure the Protestant religion, Carlisle, seconded by Halifax and Shaftesbury, proposed that the penalty for a breach of this clause, which made it illegal for a prince to marry a Catholic without parliament's approval, should be exclusion from the throne.[50] The weight of opinion was hostile to this proposition, and so Shaftesbury and his adherents let it drop. By the close of the session on 24 February contemporaries had noted other lords of a similar persuasion, including the duke of Buckingham, the earls of Clare and Denbigh, Viscounts Fauconberg and Mordaunt and Lord Holles.[51]

Much of the responsibility for the transformation of this malcontent group into a substantial party rested with the peer who was Lord Treasurer from June 1673 to March 1679. Having initially advocated comprehension Danby reverted to an orthodox Anglican policy early in 1675 that was reminiscent of Clarendon's approach to religion during the years from 1663 to 1667. The first clear sign of a change in government policy was an order of council dated 3 February 1675. This provided for the enforcement of the penal laws against Catholics and dissenters. JPs were expressly instructed to enforce the Conventicle Act and suppress all worship that was not in accordance with the Act of Uniformity. When parliament assembled on 13 April an unprecedented number of peers, twenty-eight in all, voted against giving the customary thanks to the king for his speech, which referred to the recent enforcement of the laws against dissenters. Six of the ten lords who signed the subsequent protest against giving thanks were former Parliamentarians and all voted regularly against the court later in the session.[52] This was the first time a formal protest was made against thanking the king for his opening speech.

Even more disconcerting for these lords was the introduction by Danby's brother-in-law, Lord Lindsey, two days later of a bill entitled 'An act to prevent dangers which might arise from persons disaffected to the government'.[53] Peers, MPs and all officeholders were to declare 'that it is not lawful

---

[49] Ibid., fol. 114, same to same, 27 Jan. 1674.

[50] Add. MSS 23,136, fol. 87, earl of Kincardine to Lauderdale, 20 Jan. 1674.

[51] BL, Verney MSS M/636, reel 27, Sir Ralph Verney to Edmund Verney, 8 Jan. 1674; *Cal. SP Ven.*, 38, pp. 201, 221, 228, Alberti to Doge and Senate, 16 Jan., 13/21 Feb. 1674; Swatland, 'House of Lords', pp. 244–5.

[52] Carte MSS 79, fol. 70; *LJ*, XII, 656. The former Parliamentarians were: Delamer, Paget, Salisbury, Shaftesbury, Stamford and Wharton.

[53] A copy of the bill is preserved in the Townshend Papers in the British Library (BL, Add. MSS 41,656, fols. 79–80).

upon any pretence whatsoever to take arms against the king ... or against those that are commissioned by him'. They were to swear an oath that they would 'not at any time endeavour the alteration of the government either in church or state'.[54] The penalties for refusal to subscribe to the declaration and take the oath were to be exclusion from parliament and ejection from office.

This non-resting Test Bill confirmed many of the Country peers' worst fears about the government's alleged arbitrary intentions. Shaftesbury observed in 'A letter from a person of quality to his friend in the country' that the oath was conceived by the government 'to make a distinct party from the rest of the nation of the high episcopal man, and of the old Cavalier, who are to swallow the hopes of enjoying all the power and office of the kingdom'.[55] Shaftesbury and Buckingham were particularly critical of the power the bill intended to bestow on the bishops and of their alliance with Danby's administration. Older peers remembered Archbishop Laud's influence on royal policy before the Civil War. Since the return of the bishops to the Lords in 1661 Presbyterian peers had frequently voiced their resentment of their powers within the church. This anti-episcopalianism was a marked feature of the Country party in both Houses during the mid-1670s. In 1677 Country peers attacked Danby's bill for securing the Protestant religion because too much power was to be vested in the bishops in making church appointments under a future Catholic monarch. Two years later they questioned the bishops' judicial powers, in particular whether they could participate in the impeachment trials of Danby and the five Catholic peers.[56]

Serious objections were also raised over the declaration and in particular, the clause about not taking up arms against those commissioned by the king, as this could be used to legitimise a standing army. The Test would have prevented reform of the Church of England and relief for Protestant dissenters, because the oath ruled out any change in the church, however much political expediency or 'Christian compassion to Protestant dissenters' required it. As Shaftesbury argued in the *Letter*, the bill precluded the restoration of the liturgy to what it had been under Elizabeth I, and the establishment of a broader Protestant church. Country peers also argued that the oath would remove parliament's legislative functions and reduce it to 'an instrument to raise money' since every new Act was an alteration in either church or state.[57]

[54] Ibid., fol. 79.
[55] 'Letter from a person of quality to his friend in the country', in *Parliamentary History*, IV, p. xxxix.
[56] T. Harris, *Politics under the later Stuarts*, pp. 72–3; M. Goldie, 'Danby, the bishops and the Whigs', in T. Harris, P. Seaward and M. Goldie (eds.), *The politics of religion in Restoration England* (Oxford, 1990), pp. 79–81, 82–93; Carte MSS 81, fols. 561–8.
[57] 'Letter from a person of quality ...', pp. xxxix, lv–lvii.

Although a protracted jurisdictional dispute with the Commons over *Shirley* v. *Fagg* meant that the Test Bill was still at committee stage by the prorogation on 9 June, its impact on the peerage was immediate and lasting. It assisted in swelling the numbers of the Country party, a process that is clearly discernible from voting figures. As the implications of the measure became clear, hostility to it increased from twenty-seven votes on 21 April to thirty-eight on the 23rd, whereas support declined from sixty-one to thirty-nine.[58] From the names of those who signed the four protests against the bill and from those lords cited in 'A letter from a person of quality' a formidable opposition of no fewer than thirty-two Protestant and four Catholic peers is identifiable.[59] Twenty-two of the bill's Protestant critics were of Parliamentarian ancestry, and they included Bedford, Delamer, Holles, Denbigh, Eure, Grey of Rolleston, Salisbury, Saye and Sele, Stamford, Shaftesbury, Townshend and Wharton. The remaining ten were of Royalist extraction and included several peers who, for the most part, continued to oppose government policies until the end of the decade, such as Halifax, Buckingham, Clarendon (2nd earl), Bridgewater and Carnarvon.[60] All were opposed to Danby's policies and some were sympathetic towards dissenters, notably Halifax and Buckingham. At least four, Burlington, Bridgewater, Carnarvon and Clarendon, were old 'Clarendonians', and as such had never forgiven Danby for his part in the former Lord Chancellor's impeachment.

The Test backfired on Danby, uniting his Protestant and Catholic critics, who jointly comprised a sizeable section of the House of Lords. Almost all those Protestant peers who opposed the bill voted with the Catholics to address the king to dissolve parliament in the autumn session, and their names repeatedly appear on lists of Country lords later in the reign.[61] If the king and his brother were distrusted for their associations with popery and arbitrary government, henceforth the chief minister, the architect of the Test Bill, was also viewed with the utmost suspicion because its provisions suggested that he too shared their arbitrary intentions. Danby's vigorous efforts to cure royal financial insolvency and make the king less dependent on parliament for supply, his endeavours to manage both Houses through his Court parties and his sudden reversal of the king's pro-French foreign policy were all construed by Shaftesbury's adherents as a smokescreen for popery, military rule and even the abolition of parliament itself.[62] It is no wonder then

[58] Carte MSS 79, fols. 2, 17; *Bulstrode Papers*, p. 286.
[59] 'Letter from a person of quality ...', pp. xlvii–lxvi; *LJ*, XII, 665, 668–9, 671, 677; Browning, *Danby*, III, pp. 122–5.
[60] Davis, 'The "Presbyterian" opposition', p. 15; Haley, *Shaftesbury*, p. 376; Burnet, *History*, II, 81–4.
[61] See Swatland, 'House of Lords', Appendix III, pp. 382–400.
[62] Miller, *Popery and politics*, pp. 148–9; A. Marvell, *An account of the growth of popery and arbitrary government* (1677), pp. 15–16, 40, 47, 49, 88, 155; Northamptonshire RO, Finch-Hatton MSS 2437, Richard Langhorn to Lord Hatton, 21 Dec. 1673.

that during the height of national alarm about the popish plot in December 1678 the disclosure of letters from Charles to Louis XIV, signed by both the king and Danby, which revealed that recent prorogations of parliament had been bought by French money triggered the political crisis which resulted in Danby's impeachment and imprisonment. The letters provided clear evidence of popery and arbitrary government: the issues which preoccupied the Country party for the next three years.[63]

III

A. S. Turberville and J. R. Jones have argued that nothing resembling the Whig party existed in either House until the 'Exclusion Crisis' of 1679–81.[64] Turberville has asserted that there was very little continuity between those lords who opposed the Test Bill in 1675 and those who voted for Exclusion five years later.[65] Jones portrays the Country party of 1675–9 as a heterogeneous collection of twenty to thirty peers who were not consistent opponents of the government and were only held together by their opposition to Danby.[66] More recently, Tim Harris claims that the Country party lacked the degree of leadership and cohesion needed for it to qualify as a party whilst Jonathan Scott denies the very existence of a 'Whig' party in either House![67] However, an analysis of the personnel, policies, voting behaviour and organisation of both the Country party from 1675 to 1679 and the 'Whig' party after 1680 reveals a very different picture: one of continuity, cohesion and, above all, sound and well-organised leadership in the House of Lords.

There were in fact very few significant differences between the Country and 'Whig' parties in the upper House, the first being a change of name. Irrespective of whether they voted for the Exclusion Bill on 15 November 1680, Country peers were labelled by their Court opponents 'Whigs' after the Scottish rebels of 1679. Mark Knights has recently demonstrated from his extensive study of pamphlet literature that the term 'Whig' only became common usage after the dissolution of the Oxford Parliament and that other derogatory names were also applied, such as 'Whirligigs', the 'Adverse party' and the 'Malignant party'.[68] The second difference was that following the

---

[63] Scott, *Restoration crisis*, pp. 35–6.

[64] J. R. Jones, *First Whigs*, pp. 20, 72; Turberville, 'House of Lords under Charles II', pt II, p. 58.

[65] Turberville, ibid., p. 58.

[66] Jones, *First Whigs*, pp. 20, 72.

[67] T. Harris, *Politics under the later Stuarts*, p. 63; Scott, *Restoration crisis*, p. 44.

[68] Knights, *Politics and opinion in crisis*, pp. 109–11. To avoid confusion in this study the term 'Whig' is only applied to peers from the autumn of 1680. Although the term was not used widely until 1681, Knights acknowledges that it was used from 1679. Contemporaries had no accepted definition of Whiggery. A Whig was usually someone who supported several causes:

revelations of the popish plot there was far wider support among Country peers for taking firm action to secure a Protestant succession than there had been in the mid-1670s. By the autumn of 1680 exclusion had become a central aim of most Country lords.[69]

There was remarkable continuity in terms of personnel between the Country party of 1675–9 and the later Adverse or Whig party in the Lords. Virtually every Protestant peer who was in 'opposition' in 1675 was still in 'opposition' during the years 1679–81. Forty-one Protestant lords voted against the government in 1675. Of the thirty-three still alive in 1679, twenty-seven remained in 'opposition'. These included Buckingham, Delamer, Eure, Grey of Wark, Kent, Lovelace, Manchester, Salisbury, Shaftesbury, Stamford, Suffolk, Townshend and Wharton. Four Country peers were absent after 1678 and the earls of Chesterfield and Clarendon deserted to the Court party. Thirteen of the original 1675 'opposition' voted for Exclusion as did the heirs of a further seven, making a total of twenty out of the thirty Exclusionists who voted on 15 November 1680.[70]

Such continuity is also evident when one examines Country and 'Whig' policies. Support for exclusion has been used to distinguish the 'Whigs' from earlier 'opposition' groups in parliament.[71] But as early as 10 February 1674, the earl of Carlisle, assisted by Shaftesbury and Halifax, had proposed exclusion from the succession for any prince who married a Catholic without parliament's approval.[72] In the same session the Venetian Resident noted a pro-Dutch party taking shape, in which some 'flatter' themselves 'with the hope that he [the Prince of Orange] may succeed to the Crown'.[73] The Duke of York was so perturbed by mounting opposition in parliament to his right of succession that he made overtures to several 'malcontent' lords shortly before the spring session of 1675. James offered to use his influence with the

toleration for peaceable Protestant dissenters, frequent parliaments and a Protestant succession and foreign policy. Exclusion should not be used as the sole test of Whiggery. (Kenyon, *Stuart England*, pp. 11–12; *Dictionary of historical principles*, x, p. 43; T. Harris, *Politics under the later Stuarts*, pp. 80–2, 86–94.)

[69] Scott, reacting against the traditional importance given to exclusion by historians, accords it little significance, even in 1680. In fact it was one of several solutions to the succession problem considered by the 'opposition' leadership in both Houses and was only of paramount importance for Country peers in October/November 1680, before the rejection of the Exclusion Bill. After 15 November the peers turned their attentions to limitations on a popish successor. (Scott, *Restoration crisis*, p. 20.)

[70] The thirteen Country lords were: Bedford, Delamer, Eure, Lovelace, Salisbury, Shaftesbury, Stamford, Grey, Essex, Kent, Manchester, Wharton and Sunderland. Lord Clare, who also voted for exclusion, had been a leading 'opposition' peer in 1674, but was abroad in 1675. He continued to support the Country party after this date. The heirs of the seven Country peers were: Brooke, Crew, Grey of Wark, Herbert, Howard of Escrick, Leicester and Paget.

[71] Jones, *First Whigs*, pp. 10, 17, 67, 72.

[72] *Cal. SP Ven.*, 38, pp. 220–1, Alberti to Doge and Senate, 13 Feb. 1674; Add. MSS 23,136, fol. 87, Kincardin to Lauderdale, 10 Feb. 1674.

[73] Ibid., p. 221.

king to secure toleration for Protestant dissenters and to promote 'good laws' for safeguarding subjects' rights and liberties in return for the 'Confederate' peers (Bedford, Holles, Halifax, Carlisle, Fauconberg, Salisbury and Newport are mentioned by name) refraining from questioning his right of succession in the coming session.[74] Other matters, such as Danby's Test and their vigorous attempts to persuade the king to dissolve the Cavalier Parliament so preoccupied Country peers for the two sessions of 1675 and the beginning of the 1677 session that exclusion was put on the back-burner. It was certainly not forgotten: 1676 saw the publication of a pamphlet written by Lord Holles entitled *Some considerations upon the question, whether the parliament is dissolved by its prorogation of 15 months*. This explicitly stated that acts of parliament 'can bind, limit, restrain and govern the descent and inheritance of the Crown itself, and all rights and titles thereto'.[75]

Recent research has demonstrated that until the autumn of 1680 'opposition' leaders in both Houses were not united behind exclusion.[76] It was one of many ideas considered during the period 1678–81. Halifax, Holles and Essex wanted to place limitations on the powers of a Catholic monarch. Others proposed a regency in which York should rule in name with William of Orange as regent. In 1679 Shaftesbury resurrected the question, first raised in 1667/8, whether Charles should divorce and marry a Protestant. The legitimisation of Monmouth was also discussed, but this, like divorce, depended on the king. Mark Knights has convincingly argued that a power vacuum at Court, which followed the fall of Danby, as well as mistrust of the king scuppered these schemes, so that by the autumn of 1680 exclusion was the only practical means of securing a Protestant succession.[77]

Even in 1680 exclusion was one of a number of key 'opposition' policies which were a direct consequence of the widely held belief that the king sought to impose popery and arbitrary government on the country at the expense of Protestantism, English liberties and parliament itself. Jonathan Scott claims that exclusion was not the major concern of any parliament from 1679 to 1681, arguing, like Knights, that the crisis was about the succession in general and that 'opposition' leaders proposed a number of remedies.[78] Danby's parliamentary management, notably his bribery of MPs, the king's pro-French foreign policy, his frequent prorogations of parliament (1678–80) and the existence of a standing army, Scott argues, provided the 'opposition' with evidence of the government's arbitrary intentions. He is

---

[74] Leeds Public Library, Mexborough MSS, Reresby Letters 8/5, Goodrick to Reresby, 23 Jan. 1675; *Cal. SP Ven.*, 38, p. 327, Alberti to Doge and Senate, 5 Feb. 1675.

[75] D. Holles, *Some considerations upon the question whether the parliament is dissolved by its prorogation of 15 months* (1676), p. 26.

[76] Knights, *Politics and opinion in crisis*, pp. 30, 32–5, 48–9, 64, 65, 73.

[77] Ibid., pp. 32–5, 78–87.

[78] Scott, *Restoration crisis*, pp. 17–20.

right to emphasise the significance of the popish plot revelations in the autumn of 1678 as confirming men's worst fears that French money was to be employed to render parliament redundant and enable Charles to maintain a standing army and change the religion. Therefore in the last session of the Cavalier Parliament and the three subsequent parliaments of the reign, Country peers spent the vast majority of their time promoting measures to counter the threat from popery and arbitrary government, as the 'malcontent' lords had done in 1674. These included the impeachment of Danby and the five Catholic peers, legislation against Catholics in general, the reform of the habeas corpus procedure, placing strict limitations on the powers of a popish successor (particularly after the defeat of the Exclusion Bill) and lifting restrictions on Protestant dissenters.[79]

Freedom of worship for Protestant dissenters appealed to 'Whigs' in both Houses and was especially popular with peers of Presbyterian and Parliamentarian extraction. They argued that it was vital for all persuasions of Protestants to unite to resist the challenge of popery. No fewer than twenty-four of the thirty lords who voted against the rejection of the Exclusion Bill were either Presbyterians with Parliamentarian ancestries, or those from Royalist families who had sympathised with nonconformists on earlier occasions.[80] After the defeat of the Exclusion Bill, 'opposition' peers made considerable efforts to exempt Protestant dissenters from the penal laws, voting for the repeal of the Elizabethan Sectaries Act and promoting a bill to discharge and pardon those Protestant dissenters indicted under the recusancy laws.

Most Country peers had also promoted the cause of Protestant dissenters in the mid-1670s. Anxious to re-admit Presbyterian ministers to the Church of England, they had endorsed the 1674 Comprehension Bill, and partly to facilitate further reform of the church had vehemently attacked Danby's 1675 Test.[81] No doubt many regarded toleration for Protestant dissenters like Buckingham did, when in November 1675 he sought permission of the House to introduce a bill for the ease of dissenting Protestants, as a means of widening support for the Country party among nonconformists outside parliament.[82] Country peers claimed that one reason for their unsuccessful attempt to address the king to dissolve parliament on 20 November 1675 had been to provide a House of Commons that would assist 'the dissenting Protestants ... [to] find more favour and ease'.[83] Three years later the

---

[79] Ibid., pp. 20, 38.

[80] The twenty-four peers were: Anglesey, Salisbury, Stamford, Lovelace, Paget, Rockingham, Leicester, Kent, Bedford, Shaftesbury, Herbert, Delamer, North, Grey of Wark, Clare, Manchester, Eure, Cornwallis, Howard, Wharton, Crew, Suffolk, Brooke and Essex (Add. MSS 51,319, fol. 55; Appendix 1 of this book).

[81] 'Letter from a person of quality', pp. xliv, xlviii, lvi, lvii.

[82] Yardley, 'George Villiers', pp. 226–7.

[83] 'The debate or argument for dissolving this present parliament', *Parl. Hist.*, IV, appendix vii, p. lxxvii.

marquis of Winchester and others discussed 'taking off the penal laws against the papists' in return for liberty of worship for Protestant dissenters.[84] Although Country peers channelled their energies into the investigation of the popish plot and the impeachment of Danby during the last session of the Cavalier Parliament, the plight of Protestant dissenters was not forgotten. On 2 May 1679 seven Country peers protested against a Commons' amendment to a bill to remove papists from London 'because there are thousands of dissenters that will be faithful, even to death, against the common enemies, the papists; which by the addition of the oaths to the Test, may be tempted to think themselves in interest obliged to take the papists' parts against us'.[85]

Of course not all Country lords were the friends of dissenters. The earl of Bridgewater was both an orthodox Anglican and a zealous opponent of dissent, but nevertheless joined with the Country party in the 1670s through his opposition to the administration of the earl of Danby. That Court renegade, the earl of Northampton, had also been a consistent enemy of dissent during the 1660s and 1670s, but voted for the Exclusion Bill and other 'Whig' measures. He had been closely associated with the duke of York and presumably knew better than most about his arbitrary inclinations. Similar fears were harboured by another former associate of York's, the earl of Macclesfield (Lord Gerard until 1679).[86]

Country and 'Whig' lords regarded frequent parliaments as vital for the reduction of Court corruption in the Commons (perceived to be a consequence of Danby's management) and for ensuring that firm measures could be taken against popery and arbitrary government. There was nothing novel about calls for frequent parliaments. The subject had been discussed in the Lords in 1641 during the debates on the Triennial Bill and was aired again shortly after the Restoration. On 28 January 1662 a committee chaired by Buckingham contemplated replacing the Triennial Act with a bill that required parliament to be called at least once every three years.[87] From 1674 to 1681 Country leaders asserted that new parliaments must be called regularly with sessions of several months rather than the customary few weeks.[88] Writing to the earl of Carlisle in a letter dated 3 February 1675, Shaftesbury set out his 'manifesto' for the approaching session, and near the top was a call for the dissolution of the current parliament and for frequent ones to be summoned in the future. Shaftesbury intended Carlisle to show the letter to

---

[84] Hertfordshire RO, Cowper Papers D/EP/F24, newsletter, 8 Jan. 1678.
[85] *LJ*, XIII, 549.
[86] R. W. Davis, 'The "Presbyterian" opposition', p. 20; Carte MSS 77, fols. 650–1; Seaward, pp. 66, 97; Swatland, 'The House of Lords', appendix III, pp. 382–400.
[87] Committee Minutes I, pp. 117–18; Seaward, p. 133.
[88] The king's adjournments, prorogations and dissolutions meant that the 'opposition' was unable to take adequate measures against popery and arbitrary government during the crisis of 1678–81.

other 'malcontent' lords, including Halifax, Fauconberg and Holles.[89] Although there was much talk of the desirability of frequent parliaments no bill was brought in to curtail the Crown's power to summon and dismiss them at will.[90] Instead the government's critics focused on the longevity of the Cavalier Parliament.

Country peers had very good reason to seek the dissolution of the Cavalier Parliament. By 1675 it had already been in existence for fourteen years and sessions lasted on average eight weeks, insufficient time to pass stiff legislation against popery and other national grievances. Such longevity, they claimed, had allowed parliament to become corrupted by the court through the distribution of offices, pensions, honours and money to MPs, making it subservient to the government and unrepresentative of the majority of electors.[91] This feature had been exacerbated by the earl of Danby's increasingly systematic management of the lower House. A new Commons, they thought, would be more independently minded and less susceptible to government management. It was also thought that a new House of Commons would contain fewer orthodox Anglicans, and therefore would be more sympathetic to passing legislation both to broaden the Church and to enable Protestant dissenters to worship freely.[92]

The Country party made three main attempts to 'persuade' the king to dissolve parliament, two in 1675 and the last in 1677. The first involved the orchestration of a bicameral conflict over the Lords' judicial authority in the spring session. By focusing parliament's attention on the issue of privilege instead of government business, Country leaders hoped the king would be forced to dissolve if he wanted harmony restored. Instead he opted to prorogue until the autumn. The second attempt, which was also carefully planned, came closer to success. Shortly before the adjournment on the afternoon of 20 November 1675 a young Country peer, Lord Mohun, proposed that the best way of ending the protracted privilege dispute with the Commons over *Shirley* v. *Fagg* was by addressing the king to dissolve parliament and summon a new one. Mohun had chosen his moment well because many Court lords and bishops had already vacated the chamber, leaving the Country party in the majority. In a long and elaborate speech Shaftesbury seconded the proposal. After an angry debate that lasted until about nine o'clock the question was finally put whether to address the king, but was defeated by a mere two votes.[93] The dissolutionists actually

---

[89] Haley, *Shaftesbury*, pp. 369–71; Carte MSS 38, fol. 277, Southwell to Ormond, 27 Feb. 1675.
[90] J. Miller, 'Charles II and his parliaments', *Transactions of the Royal Historical Society*, 32 (1982), p. 22, note 145.
[91] *LJ*, VIII, 33; *Parl. Hist.*, IV, pp. lxxii–lxxvi.
[92] Haley, *Shaftesbury*, p. 403; Yardley, 'George Villiers', pp. 225–7; *Parl. Hist.*, pp. 789–98.
[93] Verney Papers M/636 reel 29, Mr Fall to Sir Ralph Verney, 22 Nov. 1675; Haley, *Shaftesbury*, pp. 400–1.

outnumbered the Court party in the House, but held fewer proxies, and so lost the division! The duke of York and eleven Catholics cast their votes with the Country party in the hope that a new parliament might favour schemes to ease the restrictions on loyal Catholics.[94]

The last attempt to dissolve the Cavalier Parliament was a disastrous failure. On the first day of the 1677 session (15 February), Buckingham delivered a long speech arguing that the fifteen-month prorogation had effectively dissolved parliament since two statutes from Edward III's reign decreed that parliament must meet at least every twelve months.[95] The duke was backed by Shaftesbury, Salisbury and Wharton. A handful of other peers, including Holles, Stamford, Delamer, Bolingbroke, Halifax and Winchester, were to varying degrees sympathetic.[96] In contrast with November 1675, the duke of York and the Catholics were not prepared to aid the Country leaders, because to declare parliament dissolved was regarded by them as an invasion of the royal prerogative.[97] After some debate Buckingham's motion was laid aside and Danby's associate, Lord Frescheville, moved that he 'might be called to the bar, and then proceeded with as should be thought fit'.[98] Danby then suggested that Shaftesbury, Salisbury and Wharton might also be called to account for declaring parliament dissolved. The Court majority agreed and Salisbury and Wharton were required to seek the pardon of the king and the House, whilst Buckingham and Shaftesbury were required to do the same and also acknowledge that their actions were 'ill-advised'. None made the necessary submission or apology and all four were incarcerated in the Tower.[99] Although Salisbury, Wharton and Buckingham were released later in the summer, and Shaftesbury the following February, their imprisonment served as a warning to the Country party; not surprisingly no further attempts at dissolution were made during the life of the Cavalier Parliament.

The notion that parliaments should be summoned frequently assumed a new importance during the years 1678–81. The investigation of the popish plot and the attempt to counter the threat from popery and arbitrary government, which included securing a Protestant succession, depended on parliament sitting. Sensitive about the succession, on a number of occasions Charles prorogued and adjourned sessions of parliament in order to prevent the 'opposition' from organising an effective lobby. Deprived of a forum in which to keep the popish plot before the public, 'opposition' leaders tried to coerce the king into letting parliament meet in January 1680. Their ploy was

---

[94] BL Add. MSS 35,885, fol. 224 (division list, 20 Nov. 1675).
[95] Yardley, 'George Villiers', pp. 231–3; *Parl. Hist.*, IV, pp. 817–23; Carte MSS 79, fol. 37, Lord Wharton's notes on the debate in the House on 15 Feb. 1677; Leicestershire RO, Finch Papers PP. 41, Lord Finch's notes on the same debate.
[96] Carte MSS 79, fols. 37–43.
[97] See Haley, *Shaftesbury*, pp. 413–14.
[98] Carte MSS 79, fol. 37.
[99] Ibid., fol. 38; *Shaftesbury*, p. 419.

to launch a mass petitioning movement and thereby demonstrate that public opinion was behind their demand. Sixteen peers – Bedford, Saye and Sele, Huntingdon, Clare, Stamford, Shaftesbury, Rockingham, Kent, Eure, Holles, North, Chandos, Grey, Howard of Escrick, Herbert of Cherbury and Delamer – signed and presented a petition to Charles on 7 December 1679 in which they advised him to let parliament meet on 26 January.[100] These were among the most committed 'opposition' peers and it is worth noting that thirteen voted for the Exclusion Bill. Calls for frequent parliaments featured in the 'opposition' election campaign early in 1681 and it is likely that these were approved, if not actually orchestrated, by Shaftesbury and other 'Whig' leaders.[101]

Other reform proposals also had their antecedents earlier in the reign. The famous Habeas Corpus Amendment Bill, which received the royal assent on 27 May 1679, had been discussed by 'opposition' lords and commoners in three sessions of the Cavalier Parliament since its introduction in the Commons in April 1668.[102] The existing habeas corpus procedure, which was intended to safeguard persons from arbitrary imprisonment at the hands of the government, was open to considerable abuse. The 1679 bill rectified the most glaring deficiencies in the procedure and made it illegal to transport prisoners overseas.[103] Despite the absence of either reports of debates or division lists there can be little doubt that Country peers were the bill's promoters. It had been a Country measure earlier in the decade. The proviso about not transporting prisoners without their consent had been drafted by Shaftesbury in 1674.[104] Moreover the narrowness of the only recorded vote on the bill, fifty-seven to fifty-five, on 27 May, over whether to agree to a free conference with the Commons on the Lords' amendments, demonstrates that it was still a controversial issue in 1679. Lord Chancellor Finch's jottings clearly demonstrate that he believed it favoured prisoners and hindered legal processes, but other Court peers who were opposed to the Bill presumably did so because they perceived it as a party issue.[105]

Another concern which the 'Whigs' shared with the earlier Country party was the prospect of a standing army. As early as 1673/4 the Presbyterian earl of Denbigh wrote that 'the least appearance of a standing army is of dangerous consequence', against which the 'whole kingdom hath an irrecon-

---

[100] See Haley, *Shaftesbury*, pp. 561–2.
[101] Ibid., p. 627. The example of these peers was not followed. See Knights, *Politics and opinion in crisis*, p. 294.
[102] The sessions were: 1674, 1675, 1677.
[103] *Statutes*, V, pp. 935–8.
[104] Committee Minutes vol. 3, p. 78.
[105] Leicestershire RO, Finch Papers PP. 60, Heads of the habeas corpus bill with comments written by Lord Finch; Kenyon, *Stuart Constitution*, p. 425.

cilable antipathy'.[106] Because of war between 1672 and 1674 and the contingency of a fresh war during 1677/8 the Crown raised standing forces which were quartered close to London and to parliament. Since the heir presumptive was a Catholic with known authoritarian leanings, and since the European monarch whom Charles II sought most to emulate, Louis XIV, ruled in an arbitrary manner with the assistance of soldiers, it was not unreasonable to assume that Charles and his brother James might use military force to impose their will on the country too.[107]

Country peers voiced their disquiet about the prospect of a standing army in debates. In one speech in the spring of 1675 Shaftesbury asserted that the oath in Danby's Test Bill was 'directly establishing a standing army by act of parliament for if whatever be by the king's commission be by the king's authority then a standing army is law for the king's authority is nothing but the law'.[108] When the hysteria created by the popish plot was at its peak in the autumn and winter of 1678 the king actually possessed a peacetime standing force, which had originally been raised to fight France. Charles asked parliament for sufficient money to disband it, but the 'opposition' in both Houses, with understandable suspicion of government intentions, believed that any money voted would be employed to retain the army – a potential instrument with which to impose Catholicism on England. For this reason the Commons inserted a claim into the bill to disband the armed forces requiring the £204,462 to be paid into the Chamber of London, which was outside the government's direct control, so that the money could only be used for disbandment. Under intense pressure from the court, the House of Lords made several amendments to the bill in the committee of the whole House, including one for the payment of the money into the Exchequer. The question of whether to agree with the committee's amendments was carried by forty-three votes to thirty on 20 December 1678.[109]

In July 1679 the king formed 200 of his disbanded officers into a company of guards, and two peers who voted for exclusion, the earls of Sussex and Sunderland, complained to the king about this.[110] Essex observed that people believed the company was the 'foundation of a standing army' and 'there is nothing I do more apprehend than a mistrust men may have that any design is on foot of governing by an army, and therefore the least action of which may be construed to intend this, cannot ... but be fatal to your majesty'.[111]

---

[106] Warwickshire RO, Denbigh MSS Collection CR 2017/13, 'The steps of descent whereby of late this monarchy hath much lessened itself'.

[107] Airy (ed.), *The Essex papers*, I, p. 258, William Harbord to Essex, 15 Sept. 1674.

[108] PRO, PRO 30/24/294 (Shaftesbury Papers), fol. 1v, 'Reasons against the Test by the earl of Shaftesbury' (1675).

[109] PRO, PRO 31/3/141 fol. 107, Barillon to Louis XIV, 20 Dec. 1678.

[110] J. Dalrymple (ed.), *Memoirs of Great Britain and Ireland*, 2 vols. (1773), II, Appendix, pp. 231–2, Essex to Charles II, 21 July 1679.

[111] Ibid., p. 232.

The government's critics in both Houses expected that if James became king he would be forced to rule with a standing army because he would be unable to rely on the cooperation of his Protestant subjects. One of the clauses in the Bill of Limitations which 'opposition' peers drafted after the defeat of the Exclusion Bill was that no forces were to be raised by a popish successor without the consent of parliament.[112]

Anxieties about a standing army were compounded by the king's pro-French foreign policy. Foreign affairs was not usually a party issue in the sense that the Court and Country parties had distinct policies. Both preferred the king to pursue a Protestant, as opposed to a pro-French policy, though Country lords were more forceful in their demands that he should abandon the French alliance once the war with the United Provinces had ended in 1674.[113] Both accepted that the control of foreign policy was a fundamental part of the royal prerogative. Writing in 1673/4, even the disaffected earl of Denbigh acknowledged that 'the sole power of making war and peace be vested, and indisputably settled in his majesty; yet let him please manage this power with such temper and prudence that the spirit of the people be not dampened, nor their hearts alienated by engaging them in such wars as … run against the common stream and current of their affections and inclinations'. Obviously a war in which England was allied with Catholic France, against a Protestant country, as had occurred between 1672 and 1674, was regarded as against the 'common stream and current' of most people's 'affections'.[114]

On the few occasions when foreign affairs was an issue in the Lords disagreement generally centred on the best method of executing a particular policy. In March 1678 the Lords agreed with the Commons that the king should be addressed to declare war on France. Even Danby 'did openly declare that no man for these two years past had lived with greater apprehension of France than himself, and was more convinced of the necessity of war'.[115] Dispute arose over whether to agree with the Commons and address the king to declare war *immediately*, or whether to alter this to with all the possible speed 'as the king's occasions would permit'.[116] In a very grave and temperate debate Danby, Lord Chancellor Finch and other Court peers argued that the government was ill-prepared for an immediate declaration of war for want of the necessary money and ships. Against this Halifax, Shaftesbury, Buckingham, Holles, Essex, Wharton, Clarendon and Carnarvon used 'most of the arguments which had been urged among the Commons

[112] Harris, *Politics under the later Stuarts*, p. 85; Carte MSS 228, fol. 208.
[113] *Cal. SP Ven.*, 38, p. 391, Alberti to Doge and Senate, 9 April 1675.
[114] Denbigh MSS Collection CR 2017/13.
[115] *Hist. MSS Comm.*, 36, Ormonde MSS IV, p. 416, Southwell to Ormond, 19 Mar. 1678.
[116] Ibid., p. 417.

as ... the encouraging of our allies' and 'the great dangers we were in and the necessity of a speedy remedy'.[117]

If Country peers were more determined than others that the government should pursue a Protestant foreign policy, it was because they harboured a greater distrust of the king, who had traditionally allied himself with France. This helps to explain their efforts at persuading Charles II to commit himself to an anti-French alliance in 1677 and to declare war on France the following year. Such a course would have had the added advantage of depriving the king of the French money and troops necessary, in their eyes, for establishing popery and arbitrary government. Lord Holles, who was not slow in recognising the significance of French aid, told the French ambassador in December 1679 that 'the court will always adhere to the design of governing more absolutely than the laws of England admit, and knows that your majesty [Louis XIV] alone can facilitate the success of such a design'.[118] In March 1679, just before the opening of parliament, Shaftesbury wrote a paper in which he emphasised the threat posed by absolutist France and warned that Protestant Europe would receive no help from the English government whilst 'a popish successor' was 'so near at hand'.[119] During the debate on the Exclusion Bill 'opposition' peers emphasised the importance of pursuing an anti-French foreign policy, arguing that one consequence of James' exclusion might be an alliance of Protestant states in favour of England, rather than the anticipated alliance with France after his accession.[120] The defeat of this bill forced 'opposition' peers to adopt a more extreme approach to foreign policy than had been contemplated in the 1670s. The Bill of Limitations (considered by the Lords between late November 1680 and early January 1681) contained a clause removing foreign policy from the authority of a Catholic successor.[121]

IV

Issues alone do not account for the existence of an 'opposition' party in the Lords between 1675 and 1681. Effective leadership played a vital role too. There was no single leader of this party in the upper House. Shaftesbury was the most important, but others, notably Buckingham, Salisbury, Holles and

---

[117] Ibid.; Leicestershire RO, Finch Papers PP. 49, Lord Chancellor Finch's speech 'Concerning a war'; Yale (ed.), *Lord Nottingham's Chancery cases*, II, pp. 989–95, draft of Finch's speech on the same subject, March 1678.

[118] Dalrymple, *Memoirs*, II, Appendix, p. 261, Barillon to Louis XIV, 4 Dec. 1679.

[119] 'The present state of the kingdom at the opening of the parliament, March 6, 1679', in W. D. Christie, *A life of Anthony Ashley Cooper, first earl of Shaftesbury*, 2 vols. (1871), II, pp. 281–3, 309–14.

[120] Carte MSS 77, fols. 649–50, earl of Huntingdon's notes on the exclusion debate in the House of Lords, 15 Nov. 1680.

[121] Bodl., Rawlinson MSS A. 162, fols. 39–40.

Wharton, had a significant role to play. As a former Chancellor of the Exchequer and ex-Lord Chancellor, Shaftesbury was well versed in parliamentary management and understood the most intimate workings of government. Accustomed as he was to hard work and routine business, much of the burden of party organisation fell on his shoulders. His resolute stand against popery in 1673 and 1674 gained him a reputation for being a Protestant hero, and earned him adherents in both Houses. Until his health deteriorated towards the end of the 1670s, Buckingham was almost as important a leader as Shaftesbury. It was Buckingham rather than Shaftesbury who was a coordinating figure during the 1679 general elections.[122] The earl of Salisbury, whose father and grandfather had both been zealous Parliamentarians, was one of the most active and consistent opposition peers between 1675 and 1681. He played a leading part in the investigation of the popish plot and argued long and hard in favour of exclusion.[123] The veteran Presbyterian Baron Holles, with his extensive knowledge of the records of parliament, was frequently called upon to search out precedents to back up 'opposition' arguments in the chamber. In early 1679 it was Holles rather than Shaftesbury who drew up a programme of action for consideration by parliament, which had as its first priority the 'enacting of some laws whereby the liberty and property of the subject might be preserved'.[124] Another former Parliamentarian, Lord Wharton, also had a sound knowledge of parliamentary precedents and was an indefatigable compiler of division lists. Division lists were an extremely useful guide for the Country leadership as to the strengths of their party in the chamber.

Country and 'Whig' leaders often met for private consultations outside parliament, both before sessions and between sittings. The first recorded meeting took place at Lord Holles' London house in January 1674 amidst the intense anti-popish feeling that characterised the 1674 session. There Shaftesbury, Salisbury, Carlisle, Fauconberg, Holles, Buckingham, Halifax and others 'concerted together upon the matters which were to be proposed in the lower House, where those lords had great influence'.[125] It is likely that the four well-timed proposals made by Salisbury, Carlisle, Halifax and Mordaunt during the debate on securing the Protestant religion at the opening of the session had been planned at Holles' house.[126] The tactic of addressing the king to dis-

[122] Knights, *Politics and opinion in crisis*, p. 135; Yardley, 'George Villiers', pp. 238, 257, 333; S. E. Banfield, 'George Villiers, 2nd duke of Buckingham: an intellectual study, 1660–1687' (University of London MPhil thesis, 1978), pp. 184–91.

[123] Haley, *Shaftesbury*, p. 357; Swatland, 'The House of Lords', Appendix III; Carte MSS 77, fols. 649–51.

[124] Dalrymple, *Memoirs*, II, p. 260; Add. MSS 28,047, fol. 47, T. Knox to Danby, 23 Jan. 1679.

[125] PRO, PRO 31/3/13, fol. 47, Ruvigny to Louis XIV, 22 Jan. 1674; Airy (ed.), *Essex Papers*, I, p. 168, Conway to Essex, 27 Jan. 1674; Stowe MSS 204, fol. 23, Conway to Essex, 10 Jan. 1674.

[126] Add. MSS 23,136, fol. 87, Kincardin to Lauderdale, 10 Feb. 1674; Haley, *Shaftesbury*, pp. 357–8.

solve parliament on 20 November 1675 had also been carefully planned. This was the opinion of the earl of Bristol, a firm Court supporter in 1675, who in reply to speeches by Shaftesbury, Buckingham, Mohun and others urging a dissolution observed that their speeches were 'premeditated', the result of 'long and serious consultation and consideration before hand'.[127] Shaftesbury and several Country MPs met at his house and at St John's coffee house prior to parliament assembling in February 1677, but it is not known the extent to which similar meetings took place during the following twelve months when he was a prisoner in the Tower.[128]

Private consultations, involving both opposition peers and MPs, occurred more frequently between 1679 and 1681. In the context of the heightened political atmosphere created by the popish plot the need for regular meetings is obvious. In November 1679 Lords Chandos, Howard of Escrick, North, Grey of Wark, Kent, Huntingdon, Herbert and Shaftesbury dined together every week at the Swan Tavern where they discussed petitioning the king for parliament to meet in January 1680.[129] Similar meetings were regularly held at Lord Wharton's London home and at Shaftesbury's Thanet House during the spring and summer of 1680 as 'opposition' leaders endeavoured to maintain the momentum of their cause in the absence of parliament. It was after one meeting in March that Shaftesbury communicated information about a plot in Ireland to the privy council in order to heighten general anxieties about popery. His ploy worked, for rumours of the Irish Plot quickly became the main topic of conversation in London coffee houses. Before the opening of the 1680 parliament Shaftesbury met with several peers and MPs in order to 'consult of matters in relation to that parliament'.[130]

A primary aim of the Country leadership was the maximisation of attendance in the Lords. Letters have survived in which they requested lords to attend or make a proxy. During the autumn of 1676 Halifax wrote to the earl of Chesterfield reminding him of the approaching session.[131] Lords Holles and Shaftesbury wrote to Lord Townshend the following January outlining their design to dissolve parliament and seeking his presence on the first day of the session. But 'infirmities of body ... and the gout' had so incapacitated the old Presbyterian that he was forced to send his proxy to Shaftesbury instead.[132] In the spring session of 1675 when Shaftesbury's 'manifesto' had been widely circulated, Country lords attended more regularly

---

[127] BL, Verney MSS M/636, reel 29, W. Fall to Sir Ralph Verney, 22 Nov. 1675.
[128] *Cal. SP Dom.*, 1675–6, pp. 562–3, ? to Williamson, 18 Feb. 1676.
[129] Haley, *Shaftesbury*, pp. 559–60; *Hist. MSS Comm.*, 36, Ormond MSS IV, pp. 560–1, 565, Southwell to Ormond, 18, 25 Nov. 1679.
[130] Haley, *Shaftesbury*, pp. 569, 576; Knights, *Politics and opinion in crisis*, p. 132.
[131] BL, Althorp Papers, Halifax Correspondence, vol. I, c. 1, earl of Chesterfield to Halifax, 2 Oct. 1676 (reply to Halifax's letter).
[132] Add. MSS 41,654, fol. 30, Townshend to Lords Shaftesbury and Holles, 2 Feb. 1677.

than Court peers. On average each Country peer attended thirty-six of the forty-nine sittings as compared with thirty-two for each Court lord. But the session would anyway have been well attended because of Danby's Test Bill. Unlike the government, the Country leadership did not manage proxies on a wide scale, largely because the assiduous attendance of their adherents meant that there were fewer absentees to start with. For the two sessions of 1675 and that of 1677 the Country party held twenty-eight proxies compared with over a hundred in the hands of Court lords and bishops.[133]

Country and 'Whig' peers had connections with the 'opposition' in the Commons. Buckingham, Shaftesbury, Holles and Wharton had friends and associates in the Commons who shared similar aims, and there is evidence that the tactics used in both Houses were sometimes coordinated. As early as February 1674 the king was aware of bicameral collusion between 'opposition' leaders over measures to secure the Protestant religion when he 'clearly discovered a combination betwixt the discontented and turbulent Commons in the south east corner of our House and some hotspurs in the Upper (the e[arl] of Shaftesb[ury], the Lord Halif[ax], e[arl] of Salisb[ury] and the e[arl] of Clare being the most forward)'.[134] Such collusion was a feature of 'opposition' tactics during subsequent parliamentary sessions, in particular during the *Shirley* v. *Fagg* privilege dispute and later during the proceedings in both Houses on the legality of the fifteen-month prorogation on 15 February 1677. In early November 1678 William Russell, a close associate of Shaftesbury, moved in the Commons to address the king for the removal of the duke of York from both his presence and councils in language that closely mirrored a speech made by the earl on the same subject two days earlier. Russell's speech had been prepared after consulting with Shaftesbury. However, neither Country nor 'Whig' MPs blindly followed their leaders in the Lords. At times they pursued policies which were at variance with those of 'opposition' peers.[135]

Printed publicity, of a kind usually associated with the first Whigs, was resorted to by Country leaders to stimulate extra-parliamentary support and to influence members of both houses. Protests from the Lords' Journals were secretly printed and sold in London.[136] There was nothing new in this: protests had been distributed in the capital shortly before the Civil War.[137] Speeches delivered in the chamber were also printed and read in London

[133] See HLRO, Proxy Books 5 and 6.
[134] PRO, S.P. 29/360, fol. 391, Sir Gilbert Talbot to Williamson, 28 Feb. 1674.
[135] Haley, *Shaftesbury*, pp. 349–52, 472, 507–9. Mark Knights argues that Shaftesbury's control over MPs was weaker than J. R. Jones suggested for the period 1678–81 (*Politics and opinion in crisis*, p. 130).
[136] Add. MSS 32,518, fol. 261, Lord Keeper Guildford's memoirs.
[137] G. F. T. Jones, 'The peers' right of protest in the Long Parliament', *BIHR*, 31 (1958), pp. 211–15.

coffee houses. The printing of peers' speeches was also not a new development, but the extent to which it was used as an opposition device from 1675 was. In the autumn of 1675 Country peers inaugurated a propaganda campaign against the government. Buckingham's speech on toleration and Shaftesbury's on a dissolution from the autumn session were printed and circulated in London under the title *Two speeches*.[138] Earlier in the autumn Shaftesbury's account of the debates on Danby's Test, together with arguments used against it in the House, had appeared in a pamphlet entitled *A letter from a person of quality to his friend in the country* and sold for 12d in London.[139] Towards the end of the fifteenth-month prorogation Holles was responsible for one of several pamphlets that claimed that a prorogation in excess of twelve months dissolved parliament.[140]

Pamphlets were printed with impunity during the succession crisis, but it is impossible to link more than a small percentage with the 'opposition' leadership in the Lords.[141] Several of Shaftesbury's speeches were printed, in particular one on the state of the kingdoms (March 1679) and another delivered in the Lords on 23 December 1680 that was highly critical of the king and the duke of York, entitled *A speech lately made by a noble peer of the realm*.[142] A recently discovered letter in the Harley Papers gives a valuable insight into how this second speech came to be printed.[143] According to the writer, Lord Wharton made notes as Shaftesbury was speaking in the chamber. Wharton passed these on to the earl of Bedford, who in turn handed the speech to his son, Lord Russell. Russell despatched it to the printer, Francis Smith, by the penny post. Such an elaborate process was necessary to protect those involved as the privilege-conscious peers did not deal lightly with anyone caught publishing their proceedings.

Outnumbered in the Lords, the opposition sometimes resorted to laughably unscrupulous tactics, including the falsification of votes. Bishop Burnet describes a debate on the Habeas Corpus Amendment Bill during May 1679, where in a partially lit chamber the teller for the Contents, the notorious Lord Grey of Wark, wilfully counted one fat peer as ten. Grey's 'error'

---

138 Committee Minutes 3, p. 185, 30 April 1677; Add. MSS 29,555, fol. 261, R. Langhorn to Lord Hatton, 22 Nov. 1675; Haley, *Shaftesbury*, p. 403.

139 *Hist. MSS Comm.*, 7th Rept (1879), MSS of Sir Henry Verney at Claydon House, pp. 466–7, William Fall to Sir Ralph Verney, 11 Nov. 1675.

140 Committee Minutes 3, p. 137, 20 Feb. 1677; Holles, *The Long Parliament dissolved* (1676). Other pamphlets published by the Country party included: *Some considerations upon the question whether the parliament is dissolved* (1676) and *The grand question concerning the prorogation of the parliament* (1676).

141 O. W. Furley, 'The Whig Exclusionists: pamphlet literature in the Exclusion campaign in 1679–81', *Cambridge Historical Journal*, 13 (1957), 20–1; Haley, *Shaftesbury*, pp. 552–4.

142 See Haley, *Shaftesbury*, pp. 612–14.

143 University of Nottingham, Manuscripts Dept, Harley Papers, PW/2HY/345, ? to Harley, 8 Jan. 1681.

enabled the Country party to win the vote for a conference with the Commons by 57 to 55. At the conference the peers persuaded MPs to accept their amendments to the bill so that it was ready for the royal assent later in the day.[144] The attendance list in the Lords' *Journal* and a note in Shaftesbury's papers show that only 107 lords were present that day, lending credence to Burnet's story.[145] Intimidation may have been used to procure votes the following year. The earl of Anglesey, traditionally a rather independently minded minister, is reputed by several contemporaries to have voted for the Exclusion Bill because he was 'frightened into it by an accusation of him brought into the House of Commons by Mr Dangerfield', an informer, 'for having a hand in some of the popish conspiracies'.[146]

More often, though, 'opposition' leaders exploited both peers' prickliness over their privileges and their anxieties about the popish threat for political ends. It will be remembered that the 1675 privilege disputes with the Commons had been engineered by the Country party in order to wreck the highly controversial Test Bill and, if possible, force the king to dissolve parliament.[147] Although Country leaders did not manufacture the popish plot in the autumn of 1678, they certainly exploited it in the hope of discrediting Danby and the duke of York. It was Country leaders, not Titus Oates, who linked James' name with the plot to assassinate the king in November.[148] Shaftesbury had a knack of producing informers in parliament, like Bedloe, Dugdale and Sidway, at precisely the right moment to achieve the greatest political impact. When alarm about the plot diminished during 1680 the earl tried to revive it with further allegations of plots in Ireland and England, parading yet more so-called 'informers' before the Lords.[149]

The management tactics used by the Country leadership helped to unify the party and this is reflected in members' consistent voting behaviour. For the forty-three Country lords who are recorded as voting twice or more during the period 1675 to 1681 there was a remarkable 95 per cent consistency rate between divisions.[150] Thirty-four opposed the government in all their recorded votes. Of these extremely committed peers, twenty-four had Presbyterian and Parliamentarian ancestries, which underlines our view that religion was a primary reason for going into 'opposition' and remaining there during this period.

---

[144] Burnet, *History*, II, pp. 263–4.

[145] *LJ*, XIII, 594–5; PRO, PRO 30/24/339, 'List of the House of Lords, 27 May 1679'.

[146] *Hist. MSS Comm.*, 71, Finch MSS, II, p. 96, Daniel Finch to Sir John Finch, 13 Jan. 1681; Ormond MSS, V, p. 232, Ossory to Ormond, 1 Nov. 1679 and PRO, PRO 31/3/147, fol. 33, Barillon to Louis XIV corroborate Finch's explanation of Anglesey's reason for voting against rejecting the Exclusion Bill.

[147] See above, chapter 7, pp. 136–7.

[148] Haley, *Shaftesbury*, p. 460.

[149] Ibid., pp. 593–7.

[150] Swatland, 'The House of Lords', p. 400.

The existence of an organised 'opposition' in the Lords did at times alarm ministers. Anxious to prevent a repetition of the spring session of 1675, in which the 'opposition's' orchestration of bicameral privilege disputes had blocked the Test Bill in the Lords, Danby tried to use the Court's majority in the autumn session to delay proceedings on *Shirley* v. *Fagg* which had been revived by Lord Mohun presenting Shirley's petition on 19 October. Initially Danby had tried to persuade Shirley to delay presenting his petition, but when this had no effect he argued in the House against appointing a day for the hearing. Eager to exercise their judicial privileges the majority voted against the Lord Treasurer's advice and decided by 43 votes to 23 to proceed on the case.[151] Worse was to come. On 20 November an alliance of Country and Catholic peers, led by the duke of York, voted to address the king to dissolve the Cavalier Parliament, which Danby was systematically attempting to manage. The motion was only defeated by the last-minute arrival of the duke of Lauderdale and Lord Maynard. Since the bishops generally voted *en bloc* with the Court party, there was in reality little chance of the government losing control of the House of Lords even during the succession crisis. Even without the bishops' fourteen votes, the Exclusion Bill was defeated by a nineteen-vote majority.

Country peers did score some notable successes though. Whilst their main legislative achievement was the passage of the Habeas Corpus Amendment Bill in 1679, other bills, such as those to relieve nonconforming Protestants or to make the trial of peers less susceptible to royal manipulation, either failed in the Lords or died in the lower House. Other significant successes included the wrecking of the 1675 Test, the passage of the bill for the banishment of the earl of Danby, and the trial and execution of Viscount Stafford in 1680.

Before 1675 there had been factions of peers critical of certain aspects of government policy, but these had been fluid in composition and temporary. Factions were always more likely during wartime when feelings of national insecurity were pronounced. The development of an organised 'opposition' party in the upper House after 1675 was partly a response to the current profound fears of popery and the orthodox Anglican policies associated with the earl of Danby. Yet some of its policies, most notably relief for Protestant dissenters and frequent parliaments, had their origins in the early 1660s. The revelations of the popish plot and the succession crisis ensured that the Country party remained a powerful force in the House of Lords. It had respected leaders, who used a range of organisational strategies to maximise votes in the chamber. It also resorted to printed publicity to ensure its views were circulated beyond Westminster. In contrast with the House of

---

[151] *Bulstrode Papers*, I, 317–18, 321–2.

Commons, where it is far more difficult to identify coherent political parties because of significant membership changes resulting from the general elections of 1679 and 1681, the composition of the Lords was far more static, making it easier to pinpoint an 'opposition' party. In the Lords the Country 'opposition' of 1675–9 had the characteristics of a political party, albeit an embryonic one. Far from being a new development, the 'Whig' or 'Adverse' party of 1680/1 was in most respects a continuation of the earlier Country party. For the development of an 'opposition' party in the Lords, the period 1678–91 was far less of a watershed than previously thought.

12

Court and 'Tory' peers

The three major biographies of Charles II which have been published in recent years have incorporated specialist research on the reign, yet none offers an analysis of the development of either the Court or 'Tory' parties in the House of Lords.[1] All three historians present a traditional view of the Tory party: it emerged during the 'Exclusion Crisis' (1679–81) and bore little resemblance to previous court groups in parliament.[2] Recently discovered division lists, reports of debates and letters provide a very different picture, at least for the House of Lords. From April 1675 an organised Court group appeared in the Lords which was later transformed into what most historians term the 'Tory' party. The origins, development and characteristics of this party together with an examination of the 'Tory' party in 1680 provide the main themes of this chapter.

The nickname 'Tory' (derived from Catholic Irish bandits) was only widely used by Whigs from 1681 to denote those peers and MPs who resisted their attempts to secure a Protestant succession or impose limitations on the powers of a popish monarch. It was also applied to those who adhered to the Church of England and opposed toleration for dissenting Protestants. Mark Knights has shown that other names, such as 'Church Papists', 'Pensioners', 'God-damners', 'Yorkists' and 'Loyalists' were also applied by contemporaries to these men.[3] However, to avoid confusion we will use the better-known term 'Tory' to denote peers and bishops who favoured the hereditary succession, firmly supported the 1662 church settlement and regularly voted against the 'Whigs' in the Lords from November 1680. The term

---

[1] J. R. Jones, *Charles II*; R. Hutton, *Charles II*; J. Miller, *Charles II* (1991).

[2] J. R. Jones, *Charles II*, pp. 137–61; Hutton, *Charles II*, pp. 391–403; Miller, *Charles II*, pp. 318–46. Even more recently Tim Harris claims that political parties did not exist before 1679 (*Politics under the later Stuarts*, p. 224). Jonathan Scott goes even further, denying the existence of either a Court or a Tory party during the succession crisis (*Restoration crisis*, p. 22). I cannot accept these views, as they are based on the situation in the Commons and ignore the embryonic parties which first appeared in the Lords in 1675.

[3] *A new English dictionary of historical principles* (Oxford, 1916), X, p. 171; Knights, *Politics and opinion in crisis*, p. 109.

'Court party' is used to describe the organised group of Anglican Royalist peers who followed the earl of Danby's leadership between 1675 and 1679.

I

By far the largest group of peers to sit in the Lords was the Anglican Royalists. If the sons of Civil War Royalists are included, almost two-thirds of the temporal membership consisted of these men in 1661. Most had fought for the king in the Civil War whilst others had either attended him at Oxford, joined the exiled court or had participated in Royalist conspiracies in the 1650s. From the outbreak of the Civil War to the restoration of the monarchy these men had experienced rapid and at times violent political upheaval: the destruction of the Church of England, the execution of Charles I, the abolition of the House of Lords, military rule and experiments with the constitution. The duke of Newcastle blamed religious fanatics for shattering the stability of the traditional social order and for destroying the exalted position of the nobility within it.[4]

A wave of relief surged over Royalist peers at the restoration of the monarchy. At last they would be able to re-establish episcopacy and the Prayer Book and crush the rebels, fanatics and schismatics whom they held responsible for the disorder of the preceding twenty years. They could reasonably expect a monopoly of government offices as well as rewards for their loyalty to the Stuarts. Such high hopes quickly faded. The king pardoned and rewarded ex-Parliamentarians with offices, titles, pensions and lands, neglecting many loyal former Royalists.[5] The king selected many of his senior advisers from the ranks of his former enemies. In 1661 almost half the noble membership of the privy council consisted of former Parliamentarian peers. The earl of Northampton was horrified that the king should listen to the advice of his former enemies who, he asserted, had merely 'connived at your majesty's restoration, as a degree to their rise, and yours and the monarchy's eternal destruction, and the Church's fall'.[6] The government made no attempt to capitalise on the loyalty of former Royalist peers and create a loyal party in the House of Lords. In these circumstances it is no wonder that many peers felt aggrieved and disappointed, and highly critical of royal policies.

The king's religious policies of 1660–2 served to affront rigid Anglicans who formed the majority of former Royalist lords. Along with the bishops, they were the most forward in the House in condemning royal attempts to ease restrictions on Catholics and to retain Presbyterians within the Church

---

[4] Newcastle, *Memoirs*, p. xxiii.
[5] Burnet, *History*, I, p. 176; Seaward, pp. 196–8, 209, 211.
[6] Clarendon MSS 77, fol. 236, Northampton to Charles II, 8 Aug. 1662.

of England. Earlier in this study we have seen how these men resisted royal endeavours to secure a broad church settlement in the early years of the reign.[7] Whilst some Royalists, such as the duke of Ormond and earl of Southampton, did assist the king in these endeavours, Charles II principally relied on the votes of Presbyterian peers. Yet from 1663 to 1667 the king endorsed legislation to curb the activities of nonconformists, and, if the debate on the Five Mile Bill is a representative guide, Anglican Royalists were the court's chief adherents in the House.[8] But the tolerationist schemes during the so-called Cabal years, that culminated in the king's Declaration of Indulgence in 1672 revived Anglican Royalists' foreboding about the safety of the church in the king's hands. Once again these lords, like the earl of Chesterfield, who condemned the Declaration of Indulgence, voiced their concern in the chamber.[9]

Another area of Restoration politics where the king and former Royalists did not always see eye to eye was the land settlement. During the Civil War and Interregnum many Royalist lords had suffered the sequestration of their estates and others had been compelled to sell land in order to pay delinquency fines. Steadfast loyalty to the Royalist cause did not ensure for every Cavalier the recovery of his lands at the Restoration. In May 1660 the king decided to distinguish between those whose land had been confiscated and sold by force and those who had made voluntary conveyances, even to pay delinquency fines. Only the former, Charles argued, were entitled to resort to legal proceedings and private acts of parliament to regain possession of their lands. The new regime was on an unsteady footing, and neither Charles nor Hyde wished to antagonise prior purchasers (many of whom were men of substance, like London merchants, military officers and government officials) by impugning the validity of voluntary and legal conveyances made during the Interregnum. These provisions were incorporated in the Convention's acts for Judicial Proceedings and Indemnity and Oblivion. Largely as a result of the king's stance several ardently loyal peers, such as Winchester, Lexington, Cleveland, Clifford and Derby, were prevented from repossessing estates which they had sold in order to pay composition fines or the decimation tax.[10] In the House of Lords former Royalist peers refused to adhere to government policy on aspects of the land settlement and this is illustrated by the earl of Derby's case.

The Stanley family, from its vast estates in Lancashire, Cheshire and North Wales, had pursued a Royalist course in the Civil Wars, which had cost the

---

[7] See above, chapters 9 and 10.
[8] Robbins, 'The Oxford session of the Long Parliament', pp. 221–4.
[9] Add. MSS 19,253, fol. 199, earl of Chesterfield's autobiography.
[10] Schoenfeld, *Restored House of Lords*, pp. 111–19; *LJ*, XI, 20, 36–7, 59–60, 67–74, 87–9, 116–25, 134–49, 160–4, 177–84, 386, 396, 453.

sixteenth earl of Derby his life. To ameliorate the heavy burden of fines and confiscations, as well as to pay debts incurred in the king's cause, the Stanleys had resorted to a number of conveyances of varying degrees of legality. Determined to reclaim through compulsory repurchase the manors of Hope, Mold and Hawarden, which had been sold to pay fines, the seventeenth earl introduced a total of four private bills into parliament shortly after the Restoration. These met with such obstruction both from the government and from former Parliamentarians in both Houses that one was withdrawn (August 1660), another was set aside in the Commons (December 1660) and a third disappeared in committee in the Lords (June 1661).[11] A fourth bill passed both Houses, only to receive the royal veto on 19 May 1662.[12]

The chief supporters of Derby's bills were former Royalists and members of the episcopal bench. They believed that the extraordinary efforts and sufferings of the Stanleys on behalf of the Stuarts entitled the family to special consideration.[13] Several ex-Royalists, including Mohun, Byron, Lexington and Langdale, who sat on the committee appointed on 13 January 1662 to consider the fourth bill, thought that Derby's case would establish a precedent for themselves to follow.[14] When the bill eventually reached the third reading stage on 6 February, thirty-four peers voted against it because they believed it sought to overthrow voluntary sales which the acts of Judicial Proceedings and Indemnity had declared legal and binding.[15] Twenty-five peers entered a protest in the Journal, asserting that the alleged fraud of the purchasers, which could provide justification for overriding entry fines (the legal basis of titles to land), had not been proved by Derby's counsel.[16] That the government's policy on the land settlement was jeopardised by the passage of Derby's bill is apparent from the categories of peers who voted against it. There were leading ministers: Clarendon, Manchester and Ashley; the Lord Chancellor's close associates, Ormond, Bridgewater and Portland; the king's companions and household servants, such as Chesterfield and Berkeley of Berkeley; a large group of former Parliamentarians; and finally six Catholics.[17] For ex-Royalists this protest served to confirm their fears about Clarendon's association with Presbyterians and his neglect of their own interests.[18]

[11] Ibid., 59–62, 91–4, 96, 132, 137–8, 147, 149; Seaward, pp. 201–2; Committee Minute Book 1, pp. 23, 26, 29, 33 (11, 14, 18, 20 June 1661).
[12] *LJ*, XI, 531–2; Committee Minutes 1, pp. 100, 105 (18, 21 Jan. 1662).
[13] *Cal. SP Dom.*, 1661–2, p. 316, Derby's petition to the king, 21 March 1662; Seaward, pp. 202–3; Ailesbury, *Memoirs*, I, 5–6.
[14] Schoenfeld, *Restored House of Lords*, p. 117; Committee Minutes 1, pp. 100, 105.
[15] *LJ*, XI, 378; Carte MSS 77, fol. 520, Wharton's list of peers who voted against Derby's bill, 6 Feb. 1662.
[16] *LJ*, XI, 379.
[17] Ibid.; Carte MSS 77, fol. 520.
[18] Seaward, p. 212.

If the government's attitude to controversial conveyances made by a few loyal supporters of the Stuart cause during the Interregnum humiliated former Royalist peers, then its seemingly lenient approach towards former enemies of the Crown, particularly in the Act of Indemnity and Oblivion, merely humiliated them further. Seeking retribution for the execution of Charles I and also for their suffering in the 1640s and 1650s, a group of peers that included Lords Northampton, Lichfield, Mohun, Derby, Capel, Carnarvon, Finch, Gerard and Seymour, stiffened the terms of this bill in the Convention by increasing the number of Parliamentarians to be denied a pardon.[19] The earl of Bristol spoke for these lords when he professed to the House that 'I find myself set on fire when I think that the blood of so many virtuous and meritorious peers, and persons, and others of all ranks, so cruelly and impiously shed, should cry so loud for vengeance, and not find it from us.'[20] After this harangue, delivered on 20 July, the peers extended the scope of the bill from those who had actually signed Charles I's death warrant to include others like Vane, Lambert and Hazelrigg, who were not regicides.[21] Annoyed by this thirst for blood, the king entered the chamber on 27 July and made a plea for mercy, reminding the peers of his pledge in the Declaration from Breda to grant a pardon to all who surrendered themselves upon it, and urging that those excepted from pardon should only be regicides.[22] The king's position was largely determined by political expediency, for he had no desire to adopt a revengeful policy that might undermine the stability of the regime, and perhaps even force former-Parliamentarians into renewed rebellion. In spite of the king's intervention, conciliatory speeches by Hyde and Southampton and the votes of ex-Parliamentarians like Robartes, Northumberland, Lincoln, Hunsdon and Wharton, the wishes of the numerically stronger Royalists largely prevailed.[23] Although the Commons expunged several of the peers' amendments, the final measure was harsher than either Charles or Hyde had originally desired.[24]

Of course Royalist peers were not always at variance with royal policies. They enthusiastically supported many government-sponsored bills, particularly those designed to safeguard the powers of the Crown. The 1661 bill 'against tumults and disorders', which harked back to the petitioning of

[19] C. H. Firth (ed.), *Memoirs of Edmund Ludlow*, 2 vols. (Oxford, 1894), II, pp. 282, 286, 290–1; *LJ*, XI, 103, 113–14; *Hist. MSS Comm.*, 5th Rept, pt I, Sutherland MSS, p. 156, Andrew Newport to Sir Richard Leveson, 25 Aug. 1660; Add. MSS 27,590, fol. 16.

[20] *Somers Tracts*, VII, p. 461.

[21] Schoenfeld, *Restored House of Lords*, pp. 187–8.

[22] *LJ*, XI, 108.

[23] Ludlow, *Memoirs*, II, pp. 282, 290–1; *LJ*, XI, 114, 136, 143; *Hist. MSS Comm.*, Sutherland MSS, p. 156, Newport to Leveson, 25 Aug. 1660, p. 194, Thomas Gower to John Langley, 30 June 1660; Add. MSS 27,590, fols. 58–60; 32,455, fol. 93, rough minute book of the House of Lords, 1660.

[24] *Statutes*, V, 226–33; Schoenfeld, *Restored House of Lords*, pp. 190–3.

1640–2, and was intended to forbid the presentation of petitions to the king or parliament by more than ten persons, was promoted in committee by the ex-Royalist commander, the earl of Northampton.[25] A bill 'for the securing and preserving of his Majesty's person and government', of the same year, was sponsored by Clarendon's friend, the old Cavalier earl of Portland. A committee under his chairmanship added a clause repudiating the notion 'that both houses of parliament or either of them have a legislative power without the king'.[26]

Another measure which enjoyed the backing of ex-Cavalier peers was the highly controversial Corporation Bill. The bill was introduced in the Commons in June 1661 by Anglican Royalists who sought to remove dissenters, Presbyterians and ex-Parliamentarians from corporations. Under its provisions commissioners were to be appointed to purge corporations of all officeholders who refused to take the Oath of Allegiance and Supremacy and a declaration against using armed force against the king or any of his officers. With the blessing of the government, a committee dominated by senior ministers and ex-Cavaliers re-wrote the bill in such a way as permanently to extend the Crown's authority in corporations.[27] Although at least one former Parliamentarian minister, Lord Ashley, favoured a reduction in the power of corporations, the majority of those who approved the alteration of the bill were former Cavaliers, in particular, the earl of Portland, the duke of York, the earl of Northampton, Bishop Sheldon and the duke of Ormond.[28] On other bills, where former Parliamentarians had misgivings, like the bill to regulate the press (1662) and the bill to repeal the Triennial Act (1664) – the latter was severely criticised by Lord Wharton – former Royalists provided the king and Clarendon with the bulk of their support in the chamber.[29]

In the *Continuation* of his Life Clarendon gives the impression that he was the leader of a Royalist group in parliament.[30] He certainly was influential with a group of MPs which included many old Cavaliers. But for the Lords there is no evidence that he was the leader of a unified Court group composed almost exclusively of ex-Cavaliers.[31] The Lord Chancellor was assisted

[25] Kenyon, *Stuart constitution*, p. 361; Committee Minutes 1, p. 6 (20 May 1661).
[26] Committee Minutes 1, pp. 8–9 (25 May 1661).
[27] *LJ*, XI, 309, 311, 313, 318, 319.
[28] Seaward, p. 154; Committee Minutes 1, p. 122 (4 Feb. 1662); J. H. Sacret, 'The Restoration government and municipal corporations', *EHR*, 45 (1930), 249.
[29] Committee Minutes 1, p. 231 (4 April 1662); Carte MSS 81, fols. 22–4 (Wharton's objections to the Triennial Bill of 1664); Pepys, V, pp. 93, 10; BL, Verney MSS M636, reel 19, N. Hobart to Ralph Verney, 3 April 1664; Bodl., Rawlinson MSS A. 130, fol. 5.
[30] Clarendon, *Life*, I, pp. 313, 361; II, p. 197.
[31] Seaward, pp. 80–5; J. R. Jones, 'Court dependants in 1664', *BIHR*, 34 (1961), pp. 81–4; 33. There certainly was no exclusively Cavalier court group in the House in the early 1660s, a point which is suggested by a surviving division list on Derby's bill and another on the dispute between Oxford and Lindsey over the office of Lord Great Chamberlain (1661). On both occasions former Royalists were divided (Carte MSS 77, fol. 250; 109, fol. 317).

in his management of the Lords by some Royalists who were either close friends or kinsmen, notably the duke of York, the second earl of Portland and the earls of Southampton and Bridgewater.[32] Portland and Bridgewater were particularly active in the promotion of government legislation, chairing many committees and managing conferences with the Commons. At the same time the Lord Chancellor employed ex-Parliamentarians to manage the House, in particular four privy councillors: Ashley, Anglesey, Robartes and Manchester.[33] It is highly unlikely that Clarendon had any intention of organising a purely 'Royalist' faction in the House, since, as we have seen, former Civil War Royalists were not in sympathy with all the king's policies. Instead the government relied on the votes of different groups of peers for specific policies. Many of the earl's most vociferous critics were former Royalists, such as the duke of Buckingham and Lords Byron, Lucas, Derby, Strafford, Norwich, Paulet and Bristol.[34] Those peers who drove on Clarendon's impeachment in November 1667 were mainly of Royalist extraction: eighteen of the twenty-five lay peers who signed the protest against not omitting him on the 20th fall into this category.[35]

From the impeachment of Clarendon until the implementation of an orthodox Anglican policy in the spring of 1675 bishops and Anglican Royalist peers became increasingly concerned about the safety of the church. In part this was a consequence of the attitudes and policies of those ministers and advisers who filled the void left by Clarendon's departure. The duke of Buckingham, viewed by many contemporaries as the most influential royal adviser between 1667 and 1669, was intensely disliked by most Anglican Royalists. Neither his turbulent private life nor his association with republicans and dissenters won him many close friends in parliament. His espousal of toleration for Protestant nonconformists did nothing to endear him to rigid Anglicans.[36] The influential royal adviser, Lord Arlington, also sympathised with dissenters, as did both Lord Keeper Bridgeman and Lord Clifford, a secret Catholic, who was Lord Treasurer from 1672 to 1673.[37] Lord Ashley (created earl of Shaftesbury in 1672), who was Chancellor of the Exchequer, and Lord Chancellor from 1672 to 1673, was distrusted too because of his

---

[32] Carte MSS 32, fol. 716, O'Neil to Ormond, 14 July 1663; 47, fol. 90, Clarendon to Ormond, 21 Mar. 1664; 81, fols. 2, 224; Add. MSS 22,919, fol. 203, Morrice to Downing, 21 Mar. 1662; Bodl., Rawlinson MSS A. 130, fols. 3–4.

[33] See tables 3 and 4 and Swatland, 'Privy councillors', pp. 53, 75–7.

[34] *LJ*, XII, 141; Carte MSS 76, fol. 7, earl of Salisbury to the earl of Huntingdon, 22 Mar. 1664; 77, fols. 524–5, same to same, 13 July 1663; 217, fol. 354, Anglesey to Ormond, 20 Nov. 1666; Seaward, p. 213.

[35] *LJ*, XII, 141. The eighteen peers were: Buckingham, Bristol, Norwich, Northampton, Berkshire, Arlington, Vaughan, Teynham, Paulet, Bath, Howard of Charlton, Byron, Lucas, Berkeley of Stratton, Gerard, Windsor, Powis and Rochester.

[36] Seaward, pp. 247, 301; Yardley, 'George Villiers', pp. 148–50, 155–6.

[37] Hutton, *Charles II*, pp. 254, 280; Miller, *Charles II*, p. 135; M. Lee, *The Cabal* (Illinois, 1965), pp. 147–9, 155.

advocacy of measures to benefit nonconformists culminating in his defence of the Declaration of Indulgence in the Lords in March 1673.[38] Nicknamed 'Little Sincerity', Ashley was viewed by old Cavaliers and bishops as an unprincipled turncoat, having on several occasions since 1642 changed his allegiance for the sake of personal advancement.[39] Finally, Lauderdale, the Secretary for Scotland, aroused the enmity of bishops and former Cavaliers with his scheme for a complete union between England and Scotland, which they believed was economically disadvantageous to England, and his sponsorship of the 1669 Act of the Scottish parliament, which declared the king's supreme authority in ecclesiastical matters in that country. This act was thought to presage a general indulgence to nonconformists in England as well as in Scotland.[40]

Most notably, Anglican Royalists displayed their distrust of these ministers on religious issues. After Clarendon's fall, the government stepped up its efforts to temper the severity of the penal laws against peaceable Protestant dissenters. The king's attitude was ambivalent. On the one hand he favoured toleration for these nonconformists, yet on the other, when he received complaints about seditious conventicles, he ordered their suppression. Charles still wanted to make dissenters dependent on the royal prerogative for their freedom to worship. To this end the government inserted a clause in the 1670 Conventicle Bill, which was intended to remove all doubts about any limitations on the king's prerogative powers in ecclesiastical matters, and allow him to suspend penal laws. Bishops and Anglican Royalists were the most vociferous opponents of this clause in the House, as they were again three years later on the subject of the Declaration of Indulgence.[41] The welfare of the Church of England was placed before the exercise of the royal prerogative. Despite a strong speech from the earl of Shaftesbury, designed to appeal to the monarchist sentiments of these peers, they refused to be brow-beaten by the court over the Declaration, and the Lords voted by a majority of 33 that 'the king's answer to the House of Commons in referring the points now controverted to a parliamentary way by bill, is good and gracious'.[42] The following February witnessed bishops and Anglican Royalists voting against another government-sponsored measure in the House, a comprehension bill, because it would have enabled Presbyterian ministers to preach within the

---

[38] Haley, *Shaftesbury*, pp. 267, 320–2.
[39] Ibid., pp. 37, 39, 43, 71, 111–43; Carte MSS 243, fol. 234, Sir Richard Temple to Ormond, 16 Mar. 1675.
[40] Lee, *The Cabal*, pp. 51, 61, 63.
[41] F. Bate, *The Declaration of Indulgence, 1672* (1908), pp. 67–74; Add. MSS 36,916, fols. 169, 172, John Starkey to Sir Willoughby Aston, 3/17 Mar. 1670; Manuscript Minutes vol. 16, 14, 15, 16, 19, 21, 22, 23, 24, 25, 26 Mar. 1670.
[42] Josten (ed.), *Elias Ashmole*, IV, p. 1312.

established church.[43] It was this deep concern for the preservation of the Church of England that Danby capitalised on in 1675 as he began to construct Court parties in parliament.

II

During his ascendancy as Lord Treasurer from 1673 to 1679, politics underwent a profound transformation. Political opinions gradually became more polarised and Court and Country parties developed in both Houses. From 1675 through to Charles II's final parliament in 1681 those peers with Cavalier backgrounds, priding themselves on their loyalty to the king and affection for the Church of England, aligned themselves with his leading ministers in the Lords. At the same time the majority of peers with Parliamentarian ancestries became the government's most vociferous critics. Much of the responsibility for these two developments lay with the policies of the earl of Danby. The Lord Treasurer's recourse to traditional Anglican policies whilst appealing to bishops and former Royalists, who had seriously doubted the king's commitment to the church earlier in the reign, antagonised former Parliamentarians, who still sought a more comprehensive church.

Danby began to organise his Court parties to implement the programme of policies which were entrusted to his care by the king. His most pressing concern was always to reduce the Crown's debts which stood at £1.5 million in June 1673.[44] Since the government's annual revenue was approximately £1,375,000 and its fixed expenditure was £1,350,000, little room was left for the liquidation of this deficit.[45] This situation was exacerbated by continued royal extravagance and heavy debts resulting from England's participation between 1672 and 1674 in an expensive war with the United Provinces. In a desperate bid to reduce royal indebtedness Danby approached parliament, but without success, for the anti-popery hysteria that had dominated parliament's proceedings in 1673 and 1674 had increased suspicion of the court's intentions. In the short autumn session of 1673 the Commons had not contemplated supply because of anxieties about a standing army and the duke of York's marriage to a Catholic, and during the 1674 session both Houses were too preoccupied drafting measures against popery.[46]

The Lord Treasurer's existing religious policies intensified the Commons' distrust of the court. Never at heart a committed churchman, Danby did not

[43] HLRO, Main Papers 170, fols. 88–9 (13 Feb. 1674); Bodl., Tanner MSS 42, fol. 89, Tillotson to Sancroft, 23 Feb. 1674; 43, fol. 249, John Lowland to Sancroft, 21 Feb. 1674; Add. MSS 23,136, fol. 98, Sir Robert Moray to Lauderdale, 21 Feb. 1674.
[44] Browning, *Danby*, I, pp. 107, 112, 128–32, 208.
[45] C. D. Chanderman, *The English public revenue, 1660–88* (Oxford, 1975), p. 236.
[46] Miller, *Charles II*, pp. 224–5.

pursue orthodox Anglican policies until late January 1675. As a Buckinghamite MP he had opposed the Five Mile Bill in 1665 and had approved the unsuccessful bill of 1673 to relieve Protestant dissenters.[47] As a minister in the session of 1674 he had endeavoured to strengthen the church against popery by voting for the Comprehension Bill in the Lords.[48] But in doing so he had misjudged the mood of Anglican Royalist lords, and especially the conservative country gentry, who dominated the Commons and still believed in the inviolability of the Restoration church settlement. During the autumn and winter of 1674 Danby was undecided whether to continue to advocate comprehension as a means of uniting the country against popery or whether to court Anglicans by rigidly enforcing the laws against Catholics and Protestant nonconformists.[49] Danby, Lauderdale and the two Secretaries of State attended a series of consultations with Archbishop Sheldon and the bishops during the last fortnight of January 1675, where the government was convinced of the need rigidly to enforce the laws against papists and dissenters.[50] The government's adoption of a harsh line against nonconformists, highlighted by the introduction of Danby's Test Bill in the Lords in April, was calculated to appeal to the Anglican sentiment in parliament in the hope of obtaining supply.

However, this recourse to a rigid Anglican policy could easily have undermined the government's influence in the upper House by alienating a substantial section of its adherents there, who preferred a more comprehensive church. Many of its managers and men of business, who dominated debates and proceedings in committee, were Presbyterians and former Parliamentarians and they included Shaftesbury, Robartes, Anglesey, Wharton, Holles, Fauconberg and Carlisle. Largely because of anxieties over popery several of these men had been highly critical of the court in the 1674 session. The king's prorogation of parliament before any anti-Catholic legislation had passed both Houses, coupled with his failure to take adequate safeguards against popery – particularly at court and in the capital – during the remainder of the year, merely increased the disaffection of Presbyterian peers.[51] By early 1675 it was apparent to Danby that Shaftesbury's 'Malcontent' group had significantly grown in size, with the addition of Lords Newport, Bedford, Bridgewater, Dorset, Ailesbury, Arlington, Ormond, the second earl of

---

[47] *Letter from a person of quality to his friend in the country*, p. xl; Bate, *Declaration of Indulgence*, p. 114; Yardley, 'George Villiers', p. 221.

[48] M. Sylvester (ed.), *Reliquiae Baxterianae*, III, 109.

[49] Miller, *Charles II*, p. 241; BL, Stowe MSS 207, fol. 98, Thynne to Essex, 26 Jan. 1675; Mexborough MSS, Reresby Letters 8/6, G. Copley to Reresby, 10 Nov. 1674; 8/5, Sir Henry Goodrich to Reresby, 21 Jan. 1675.

[50] Miller, *Charles II*; Reresby Letters 8/5, Goodrich to Reresby, 21 Jan. 1675; Leicestershire RO, Finch Papers, Ecc. 2, proceedings in the privy council on enforcing the laws against dissenters, Jan. 1675.

[51] Haley, *Shaftesbury*, pp. 361, 368.

Clarendon, and even Danby's former patron, Buckingham.[52] At the same time there was a strong possibility of the duke of York and his group of assorted Catholic peers and Protestant friends, such as Peterborough, Huntingdon and Anglesey, cementing an alliance with the Presbyterians. At a series of meetings with prominent Presbyterian peers James promised to use his influence to procure a liberty of conscience in return for their not questioning his right of succession in the House of Lords.[53]

Soon there were clear signs that Shaftesbury was organising his adherents in readiness for the approaching session, which was to commence on 13 April 1675. In a widely publicised letter to Lord Carlisle, dated 3 February 1675, the earl proposed that the best method of lessening the threat from popery was through new and frequent parliaments.[54] Danby greeted the ex-Lord Chancellor's design with considerable consternation.[55] In an earlier memorandum he had stated that a new House of Commons would not only contain a higher proportion of disaffected members, but would also be less likely to vote financial supplies.[56] Danby feared that if supplies were refused in the ensuing session Charles might yield to pressure from the 'opposition' and summon a new parliament. During the winter there had been rumours that the Presbyterians had offered Charles money in return for a dissolution. The possibility of a dissolution could be reduced if the Lord Treasurer were able to control both Houses.

Control over parliament became even more imperative when Danby's personal safety appeared to be jeopardised by the activities of his two main rivals at court, Lords Ormond and Arlington, who were conspiring to remove him from office. Arlington was envious and resentful of Danby's rise to power, and was bitter about the recent decline in his own influence at court following his disastrous Dutch embassy.[57] Ormond disliked Danby, believing him responsible for his failure to return to the lucrative office of Lord Lieutenant of Ireland.[58] In January Ormond was in close liaison with Danby's opponents, including the prominent Presbyterian, the earl of Bedford.[59] Shortly before parliament assembled there were rumours that Arlington and his associates intended to impeach the Lord Treasurer for financial irregularities.[60] These rumours were not groundless, as subsequent

[52] Ibid., p. 368; Miller, *Charles II*, p. 242; *Cal. SP Ven.*, 38, pp. 318–19, 357, 390–1, Alberti to Doge and Senate, 27 Nov. 1674, 5 Feb., 9 April 1675.
[53] Miller, ibid., pp. 240–2; Carte MSS 72, fol. 257, Southwell to Ormond, 23 Jan. 1675; Reresby Letters 8/5, Goodrich to Reresby, 23 Jan. 1675; *Cal. SP Ven.*, 38, p. 391.
[54] Haley, *Shaftesbury*, pp. 369–71.
[55] Copies of Shaftesbury's letter quickly circulated at court (Carte MSS 38, fols. 276, 277–8).
[56] Add. MSS 28,042, fol. 17. Browning dates this memorandum to Dec. 1673 (*Danby*, II, p. 64).
[57] Miller, *Charles II*, pp. 234, 236; Haley, *Shaftesbury*, p. 349; Browning, *Danby*, I, pp. 141–4.
[58] Browning, ibid., p. 145. The post was held by the earl of Essex.
[59] Ibid., pp. 149–51; Carte MSS 38, fol. 238, Sir George Lane to Ormond, 23 Jan. 1674.
[60] Haley, *Shaftesbury*, pp. 372–3; Browning, *Danby*, I, pp. 155–9.

events were to show: Arlington's friends commenced their attack on Danby in the Commons on 26 April.[61]

The obvious solution to Danby's problems was to turn to Anglican Royalists for assistance. Including the bishops they comprised just over half the House in 1675.[62] Danby made careful calculations of the degree of support the government might reasonably expect from the Lords in the approaching session. In addition to the bishops, forty-nine individuals are named on his pre-sessional lists of peers likely to support the Test Bill, and the vast majority had Royalist roots.[63] The king's opening speech was designed to appeal to the Anglican and Cavalier sentiments of these men. After referring to 'the pernicious designs of ill men' who wanted to compel him to dissolve parliament, Charles stressed his past obligations to his Cavalier friends, asserting that he 'will leave nothing undone that may show the world my zeal to the Protestant religion as it is established in the Church of England, from which I will never depart'.[64] Two days later ex-Cavalier peers had further testimony of the king's sincerity when the earl of Lindsey presented 'An act to prevent dangers which might arise from persons disaffected to the government'.[65] Danby made no secret of the fact that the bill was intended to give Anglicans and former Royalists a monopoly of offices in church and state.[66] It placed restrictions on Presbyterians and Catholics, prescribing dismissal from office and ejection from parliament as a penalty for refusing to declare that it was unlawful to alter the government in church and state. The old Cavaliers' ingrained belief in obedience to the monarchy was appealed to, for the bill required all officeholders, peers and MPs to swear that taking up arms against the king was illegal.

Though the bill failed to pass the Lords because a protracted privilege dispute with the Commons forced the king to prorogue, it did nevertheless achieve Danby's immediate aim of providing the government with a substantial following among Anglican and Royalist lords. Obviously not all the peers on Danby's pre-sessional lists supported the bill (Bridgewater, Petre, Clarendon, Berkshire and Dorset are known to have voted against it), but the vast majority did. A total of 53 peers and bishops voted for the bill's commitment on 26 April.[67] From surviving division lists it is apparent that most of those peers listed by Danby remained the government's staunchest adherents both during his ministry and in the period 1679 to 1681 when there

---

[61] Browning, ibid.
[62] This calculation is based on the lists of peers and bishops in Appendixes 1 and 2.
[63] Add. MSS 28,091, fols. 161, 175, 177.
[64] *LJ*, XII, 653–6.
[65] *Cal. SP Ven.*, 38, pp. 393–4, Alberti to Doge and Senate, 16 April 1675; Add. MSS 41,656, fols. 79–80, a copy of the Test Bill.
[66] Haley, *Shaftesbury*, p. 380; *Cal. SP Ven.*, 38, p. 391, Alberti to Doge and Senate, 9 April 1675.
[67] Carte MSS 79, fols. 2, 17.

was a power vacuum at court and no strong Court leader in the Lords, apart
from the king, who attended debates as zealously as ever.[68] From 1675 the
government could normally rely on the votes of between thirty and forty temporal peers, in the main ex-Cavaliers, and on almost all the fourteen to
sixteen bishops who regularly attended.

III

Like most political parties Danby's Court party was a coalition. It contained
several of the king's closest friends and bedchamber servants, prominent ministers and privy councillors, lord lieutenants, military commanders, peers in
receipt of royal bounty and pensions, the Lord Treasurer's friends and
kinsmen, most bishops and many who had no close connection with the
court. Most shared Royalist ancestries and were deeply conservative men,
believing that a strong monarchy and the established church were essential
prerequisites for stable government. In their view the Civil War and
Interregnum had demonstrated that religious and political innovation result
in disruption and dislocation.[69] They regarded the continuance of the
Cavalier Parliament, the rigid enforcement of the laws against Protestant dissenters and Catholics and the pursuit of an anti-French foreign policy as
crucial if this order and stability were to be preserved. Danby recognised this,
and having won their confidence with his Test Bill, continued to pursue
related Anglican policies to retain their allegiance.

The government's renewed commitment to the established church was regularly reaffirmed after 1675 by the king and his Lord Chancellor in their
speeches at the opening of parliamentary sessions. On 15 February 1677 Lord
Chancellor Finch delivered a long oration to the assembled Houses, appealing to conservatives to maintain the peace of the state and the church against
innovations. Nonconformists, particularly Catholics, were prosecuted more
vigorously than at any time since the early 1660s. Following rumours of
popish risings in the summer of 1676 the government issued further instructions for the enforcement of the recusancy laws. In several counties JPs and
lord lieutenants who refused to enforce the penal laws were dismissed. The
Presbyterian lord lieutenant of Norfolk, Lord Townshend, who was tolerant
towards dissenters, was replaced by the Anglican Viscount Yarmouth in
1676. Peers who sympathised with dissenters were struck off the Privy
Council Register: the bishops of London and Durham replaced Lords Halifax
and Holles in January 1676.

---

[68] See Swatland, 'The House of Lords', Appendix III.
[69] See Newcastle, *Memoirs*, p. xxiii and Add. MSS 28,046, fol. 49, a speech by Lord Gerard,
   21 Mar. 1679.

Halifax and Holles had also been prominent in the 1675 campaign to persuade the king to dissolve the Cavalier Parliament. Danby and members of the Court party believed a new parliament would contain a higher proportion of ex-Parliamentarians and dissenters than the existing one, and therefore might threaten the church settlement.[70] Lord Maynard expressed his concern about a possible dissolution in a letter to Danby in August 1676. He suggested that if papists and Presbyterians succeeded in their campaign 'our Church [would] be destroyed ... and our protestant religion would soon run the same fate'.[71]

Danby deployed a variety of strategies to ensure that the existing parliament was retained. In the summer of 1676 he persuaded the duke of York not to question the legality of the fifteen-month prorogation when parliament assembled in the following February. James was the chief exponent of dissolution at court. He believed that a new House of Commons would be more sympathetic to dissenters and Catholics, and thought it would willingly vote money in return for toleration![72] Still smarting from their defeat on 20 November 1675 over the question of addressing the king to dissolve parliament, Country peers planned to renew their endeavours in the approaching session. Danby was well informed of their intentions.[73] He dealt with the arguments of pamphlets backed by Shaftesbury, such as *The grand question concerning the prorogation of the parliament* in *A paquet of advices and animadversions*.[74] This pamphlet defended the church and attacked 'opposition' leaders, portraying them as eager to revive 'the old faction of forty-one'.[75] According to one observer, the effect of *A paquet of advices* was to deter sixteen to twenty peers from joining with those Country leaders who asserted on 15 February 1677 that parliament was dissolved by virtue of the long prorogation.[76]

Danby instructed Court peers and bishops to attend on the first day of the new session. Sixty-six court peers, with twenty-three proxies in reserve, were present on 15 February; compared with only thirty-eight 'opposition' peers, holding six proxies.[77] Danby briefed government lords well before the start

[70] This was also the view of most bishops (*Cal. SP Ven.*, 38, p. 416, Alberti to Doge and Senate, 4 June 1675).
[71] BL, Egerton MSS 3,330, fols. 21–2, Maynard to Danby, 14 Aug. 1676.
[72] Miller, *Charles II*, p. 248.
[73] *Cal. SP Dom.*, 1676–7, p. 459, Danby to Conway, 20 Dec. 1676.
[74] Cited by Haley, *Shaftesbury*, pp. 414–15.
[75] *Cal. SP Dom.*, 1676–7, pp. 476, 506, 521, letters of Thomas Barnes, 30 Dec. 1676, 13 Jan., 28 Jan. 1677.
[76] Add. MSS 28,047, fol. 119.
[77] *LJ*, XIII, 36–7; Proxy Book 6 (proxies entered before 15 Feb. 1677); BL, Stowe MSS 210, fol. 433, Coventry to Essex, 26 Dec. 1676; 217, fol. 2, Essex to Coventry, 2 Jan. 1677; Longleat House, Coventry Papers, Coventry to the earl of Suffolk, 12 Feb. 1677; *Cal. SP Dom.*, 1676–7, p. 544, Williamson to the earl of St Albans, Lord Crofts and the marquis of Worcester, 9 Feb. 1677.

of the session so they had sound arguments to counter any claims that parliament was dissolved by the long prorogation.[78] Immediately after
Buckingham's long speech declaring parliament dissolved Lord Chancellor
Finch stood up and recited carefully prepared precedents to counter the
duke's assertion.[79] The upshot of two days' debates was that Buckingham,
Salisbury, Wharton and Shaftesbury were sent to the Tower where the first
three remained for several months, and Shaftesbury until early 1678. As a
result of Danby's efforts the Country party was significantly weakened and
demoralised by the incarceration of its leaders, serving to strengthen the government's grip on the chamber.

During the same session the Lord Treasurer made a concerted effort to
reduce anxieties caused by the religion of the duke of York and papists in
general. To alleviate former Cavaliers' anxieties about the Church of England
after the king's death Danby promoted a measure to limit the powers of a
popish successor. On 1 March 1677 John Dolben, bishop of Rochester, introduced in the Lords a bill for 'securing the Protestant religion'.[80] The bill provided for the education of children from the royal family in the Protestant
religion and drastically restricted a future Catholic monarch's prerogative to
make church appointments. A second bill for 'the more effectual conviction
and prosecution of Popish recusants' was intended to allay fears about the
activities of Catholic extremists. All Catholics who took the Oath of
Allegiance and paid a fee could have their names entered on a register and
were to be relieved of all penalties apart from the shilling-a-week fine for non-
attendance at church. At the same time Catholics were not to hold offices,
carry weapons, reside at court or have their children educated abroad. As the
Lord Chancellor explained to both Houses, it was the government's intention
to distinguish between 'mistaken souls who deserve to be pitied' and
'designing men who deserve to be punished'.[81] Without the presence of the
four Country leaders both bills passed rapidly though the Lords only to
founder in the Commons, where the court had less influence.[82] Until his
impeachment in late December 1678 Danby continued to take a firm line
against disloyal Catholics. During the autumn of 1678 he led the investiga-
tions on the privy council and in the Lords into the popish plot, advising the
king to vigorously enforce the penal laws to lessen popular fears of popery.[83]

[78] Carte MSS 79, fols. 37–43. Court lords who argued against dissolution were: Ailesbury,
    Frescheville, Bristol, Arundel of Trerice and the bishop of Salisbury.
[79] Finch's speech is printed in Yale (ed.), *Lord Nottingham's Chancery cases*, II, pp. 982–9.
[80] HLRO, Main Papers, 1 March 1677; M. Goldie, 'Danby, the bishops and the Whigs', in
    Harris, Seaward and Goldie (eds.), p. 84.
[81] *LJ*, XIII, 37.
[82] Goldie, 'Danby, the bishops and the Whigs', p. 85.
[83] Kenyon, *Popish Plot*, pp. 58–76, 80–201.

Danby also pursued an anti-French foreign policy which was popular with his Anglican cohorts in parliament. Fears of absolutist France were not restricted to Country peers and MPs, as the debates on a possible war with that country in 1678 indicate.[84] Court peers too were alarmed at reports of French armies sweeping across Flanders in the spring and summer. French victories increased mistrust of Charles II, particularly since English regiments were serving in the French army. Danby advised the king to abandon the French alliance and so regain the goodwill of the lower House. He urged him to agree to a Commons' address for an offensive and defensive league with the United Provinces and France's other European enemies. In March 1678 Danby told the Lords that Charles favoured such an alliance and was prepared to engage in a war against Louis XIV. The Lord Treasurer additionally declared 'that no man for these two years past had lived with greater apprehensions of France than himself and was more convinced of the necessity of war'.[85] Not every Court lord viewed the prospect of another war and the high taxation it would entail with enthusiasm. In a private memorandum Lord Finch argued against fighting France, on the grounds of cost and the impact on trade.[86] The duke of Newcastle was also opposed to war, declaring 'I do not see how it is possible to have it with any hope of success.'[87] However, a majority of the House, including many Court lords, voted for the king to declare war 'with all the expedition that may consist with the safety of your majesty's affairs'.[88]

In all political parties it is difficult to determine the relative importance of ideology as opposed to self-interest when accounting for political allegiances. The Court party was no exception. To those peers who were intensely interested in politics, the Anglican policies pursued by the Lord Treasurer provided the key to their voting behaviour. This was certainly true of the earl of Lindsey, who stated in a letter to Danby, 'I do really believe God hath raised you to this eminency of condition to save a tottering monarchy, which if your counsel is not followed ... will be quickly changed into an anarchy of confusion.'[89] Another staunch adherent, Lord Maynard, asserted that the 'good and happiness of the king, the Church and kingdom depend upon you'.[90] For the majority of Court lords Danby's policies, which appealed to

---

[84] Yale (ed.), *Lord Nottingham's Chancery cases*, II, pp. 989–95; *Hist. MSS Comm.*, Ormonde MSS, IV, pp. 415–18, Southwell to Ormond, 16/19 Mar. 1678; BL, Verney MSS, M636, reel 31, Ralph Verney to Edmund Verney, 18 Mar. 1678.

[85] *Hist. MSS Comm.*, Ormonde MSS, IV, p. 415.

[86] Finch Papers, PP. 49, Lord Finch's notes 'Concerning a war', *c.* March 1678.

[87] Reresby Letters, 13/10, Newcastle to Reresby, 8 May 1678.

[88] *LJ*, XIII, 185–6.

[89] *Hist. MSS Comm.*, 38, 14th Rept, Appendix pt ix, Lindsey MSS, p. 377, Lindsey to Danby, 25 August 1675.

[90] BL, Egerton MSS 3,330, fols. 21–2.

their conservative outlook, rather than the perennial ones on patronage, friendship and kinship, determined their loyalty to his party.

Nevertheless the acquisition of a court post or office in the administration, particularly if Danby had been involved in bestowing the post, helped to cement party loyalties. Between 1675 and 1678 two-thirds of lord lieu-tenancies, posts at court and seats on the privy council were enjoyed by Court lords.[91] The overwhelming majority of peers promoted to offices during Danby's ministry had Royalist ancestries. In marked contrast with Clarendon, who had encouraged the king to reward a significant number of ex-Parliamentarians, Danby did his utmost to ensure that former Cavaliers received due recognition for past sufferings in the Royalist cause. The former Royalist officer, the earl of Northampton, was made Constable of the Tower of London in 1675 and Lords Frescheville, Yarmouth, Newcastle and Norreys were given lucrative local offices. For similar reasons Lords Strafford and Berkeley of Berkeley were sworn privy councillors during Danby's ascen-dancy.[92]

Danby did not extensively use pensions as a means of buying peers' votes. Bribing peers in this way was generally unnecessary since the government normally mustered a majority in the Lords. Under Danby the government could usually rely on the votes and proxies of the bishops. Even when tax yields increased in the late 1670s the Treasury did not have surplus money to shower indiscriminately on peers, and especially to buy off 'opposition' lords.[93] Pensions were generally only given as rewards to loyal Anglican Royalists, and even then very sparingly. The earl of Northampton and Lord Arundel of Trerice both received pensions of £1,000 in 1676 for services ren-dered to the Crown. Very few peers were court dependants. Between 1675 and 1679 no more than two dozen peers are recorded as receiving pensions.[94] Through the Lord Treasurer's efforts to reduce expenditure many of these were either reduced or not paid at all. No Court peer relied exclusively on a pension or a salary, which were sometimes insufficient even to meet day-to-day expenses. Despite an annuity of £100 the earl of Marlborough was so impoverished in 1677 that he wrote to Danby offering to sell his earldom.[95] The earl of Sunderland's salary of £1,000 as a gentleman of the bedchamber was inadequate for his lavish life-style, and certainly did not deter him from voting for the Exclusion Bill.[96]

[91] See Swatland, 'House of Lords', Appendix I.
[92] PRO, P.C. 2/64, fol. 1; 66, fol. 1.
[93] Chanderman, *English public revenue*, pp. 231–8.
[94] *Calendar of Treasury Books*, 1672–5, pp. 365, 370, 380, 381, 387, 440–1, 482, 555, 573, 585, 617, 676, 725, 728, 731, 754, 783, 795, 845; 1676–9, pp. 111, 139, 152, 177, 206, 278.
[95] BL, Egerton MSS 3,330, fol. 101, Marlborough to Danby, 23 April 1677.
[96] J. Kenyon, *Robert Spencer, earl of Sunderland* (1958), p. 16; Add. MSS 51,319, fol. 55, division list on the Exclusion Bill.

Of greater significance in retaining allegiances were the bonds of kinship. Kinship traditionally had a powerful influence on shaping political loyalties in the House because many peers were related through blood or marriage. The nucleus of Danby's Court parties in both chambers consisted of his close friends and relatives.[97] His most stalwart adherent in the upper House was his brother-in-law, the earl of Lindsey. It was Lindsey who was entrusted with the introduction of the Test Bill in April 1675 and who defended Danby during the proceedings on his impeachment and attainder in 1678 and 1679.[98] The Lord Treasurer's marriage into the Bertie family assured him the loyalty of a further three peers, Lord Norreys, Viscount Campden and Lord Noel. Almost all Danby's relatives were Anglican Royalists, and would probably have endorsed his policies irrespective of ties of kinship.[99]

Notwithstanding the appeal of Danby's policies and the importance of offices, posts, pensions and the bonds of kinship to focus and strengthen the loyalties of Court peers, the government's control over the House of Lords was not watertight. Even with the bishops' votes divisions were at times extremely close, as those recorded on Danby's 1676 Test Bill and the second Test Bill indicate.[100] On 20 November 1675 the combined forces of Country and Catholic peers very nearly defeated the Court party in the Lords on the question of addressing the king to dissolve parliament.[101] Outnumbered, the Court only managed to defeat the motion by two proxy votes. Earlier in the year Danby had been forced to abandon his Test because Country and Catholic lords had fomented a protracted privilege dispute with the Commons, which brought all other parliamentary business to a standstill. In order to maintain the government's superiority in the Lords, the Lord Treasurer resorted to some of the techniques and practices which he used in his management of the Commons.

Danby made the most concerted efforts of any of Charles II's ministers to manage the House of Lords. He was the first minister to resort to whipping on a significant scale in the Lords. He drew up lists of probable court supporters in the Lords before parliament assembled in April 1675.[102] Later, he estimated how many votes the government could muster were the 'opposition' to force a division on the legality of the fifteen-month prorogation when parliament met in February 1677. Peers noted for their erratic atten-

---

[97] Browning, *Danby*, I, pp. 118, 167–8.
[98] *Hist. MSS Comm.*, Lindsey MSS, pp. 419–20, Lindsey to Danby, 4 Sept. 1680; Add. MSS 28,091, fols. 134, 140.
[99] Add. MSS 28,091, fols. 134, 139–40; 29,572, fol. 112, C. Hatton to Lord Hatton, 15 April 1679; Browning, *Danby*, I, pp. 167–8.
[100] *Bulstrode Papers*, p. 287; Swatland, 'Further recorded divisions in the House of Lords', p. 108.
[101] Carte MSS 79, fol. 19.
[102] Add. MSS 28,091, fols. 161, 175, 177; *Cal. SP Ven.*, 38, p. 391, Alberti to Doge and Senate, 9 April 1675.

dance were urged to be present at the beginning of the session.[103] At least six peers and all the bishops were instructed either to attend on 15 February or to return proxy forms.[104] Danby duly obtained the support he desired, but it may of course be that some of those written to had already decided to attend or assign proxies.

The most novel feature of Danby's management was his exploitation of proxies. Occasionally Clarendon had endeavoured to obtain the proxies of absent peers, but his attempts had usually been confined to a few absentee royal officials.[105] Danby's management of proxies was altogether more systematic. Several weeks before every session from 1675 to 1678 the two Secretaries of State wrote to likely absentees desiring them to sign and return proxy forms.[106] In contrast with the practice of Clarendon's administration, they were usually asked to leave the name of the recipient blank, allowing Danby to nominate proxies. In October 1675 Secretary Williamson wrote to the earl of Suffolk, a capricious and inconsistent courtier, whose loyalties were divided between serving the king and the Country party. Suffolk was commanded to sign a blank proxy form, which was duly assigned to Danby's associate, Lord Maynard.[107] From 1675 to the autumn of 1678 the Lord Treasurer obtained on average ten to fifteen proxies per session.[108] For the five sessions during this period the government controlled three-quarters of registered proxies. All these were held by loyal Court peers and bishops, and 52 per cent of all proxies were in the hands of privy councillors.[109] This allowed the Court party to win close divisions, the most notable being on 20 November 1675, when its sixteen proxies enabled it to defeat the attempt to address the king to dissolve parliament.[110]

Danby's exertions did not cease at proxies: he made considerable efforts to ensure that those Court lords who attended were informed of the government's business in the House. Like the leaders of the Country party, he

---

[103] BL, Stowe MSS 210, fol. 433; Add. MSS 25,125, fol. 118, Coventry to Suffolk, 12 Feb. 1677; *Cal. SP Dom.*, 1676–7, p. 544.

[104] BL, Stowe MSS 210, fol. 433; Add. MSS 25,125, fol. 118; *Cal. SP Dom.*, 1676–7, pp. 459, 544; *Calendar of Treasury Books*, 1676–9, p. 425; *Hist. MSS Comm.*, 45, Manuscripts of the duke of Buccleuch and Queensberry, vol. I (1899), p. 324, William Montagu to Lord Montagu, 18 Jan. 1677.

[105] Clarendon MSS 79, fol. 109, Orrery to Clarendon, 12 Mar. 1662; Carte MSS 33, fol. 718, Lady Devonshire to Ormond, 23 Nov. 1664; 51, fol. 18, Ormond to Anglesey, 18 Dec. 1666.

[106] BL, Egerton MSS 3,329, fol. 6, Harbord to Danby, 2 Mar. 1675; BL, Stowe MSS 217, fol. 2, Essex to Coventry, 2 Jan. 1677; Add. MSS 25,125, fol. 118, Coventry to Suffolk, 12 Feb. 1677; *Cal. SP Dom.*, 1676–7, pp. 459, 544; *Hist. MSS Comm.*, 13th Rept, Appendix, Portland MSS, II, p. 153, Albemarle to Newcastle, 19 Nov. 1675.

[107] *Cal. SP Dom.*, 1675–6, p. 343, Williamson to the earl of Suffolk, 11 Oct. 1675; Proxy Book 5, Oct. 1675.

[108] See Proxy Books 5 and 6.

[109] Ibid.

[110] Add. MSS 35,865, fol. 224, division on 'whether to address the king to dissolve parliament', 20 Nov. 1675.

chaired private meetings to coordinate tactics in both Houses before and during a session. Often these were attended by senior ministers, parliamentary managers and MPs. On 19 April 1675 Danby, Anglesey and Finch met to discuss objections to the oath in the Test Bill.[111] Two years later Danby, Finch, Lauderdale and Ormond met several times to prepare for the 1677 parliamentary session.[112] When extremely important issues were under debate, the Lord Treasurer even provided government supporters with written arguments to use in the House. Among his manuscripts in the British Library are three copies of papers containing arguments relating to his Attainder Bill of April 1679, five copies of notes for conferences on the same bill and seven identical sheets demonstrating the validity of his royal pardon.[113]

The impact of this management on Court peers is reflected in their voting behaviour. An analysis of the same twenty-eight divisions and protests referred to in the previous chapters reveals that the fifty-eight Court lords (not bishops) recorded as voting twice or more between 1675 and 1681 supported the king's ministers in at least eight out of ten divisions, and many voted with the government on every issue. This does not mean the House was always split along party lines. Non-controversial private bills and judicial cases, where the court did not give directions to peers, witnessed members voting according to their consciences or on the merits of the case. The distinctions between parties were completely blurred on the question of giving relief to a petitioner in the case of *Darrell* v. *Whitchott* in July 1678: eight Court lords and ten Country lords protested against giving relief.[114]

On the whole, however, Court lords were slightly less consistent in their voting behaviour than their Country opponents. There are several explanations for this. Court peers were at their most inconsistent during the autumn of 1678 when hysteria created by the popish plot was at its height and in the spring of 1679 following the fall of their leader, the earl of Danby. Several traditional government supporters were so concerned for the king's safety in November 1678 that they temporarily sided with the 'opposition' in proposing drastic remedies. Nine voted with the Country party on 15 November in the division for annexing the declaration against transubstantiation to the Oaths of Allegiance and Supremacy in the second Test Bill as a means of preventing papists from sitting or voting in the House of Lords.[115] The dismissal of Danby deprived the government of its most able parliamentary manager in the House at a time when he was most needed to unify and direct the

---

[111] Add. MSS 40,860, fol. 86 (Anglesey's diary), 19 April 1675.
[112] *Cal. SP Dom.*, 1676–7, p. 480, notes by Secretary Williamson.
[113] Add. MSS 28,047, fols. 207–17, 246.
[114] Carte MSS 81, fol. 365; *LJ*, XIII, 273.
[115] Chatsworth House, Devonshire Collection, Group 1/C, newsletter to the earl of Devonshire, 16 Nov. 1678; Dr Williams' Library, Morrice MSS, Entering Book P, p. 95; Carte MSS 81, fol. 380.

Court party. Although Lord Chance"or Finch and, to a lesser extent, Lord
Robartes and the earl of Bath, attempted to lead the Court party, none had
the abilities or personal following enjoyed by Danby, and there is little evidence that they used the range of managerial techniques employed by him.[116]

Paradoxically, continued loyalty to Danby was a further cause of disunity
within the Court party towards the end of the 1679 parliament. Danby was
in the Tower awaiting trial following his impeachment. Most 'opposition'
peers, and a few Court lords wanted a speedy trial before any prorogation
of parliament, whilst Danby's friends preferred delay in the hope that he
would be released when passions had calmed. A rift in the Court party was
apparent during a vote on 10 May 1679 for establishing a joint committee to
consider the method of proceeding in the trials of Danby and the five
Catholic lords, impeached for their alleged involvement in the popish plot.
Fifteen Court lords, including the Lord Chancellor and the Lord
Chamberlain, joined with thirty-six country peers in voting for the committee
because they believed if MPs were preoccupied in this business, the passage
of the first Exclusion Bill would be impeded in the Commons.[117] However, a
majority of Court peers (including all Danby's friends) and all but two
bishops voted the opposite way, anxious to prevent any cooperation between
the Houses on the impeachment procedure. They carried the day by fifty-four
votes to fifty-two.[118]

Among the most reliable members of the Court party were the bishops. With
few exceptions they consistently voted as the government desired on most
issues between 1675 and 1681.[119] With the lay membership of the Court and
Country parties finely balanced, the bishops' votes were vital in ensuring that
the government retained control of the Lords. Prior to 1675 the bishops had
not always supported the government there, particularly when the king had
sought to mitigate the severity of the Uniformity and Conventicle Acts. As
recently as 1674 the bench had been sharply divided over a Comprehension
Bill. In January 1675 Danby had effected a *rapprochement* between the
bishops and the court during the consultations at Lambeth Palace over the
enforcement of the penal laws. A consequence of the government's adoption
of Anglican religious policies at this time was Archbishop Sheldon's return
to favour at court after eight years of frosty relations with the king.[120] Thus

[116] Add. MSS 28,049, fol. 20, Bath to Danby, 1 April 1679; Carte MSS 79, fol. 164, proceedings
at the Oxford Parliament, 21–22 Mar. 1681; Leicestershire RO, Finch Papers, PP. 65, brief
notes of speeches made in the privy council by Lord Chancellor Finch and Lord President
Radnor, 31 Dec. 1680.

[117] Haley, *Shaftesbury*, p. 523; Chatsworth, Halifax Collection, Group E/7, Algernon Sidney to
Henry Savile, 12 May 1679; Add. MSS 28,049, fol. 47; *LJ*, XIII, 564, 567.

[118] Carte MSS 103, fol. 270.

[119] See Swatland, 'House of Lords', Appendix III.

[120] R. Beddard, 'The Restoration Church', in J. R. Jones (ed.), *The Restored monarchy*,
pp. 171–2.

years of royal inconstancy towards the church, which had made bishops suspicious of the king, were followed by a return to orthodox Anglican policies under Danby.

This new relationship was immediately evident when the bishops vigorously defended the Lord Treasurer's Test Bill, and in doing so earned themselves the epithet 'dead weight' from the earl of Shaftesbury.[121] During the autumn session of 1675 the votes and proxies of sixteen bishops helped to defeat the motion to address the king to dissolve the Cavalier Parliament. In fact the bishops' attendance was higher that autumn than at any time since 1664 (see table 1). Apart from the bishop of Durham, the bishops stood by Danby on 27 December 1678 when the House rejected an 'opposition' motion that the earl should be imprisoned in the Tower after his impeachment by the House of Commons.[122] The central role played by the bishops in the politics of the chamber was underlined on 14 April 1679 when the House voted by a very narrow margin to agree with the Commons and accept the bill for Danby's attainder. The Country party was only able to win the division because six bishops who had previously voted against the bill were persuaded by the court to absent themselves before the vote took place.[123]

As in the 1660s, the management of the bishops owed more to the industry of the archbishop of Canterbury and bishop of London than to government ministers. There were two archbishops of Canterbury during Danby's ministry, the ailing Sheldon (1663–77) and the energetic Sancroft (1678–91). Until Sheldon's death, Henry Compton, bishop of London, was the driving force behind the organisation of the bishops in the upper House. It was Compton who reminded Sheldon of the need to despatch circular letters to bishops in January 1677 giving them 'timely notice of sending their proxies up in good time' if they could not attend in person.[124] The continuation of this practice under Sancroft ensured that bishops attended in good numbers or registered proxies. For the five sessions from 1675 to 1678 bishops registered an average of seven proxies each session, whilst attendance averaged thirteen each sitting.[125] The bishops were among the king's most loyal adherents during the succession crisis. Anxious to maintain the lawful succession all fourteen bishops present in the chamber on 15 November 1680 joined with Court peers in rejecting the Exclusion Bill after its first reading.

---

[121] *Letter from a person of quality* ..., p. xiv.
[122] Carte MSS 81, fol. 405, division list, 27 Dec. 1678.
[123] *LJ*, XIII, 514–16; Browning, *Danby*, I, pp. 326–9; Haley, *Shaftesbury*, p. 509; Add. MSS 29,572, fol. 112.
[124] Bodl., Tanner MSS 40, fol. 44, Compton to Sheldon, early Jan. 1677; fol. 51, draft letter from Sheldon to the bishops about the meeting of parliament, 16 Jan. 1677.
[125] See Proxy Books 5 and 6 and table 1, p. 35.

IV

No consideration of government supporters in the Lords can be complete
without discussing the 'Tories'. It has been asserted recently by one historian
that in contrast with members of the Court party most 'Tories' were independent peers, with few holding offices in the central administration.[126]
However, an analysis of the membership of the 'Tory' party reveals a different picture. Few 'Tory' peers were genuinely independent of the court or the
government: three-fifths of those lords who voted against the Exclusion Bill
held court offices or posts in the administration.[127] Of these, fourteen were
privy councillors and a further eight were former privy councillors who had
lost their posts following the king's re-organisation of the council in 1679.[128]

It is unhelpful to make a distinction between Court lords of the period
1675–9 and the so-called 'Tory' lords of 1680–1, since they were normally
the same men. In fact over 70 per cent of those Court peers who voted
against Danby's attainder bill in April 1679 remained consistently loyal to the
government in the Lords during the autumn of 1680.[129] Court and 'Tory'
lords were intensely conservative, sharing the same characteristics: a deep
respect for the monarchy, its prerogatives, the established church and the law
and an abhorrence of dissent, political instability and social upheaval.
The main difference, though, was the political situation of 1680/1. The
popish plot heightened men's anxieties about the succession, and both the
opposition's exploitation of the plot and the activities of dissenters in the corporations aroused fears among Tories that the 'Whigs' wished forcibly to
overthrow the established order in church and state.[130] For many former
Royalist peers the succession crisis forced them to state openly opinions
which they had long retained about the monarchy. There was nothing particularly new about these views (expressed by 'Tory' lords in the debate on
the Exclusion Bill): several had already been voiced earlier in the reign. The
notion that it was unlawful to alter the hereditary succession, which both
Newcastle and Ailesbury emphasised in their speeches, had medieval
antecedents, and had been deployed by Lord Keeper Finch in 1674 when
'Malcontent' peers had proposed exclusion as the penalty for a prince who
married a papist without parliament's consent. Likewise the idea of obedience, even to a popish monarch, had been expounded on the same occasion
by the archbishop of York and the bishop of Winchester. They contended

[126] J. R. Jones, *Charles II*, pp. 137–8.
[127] Swatland, 'The House of Lords', Appendix I.
[128] Swatland, 'Privy councillors', pp. 75–7.
[129] Carte MSS 81, fols. 4, 588 (division list, 14 April 1679); fol. 654; Add. MSS 36,988, fol. 189;
51,319, fol. 55; Northamptonshire RO, Finch-Hatton MSS 2893 A–D (division lists on the
Exclusion Bill, 15 Nov. 1680); Carte MSS 81, fols. 4, 669 (division list on appointment of a
joint committee, 23 Nov. 1680).
[130] Miller, *Charles II*, p. 320; Knights, *Politics and opinion in crisis*, pp. 202, 357.

that by 'divine law, obedience and submission were due not only to a Popish king, but to a tyrant and even to a pagan'.[131]

An analysis of the surviving division lists on the Exclusion Bill demonstrates that there was a high degree of continuity between Danby's Court party and the membership of the 'Tory' party. There are three extant lists of lords who voted to reject the bill after its first reading.[132] In terms of numbers and names each list is slightly different and none exactly accords with the final vote of sixty-three to thirty. After eliminating known absentees, one is left with a total of fifty-three peers, of whom forty-nine actually voted against the bill. Of these fifty-three, no fewer than thirty-eight had been members of Danby's party. Ten had previously voted with the 'opposition' and four had succeeded to titles after Danby's impeachment.[133] Of these ten peers eight had not permanently deserted the 'opposition' for they voted against the government in subsequent divisions.[134] The composition of the Court and 'Tory' parties was almost identical: 74 per cent of Court lords in 1675 and 75 per cent of 'Tories' in 1680 were either ex-Royalists or their descendants.[135]

The decisive factor in the defeat of the Exclusion Bill was the attitude of these Anglican peers, who prided themselves on their loyalty to the monarchy and the Church of England. All would have echoed the earl of Yarmouth when he wrote in March 1680: 'My love to the Crown, the lawful successor and the Church I shall never warp.'[136] Danby's Anglican policies, coupled with the king's renewed commitment to the Church of England since 1675, had brought these men into a close alliance with the Crown. Those whose speeches have survived from 15 November 1680 emphasised their firm commitment to the principle of hereditary succession.[137] The earl of Ailesbury expounded the divine-right theory, asserting that exclusion was 'against the law of God and nature'. The aged duke of Lauderdale expressed his concern that the monarchy might become elective since the exclusion of the duke of York would create a precedent for parliament to depose kings. Equally important to 'Tory' lords were memories of the Civil War. Both Yarmouth and Ailesbury declared that exclusion could result in anarchy and bloodshed, since James would probably invade in order to protect his rightful inheritance after the death of Charles II. To Ailesbury the prospect of this posed a much greater threat of 'insecurity ... than to suffer him to reign', especially

---

[131] *Cal. SP Ven.*, 38, p. 221, Alberti to Doge and Senate, 13 Feb. 1674.
[132] Add. MSS 36,988, fol. 189; Carte MSS 81, fols. 4, 654; Northamptonshire RO, Finch-Hatton MSS 2893, A and C.
[133] The ten 'opposition' peers were: Bridgewater, Burlington, Carlisle, Carnarvon, Chesterfield, Clarendon, Fauconberg, Mulgrave, Newport and Scarsdale. The four who had succeeded to titles were: Berkshire, Deincourt, Rutland and Thanet.
[134] See Swatland, 'The House of Lords', Appendix III.
[135] These percentages are derived from the lists of peers in Appendix 1 of this book.
[136] Add. MSS 36,988, fol. 154, Yarmouth to Sir R. Clayton, 7 Mar. 1680.
[137] De Beer, 'House of Lords in the parliament of 1680', pp. 32–6.

as 'he may exercise this religion in private' and not force it upon the nation.[138]

Whilst the earl of Huntingdon's notes on the debate give the 'Tory' arguments against exclusion, they are too incomplete to enable one to judge whether Halifax had a decisive impact on the final division. Traditionally it has been assumed that his eloquence and rhetoric played a vital part in the rejection of the bill. It is unlikely that his speeches did more than rally a few waverers. Most lords had decided how they would vote before the bill was presented to the Lords. From a detailed assessment of likely government adherents, the earl of Conway accurately predicted the outcome of the vote, for on 9 November he wrote: "tis certain it will not pass the House of Lords, for by the largest computation they are but thirty of the temporals, which is all be for it ... and we shall be fifty now sitting against it, besides the bishops'.[139] The king's highly publicised stand against the bill probably deterred less committed peers from joining the 'opposition'. Charles informed the privy council that he expected the Lords to reject the bill after its first reading. He was present throughout the lengthy debate on the 15th, expressing his approval of those who spoke against the bill and glaring at those whose speeches displeased him.

The decisive action of the 'Tories' in voting against the Exclusion Bill denied the 'opposition' the possibility of altering the succession by an act of parliament, since it was now apparent that the vast majority of the House of Lords would never consent to such a measure. The central role played by these lords on this occasion served to underline their importance in ensuring that Charles II retained control of the upper House during this period of crisis. On other controversial issues that winter, such as the imprisonment of Lord Chief Justice Scroggs (7 January 1681) or the trial of the informer Edward Fitzharris (26 March 1681) 'Tory' lords and bishops voted decisively as the government directed.[140]

The creation of this loyal party owed much to the Anglican policies and management of the earl of Danby. From 1675 it had been essential for the Crown to maintain a working majority in the Lords since it was unable to exert much influence over the Commons, where court groups lacked cohesion.[141] Danby's management of the upper House had helped to provide this majority, without which the court would have been powerless to resist the challenges of the Country party. Danby's policies appealed to the conservative

---

[138] Ibid., p. 36. The issue of a civil war was a major theme in printed 'Tory' propaganda. See Knights, *Politics and opinion in crisis*, pp. 320–1.

[139] *Hist. MSS Comm.*, Ormonde MSS, V, p. 486, Conway to Ormond, 9 Nov. 1680.

[140] Carte MSS 81, fols. 656–7; Haley, *Shaftesbury*, p. 617; *LJ*, XIII, 755; Swatland, 'The House of Lords', Appendix III.

[141] In contrast with the Lords the composition of Court groups was constantly shifting in the Commons. See Knights, *Politics and opinion in crisis*, pp. 9, 354.

inclinations of Anglican Royalists, both lay and clerical, and brought them into a close partnership with the Crown, a partnership which survived the popish plot revelations, the absence of a united ministry after Danby's dismissal and the crisis over the succession, and lasted into the reign of James II.

13

Conclusion

The House of Lords was unquestionably a powerful force in Charles II's reign. Few writing in 1659 could have predicted that a defunct institution would rise phoenix-like from the ashes of 1649 to assume such a vigorous part in the politics of later Stuart England. Turberville was correct when he wrote, 'It is clear that the House of Lords emerged from the testing time of the Restoration a much stronger body than might have been anticipated in 1660. The House succeeded in re-establishing itself as an ... integral part of the mechanism of the state.'[1] How the House of Lords exercised its responsibilities between 1660 and 1681 vindicated those who had emphasised the need for a second chamber during the Interregnum.[2]

The Lords provided the most powerful section of the country with an arena for the detailed discussion of national and local issues in the same way as the Commons did for the gentry. Although only a minority, especially privy councillors, played a decisive role in shaping legislation in committee, virtually all peers were involved at some time in discussing legislation that had a direct bearing on their estates or localities. Disaffected magnates too, such as the duke of Buckingham and the earl of Shaftesbury, were able to let off steam in debates rather than in armed uprisings. During the popish plot and succession crisis the Lords acted as a safety-valve for the government, in that 'opposition' peers were usefully preoccupied at Westminster investigating the plot and framing legislation against popery.[3]

The Lords' function as a second chamber in the legislative process was of enormous importance. Long before Charles II's reign the upper House had ceased to initiate the bulk of legislation. Nevertheless between 1660 and 1681 a third of all acts of parliament (in the main private bills) were conceived there. Like the present-day House of Lords, Charles II's imposed a check on the activities of the Commons. On many occasions it skilfully revised or

[1] Turberville, 'The House of Lords under Charles II', p. 74.
[2] William Prynne, *A plea for the House of Peers* (1658); C. H. Firth (ed.), 'A letter from Lord Saye and Sele to Lord Wharton', *EHR*, 10 (1895), 106–7.
[3] Kenyon, *Popish Plot*, pp. 81–203; Haley, *Shaftesbury*, pp. 452–528.

rejected those Commons' bills which it considered not to be in the interest of the king, the nobility or the nation as a whole. Since the lower House received more bills than it could reasonably pass, the Lords, with its smaller volume of legislation, was able to function more effectively, passing a higher proportion of those bills initiated there than the Commons was able to do. This situation also owed much to the Lords' committee system, and particularly to the expertise of the 'men of business' who chaired committees, many of whom had served apprenticeships in the Commons.

In contrast with the Commons, which was not a court of law, the upper House made a significant contribution to the administration of justice in Restoration England. As the highest court, the Lords received a multitude of petitions on a wide range of subjects, including disputes over land, inheritance and debts. The peers adhered to established judicial procedures that were fair and equitable. The House functioned more efficiently than before 1649, reaching a decision in about half of all error cases and in 60 per cent of all Chancery appeals.[4] This was a consequence of both the expertise of legally minded members and the absence of a protracted national crisis until 1678 to distract it from the demands of litigation. During the popish plot and succession crisis years the House continued to hear legal cases, though at a reduced rate.[5] Nevertheless this high court was unable to function as effectively as in later reigns for sessions were short and not necessarily held annually, which prevented the determination of every case brought before it.

Especially in moments of crisis the Lords proved to be an indispensable ally for the king and his ministers. Although no rubber-stamp for royal policies, it was generally more receptive to the king's desires than the Commons. This was a consequence of many factors, including the king's creation and promotion of peers, the presence of a substantial number of privy councillors and ministers to manage the House, the conservative outlook of most lords and the fact that Charles could normally count on the votes of the twenty-six bishops who sat in the chamber. The Lords displayed a greater willingness to protect the king's prerogatives than the Commons. Particularly those peers with Royalist ancestries thought that any diminution in the powers of the Crown would have dangerous consequences for both the monarchy and their own standing in government and society. One reason why the peers so decisively rejected the Exclusion Bill's claim to alter the hereditary succession was that they feared another republic with all the concomitant upheavals in government and society.[6]

[4] Hart, *Justice upon petition*, p. 242.
[5] See table 5.
[6] See in particular the earl of Chesterfield's speech in Add. MSS 19,253, fols. 197–8 and the speeches of the earls of Ailesbury and Yarmouth in De Beer, 'The House of Lords in the parliament of 1680', 32–6.

The Lords usually responded more favourably to the king's religious initiatives than the Commons. This was essentially because of the presence of a substantial group of Presbyterian peers, who wished to reduce the legal restrictions on nonconformists. Of course the greater ease with which the government could manage the Lords was also highly significant. Between 1660 and 1662, when the legislation that constituted the church settlement was before parliament, the House of Lords normally adhered to royal policy by tempering the severity of much of the legislation formulated in the Commons. At this time approximately half the House preferred the establishment of a broad Church of England, that closely resembled the Elizabethan and Jacobean Church and incorporated moderate Presbyterian ministers. After 1662 most of the parliamentary endeavours to modify the church settlement in the interests of peaceable nonconforming Protestants originated in the upper House. Whilst none succeeded, it is significant that some of the peers' proposals, such as the repeal of the assent and consent clause in the 1674 Comprehension Bill, anticipated the provisions of the 1689 Toleration Act.

Religion was the root cause of one of the most far-reaching developments in parliamentary politics during the reign: the emergence of political parties in the 1670s. The House of Lords had rarely been a united body before this decade: during the 1620s and 1660s proceedings had become increasingly influenced by competing court factions. A number of factors, most notably pronounced anti-Catholic phobia, anxieties about the church and the succession, and the orthodox Anglican policies of the earl of Danby, account for the development of organised political parties in the House of Lords from 1675. The Court and the Country parties had definite aims and a discernible organisation extending beyond the confines of Westminster. In general their membership reflected the Civil War divisions in the country: former Parliamentarians composed the hard core of the Country party whilst former Royalists and those from Royalist families comprised the bulk of Danby's Court party. In chapters 11 and 12 it was argued that there was very little to distinguish the Court and Country parties from the later 'Tory' and 'Whig' parties. There was little difference in terms of personnel and policies, and the one major development, the prominence given to the issue of the royal succession, was in reality a change in emphasis, for exclusion had been broached in the Lords as early as 1674, and only assumed a greater significance from 1679.

At times the activities of the Court and Country parties brought the houses of parliament into conflict with one another. Since the Restoration, bicameral relations had not been harmonious. Various factors, not least the peers' extreme sensitivity towards their privileges and those of their House and the manoeuvrings of factions, had often resulted in bicameral disputes during the 1660s. During these disputes the upper House vigorously resisted encroachments on its powers and privileges. The House had considerable success in defending its appellate jurisdiction when this was questioned in 1675, and steadfastly refused to recognise all the Commons' claims in the sphere of finance. The peers' stance was decisive in several constitutional wrangles, notably those surrounding the impeachments of Clarendon and Danby. In fact from 1660 to the end of the century the Lords had such a crucial impact on the course of bicameral conflicts that its intervention came to be feared and resented by the Commons.[7]

This does not mean, however, that the House of Lords was the dominant or more important chamber: both Houses had separately distinctive responsibilities and personalities which yet closely interacted with those of the other. There was a multitude of connections between the two Houses, involving kinship, patronage, religion, faction, party and elections. It should not be forgotten that through their electoral influence peers helped to determine the composition of approximately 25 per cent of the Cavalier Commons. Although the Commons supplied the Crown with money, it should not be assumed that its financial responsibilities necessarily rendered it more important for the government than the Lords. Professor Chandaman has demonstrated that from the 1670s the Crown's ordinary sources of revenue were yielding far more than they had done in the 1660s, making parliamentary supplies less significant, and from 1679 the government survived without them.[8] From the king's perspective the Lords was a vital component of the parliamentary triumvirate, because it could restrain the more aggressive Commons, was more sympathetic to his religious policies and generally defended his prerogatives.

Several major developments in Charles II's House of Lords had a profound impact upon parliamentary politics after the king's death. Most significant was the emergence of organised political parties in the 1670s and the continuing association of the Whigs with the aspirations of Protestant dissenters and the corresponding association of the Tories with the established church. The solid alliance between a majority of the House of Lords and the Crown that characterised the last ten years of the reign survived the upheavals of James II's reign to become a significant feature of eighteenth-century parliamentary politics. In addition several of the management techniques used first by Danby to control the upper House, such as whipping and compiling pre-sessional lists, were employed by chief ministers, such as the earl of Oxford and Sir Robert Walpole in the eighteenth century.[9] These were just a few of the legacies bequeathed by members of Charles II's House of Lords to their descendants in the reigns of later monarchs.

[7] Kenyon, *Stuart England*, p. 189.
[8] Chandaman, *English public revenue*, pp. 33, 270–3, 277.
[9] C. Jones, "'The Scheme Lords, the Necessitous Lords, and the Scots Lords", the earl of Oxford's management and the "Party of the Crown" in the House of Lords, 1711–14', in C. Jones (ed.), *Party and management in parliament*, p. 143.

Temporal members of the
House of Lords

Approximately 150 peers were entitled to sit in the House of Lords at any one time during the reign. This appendix records all 262 peers who were eligible to sit during the period 1660 to 1681. Most of the information used in its compilation is derived from the *Journals of the House of Lords*, the *DNB* and *The Complete Peerage*. Professor Henning's three volumes on the members of the House of Commons were extremely useful for studying a lord's influence in parliamentary elections.[1]

In addition to these works of reference, the principal sources for categorising peers on religious grounds are as follows: *Calendar of State Papers Domestic: Charles II*; *Calendar of State Papers Venetian, 1660–1675*; E. Hyde, *The continuation of the life of Edward, earl of Clarendon*; G. Burnet, *A History of my own time*; *The Bulstrode Papers*; Browning, *Danby*, vol. III; Bate, *Declaration of Indulgence*; Davis, 'The "Presbyterian" opposition and the emergence of party in the House of Lords in the reign of Charles II', in C. Jones (ed.), *Party and management in Parliament, 1660–1784* (Leicester, 1984), pp. 1–35; Green, *The re-establishment of the Church of England, 1660–1663*; Haley, *The first earl of Shaftesbury*; Kenyon, *The Popish Plot*; Lacey, *Dissent and parliamentary politics in England, 1661–1689*; Miller, *Popery and politics in England, 1660–1688*; Pepys, *Diary*; Seaward, *The Cavalier Parliament and the reconstruction of the old regime, 1661–67*; Carte MSS 81, fol. 83 (Lord Wharton's list of lay peers, 1660); Huntington Library, Ellesmere MSS 8418 (division list, 20 Nov. 1675); Add. MSS 28,091, fols. 161, 175, 177 (pre-sessional lists on Danby's Test Bill, April 1675). Less frequently used sources are cited in the notes.

It has not proved possible to discover the religious views of every peer. Where the evidence is inconclusive or insufficient a question-mark has been used. Those categorised as 'Presbyterians' are not only the few who attended nonconformist meetings, but Anglicans who favoured broadening the Church of England to include Presbyterian and moderate Independent

---
[1] Henning (ed.), *House of Commons, 1660–1690*, 3 vols.

ministers. Some also advocated toleration for peaceable Protestants who refused to conform to the church. Rigid Anglican peers were the staunchest defenders of the Restoration church settlement and under no circumstances would contemplate making concessions to Protestant dissenters. It is much easier to identify Catholic lords by their recusancy and exclusion from the House after the passage of the Second Test Act in 1678.

The evidence for political allegiances can also be inconclusive. Since very few speeches and records of debates exist for the period, manuscript division lists, dissents and protests in the *Journals* are often the only guide to political opinions and party allegiances. None of these provides an entirely accurate record of voting behaviour. Lists of dissenting and protesting peers only include those who voted with the minority side and bothered to sign the manuscript journal. Division lists, though they usually give both sides in a vote, can contain errors. Clyve Jones and Richard Davis in *A register of parliamentary lists, 1660–1761*[2] have described at length how these unofficial lists were compiled and the types of errors which they may contain. Tellers and note-taking peers sometimes made mistakes when counting.[3] When more than one division list survives for the same vote, comparisons have been made. Party designations have, where possible, been verified by reference to other sources, such as the earl of Shaftesbury's lists of lay peers (1677–8).[4]

Even allowing for minor inaccuracies, it is clear from twenty-eight division lists and protests on key issues that the Protestant membership of the chamber was divided into two organised political parties during the years 1675 to 1681. (An explanation of each division and protest is in Swatland, 'House of Lords', pp. 383–400.) Peers have only been given a party designation if they are recorded as voting at least twice during this period. Catholics have not been categorised as Court or Country, since on religious issues they tended to pursue their own independent line, and of course from late 1678 the vast majority no longer sat in the House.

---

[2] D. Hayton and C. Jones (eds.), *A register of parliamentary lists, 1660–1761* (University of Leicester History Dept, Occasional Publication no. 1, 1979), pp. 5–19.

[3] See Swatland, 'Further recorded divisions in the House of Lords, 1660–81', *Parl. Hist.*, 3 (1984), 179–80.

[4] K. H. D. Haley, 'Shaftesbury's lists of the lay peers and members of the Commons, 1677–8', *BIHR*, 43 (1970), 86–101.

1	2	3	4	5	6	7	8	9	10	11	12
L	Abergavenny	1614	1641	1662	–	–	–	C	R	–	–
L	Abergavenny	?	1662	1666	–	–	–	C	R	–	–
L/E	Ailesbury[1]	1626	1663/6	1685	MP	PC	E	A	(P/R)	Ct	T
D	Albemarle	1608	1660	1670	MP	PC	E	Pr[2]	R/P	–	–
D	Albemarle	1653	1670	1688	MP	PC	E	A	(R/P)	Ct	T
E	Anglesey	1614	1661	1686	MP	PC	E	Pr	P	Ct	W?
L/E	Arlington	1618	1665/72	1685	MP	PC	E	Pr/A	R	Ct	T
L	Arundel of Trerice	1616	1665	1687	MP	–	E	A	R	Ct	T
L	Arundel of Wardour	1606	1643	1694	–	–	E	C	R	–	–
L	Astley	1609	1644	1662	–	–	–	A?	R	–	–
L	Astley	1654	1662	1688	–	–	–	A	(R)	Ct	T
L	Audley	1617	1633	1684	–	–	–	C	R	–	–
E	Banbury	1631	1646	1674	–	–	–	–	–	–	–
E	Bath	1628	1661	1701	–	PC	E	A	R	Ct	T
E	Bedford	1613	1641	1700	MP	–	E	Pr[3]	P/R	Cy	W
L	Belasyse	1614	1645	1689	MP	–	E	C	R	–	–
L/E	Berkeley of Berkeley	1627	1658/79	1698	–	PC	E	A?	R	Ct	T
L	Berkeley of Stratton	1606	1658	1678	MP	PC	–	A	R	Ct	–
E	Berkshire	1590	1626	1669	MP	PC	E	C	R	–	–
E	Berkshire[4]	1615	1640/69	1679	MP	–	–	C	R	–	–
E	Berkshire	1619	1679	1706	MP	–	–	A	R	Ct	T
E	Bolingbroke	1634	1646	1688	–	–	E	Pr	(P)	Cy	–
E	Bridgewater	1623	1649	1686	–	PC	E	A	R	Cy	W
E	Bristol	1621	1641/53	1677	MP	–	E	C	R	–	–
E	Bristol	1635	1677	1698	MP	–	–	A	(R)	Ct	T
L	Brooke	1638	1658	1677	–	–	E	Pr[5]	(P)	Cy	–
L	Brooke	1643	1677	1710	MP	–	E	Pr	(P)	Cy	W
L	Bruce	1599	1641	1663	–	–	E	Pr?	P/R	–	–
D	Buckingham	1628	1628	1687	–	PC	E	Pr	R	Cy	W
E	Burlington[6]	1612	1644/64	1697	MP	–	–	Pr?	R	Cy	W
L	Butler of Moore Park	1634	1665	1680	MP	PC	E	A	(R)	Ct	T
L	Butler of Weston	1639	1673	1686	MP	–	–	A	(R)	Ct	T
L	Byron	1605	1652	1679	–	–	E	A	R	Ct	–
L	Byron	1636	1679	1695	–	–	–	A	(R)	Ct	T
V	Campden	1628	1643	1682	MP	–	E	A	R	Ct	–
E	Cardigan[7]	c. 1580	1628/61	1663	–	–	–	C	R	–	–
E	Cardigan	1607	1663	1703	–	–	–	C	R	–	–
E	Carlisle	1612	1622	1660	–	–	–	A?	R	–	–
E	Carlisle	1629	1661	1685	MP	PC	E	Pr	P	Cy/Ct	–
E	Carnarvon	1632	1643	1709	–	–	–	Pr?[8]	(R)	Cy	–
L	Carrington	1598	1643	1665	–	–	–	C	R	–	–
L	Carrington	1621	1665	1701	–	–	–	C	R	–	–

1	2	3	4	5	6	7	8	9	10	11	12
L	Chandos	1621	1655	1676	–	–	–	Pr	R	–	–
L	Chandos	1642	1676	1714	–	–	E	Pr	(R)	Cy	W
E	Chesterfield	1634	1656	1714	–	PC	E	Pr?	(R)	Cy/Ct	T
E	Clare	1595	1637	1666	MP	–	E	Pr	P/R	–	–
E	Clare	1635	1666	1689	MP	–	E	Pr[9]	(P/R)	Cy	W
E	Clarendon[10]	1609	1660/1	1674	MP	PC	E	Pr/A[11]	R	–	–
E	Clarendon	1638	1674	1709	MP	PC	E	A	(R)	Cy/Ct	T
E	Cleveland	1591	1626	1667	–	–	E	A	R	–	–
L	Clifford	1630	1672	1673	MP	PC	–	C	R	–	–
L	Colepeper	1600	1644	1660	MP	PC	–	A?	R	–	–
L	Colepeper	1635	1660	1689	–	–	–	A	(R)	Ct	–
V/E	Conway	1623	1655/79	1683	–	PC	–	A	R	Ct	T
L	Conyers-Darcy[12]	1599	1654/80	1689	–	–	–	A?	R	Ct	–
L	Conyers	1622	1680	1692	MP	–	–	A?	R	Ct	T
L	Cornwallis	1610	1661	1662	MP	PC	E	A?	R	–	–
L	Cornwallis	1632	1662	1673	MP	–	–	A	(R)	–	–
L	Cornwallis	1655	1673	1698	–	–	E	Pr	(R)	Cy	W
L	Coventry	1606	1640	1661	MP	–	–	A?	R	–	–
L	Coventry	1628	1661	1680	–	–	E	A?	R	Ct	–
L	Coventry	1654	1680	1687	–	–	E	A?	(R)	Ct	T
L/E	Craven	1606	1627/65	1687	–	PC	–	Pr[13]	R	Ct	T
L	Crew	1598	1661	1679	MP	–	–	Pr[14]	P	Cy	–
L	Crew	1623	1679	1697	MP	–	–	Pr	P	Cy	W
L	Crofts	1611	1658	1677	–	–	–	A	R	Ct	–
L	Cromwell	1624	1653	1668	–	–	–	A?	R	–	–
L	Cromwell	1653	1668	1682	–	–	–	A	(R)	Ct	T
D	Cumberland	1619	1644	1682	–	PC	E	Pr?	R	Ct	T
L	Dacre	1619	1630	1662	MP	–	–	Pr	P	–	–
E	Danby[15]	1632	1673/4	1712	MP	PC	E	A	(R)	Ct	–
L	Deincourt[16]	1654	1680/1	1707	MP	–	–	A	(P)	Ct	T
L	Delamer	1622	1661	1684	MP	–	E	Pr	P	Cy	W
L	Delawarr	1626	1628	1687	–	–	–	A	P	Ct	–
E	Denbigh[17]	1608	1628/43	1675	–	–	–	Pr[18]	P	Cy	–
E	Denbigh	1640	1675	1685	–	–	E	A?	(P)	Ct	T
E	Derby	1628	1651	1672	–	–	E	A	R	–	–
E	Derby	1655	1672	1702	–	–	E	Pr	(R)	Cy	W
E	Devonshire	1617	1628	1684	–	–	E	Pr[19]	R	Cy	–
M	Dorchester	1607	1645	1680	MP	PC	–	C?	R	Ct	–
E	Dorset	1622	1652	1677	MP	–	E	Pr[20]	(R)	Cy	–
E	Dorset[21]	1638	1675/7	1705	MP	–	E	A?	(R)	Ct	T
E	Dover[22]	1580	1621/8	1666	MP	–	–	Pr?	P	–	–
E	Dover[23]	1608	1640/66	1677	–	–	–	Pr	P	–	–
E	Essex[24]	1632	1649/61	1683	–	PC	E	Pr	(R)	Cy	W
L	Eure	?	1652	1672	MP	–	–	Pr	P	–	–
L	Eure	?	1672	1707	–	–	–	Pr	P	Cy	W
E	Exeter	1628	1643	1678	–	–	E	Pr?	P	Cy	–
E	Exeter	1649	1678	1700	MP	–	E	Pr?	(P)	Cy	–

1	2	3	4	5	6	7	8	9	10	11	12
V	Fauconberg	1628	1653	1700	–	PC	E	Pr	P	Cy	W
L	Ferrers	1650	1677	1711	–	–	E	A	(R)	Ct	T
E	Feversham	1599	1676	1677	MP	–	–	A	R	Ct	–
E	Feversham[25]	1641	1673/7	1709	–	–	E	A?	–	Ct	T
L	Finch	1584	1640	1660	MP	–	–	A	R	–	–
L	Finch	1621	1674	1682	MP	PC	–	A	–	Ct	T
L	Fitzwalter	1646	1670	1679	–	–	–	Pr	(P)	Cy	–
L	Frescheville	1606	1665	1682	MP	–	–	A	R	Ct	–
L	Gerard of Bromley	1634	1640	1667	–	–	–	C	(R)	–	–
D	Gloucester	1640	1640	1660	–	PC	–	–	(R)	–	–
L	Grey	1657	1676	1679	–	–	–	Pr	(R)	Cy	–
L	Grey of Wark	1593	1624	1674	MP	–	–	Pr	P	–	–
L	Grey of Wark	1630	1674	1675	–	–	–	A?	(P)	–	–
L	Grey of Wark	1655	1675	1701	–	–	E	Pr	(P)	Cy	W
V/E	Halifax	1633	1668/79	1695	MP	PC	E	Pr[26]	(R)	Cy/Ct	T
L	Hatton	1605	1643	1670	MP	PC	–	Pr?	R	–	–
L	Hatton	1632	1670	1706	MP	–	–	A	(R)	Ct	T
L	Herbert of Cherbury	1633	1655	1678	–	–	E	Pr[27]	(P/R)	Cy	–
L	Herbert of Cherbury	1640	1678	1691	MP	–	E	Pr	(P/R)	Cy	W
V	Hereford	1617	1654	1676	–	–	E	Pr	P	Cy	–
E	Holland[28]	1620	1649/73	1675	–	–	–	Pr	P/R	–	–
L	Holles	1599	1661	1680	MP	PC	–	Pr	P	Cy	–
L	Holles	1627	1680	1690	MP	PC	–	Pr	P	Cy	–
L	Howard of Escrick	?	1628	1675	MP	–	–	Pr	P	Cy	–
L	Howard of Escrick	1625	1675	1678	–	–	–	–	P	Cy	–
L	Howard of Escrick	1630	1678	1694	MP	–	–	Pr	P	Cy	W
L	Hunsdon	?	1677	1692	–	–	–	C	(R)	–	–
E	Huntingdon	1651	1656	1701	–	–	E	A?[29]	(P)	Ct/Cy	W
E	Kent	1645	1651	1702	–	–	E	Pr	(P)	Cy	W
L	Langdale	1617	1658	1662	–	–	–	C	R	–	–
L	Langdale	1628	1662	1703	–	–	–	C	R	–	–
D	Lauderdale[30]	1616	1674	1682	–	PC	–	A?	P/R	Ct	T
E	Leicester	1595	1626	1677	MP	PC	–	Pr	P	Cy	–
E	Leicester	1619	1677	1698	MP	–	–	Pr	P?	Cy	W
L	Leigh	1595	1643	1672	MP	–	–	A?	R	–	–
L	Leigh	1652	1672	1710	–	–	E	A?	(R)	Ct	T
L	Lexington	1594	1645	1668	MP	–	E	A	R	–	–
E	Lincoln	1600	1619	1667	–	–	–	Pr	P	–	–
E	Lincoln	c. 1652	1667	1692	–	–	–	Pr?	(P)	Cy	–

1	2	3	4	5	6	7	8	9	10	11	12
E	Lindsey	1608	1642	1666	MP	PC	E	A	R	–	–
E	Lindsey	1630	1666	1701	MP	PC	E	A	(R)	Ct	T
E	Loughborough	1610	1643	1667	–	–	E	A	R	–	–
L	Lovelace	1616	1626	1670	–	–	–	A	R	–	–
L	Lovelace	1642	1670	1693	MP	–	E	Pr	(R)	Cy	W
L	Lucas	1606	1645	1671	–	–	–	Pr	R	–	–
L	Lucas	?	1671	1688	–	–	–	A	(R)	Ct	T
E	Macclesfield[31]	1618	1645/79	1694	–	–	E	A/Pr	R	Ct/Cy	W
E	Manchester[32]	1602	1626/42	1671	MP	PC	E	Pr	P	–	–
E	Manchester	1634	1671	1683	MP	–	E	Pr	(P)	Cy	W
E	Marlborough	1618	1638	1665	–	–	–	–	R	–	–
E	Marlborough	1612	1665	1679	–	–	–	–	R	–	–
L	Maynard	1623	1640	1699	–	PC	–	A	P/R	Ct	T
E	Middlesex	1625	1651	1674	–	–	–	–	(P)	–	–
L	Mohun	1620	1641	1665	MP	–	E	Pr?	R	–	–
L	Mohun	1645	1665	1677	–	–	E	Pr	(R)	Cy	–
E	Monmouth	1596	1639	1661	MP	–	–	–	R	–	–
D	Monmouth	1649	1663	1685	–	PC	E	Pr?	(R)	Ct/Cy	W
V	Montagu	1610	1629	1682	–	–	E	C	R	–	–
L	Montagu	1616	1644	1684	MP	–	E	Pr	P	–	–
V	Mordaunt	1626	1659	1675	–	–	E	A?	R	Cy	–
V	Mordaunt	1658	1675	1735	–	–	–	Pr?	(R)	Cy	W
L	Morley	1636	1655	1700	–	–	–	C	(R)	Ct	T
L	Mowbray	1655	1678/84	1701	–	–	–	A	(R)	Ct	T
E	Mulgrave	1647	1658	1721	–	–	–	Pr	(P)	Cy	W
D	Newcastle	1593	1628/65	1676	MP	–	E	A[33]	R	Ct	–
D	Newcastle	1630	1676	1695	MP	PC	E	A	(R)	Ct	T
E	Newport	1597	1628	1666	–	–	E	Pr[34]	R	–	–
E	Newport	1630	1666	1675	–	–	–	–	(R)	–	–
E	Newport	1633	1675	1675	–	–	–	–	(R)	–	–
E	Newport	?	1675	1679	–	–	–	–	(R)	–	–
V	Newport[35]	1619	1651/75	1708	MP	PC	E	Pr	R	Cy/Ct	–
L	Noel	1641	1681	1689	–	–	–	A	(R)	–	–
D	Norfolk[36]	1627	1652/60	1677	–	–	–	C	R	–	–
D	Norfolk[37]	1628	1669/77	1684	–	–	E	C	R	–	–
L	Norreys	1653	1675	1699	–	–	E	A	(R)	Ct	T
L	North	1582	1600	–	–	–	–	Pr	P	–	–
L	North	1602	1666	1677	MP	–	–	Pr	P	Cy	–
L	North and Grey[38]	1635	1673/7	1691	–	–	E	Pr	(P)	Cy	W
E	Northampton	1622	1643	1681	MP	PC	E	A[39]	R	Ct	–
E	Northumberland	1602	1632	1668	MP	PC	E	Pr	P	–	–
E	Northumberland	1644	1668	1670	–	–	–	–	(P)	–	–
E	Norwich	1588	1644	1663	MP	PC	–	A	R	–	–
E	Norwich	1615	1663	1671	–	–	–	A?	R	–	–
E	Nottingham	1610	1642	1681	–	–	–	Pr	P	–	–
D	Ormond[40]	1610	1660	1688	–	PC	E	A?	R	Ct	T
E	Oxford	1627	1632	1703	–	PC	–	A?	R	Ct	T

1	2	3	4	5	6	7	8	9	10	11	12
L	Paget	1609	1628	1678	–	–	E	Pr	R/P	Cy	–
L	Paget	1637	1678	1713	–	–	E	Pr	(R/P)	Cy	W
L	Paulet	1615	1649	1665	MP	–	E	A	R	–	–
L	Paulet	1641	1665	1679	MP	–	E	A?	(R)	Ct	–
E	Pembroke	1621	1650	1669	MP	–	E	Pr[41]	P	–	–
E	Pembroke	1640	1669	1674	MP	–	(E)	–	P	–	–
E	Pembroke	1653	1674	1683	–	–	E	–	(P)	–	–
E	Peterborough	1623	1643	1697	–	PC	E	A	P/R	Ct	T
L	Petre	1626	1638	1684	–	–	–	C	R	–	–
E	Plymouth	1657	1675	1680	–	–	–	A?	(R)	–	–
E	Portland	1605	1635	1663	MP	PC	E	A	R	–	–
E	Portland	1609	1663	1665	–	–	–	A?	R	–	–
E	Portland	1639	1665	1688	–	–	–	–	(R)	–	–
L	Powis	1600	1656	1667	MP	–	E	C	R	–	–
E	Powis[42]	1626	1667/74	1696	–	–	–	C	R	–	–
E	Radnor[43]	1606	1625/79	1685	–	PC	E	Pr	P	Cy/Ct	T
D	Richmond[44]	1639	1645/60	1672	–	–	–	–	(R)	–	–
E	Rivers	1628	1654	1694	–	–	–	C?[45]	R	Cy	W
E	Rochester	1647	1658	1680	–	–	–	Pr	(R)	–	–
L	Rockingham	1630	1653	1689	–	–	E	Pr?	(R)	Cy	W
E	Rutland	1604	1641	1679	MP	–	E	Pr?	P	–	–
E	Rutland[46]	1638	1679/79	1711	MP	–	E	A?	(P)	Ct	T
E	St Albans[47]	1604	1643/60	1684	MP	–	–	C?	R	Ct	T
E	Salisbury	1591	1612	1668	MP	–	E	Pr	P	–	–
E	Salisbury	1648	1668	1683	MP	PC	E	Pr	(P)	Cy	W
E	Sandwich	1625	1660	1672	MP	PC	E	Pr[48]	P	–	–
E	Sandwich	1648	1672	1688	MP	–	–	–	(P)	–	–
L	Sandys	1626	1649	1666	–	–	–	Pr?	P/R	–	–
L	Sandys	?	1668	1680	–	–	–	Pr?	(P/R)	Cy	–
V	Saye and Sele	1582	1624	1662	–	PC	–	Pr	P	–	–
V	Saye and Sele	1603	1662	1674	MP	–	–	Pr	P	–	–
V	Saye and Sele	1641	1674	1698	–	–	–	Pr	(P)	Cy	–
E	Scarsdale	1612	1655	1681	–	–	–	Pr	P	Cy	W
L	Seymour	1590	1641	1664	MP	PC	E	A	R	–	–
L	Seymour	1621	1664	1665	MP	–	–	A	R	–	–
E	Shaftesbury[49]	1621	1661/72	1683	MP	PC	E	Pr	R/P	Cy	W
E	Shrewsbury	1623	1654	1668	–	–	–	C	R	–	–
E	Shrewsbury	1660	1668	1718	–	–	–	A	(R)	–	–
D	Somerset[50]	1587	1641/60	1660	MP	PC	E	A	R	–	–
D	Somerset	1633	1671	1675	MP	–	–	A?	(R)	–	–
D	Somerset[51]	1638	1665/75	1678	MP	–	E	A?	(R)	Ct	–
E	Southampton	1608	1624	1667	–	PC	E	Pr	R	–	–
V	Stafford	1612	1640	1680	–	–	–	C	R	–	–
E	Stamford	1600	1628	1673	MP	–	E	Pr	P	–	–
E	Stamford	1653	1673	1720	–	–	E	Pr[52]	(P)	Cy	W
L	Stanhope	1595	1621	1675	–	–	–	–	–	Ct	–
L	Stourton	1594	1633	1672	–	–	–	C	R	–	–
L	Stourton	c. 1638	1672	1685	–	–	–	C	(R)	–	–

1	2	3	4	5	6	7	8	9	10	11	12
E	Strafford	1626	1642	1695	–	PC	–	Pr[53]	R	Ct/Cy	–
E	Suffolk	1619	1640	1688	–	–	–	Pr	P	Cy	W
E	Sunderland	1641	1643	1702	–	PC	–	A?	(R)	Ct/Cy	W
E	Sussex	1647	1659	1671	–	–	–	–	(R)	–	–
E	Sussex[54]	1654	1662/74	1715	–	–	–	A	(P)	Ct	T
L	Teynham	1616	1621	1673	–	–	–	C	R	–	–
L	Teynham	?	1673	1689	–	–	–	C	(R)	–	–
E	Thanet	1608	1631	1664	–	–	E	A	R/P	–	–
E	Thanet	1631	1664	1679	–	–	E	A?	(R/P)	Ct	–
E	Thanet	1638	1679	1680	MP	–	E	A?	(R/P)	Ct	–
E	Thanet	1641	1680	1684	MP	–	–	A	(R/P)	Ct	T
L	Townshend	1630	1661	1687	MP	–	E	Pr	P	Cy	–
L	Vaughan	1606	1643	1686	MP	PC	E	A[55]	R	Ct	–
L	Vaux	1588	1595	1661	–	–	–	C	–	–	–
L	Vaux	1591	1661	1663	–	–	–	C	–	–	–
L	Ward	1614	1655	1670	–	–	–	A	R	–	–
L	Ward	1631	1670	1701	–	–	E	A	(R)	Ct	T
E	Warwick	1616	1659	1673	MP	–	E	Pr	P	–	–
L	Wentworth	1613	1640	1665	MP	PC	E	A	R	–	–
E	Westmorland	1602	1629	1666	MP	–	E	Pr	R/P	–	–
E	Westmorland	1635	1666	1691	MP	–	–	Pr	(R/P)	Cy	W
L	Wharton	1613	1625	1696	–	–	E	Pr[56]	P	Cy	W
L	Widdrington	c. 1630	1651	1675	–	–	–	C	R	–	–
L	Widdrington	1656	1675	1695	–	–	–	C	(R)	–	–
L	Willoughby	1613	1618	1666	–	–	–	Pr	P	–	–
L	Willoughby	1616	1666	1673	–	–	–	Pr[57]	P	–	–
L	Willoughby	1639	1673	1674	–	–	–	Pr?	(P)	–	–
L	Willoughby	1643	1678	1678	–	–	–	–	(P)	–	–
L	Willoughby	1650	1678	1679	–	–	–	–	(P)	Ct	–
L	Willoughby	1602	1679	1692	–	–	–	Pr[58]	P	Cy	W
M	Winchester	1598	1629	1675	MP	–	E	C	R	–	–
M	Winchester	1630	1675	1699	MP	PC	E	Pr[59]	(R)	Cy	W?
E	Winchilsea	1628	1639	1689	–	–	E	A	R	Ct	T
L	Windsor	1627	1660	1687	–	–	E	A	R	Ct	T
M	Worcester	1603	1646	1667	–	–	–	C	R	–	–
M	Worcester	1629	1667	1700	MP	PC	E	A	R	Ct	T
L	Wotton	1635	1650	1683	–	–	–	A	(R)	Ct	T
E	Yarmouth[60]	1631	1673/9	1683	MP	–	E	A	(R)	Ct	T
D	York	1633	1644	1701	–	PC	E	A/C[61]	(R)	–	–

Key

1 Noble rank

- L Baron
- V Viscount
- E Earl
- M Marquis
- D Duke

2 Title in the English nobility. The earls of Guildford and Brecknock are listed under their better-known titles as the duke of Lauderdale (Scottish nobility) and the duke of Ormond (Irish nobility)
3 Date of birth
4 Date of succeeding to a title
5 Year of death
6 Member of the Commons before elevation to the Lords
7 Privy Councillor at some point during the period 1660 to 1681
8 Exerted electoral influence
9 Religious leanings
   Pr   Presbyterian
   Pr? Probable Presbyterian
   A   Rigid Anglican
   A?   Probable Rigid Anglican
   C   Catholic
   C?   Probable Catholic
10 Civil War and Interregnum allegiances
   P   Parliamentarian
   R   Royalist
   R/P Changed allegiances at least once between 1642 and 1659
   NB. Letters in brackets denote lords who were descended from Royalist or Parliamentarian families
11 Party allegiances 1675–79
   Ct   Member of the earl of Danby's Court party
   Cy   Member of the Country party
   Cy/Ct Changed party allegiance from Country to Court
   Ct/Cy Changed party allegiance from Court to Country
12 Party allegiances 1680–1
   T   Member of the 'Tory' party
   W Member of the 'Whig' party

[1] Baron Bruce, 1663–6.
[2] Hutton, pp. 90, 96; A. G. Matthews, *Calamy revised* (Oxford, 1934), p. 325.
[3] Matthews, ibid., pp. 384, 484.
[4] Baron Howard of Charlton, 1640–69.
[5] Lord Brooke was active on behalf of Presbyterian ministers in the Convention (HLRO, Main Papers, 12 July 1660).
[6] Baron Clifford, 1644–64.
[7] Baron Brudenell, 1628–61.
[8] BL, Verney MSS M/636/19, Hobart to Verney, 3 Apr. 1664.
[9] Add. MSS 30,013, fol. 28, Lord Paget to John Swinfen, 26 Nov. 1681; Nottingham University, Cavendish MSS PwL, 143, Clare to the countess of Ogle, 4 Nov. 1675.
[10] Baron Hyde, 1660.
[11] Until early 1663 he advocated a broad church that incorporated peaceable Protestant nonconformists (see Seaward, pp. 162–95).
[12] Lord Darcy, 1654, created Lord Conyers and Darcy in 1680.
[13] 'The Craven papers' (National Register of Archives, 1966), p. 60.
[14] Valuable insights into his religious beliefs are in his letters to his friend, John Swinfen (Bedfordshire RO, Lucas Collection L30/20/1–19).
[15] Viscount Latimer, 1673.

16 Earl of Scarsdale, 1681.
17 Baron Fielding, 1628–43.
18 For his patronage of Presbyterian ministers, see Matthews, *Calamy revised*, pp. 328, 342.
19 Ibid., p. 55; Nottingham University, Cavendish MSS PwL 76, Devonshire to Newcastle, n.d.
20 Kent Archives Office, U269 (Sackville MSS) C. 20, fol. 89, 036, fol. 82.
21 Earl of Middlesex, 1675.
22 Viscount Rochford, 1621–8.
23 Baron Hunsdon, 1640–66.
24 Baron Capel, 1649–61.
25 Created Lord Duras in 1673.
26 H. C. Foxcroft, *A character of the Trimmer* (Cambridge, 1946), pp. 30, 51, 55.
27 Herbert was a close friend of Quakers (see *DNB*, 26, p. 180).
28 Earl of Warwick, 1673.
29 Although a 'Whig', he did not hold Presbyterian religious views, remaining firm to the Church of England (see Huntington Library, Hastings MSS, Huntingdon to Gery, 4 Mar. 1681).
30 Earl of Guildford in the English nobility, 1674.
31 Lord Gerard of Brandon, 1645–79. Until 1679 Macclesfield was staunchly Anglican, protesting against the alterations to the Additional Uniformity Bill in 1663 and supporting the 1675 Test. During the spring of 1679 he joined the 'opposition' in the House.
32 Baron Kimbolton, 1626–42.
33 See Newcastle, *Memoirs*, p. xxiii.
34 Friends' House Library, A. R. Barclay MSS I, fol. 40, Edward Burrough to Francis Howgill, 24 Sept. 1658.
35 Baron Newport, 1651.
36 Earl of Arundel, 1652.
37 Baron Howard of Castle Rising, 1669, created earl of Norwich, 1672.
38 Created Lord Grey of Rolleston in 1673. He succeeded to his father's title as Lord North in 1677 and was known as Lord North and Grey.
39 See Clarendon MSS 77, fol. 236 for his attitude towards dissenters in the early 1660s.
40 Earl of Brecknock in the English nobility, 1660. In the early 1660s he assisted Clarendon to modify Commons' bills on the Church. Later he was an opponent of Danby and was critical of the 1675 Test Bill. Though not a rigid Anglican he was 'firm in the Protestant religion' (Burnet, *History*, I, p. 170).
41 Pembroke was a Quaker sympathiser, if not a Quaker himself. (See *Hist. MSS. Comm.*, 78, Rawdon-Hastings MSS, p. 150, J. Jaques to the earl of Huntingdon, 27 Apr. 1665.)
42 Created earl of Powis, 1674.
43 Baron Robartes, 1625–79.
44 Earl of Lichfield, 1645–60.
45 Although brought up in a Catholic family, Rivers does not appear to have practised this religion during the reign. He subscribed to the oaths and declaration in the 1678 Test Act and followed the Country leadership in the Lords.
46 Created Lord Manners of Haddon in 1679.
47 Lord Jermyn, 1643–60. A secret Catholic, St Albans subscribed to the 1678 Test Act. (See Kenyon, *Popish Plot*, p. 38; R. Ollard (ed.), *Clarendon's four portraits*, 1989, p. 126.)

48 R. Ollard, *Cromwell's earl* (1994), pp. 10, 20, 36; Harris, *Sandwich*, II, pp. 199, 291.
49 Baron Ashley, 1661–72.
50 Marquis of Hertford, 1641–60.
51 Baron Seymour of Trowbridge, 1665–75.
52 Huntington Library, Hastings MSS, Huntingdon to Gery, 4 Mar. 1681.
53 *Hist. MSS Comm.*, MSS of the marquis of Bath, II, pp. 152, 155–6.
54 Lord Dacre, 1662, created earl of Sussex, 1674.
55 See T. S. Williams, 'Richard Vaughan, 2nd earl of Carbery, 1660–86' (University College of Wales, MA thesis, 1936), pp. 96, 131–7.
56 Jones, *Saw-pit Wharton*, pp. 1, 5, 175, 192.
57 P. J. W. Higson, 'A neglected revolution family, the Lancashire Lords Willoughby of Parham and their association with Protestant dissent, 1640–1765' (University of Liverpool PhD thesis, 1971), pp. 25–30.
58 Ibid., pp. 12, 13, 30–3.
59 See Hertfordshire Record Office, Cowper papers, D/EP/F24, anonymous letter to Sir William Cowper, 8 Jan. 1678.
60 Viscount Yarmouth, 1673–9.
61 James became a secret Catholic in 1669 and ceased to take Anglican communion from Easter 1673.

The bishops, 1661–1681

All twenty-four English and Welsh bishops and the archbishops of Canterbury and York were entitled to sit in the Lords. This appendix lists the sixty-five clerics who sat there for the period 1661 to 1681. The bishops were an important element in the chamber, since they comprised one-sixth of the membership and therefore could determine the outcome of divisions. Their attendance record was better than that of the peers, averaging 50 per cent for this period as compared with 41 per cent for the peers. They were instructed to attend by the archbishop of Canterbury or the bishop of London in order to defend the interests of the Church in parliament.

However, they were not a homogeneous group. Although they generally supported the court in the chamber, there were occasions, most notably when the king sought to alter the Restoration church settlement in the 1660s, when they were divided. Whilst the majority were staunch defenders of the established church, approximately a quarter supported attempts to broaden it by making concessions to moderate nonconformists.

The following sources were used in the compilation of this appendix: *DNB*; *Journals of the House of Lords*; E. Berwick (ed.), *The Rawdon papers*; G. R. Cragg, *From puritanism to the age of reason*; I. M. Green, *The re-establishment of the Church of England*; Haley, *The first earl of Shaftesbury*; T. Harris, P. Seaward and M. Goldie (eds.), *The politics of religion in Restoration England* (Oxford, 1991); P. Seaward, *The Cavalier Parliament and the reconstruction of the old regime, 1661–1667*; J. Spurr, 'The Church of England, comprehension and the 1689 Toleration Act', *EHR*, 104 (1989), 927–46; N. Sykes, *From Sheldon to Secker* (Cambridge, 1959); R. Thomas, 'Comprehension and Indulgence', in G. F. Nuttall and O. Chadwick (eds.), *From uniformity to unity* (1962); Bodl., Tanner MSS 42, fol. 89; 43, fol. 249; 44, fol. 196; Add. MSS 23,136, fol. 98.

	1	2	3	4	5
Barlow, Thomas	1607	1675	Lincoln	1691	Yes[1]
Barrow, Isaac	1614	1669	St Asaph	1680	No
Beaw, William	1616	1679	Llandaff	1706	No
Blandford, Walter	1619	1665	Oxford	–	Yes
		1671	Worcester	1675	Yes
Brideoak, Ralph	1613	1675	Chichester	1678	Yes
Charleton, Guy	1605	1672	Bristol	–	No
		1679	Chichester	1685	No
Compton, Henry	1632	1675	London	1713	No
Cosin, John	1594	1660	Durham	1672	No
Creighton, Robert	1593	1670	Bath and Wells	1672	No
Crew, Nathaniel	1633	1671	Oxford	–	Yes
		1674	Durham	1721	Yes
Croft, Herbert	1603	1662	Hereford	1691	Yes[2]
Davies, Francis	1605	1667	Llandaff	1675	No
Dolben, John	1625	1666	Rochester	–	Yes
		1683	York	1688	Yes
Duppa, Brian	1588	1660	Winchester	1662	No
Earle, John	c. 1601	1662	Worcester	–	No
		1663	Salisbury	1665	Yes
Fell, John	1625	1676	Oxford	1686	No
Ferne, Henry	1602	1662	Chester	1662	No
Fleetwood, James	1603	1675	Worcester	1683	No
Frewen, Accepted	1588	1660	York	1664	No
Fuller, William	1608	1667	Lincoln	1675	Yes
Gauden, John	1605	1660	Exeter	–	Yes
		1662	Worcester	1662	Yes
Glenham, Henry	1603	1667	St Asaph	1670	No
Griffith, George	1601	1660	St Asaph	1666	Yes
Gulston, William	1640	1679	Bristol	1684	No
Gunning, Peter	1614	1670	Chichester	–	No
		1675	Ely	1684	No
Hacket, John	1592	1661	Coventry and		
			Lichfield	1670	No
Hall, George	1612	1662	Chester	1668	No
Henchman, Humphrey	1592	1660	Salisbury	–	No
		1663	London	1675	No
Henshaw, Joseph	1603	1663	Peterborough	1679	No
Hyde, Alexander	1598	1665	Salisbury	1667	No
Ironside, Gilbert	1588	1661	Bristol	1671	Yes[3]
Juxon, William	1582	1660	Canterbury	1663	No
King, Henry	1592	1642	Chichester	1669	Yes
Lamplugh, Thomas	1615	1676	Exeter	1691	Yes[4]
Laney, Benjamin	1591	1660	Peterborough	–	Yes
		1663	Lincoln	–	Yes
		1667	Ely	1675	Yes
Lloyd, Hugh	1586	1660	Llandaff	1667	No
Lloyd, Humphrey	1610	1673	Bangor	1689	No

	1	2	3	4	5
Lloyd, William	1627	1680	St Asaph	1717	Yes[5]
Lloyd, William	1637	1675	Llandaff	–	No
		1679	Peterborough	1710	No
Lucy, William	1594	1660	St Davids	1677	No
Mews, Peter	1619	1673	Bath and Wells	1706	No
Monck, Nicholas	1610	1661	Hereford	1661	No
Morgan, Robert	1608	1666	Bangor	1673	No
Morley, George	1597	1660	Worcester	–	Yes
		1662	Winchester	1684	Yes
Nicholson, William	1591	1661	Gloucester	1672	Yes
Paul, William	1599	1663	Oxford	1665	No
Pearson, John	1613	1673	Chester	1686	Yes
Piers, William	1580	1632	Bath and Wells	1670	Yes[6]
Pritchet, John	1605	1672	Gloucester	1681	No
Rainbow, Edward	1608	1664	Carlisle	1684	No
Reynolds, Edward	1599	1661	Norwich	1676	Yes
Roberts, William	1585	1637	Bangor	1665	No
Sancroft, William	1617	1678	Canterbury	1693	No
Sanderson, Robert	1587	1660	Lincoln	1663	Yes
Sheldon, Gilbert	1598	1660	London	–	Yes[7]
		1663	Canterbury	1677	No
Skinner, Robert	1591	1641	Oxford	–	No
		1663	Worcester	1670	No
Sparrow, Anthony	1612	1667	Exeter	–	No
		1676	Norwich	1685	No
Sterne, Richard	1596	1660	Carlisle	–	No
		1664	York	1683	No
Thomas, William	1613	1678	St Davids	1683	Yes
Walton, Brian	1600	1660	Chester	1661	No
Ward, Seth	1617	1662	Exeter	–	No
		1667	Salisbury	1689	No
Warner, John	1581	1638	Rochester	1666	No
Wilkins, John	1614	1668	Chester	1672	Yes
Wood, Thomas	1607	1671	Coventry and Lichfield	1692	Yes
Wren, Matthew	1585	1638	Ely	1667	No

Key
1 Date of birth
2 Date of appointment to diocese
3 Diocese
4 Year of death
5 Supporter of a broader Church of England than was created by the Restoration church settlement

[1] Bodl., MS B.14.15, Linc., pamphlets collected and annotated by Bishop Barlow on the comprehension initiatives of 1667/8; Bodl., MS Eng. Lett. C. 328, fol. 509, Barlow to Francis Parry, 8 Jan. 1669.

[2] See Herbert Croft, *The naked truth* (1675) and J. Spurr, 'Anglican apologetic and the Restoration church' (unpublished University of Oxford DPhil thesis, 1985), pp. 114–21.

[3] *Several tracts relating to the great Acts for comprehension* (1680), IV, p. v.

[4] A. G. Matthews, *Calamy revised* (Oxford, 1934), p. 276.

[5] Horwitz, 'Protestant reconciliation', pp. 206–7.

[6] W. G. Simon, 'Comprehension in the age of Charles II', *Church History*, 31 (1962), 442.

[7] Following his appointment as archbishop of Canterbury in 1663 Sheldon became a firm adherent of the Restoration church settlement. As bishop of London he had supported Clarendon's attempts in the Lords to secure a broad Church of England, that included Presbyterian ministers. See *Hist. MSS Comm.*, Hastings MSS, iv, pp. 129–30.

INDEX

Cambridge Studies in Early Modern British History